GW01018579

FACE-TO-FACE

FACE-TO-FACE

BLACKS IN AMERICA: WHITE PERCEPTIONS AND BLACK REALITIES

Rose L. H. Finkenstaedt, Ph.D.

WILLIAM MORROW AND COMPANY, INC.

New York

It is the policy of William Morrow and Company, Inc., and its imprints and affiliates, recognizing the importance of preserving what has been written, to print the books we publish on acid-free paper, and we exert our best efforts to that end.

Library of Congress Cataloging-in-Publication Data

Finkenstaedt, Rose L. H.
    Face-to-face : blacks in America : white perceptions and black
realities / Rose L. H. Finkenstaedt.
        p.   cm.
    Includes bibliographical references.
    ISBN 0-688-12383-X
    1. United States—Race relations.   2. Racism—United States.
3. Afro-Americans—Race identity.   4. Afro-Americans—Segregation.
I. Title.
E185.615.F52   1994
305.8'00973—dc20   93-39675
                                                              CIP

Printed in the United States of America

First Edition

1   2   3   4   5   6   7   8   9   10

BOOK DESIGN BY MICHAEL MENDELSOHN / MM DESIGN 2000, INC.

This book is dedicated to my children,
Isabel Luke Finkenstaedt
and James Clements Finkenstaedt, Jr.

CONTENTS

INTRODUCTION

I f, as a method of labor exploitation, slavery was a precondition for the development of American capitalism, then as an institution slavery obstructed the centralization that was necessary for the growth of industry. It had to be wiped out: the North forced the South to submit to the hegemony of one economic system. Nevertheless, the reassembled Union perpetuated—in fact, accentuated—the ideology of racism, or of white supremacy, which underlay the process of black enslavement and differentiated it from other like practices in other sections and cultures of the world. Racism was the expedient by which the modern industrial state was able to rise to power in an extraordinarily short period.

The black has, in effect, been responsible for the material success of America. His relegation to outcast status was the means by which the nation reunited, centralized its territory and economy, consolidated a heterogeneous work force and burst on the international scene in two world wars as a productive giant. Racism made possible America's development, its self-proclaimed political democracy and its majority consensus, which is based on a middle-class norm. Not only did racism (the justification of the social, political and economic debasement of black people) provide the country with a ready supply of cheap labor, but it also reduced class antagonism that might have been an impediment to capitalistic growth. The fact that blacks were branded as nonequals gave all whites the illusion that they were equal in kind: blacks set a bottom limit to an otherwise dispersed and incoherent population over which rich and poor, worker and entrepreneur could feel a sense of solidarity in idea. They were the foundation that served, in the absence of institutionalized European classism, to hold the nation together.

The black has also been a factor in the intensification of America's idealistic nationalism, which has united the country and inspired its people. Racism has served as a substitute for the historical experience which Americans deny in their fixation on and, paradoxically, negation of the present. Because the black, who was neither European nor Christian, was culturally unacceptable, he was the means by which whites could relate to the western tradition which they would transcend but by which they were conditioned: by rejecting him they affirmed their historical roots; they could look to the future. Because the black was described as a lower human species representing the brute id, he was treated, symbolically, as the evidence of a natural order in which whites claimed a lofty rank: through him whites had a progressively worthy place in an assumed universal order of things. If America was not an ideological society, still it presumed to be an ideology in itself. America was supposed to be the culmination of occidental civilization and, therefore, the exemplar of mankind. In this sense, the black played an essential role in its reason for being.

White Americans, already conditioned by Judeo-Christianity, and especially by the Protestant Reformation, were disposed to view existence as a battle of man against nature, or of mind and soul against body. Because they looked at the world in terms of right against wrong, they felt obligated to master their environment, perhaps as a sign that they were mastering their lower animalistic instincts. The good and the successful were those who prevailed over not just natural but human difference. Through pronounced binary opposition, white Americans claimed their increasing right to the earth. Racism—the degradation of blacks, who were associated with unrefined brute nature—was evidence of both the material and the moral superiority of white people—for the two went together. Racism justified Americans pragmatically as the vanguard of the race of man—as the French writer Madame de Staël had actually called them. To dominate different humans as well as things was to prove their innate worthiness, through which they would progressively reveal themselves as the universal good of mankind.

Traditionally, Americans have used economic criteria as the measure of individual worth. It was the materialistic ethic, the association of worldly success with divine election, that undermined the validity of the Puritan concept of grace. It was the Constitution's identification of race and property that institutionalized the then evident dichotomy between the profession and the practice of human rights. As an abstract object, a thing to be owned, the black slave could be used as a staple in James Madison's organization of property relations, which involved different segments of the population. His racial exploitation was instrumental to the maintenance of social stability on both economic and ideological levels. The man who owned property was inherently an individual of merit; the individual who *was owned* was a nonentity inherently so designated by his color. Those who were distinguished neither by possession nor by color acquiesced to the existing order—unjust as it might have been to them—simply through the fact that they profited ideologically from racial divisiveness.

With the rise of the industrial state and the relegation of freed black men and women to outcast status, society seemed to function almost exclusively on materialistic terms. The spectacular achievements of capitalism subjected all America to the success ethic, which depended on the unacceptability of failure, and failure was epitomized by its association with a historical minority. In postindustrial times, this minority consists of unassimilable poor people whose condition—it is rationalized—is not necessarily caused by their skin color. The modern poor, in other words, are theoretically not the product of racially discriminatory practices: they are simply men, women and children who are unable to meet the demands of materialistic society and who do not enjoy its benefits because of their innate disabilities; therefore, by the inevitable logic of the system, they deserve their lot. However, since it is the blacks alone of all ethnic and national groups who have been intentionally deprived, the minority poor are in fact disproportionately made up of blacks. As their dispossession was an essential factor in the rise of industrial wealth, so their present marginality poses a potential threat to the continuing prosperity of America.

The culture that has historically excluded blacks on the one hand has, on the other, accentuated their difference and thus has deprived them of their identity. To exist in spite of the materialistic standards that govern American society is necessarily to create an alternate way of life. In the process of doing so, blacks, unlike immigrants, have tried to establish their own set of values and call into question those of the majority.

Blacks, of course, have responded in various ways to conditions in the United States. After the Civil War, when they were emancipated as a race, they were all—the free as well as the freed, the professional as well as the peasant—put in the same class socially. They were subject to the restrictions of institutionalized segregation, or second-class citizenship. With the rise of the industrial state, blacks self-consciously attempted to develop racial leadership in order to deal with an oppressive social order, and they introduced several methods of resistance.

One of these was economic nationalism, by which black entrepreneurs and professionals tried to lead black communities to a degree of autonomy. But in a white-controlled capitalistic system this was doomed—at the most—to minor success. Integrationism was another: black leaders believed that the moral elevation of the race would be a solution to the separatism that condemned blacks to outcast status. Integration entailed the sacrifice of the communal identity that blacks had developed through centuries of racist exclusion. Revolt, including riot, was a desperate act of resistance to the white hegemony, which, in the face of massive and concerted white repression, was doomed to failure. The culture of poverty (involving all kinds of nonbourgeois amoral behavior patterns, from drug dealing to committing crimes to adolescent motherhood to single-woman households) is a challenge to prevailing standards as well as to the consumer economy—as long as a disproportionate percentage of the poor are black.

Actually, it was the emergence of a communal black culture that not only differentiated black people from the materially oriented middle-class majority, but also enabled them to adapt to an inimical environment. White American culture, which was never able to liberate itself from that of Europe, has been lost in the exigencies of the pragmatism of the success ethic, as white intellectuals, including Norman Mailer, Thomas Pynchon and Don DeLillo, have indignantly or pessimistically pointed out. However, these social critics are themselves subject to the demands and rewards of the postindustrial machine: they willingly play the role of a strategic elite within the existing order, and, quite naturally, they would preserve their favored status. Blacks, however, who have produced the only indigenous American art form in their music, have as a whole been put outside the system. No matter how many of them individually do and will join the orthodox mainstream, they have achieved a sense of community that has little to do with that of pluralistic white groups, which are included in the middle class. A feeling of solidarity is common to black folk from the South to the North, from the church to the bar, from the rural settlement to the slums. The fact that blacks complain about their race's not sticking together, a sentiment that is not common to ethnic associations, testifies to a strong consciousness of black solidarity.

In the first place, blacks' cultural difference is based on their African heritage, as distinguished from whites' European heritage. Insofar as blacks affirm their roots, they can transcend the modern sense of alienation, which calls into question the binary opposition between spirit and matter on which occidental civilization is based, from which that civilization derives its ethical bias and which would oppose the mind to the body and the rationalized to the unspoken word. Second, black culture is founded on a recognized value system which turns that of official white America upside down—or right side up. Whites founded their system of oppression on universal human rights; blacks could, therefore, make a claim to the moral essence of America by demanding their rights. And, third, black culture is based on certain techniques of survival that blacks have developed through the ages and which are themselves potential art forms. The trickster, the con man, the so-called signifying monkey might have pretended to submit to the white man's authority, but at the same time the trickster availed himself of the latter's skills—and often goods—and converted them to his own uses.

Nowadays, for instance, the black has—despite himself—been integrated. As there are many Americans—Anglo ethnics in particular—with hidden black blood, so there are practically no African Americans left who do not have some kind of white forebears. The mulatto is the trickster *par excellence:* he is Brer Rabbit at the same time as he is Farmer Brown; he is the white-black, the player, the illusionist, who can envision a truth behind the façade of an ethic oriented to results, who can turn appearance back on itself and promote the collusion between process and being.

In this book, I have tried to present face-to-face the white and black trends in contemporary culture. Part I is a summary of the economic, political and social effects of segregation that have resulted in the emergence of an industrially unassimilable class (a class that has no place in postindustrial society) of ghetto blacks. Part II analyzes blacks' reactions to this secondary form of slavery, from those of Booker T. Washington and W. E. B. DuBois to those of Martin Luther King, Jr., Malcolm X and the black rebels of the 1960s. Part III is an examination of the stereotypes, most with sexual implications, by which whites have instituted the dogma of their superiority and, therefore, authorized the exploitation and control of black people. These stereotypes are so intimately embedded in the fabric of white American culture that intellectuals repeat and perpetuate them to this day. And, finally, Part IV is an account of blacks' struggle to achieve their own cultural autonomy, particularly with respect to these stereotypical themes that represent the bias of white supremacy—themes which have been or can be turned against them and yet which, on a symbolic level, have been instrumental in the development of the blacks' cultural self-definition.

PART I

SEGREGATION AND POVERTY IN INDUSTRIAL AND POSTINDUSTRIAL AMERICA

CHAPTER 1

CULTURAL AND ECONOMIC SEGREGATION

Operation of the American industrial state depends upon the cohesiveness of a "democratic" middle class, which is committed not only ideologically to uphold the system, but also economically to support it as a consumer market. There can be few dissidents. Even intellectuals have become apologists for a status quo in which they enjoy a privileged position. The working class does not constitute a possible source of conflict[1]—as former radicals supposed it would. It is middle class itself: the principle of egalitarianism has conferred on the working class a kind of status; it is tied to the consumer market. Immigrants have been comfortably assimilated into the cultural mainstream. Indeed, all sorts of separate interest groups are integrated in a social organization whose dominant aim, says sociologist John Dollard, "seems to be to middle-class-ify all of its members."[2] Since the effect of mass production, mass consumption and the mass media is standardization or "regimentation on a vast scale,"[3] there is practically no one to contest the industrial regime. Every individual and every association—no matter how self-seeking his or its goals—show an inclination to conform to the establishment.

Obviously, class equality exists only in idea and not in fact. It is the product of the practical politics and economics of the consumer state: it is the effect of an ethic which, like that of the American materialist, tends to disguise ideals in the form of things. The ideology of America is arbitrary because it has never been satisfactorily defined: it is assumed to be a self-evident good. Actually, the middle-class majority is made up of all kinds of divergent, self-centered and conflicting groups. But even if this majority does not constitute a bloc, it is supposed to represent American democracy. As such it is a morally charged term: the

middle class is a value in itself. And as prosperity has presumably confirmed the virtue of the American order, any other system dominated
by any other class is considered to be undemocratic and inferior.

It was, of course, the degradation of an out-class that made possible
the consolidation of the in-class. The black has historically represented
the minority that, by contrast, defined the acceptable majority. He was,
in fact, the constant throughout centuries of American experience because he was always treated as the antithesis of the American norm.
Certain Marxist dialecticians such as Herbert Marcuse and Jean-Michel
Palmier considered him the true American revolutionary: he would incarnate the "new proletariat . . . a real danger for the world system of
capitalism."[4]

Some blacks have become as influential members of the middle class
as individuals of any other group. These belong chiefly to the technocratic and intellectual elites. "The . . . exception to [the] picture of ethnic separation is the compartment marked intellectuals and artists," says
sociologist Milton Gordon.[5] Black intellectuals can be as much apologists for the industrial state as immigrant and native whites. But collectively as a race, blacks are more and more disadvantaged especially as
many of their racial family enjoy the privileges of status. This is a phenomenon that has already occurred in American history. After the
American Revolution, segments of the free black population were able
to prosper materially even as the institution of slavery hardened and
spread throughout the South. After Reconstruction, the economic, political and social prowess of individual blacks caused class divisions
within the community while, concurrently, Jim Crow prevailed on a
national level.

In effect, the most consistent theme of American history involves
white Americans' treatment of the black. "The most distinctive feature
of United States history is Afro-American slavery and its consequences.
. . . It is . . . at the heart of our *cultural* experience."[6] America seems to
owe its continuity and coherence to the presence of the black. His exploitation has been an essential element in the country's rise to world
power. It provided the South with marketable capital; it made possible
whites' conquest and domination of the wilderness and its resources—
which was the precondition of industrial organization—and it provided
necessary labor to develop the economy. "One could even argue that
the institution of Negro slavery helped provide the capital on which the
Industrial Revolution was based."[7] As the ground on which the original
American federation was established, slavery made for the social co-

hesiveness of whites. It is a question, said one critic, "whether the government which [the founders] set up necessarily implies the continued existence of an illiterate peasantry"[8] or whether its very institution depended on slavery. Certainly this "was the cause of two of the three great compromises that entered into the making of the Constitution. . . ."[9] And, certainly, "the degradation of non-whites frequently served to bind together the white population. . . ."[10]

If, as the historian Louis Hacker contended, *"our climate has always been capitalist,"*[11] and so profit oriented, then the large-scale organization of slavery at the expense of the small farmer was implicit in southern expansionism and land speculation. Later, emancipation and the defeat of southern agricultural feudalism cleared the way for the triumph of northern industrialization. But it was the reunion of the North and the South, which depended on black peonage, black disfranchisement and black segregation, that stimulated capitalistic development. The assumption of black inferiority, sustained by forced black subservience, sanctioned whites' identification of might and right. Because of the black's rejection, white workers—both immigrant and native—were integrated relatively peacefully into the economic process that led to America's strength. The disadvantaged freed man, "no longer . . . the property of the individual master . . . [was] considered the slave of society," said sociologist, critic and educator W. E. B. DuBois.[12] As J. C. Calhoun's grandson prophesied in 1883, southern conflict—like that of the North—would "not assume the form of labor against capital, but of race against race."[13]

Recently, poverty and unemployment—which have drastically increased in the black community—constitute the economic bottom floor above which the middle class comes together. Poverty and unemployment provide a moral, cultural and economic norm. Blacks are reproached for their understatus, a reproach which dialectically justifies whites' advantages. Black victimization, wrote the militant Stokely Carmichael, "takes place . . . first . . . in fact and deed, then . . . in the official recording of those facts."[14] George Bernard Shaw commented that America "has relegated the Negro to be a bootblack and now condemns him because his hands are dirty."[15] It is this kind of pragmatic thinking that dominates the industrial approach.

Since it is blacks—particularly working-age black youths—who make up a disproportionate percentage of the unemployed and of the criminal population, and since it is black families that are most severely dislocated, color has come to assume "the characteristics of a cultural norm."[16] America has been moving "toward two societies, one black, one white—separate and unequal."[17] The material plenty of the one is balanced by the material penury of the other. The black suffers not simply from a general—even class—struggle to get by, but from his particular situation as a "poor race in a land of dollars."[18] Yet the well-being of the white majority depends on the black's deprivation. Indeed, culturally, the black is the dialectical perpetrator of middle-class standards that facilitate the operation of industrial and post-industrial America. He is the out-class, the have-not by whom a heterogeneous people has been consolidated into a universalist democracy with nothing in common but its difference to him. To be "human and universal . . . in the white folks' . . . cultural philosophy means 'universally white.' "[19]

In effect, the black represents the bonds of history that industrial culture has assumedly overcome by its material prowess. Theoretically, industrial culture has liberated man from his primeval battle to survive against nature. Industrial America, which has created and enlarged middle-class welfare, is an ahistorical state: it denies the past and its dependence on it. Standardization and middle-classification constitute a rejection of historical roots. The modern impoverished black minority, which bears its and its country's history in its color, which started as the slave labor force of a white bourgeois elite in order to become the economic victim of a heterogeneous white public, incarnates the evolution of middle-class democracy.

Only blacks remain in their relative group integrity to represent American history with its changing values and social order. The Anglo-Saxons, who settled the country and set its social tone, have suffered a decline of power. Protestant morality, the basis of the cultural standard that stresses industry, thrift and self-reliance—the preconditions of the industrial ethic—no longer obtains. The idea of opportunity, the mood of optimism, which persisted in various forms throughout America's rise to power, have been deflated by the close of the frontier, the impersonal structure of the managerial state and the more or less traumatic experiences such as the Vietnam War, that have characterized American foreign policy in the twentieth century.

Nevertheless, the black remains the preserver of the old heritage. Because he is the only American who must reach out beyond his own group "for absolute identification," as the black reporter Louis Lomax pointed out, he is the only American "unwilling to make even the slightest compromise in the American creed."[20] He upholds the principles on which the country was founded: he has "no ideology other than that of democracy,"[21] wrote Frederick Patterson, a black commentator. "The American Negro believes in democracy,"[22] Langston Hughes, the poet, affirmed. Blacks are "passionate believers in democracy [and] the broader American ideals." They are idealists whose "true source of power" lies in their "ability to suffer even death for the attainment of [their] beliefs,"[23] says novelist Ralph Ellison. Culturally, the black is "more like the white 'old American' than [are] any other sub-groups,"[24] as sociologist Lloyd Warner remarked. He has not only developed a "folk tradition," but he has also maintained that "of the gentleman,"[25] according to black social thinker E. Franklin Frazier. In fact, he is perhaps more American than most whites since "his aboriginal culture was smashed":[26] he was forcibly cut off from his African heritage. As DuBois summed up, "There is nothing so indigenous, so 'made in America' as we."[27]

Writer James Baldwin pointed out, "In our image of the Negro breathes the past we deny."[28] And since this past incarnates the dichotomous confluence of humanitarianism and racism, of the ideal of equal rights and the practice of oppression—and the dependence of the one on the other—it represents American reality. Naturally, white Americans will not accept it. The "organic-racist view of man . . . stands in sharp opposition to most [American] value orientations."[29] Gunnar Myrdal, the Swedish sociologist, claims that racism indicates Americans' *"need for a defense . . . against their national creed."*[30] In effect, racism is intentional: it is a coherent policy that served pragmatically to expedite the functioning of the diverse industrial state by consolidating diverse Americans. It is, therefore, as DuBois saw, a "deliberately cultivated and encouraged state of mind."[31] Only Indians, who were progressively eliminated, and blacks have "never been included in the original *consensus universalis* (universal consensus) of the American republic."[32] Capitalistic democracy depended on the black: had he not been brought to America in the beginning of its history, he would have had to be invented. In a real sense, he *was* invented. Black is an abstraction which stands outside the existence of black individuals. In other words, black is a category which misrepresents the person in himself.

It was the South that, after the Civil War, exploited the racist ideology. The South stressed the doctrine that "Negroes belonged to a separate and inferior species,"[33] the concept by which slavery had been rationalized and to which the North was culturally habituated. The

South consequently instituted segregative practices to which the North, convinced of Negro inferiority, acquiesced.

Segregation, based on this postulate of black inferiority, was the means of northern and southern reunion. It was "second-class citizenship," as black leader Malcolm X said, "a modified form of slavery."[34] The middle class was devastated in the South; it was threatened by urbanization, industrialization and immigration in the North; but it could be brought together by racism, which had historically bolstered cultural attitudes. In the South, "biological inferiority,"[35] a relic of slavery, consolidated the white majority and accorded it economic, sexual and prestige gains.[36] Segregation made it possible to avoid a clash between rising sectors of society—such as middle-class strivers, new entrepreneurs and boisterous agrarians—and the old declining aristocrats. Negro subservience was the means of uniting whites.[37]

In the North, segregation occurred at a time when immigrants and the industrial new rich were threatening past structures and values. Belief in Negro inferiority had an opportunistic dimension: it was a way of affirming nativist group interests without disturbing traditional cultural norms. And so, by the 1880s, as the sociologist Robert Wiebe remarked, scarcely any Americans "still doubted the Negro's proper place."[38] He was "the national scapegoat in the reconciliation . . . of North and South,"[39] says historian C. Vann Woodward. According to black writer Amiri Baraka, racism is "the basic social organization of this society."[40]

Moreover, segregation provided a cultural ground on which a new white social order could be based. Aimed uniquely at the black, his separation was self-perpetuating. Racism, founded on color, is "the most effective single instrument for keeping people down that has ever been found"[41]—as one sociologist, Michael Harrington, pointed out— not just because the black inherits and bequeaths his visibility, but because prejudicial attitudes tend automatically to reproduce themselves, as children assume the bias of their parents.[42] As Mydral remarks, the practice of segregation *"constitute[s] an added motive for every individual white group to maintain [it]."*[43]

Although the South initiated the rule of segregation, it was methodologically the invention of the North, which had in many ways adopted the practice after its own emancipation of slaves. All the North had to do was to give its already established approval to the idea of black inferiority for the policy to flourish. After the Civil War the North soon lost interest in its enforcement of black protection. The North preferred not just to abandon the black, but to justify its infidelity by supporting the South in the assumption that he was incompetent. Of course the North had always entertained racist attitudes. Abraham Lincoln, with his capitalistic Continental vision, had reflected northern opinion when, as victorious president, he endorsed simultaneously the doctrines of human equality and of black inferiority. He did not believe the black was as capable as the white. He also associated democracy with majority will, which had been oriented to racist bias throughout American history. Whites for centuries had implicitly condoned racist slavery. Most of them had been schooled through generations of slavery to think of blacks as lesser human beings: even the abolitionists were prejudiced, as Frederick Douglass discovered. If might meant right, then blacks should be required to submit to white hegemony.

Andrew Jackson brought the question of black rights closer to the capitalistic ethic of laissez-faire. He evaded the issue of the blacks' suffrage, vetoed a bill giving the blacks the vote in Washington, D.C.—on which he was overruled—and challenged the freed but totally dispossessed slave to make good in an open market controlled by advantaged whites. If the poor, illiterate, landless peasant could not rise to middle-class status by his own efforts, then he would have proved himself by the law of nature to be inferior to those who were better off than he. Success was the *a posteriori* sign of spiritual worth. In effect, Jackson, a lower-class white seeking opportunity for his own group, made it clear that his was "a white man's government intended for white men only,"[44] as certain leaders proclaimed. His position reflected that of the South.

It was the Supreme Court, dominated by northern Republicans, that officially sanctioned and thus nationalized the practice of segregation. Before its decision, the South had resisted black Reconstruction rights on a state and community level. It tried to reduce the black to servitude by undermining local leaders; it attacked individuals and it dissembled its policy. But the Supreme Court universalized the doctrine of black inferiority. Quite naturally it rationalized its ruling that blacks and whites constituted separate societies. In keeping with the American idealistic tradition, the justices came up with the concept of "separate but equal"[45] to moralize their decision. In fact, as most observers realized, the practice affirmed the dominance of the white majority. It "confirmed the white majority's habits, customs, traditions and way of life."[46] It "helped place the stamp of inferiority on black men and labeled them irrelevant."[47] As the liberal newspaper *The Nation* reported, "The Ne-

gro will disappear from the field of national politics. Henceforth, the
nation, as a nation, will have nothing to do with him."[48]

The very argument of Jim Crow—or segregation—was based on
liberal economic concepts, although in practice, in an increasingly industrialized state, Adam Smith's mercantile theory of laissez-faire had
been outmoded. It was, in fact, founded on two contradictory notions:
the first, pragmatic, that "no connection existed between economic behavior and moral conduct"[49] clashed with the second, evaluative, that
sin was the cause of poverty and failure. Both coincided in their sanction
of exploitation—one methodologically and the other ideally—and both
endorsed the concept that might was right. In any case, the illusion of
equal opportunity in a free market persisted in the public mind.

In upholding the tradition of laissez-faire, the Court, of course, minimized the implications of racial bondage to which it was subjecting the
black. To deny a man a hotel room on the basis of color was not to
enslave him, it argued. If a Negro legislature (at that point there were
conveniently none in America) "should enact a [separate but equal] law,
whites, who were endowed by nature with dynamism, energy and ambition, would not consider themselves inferior."[50] But as Booker T.
Washington observed, "The courts in no section of the country would
uphold a case where negroes sought to segregate white citizens."[51] Indeed, in the Reconstruction South, when blacks had access to state leg-
islatures, they had never taken advantage of their numbers and their
power to impose their racial will. They showed no inclination to dominate their former masters: they were instrumental in enacting measures
to benefit poor whites as well as blacks.[52]

Nevertheless, segregation legally denied blacks jobs, schooling, ad-
equate housing and civil rights. It was an essential factor in reducing
them, who had struggled to emerge from slavery, to an underclass condition. Segregation authorized white might.

Naturally, there was an obvious discrepancy between segregation,
which was the open practice of racism, and democratic theory, for
which the North had—in principle for the good of the Union—fought
a long and bloody war. But as critic James Comer observes, "The white
mind operates consciously and unconsciously to deny that white racism
gives whites an unbeatable social, psychological and economic advantage over blacks."[53] White thinking clings stubbornly to the idealism on
which the country was presumably founded: it tries to justify itself not
just by the materialistic ethic that upholds whatever prevails as right,
but by transcendent standards.

So the discrepancy between officially sanctioned race discrimination and the ideal of equal rights demanded a defensive ideology. As the new segregation laws were legitimized, science, social science and philosophy were enlisted in a campaign to prove that blacks were, in fact, inferior to whites and that Jim Crow, therefore, was a rationally, not expediently founded policy.

Biological science, for instance, came to the conclusion that the Negro was a lesser man than the white. Its "stamp . . . on . . . ideas convinced many Americans, North and South, that whatever equality meant, it did not mean that the Negro was equal to the white man."[54] Inequality was a principle associated with racial inferiority which—by dialectical extension—affirmed the ideal of the democracy of a higher order of Americans. The *Dictionary of Races,* purportedly based on objective criteria and commissioned by President Theodore Roosevelt, stressed inheritance as the "critical element in determining racial affiliation."[55] Blacks produced a lesser species of man, and so should be dispossessed and separated. The study asserted, however, that new immigrants from southern and eastern Europe were not as evolved as Anglo-Saxons, who were from the most progressive sections of Europe.[56] As the ethnics were assimilated, the *Dictionary* was discredited.

Neo-Darwinian philosophers also produced theories supporting racial discrimination. The late nineteenth century was a period of Anglo-Saxon supremacy and, therefore, the evolutionary concept was expanded to hypothesize that there had been an original battle of mankind in which the most worthy race—God's and nature's favored Anglo-Saxon—had prevailed. By virtue of the Anglo-Saxon's victory and of the Anglo-Saxon's assumed position as the moral and economic vanguard of humanity, he was obligated to dominate his inferiors. White America's very rise to industrial power involved the mastery of those who were other than its representatives. "The race integrity ideology of the white man . . . is bound up with a Master Race complex. . . ."[57] His mission, his insistence that he had the most developed "instinct of progress,"[58] compelled him to conquer those whom he considered backward, undemocratic, unworthy—mostly colored—peoples. Racism was thus an essential factor in the emergence of the interventionist state on both economic and noneconomic levels: industrialism brought with it imperialism against all kinds of nonwhite peoples.

Sociologists also endorsed the theory of Anglo-Saxon supremacy during the 1890s. Many of the devoted champions of democracy—like the sociologists Charles Copley and Lester Ward—were subject to race prejudice.[59] Herbert Croly's father, David, wrote an antiblack pamphlet, and Croly's New Nationalism was opposed to pluralism.[60] Intellectuals of the day tended to point to the black—over foreign, noncolored newcomers—as the least qualified and least assimilable of all human groupings. This opinion, of course, facilitated ethnic integration, again at the expense of the black: new immigrants were preferable as industrial laborers.[61]

Politicians propagated racist ideas while at the same time maintaining the idea of equality on the pretext that they were endorsing the principle of free enterprise. If blacks could not succeed by their own efforts, they deserved the lower social place to which they were *a priori* assigned. President Taft, for example, righteously insisted that blacks compete in a white-controlled market, "base their hope on the results of their own industry, self-restraint, thrift and business success" and rely on the "aid and comfort and sympathy"[62] of their white southern rulers. He also relieved the few blacks who had remained in official Republican ranks of their political jobs. Woodrow Wilson introduced segregation to the federal bureaucracy. He was influenced, he said, by the suggestion of "several of the heads of departments." But, he insisted, he was acting in the "interests of the Negroes,"[63] by whose disfranchisement and segregation, he wrote elsewhere, "the South has rid itself of the only obstacle which kept it from enjoying the fruits of . . . nationalism and prosperity."[64] Warren Harding, who was presumed himself to have black blood, came out vigorously against "racial amalgamation." It was not a question of social equality, he claimed, but one of "fundamental, eternal and inescapable difference" between white and Negro.[65]

Inevitably, historians followed the trend—even to the point of revising the theory of the cause of the Civil War. University professors maintained that it was fought not over slavery, but over the issue of secession. The historian Francis Parkman had, like Roosevelt, an Anglo-Saxon supremacist view of the past. Although certain scholars like Hermann von Hoist and James Schouler interpreted black bondage, the one as a "slavocratic," the other as a "race," practice,[66] many northern academics followed the lead of southern apologists who treated slavery as the only method of preserving superior white culture. During Reconstruction, historian James Ford Rhodes spread the legend of blacks' venality and incompetence. They constituted "one of the most inferior races of mankind."[67] Apparently he was trying to conciliate his southern colleagues. Historian Claude Bowers endorsed the Ku Klux Klan, as the historian Ulrich Phillips did slavery itself.[68] Henry Steele Commager and Samuel Eliot Morison suggested that "Sambo" might have "suffered less than any other class in the South from its 'peculiar institution.' "[69] Historians William Dunning and—to a lesser extent—Arthur Schlesinger, Jr., pretended that the Civil War had little to do with the institution of slavery.

Reformers tended at best to paternalize, at worst to debase black people. "Committed to the doctrine of advancing social justice and equality of opportunity," said the historian Merle Curti, they "devoted little attention to an important limitation on political democracy—the denial of suffrage to Negroes in the South."[70] They had, in effect, "contempt for Negroes,"[71] as DuBois remarked. They worked "not [for] the liberation of the black, but the fortification of the white."[72] Even the most self-conscious of the progressives, such as Oswald Garrison Villard, grandson of the abolitionist William Lloyd Garrison, expected Negroes to be humble and thankful for any attentions given them. White liberals were inclined to blame blacks for sectional strife, for graft under Reconstruction regimes and for southern lawlessness. And boss machines, the reform mafias of which Anglo-Saxon progressives disapproved, benefited ethnics at the expense of the blacks.

The idea of black inferiority, the justification of segregation, was, therefore, reinforced on all levels of society. The black was considered to be "little . . . better than a beast."[73] And this idea was propagated until it was accepted as the expression of democratic majority opinion.

Segregation was, of course, methodically necessary to the South's rehabilitation. It was a factor in the relative redress of the southern economy, which had been decimated by defeat. Segregation kept the blacks—who for the most part had remained in the South and whose labor was necessary in the fields—from uniting with poor whites on a class basis during a proposed alliance of farmers and sharecroppers. Jim Crow was the conservative planter's response to Populism: Negrophobe elements entered the ruling party. The doctrine of racial inferiority gave confidence to a "numerically preponderant poor-white population [which] feared the economic competition and the social and political power of the large black population,"[74] wrote public servant Ralph Bunche. Segregation accompanied the rise of town-based strivers, such as Henry Grady, who were trying at the expense of the Negro to construct a New South in collaboration with northern business interests and often with redneck Negro-baiting demagogues. Jim Crow "followed a route marked by the newly assertive Southern white farmers and townsmen."[75]

The slave, once freed, at first looked to his former master for protection from, if not for a base in, an uprooted social order. But the planter felt threatened by a Populist movement that would unite poor whites and Negroes. So he sacrificed blacks to the expedient of white solidarity. He wanted to keep blacks in a subservient position so they would have to depend on him. He could exploit them as workers and servants as long as they remained in a state of insecurity in a world in which he alone could shelter them. Consequently, the planter encouraged animosity between lower-class whites and blacks. Nevertheless, he—prodded especially by his women[76]—refused to sanction lynching and mob rioting against his self-appointed wards: this again was a method of making them dependent on him. Indeed, the gentleman farmer could afford to denounce terrorism as long as there were others who used it to degrade blacks. It was the planters, however, who failed Booker T. Washington in crises of disfranchisement and segregative abuse.[77] Obviously, they were not eager to promote Negro self-reliance.

In effect, segregation led to the entrenchment of the ruling elite and to white social cohesion, known as democracy. It was an authorized outlet for the frustrations of ignorant white rednecks because it disempowered the black politically, socially and economically, and protected them from any competition with him. They enjoyed a sense of status by which they could coexist harmoniously with the upper stratum. The abasement of the Negro was an essential factor "in the reconciliation of estranged white classes and the reunion of the Solid South."[78]

Evidently, the South could assert a voice in national affairs only if it was united. Its solidarity, which it manifested particularly in religious and racial fundamentalism, was based on racism. The North would not invest in a troubled social order; the North also could not economically progress in a sectionally antagonistic political state. In effect, southerners allowed northerners to intervene in their affairs—indeed, to colonize them—in exchange for a regional license to degrade freed blacks. The Redeemers, said Woodward, were eager to "cooperate with *economic* carpetbaggers" for white supremacy.[79] "The South became a satellite of the dominant region . . . a bulwark instead of a menace to the new order"—of industrialism.[80] In the name of states' rights it assumed the "freedom to oppress" and to flout federal law.[81] The North, meanwhile, sanctioned racist segregation in principle in the South—and in practice in the North—in order to expedite its capitalistic development. In many ways industrial interests were responsible for the blacks' abasement. As Dollard points out, white solidarity, the political assertion of the poor white and the caste system—all effects of segregation—were the result of "Northern interference in the South."[82]

And yet, while on the one hand segregation served the interests of the growing industrial state, on the other, paradoxically, it was not compatible with southern tradition. As an ideology, it bolstered the racism that was the justification of slavery; as a practice, it was at variance with folk customs. It was a form of social organization which was new to the region; in effect, it was imposed on the south. Psychologist Joel Kovel, for instance, claims that segregation was forced on the people. It represented an "effort to accommodate southern culture to the dominant mainstream."[83] Jim Crow stood for legislation that actually changed southern habits: it was, therefore, proof that habits and opinions can be drastically modified by legal means—despite the argument of modern liberals and segregationists who insist that laws cannot change popular attitudes. In fact, culture feeds on transformation. Before segregation was enforced, blacks had lived and worked and played alongside whites; the segregation laws deliberately isolated black people. And this separation created a "lower-class society," a "dark America of the rural and of the urban Negro."[84] White America meanwhile took pride in being basically a middle-class society. Color began, pragmatically, to serve as a substitute for class.[85]

Moreover, unlike feudalistic slavery, which was controlled by definite laws and customs, segregation did not assign the black to a fixed place in the hierarchy of labor relations. It was flexible and inconsistent. The preacher could work as a bricklayer, the professor as a butler. The Jim Crow statutes, which the Supreme Court pretended were irrelevant to color discrimination, increased racism by bureaucratizing it in public institutions.[86] Those laws were "effective means of tightening and freezing—in many cases instigating—segregation and discrimination."[87] As historian Maury Maverick puts it, "Out of economic and political conflict there was born a race prejudice even greater than existed before the Civil War."[88] The caste color line was a "catalyst to widen differences and engender conflicts."[89] People who had no animosity toward blacks, who had never owned slaves, were encouraged by law to become hostile, especially as blacks were eliminated from the sphere of relationships that obtain in the ordinary course of existence—those of buyer and seller, of worker and worker, of student and student. "With a Negro you couldn't be close friends like you can with another white man . . ." remarks one of Sherwood Anderson's southern crackers in "The Man Who Became a Woman." "There's been too much talk about the difference between whites and blacks. . . ."[90] Whites became obsessed about, often fearful of, the race they were persecuting. Thomas Wolfe's lower-middle-class mother in *Look Homeward, Angel* was afraid of the Negroes on whom her son and his gang "made war."[91]

Whereas Jim Crow was imposed on the South, it existed *de facto* in the North. The social order was founded on segregation by class and especially by caste. Because northern industrial democracy still upheld the principle of laissez-faire opportunity, the practice of segregation amounted to social indifference: northern racism was what Kovel calls "*aversive.*" It was the "organization *of . . . racial relations . . . modern and abstract.*"[92] Unlike southerners, northerners did not openly act out the part of race masters. The economy was focused on the profit principle and the social system, which reflected this interest, expressed its racial bias in institutionalized economic terms. Since the black was the most deprived of all ethnic and occupational groups—particularly as he migrated en masse from the South to northern cities—he occupied the poorest of available slums, quite separated from the middle class.

In fact, the impoverished, uneducated black rural laborer made up a caste of permanent underprivileged. He inhabited slums not just because he could not afford the rent for proper housing, but because the cities to which he came were already ghettoized.[93] He was unqualified for productive jobs not just because he lacked the training but also because white workers refused to admit him into their unions.[94] Because he faced an impersonal system and not individuals, he was unable to fight for his rights. The more he failed to succeed, the more he was subject—as a group—to the hostility of a politically active white majority which refused to consider him as a first-class citizen.

The antiblack climate of the North discouraged Negroes from leaving the South, where at least everyone was relatively equally deprived. In the closed environment of the North, "racial lines were . . . more and more tightly drawn."[95] Even interracial communities imposed limits on the influx of nonwhites.[96] And as *de facto* Jim Crow boundaries were defined, blacks were caught behind bars.[97] "Whoever heard of integration between a mop and a banker," asked a cleaning man.[98] Blacks were exploited by what theologian Reinhold Niebuhr called the "publicans,"[99] the better citizens who hardly saw them, but whose indifference to them entrenched them in their lower status. "The social isolation of the northern urban Negro is, for very large numbers, more complete than it ever was for the Negro rural resident in the South."[100]

Therefore, segregation, the application of the concept of black inferiority, was an essential ingredient in the historical and social fabric of American culture. "Racist assumptions of white superiority have been so deeply ingrained in the structure of society that it infuses its entire functioning, and is so much a part of the national subconscious that it is taken for granted and is frequently not even recognized,"[101] writes Carmichael. But these assumptions were purposeful. It is obvious, says Myrdal, that whites *"really want . . . to keep Negroes in a lower status."*[102] It is also obvious that segregation, based on the illusion of separate but equal, has allowed whites to reconcile the concepts of democracy and exclusivity and thus to reject their responsibility for having committed black people to social bondage. They have simply accepted the fact of blacks' lower status as if they had had nothing to do with it—and *a posteriori* they have profited from the situation.

Segregation is a totalistic policy that has affected every facet of blacks' existence. It has provided for their disfranchisement, for their disqualification in the labor market, for their inadequate housing, for their ill-funded schools and inferior education and for their exclusion from proper recreational, medical and transportation facilities. It has even permitted whites to refuse them entry to white Christian churches. Indeed, segregation perpetuates segregation.

With respect to education, for instance, blacks, South and North, in rural as well as urban environments, have been deprived of the means not simply to succeed but to survive in industrial America. Since opportunity depends increasingly on proper training, schooling is an essential prerequisite for all Americans. But in the South, states simply did not allocate the same resources to black schools as to white. Since the turn of the century, the Southern Education Board has done "its work of promoting white education"[103] while it seized the school funds allotted by the federal government to blacks. As a black sharecropper remarked, we got "mighty little [to start our schools] from the state government."[104]

In the North, schools in the ghetto—to which blacks are relegated—have necessarily received less money than those in middle-class districts, since poor blacks pay less in taxes. "Statewide equalization of per pupil property tax bases"[105] does not benefit schools in central cities, which have fewer pupils and in which educational standards are disastrously low. As the educator Robert Hutchins pointed out, segregation on the basis of color is especially damaging, for achievement is conditioned by racial background more at the end of the school process than at the beginning.[106] The black child loses ground as he advances, not because his schools are less exacting but because his environment—as he matures—is less conducive to study.[107]

Moreover, since education is linked so intimately to economic gain, education is a source of particularly strong levels of public opinion in both the South and the North. White people do not want their children to go to school with blacks: they are afraid not just of racial intermingling, but also of the effects of lower educational standards. Habitually, the middle-class majority is apathetic: it is indifferent to the plight of the black. But it can be aroused to irrational—especially violent—action on the issue of schooling.[108] Regardless of existing laws, which in principle have redressed school inequities, it seems that it would be difficult to enforce the practice of equal education by any means. Since the end of the Civil War, states with "substantial racial differences"[109] have established or approved separate schools: even where desegregation was significant, "the proportion of white schoolmates for the average black child increased only .03."[110] As in New York, "in the minds of most Negroes . . . the problem of education is the problem of segregation."[111]

Black children inherit their disadvantage. They have been deprived of the opportunity to qualify for productive jobs. In the ghetto in particular they seem unable to adapt to, much less achieve in, their schools. Inadequate performance, of course, breeds teacher indifference, which, in turn, increases the resistance of pupils. Negro students are often dismissed as irremediably ineducable, and the fact that they are so treated tends to condemn them to incompetence. They are unmotivated and ill prepared. As the sociologist Kenneth Clark pointed out, "The child of whom little is expected produces little."[112] Ghetto schools have been turning out functional illiterates to a postindustrial "knowledge-intensive"[113] labor market. Moreover, black self-help projects—such as the drive to upgrade community schools in New York by assigning black teachers to black students—roused the indignant opposition of a Jewish-controlled teachers' union led by Albert Shanker, which wanted to preserve educational posts for its members.[114] Again, many years ago in Fulton, Ohio, Negro instructors were fired when they staged a boycott in order to teach in a segregated school.[115]

Quite naturally, the practice of segregation blocked the chances of success of Negro entrepreneurs. It consigned them to the financially limited consumer market of their own race. In general, blacks did not and do not have enough buying power to enable the few exceptional black capitalists to make it rich. "There are no important commercial and industrial enterprises in Negro communities . . ." wrote Frazier.[116] Negro businesses have suffered from the competitive disadvantage of size, from credit difficulties and from the fact that traditionally their executives have been refused entrance to business schools and to apprentice training.[117]

But more disastrous for the Negro group as a whole, segregation has closed out potential job openings. It was the source of labor discrimination in the North as in the South. In Boston, for instance, in 1950, blacks had a lower occupational status than whites even when they were more educated than members of other minorities. There were also "disparities in the relative earnings of blacks and whites at higher occupational levels," according to sociologist Stephen Thernstrom. He concludes, "The economic status of Negroes in Boston from the late nineteenth century to 1940 . . . was much too low to be explained as the result of their educational deficiencies"[118] and the disadvantages of their ghetto housing or family conditions. It was caused by deliberate racial discrimination.

This type of discrimination, however, has been a positive factor in the development of the industrial state. Because of it, Negroes could be used as a buffer between white workers and their managers whenever the former became too demanding. DuBois spoke of the unfair utilization of the Negro as a poorly paid but irregularly employed labor reserve during the period of industrial growth.[119] For Jim Crow provided the capitalist with a constant supply of jobless Negroes of which he could avail himself in order not just to keep wages down, but also to break up strikes. Indeed, segregation was an invaluable means of domesticating white labor whose militancy was a potential obstacle in the operation of political capitalism. Even in times of labor harmony, the presence of a perpetually disadvantaged segment of the population was a benefit to business, which, to profit, had to keep group tension at a minimum. Whites could always count on the fact that blacks were the last to be hired and the first to be fired. Color, unlike ethnicity, was the "*single* identifying characteristic."[120]

As a critic says, racism relaxed "the relationships between the middle and upper classes on the one hand and the lower classes on the other."[121] The sociologist George Frederickson writes, "My assumption is that economic discrimination along racial lines would not have developed and persisted in the industrial era to the extent that it did had it not served . . . the material interests of industrial capitalists and skilled white workers."[122] Prejudice, said A. Philip Randolph, the black labor leader, "is the chief weapon in the South which enables the capitalists to exploit both races."[123] "The white worker has felt . . . less a proletariat . . . than his counterpart in Europe because of the existence of a black proletariat . . . beneath him."[124] The race view, observed sociologist Talcott Parsons, "provides a floor below which [low-stratum] people cannot fall."[125]

In the South blacks, of course, were excluded from most industries. The opinion prevailed that there was an "incompatibility between black labor and advanced technology."[126] As DuBois remarked, labor segregation was instituted to remove the Negro from competition with skilled and unskilled whites. Indeed, the campaign "which culminated in the Atlanta Massacre of 1906 [when whites butchered blacks] was an attempt [of] politicians, to arouse the prejudices of the rank and file of white laborers and farmers against the growing competition of black men [and force them] back to subserviency."[127]

Paradoxically, it had been radical Reconstruction after the Civil War that had prevented the organization of a southern black industrial work force. Republicans were exponents of free enterprise. The exslaves, consequently, had no place in the labor market: the pattern "was one of economic segmentation rather than competition, or cooperation between white and black workers."[128] And since the presence of blacks protected whites from class resentment, and from class consciousness, there was no union agitation in the South. Blacks stayed on the farm, reduced mostly to peonage, the practical field hands of their former masters. The white landlord "don't want no damn white man on his place," said a sharecropper. "He gets a nigger, that's his glory. He can do that nigger just like he wants to and that nigger better not say nothin against his rulins."[129]

In the North job segregation was effective as a means of integrating a white work force which was troubled by the influx of immigrants not accustomed to factory employment and by the stress of industrial organization. Foreigners were not used to the new labor management.[130] The very institution of unions diverted workers from assuming a militant class posture. Segregation allowed—and encouraged—these associations to practice racial discrimination. "The American working class [was] split by the color line."[131]

Skilled workers jealously protected themselves from black competition, thereby effectively closing off opportunity for blacks in the higher echelons of labor. As DuBois realized, "Union labor had not welcomed

Negro workers since the collapse of the Knights of Labor."[132] The socialist Eugene Debs's American Railroad Union refused to admit Negroes, but accepted "the Hungarian, Polander, Italian, Chinaman," reported Richard Davis,[133] a black organizer. Labor leader Samuel Gompers of the American Federation of Labor was a racist who claimed that blacks did not "understand the philosophy of human rights."[134] By 1900 "most unions excluded blacks . . . a dozen openly, the majority by subterfuge."[135] Even the most liberal drew the color line. The Jewish-dominated International Ladies' Garment Workers' Union discriminated against blacks in New York City.[136]

Moreover, capitalists hired blacks as scabs in labor strikes, a practice that accentuated racist prejudice among white workers. Indeed, the only groups that sought black participation were certain segments of the Wobblies, whose policy was to bridge the gap "between white workers and black,"[137] and, later, during the Depression, the Congress of Industrial Organizations (CIO). But the leftist affiliations of both alienated black leaders who did not trust socialism.

With the solidification of the industrial state, segregation had led to what the sociologist Richard Edwards calls the fractionalization of the labor market.[138] Although the primary, or skilled, group shares the same interests with the secondary, or low-skilled, low-paid, casual section, the two groups remain divided and are, therefore, subject to tight corporate control. Negroes in particular have been consigned by deprivation due to race to the least satisfying types of employment. In Chicago, for instance, two thirds of the black work force was below the job ceiling.[139] In New York, in the 1960s, as Clark has remarked, one of the causes of the ghetto pathology is "the status of the jobs held."[140] The black man has no voice in bargaining because he has no power; he has no chance to rise except during labor shortages which depend on external factors like world wars.

And if in principle trade unions have taken a liberal tack and "seek to convert the Negro problem . . . into a relatively simple one of class conflicts and interests,"[141] in fact their efforts to transcend racism by ignoring it have resulted in the idea that the black is incompetent. It is he who is excluded from the primary job market and he who holds the most menial, the most temporary occupations. Discrimination actually penalizes the whole labor force because it "results in a surplus labor force whose chief characteristic is its employment at low wages." Discrimination brings "greater inequality among whites," and, at the same time, expedites the functioning of the industrial state.[142]

Because the Negro was used on a practical level to bring labor and capital together, he has ideologically served as a safeguard against the influence of Marxist doctrine. Class agitation—and the threat of class revolution—was what the capitalist feared most of all in his industrial projects. Indeed, the Marxist menace has until very recently hung over the industrial operation. Despite the agitation of ethnic intellectuals, however; despite the tenacity, even militance of mainly immigrant pre–World War I strikers—particularly in cities like Paterson, New Jersey, and Lawrence, Massachusetts—Marxism was a lost cause as long as there was an outcast labor class of blacks. This was not simply because the philosophy was uncongenial to the principles of American materialism. Rather, Marxism was unable to propagate the ideas of classlessness and social justice as long as workers accepted and welcomed caste difference. The workers were capitalists on the make who would not sink below a certain level: they had more than their chains to lose.[143]

The left, in fact, seemed to share the color bias of American labor: its strategy was not in tune with its ideological goals. Communists neither knew nor appreciated "the complex nature of Negro life."[144] At first the socialist movement hardly appeared to be radical. Blacks were an embarrassment to the movement and they were "rarely mentioned."[145] It did not seriously try to explore the revolutionary potential of the Negro masses until the 1920s—when it was closely identified with ethnics. Then as the movement enlisted blacks' participation, it implicitly discriminated against them with the arrogance of the intellectual clique that it represented.[146] As the historian Harold Cruse observes, whereas immigrant groups were encouraged to practice cultural nationalism, Negroes were criticized for so doing.[147] The "denial of black nationalism" caused one party member to "gag."[148] Nationalism and the black folk culture were considered to be "diversionary."[149] The central committee of the Communist party refused to accept even the idea that blacks could have a special, positive identity. Inside the brotherhood of Communists "they didn't see us,"[150] said Ellison's invisible man. The black writer Claude McKay had to resign from the board of the *Liberator* because of the intervention of Mike Gold, the editor of the *New Masses*.[151] Richard Wright broke with the Communists because "they . . . feared a man who stood alone."[152]

In the South, the Communists acted like an alien power in a strange country. They invaded the region, disseminating propaganda rather than working with the people for social equality. In the North, they laid plans to take over unions, which were already segregated, by opposing the incumbent leaders. The Communists withdrew from popular movements, from leftist non-Communist groups and from the public in general, and operated in a closed system. "Victims of a narrow exclusivism," they pretended to be the "sole guardians of the truth."[153]

Abruptly, the Communists changed tactics during Franklin Roosevelt's New Deal and infiltrated all kinds of organizations and dictated to their adherents. They defended Negro rights in the abstract—for their own ends. They denounced British colonial imperialism during the period of the Germano-Soviet pact in the Second World War and then immediately reversed their anti-British position when Hitler invaded Russia. They ignored black rights. "So isolated did we become from Negro life," wrote John Gates, an ex-Communist, ". . . that when the United States Supreme Court . . . handed down its historic decision on school segregation we were taken completely by surprise."[154] The Communists were, in effect, inept.

With this record, it was inevitable that the Communists attracted little Negro support. Blacks as a rule did not trust their appeal to social justice. And yet during the Depression they did win to some extent "the admiration of the Negro masses by default," masses who identified—albeit passively—with Communist goals.[155] But the Communists were doctrinaire with respect to the class struggle; their idea of progress and of the regulation of human rights was based on certain historically assumed rules which reflected Eurocentric values. They expected blacks to comply with their will. As Cruse points out, the left wing served the role of "political surrogate for the social *aims* of the Negro middle class over the social *necessities* of the Negro working class."[156]

Even DuBois, a radical sympathizer, realized that "the program of the American Communist Party was inadequate for our plight."[157] It certainly was not effective as a means of frightening a racist American society into abandoning its flagrant racist practices. No matter how many worthy causes the Communists sponsored, they achieved few positive results. In effect, they were blocked by their own inherent ideological contradictions—including those which promoted the idea of a proletarian revolutionary force; they were victims of the doctrine of white superiority, which made them impotent before the realities of capitalist rule.

CHAPTER 2

POLITICAL AND SOCIAL SEGREGATION

Politically, segregation almost totally disempowered the Negro. He had looked optimistically toward three principles following his emancipation: property, suffrage and education. As sociologist August Meier writes, "Republican politicians and . . . industrialists might use the Negro vote and the Reconstruction amendments to . . . perpetuate their power, but to Negroes the issues were moral ones. . . ."[1] They, indeed, had faith in their country's ideals, but this faith was misplaced: they were deprived of their own rights.

By means of deliberate subterfuge in the South—such as property and literacy requirements, the grandfather clause (both of which limited suffrage to whites), the white primary, the poll tax—the black was almost completely disfranchised.[2] By 1910 he had lost his vote in virtually every southern state. In the North, where, with the exception of Grover Cleveland's administration, government was firmly in the hands of emancipators, the victorious Republicans, the black was arbitrarily deprived of his rights.[3,4] Obviously, such a policy was hard to reconcile with the rationalization "separate but equal."

Even before the Civil War, "Northerners denied [in blacks] what was allowed for in white aliens and male children—the possibility of political maturation."[5] There were, of course, far fewer Negroes in the North than in the South and they had fewer social relations with whites. Most northern states had limited their suffrage in the early part of the nineteenth century. Nevertheless, the black upper middle class in northern cities had always participated in civic affairs. It had a recognized status.

With segregation, however, the black's political power was severely restricted. He was deprived of the vote both directly and insidiously.

38

New states, like Oklahoma, disfranchised him whose migration it had once encouraged. Whites who favored suffrage for educated Negroes were able to cut down voting in the slums where underprivileged blacks were bunched in segregated blocks. Bosses organized their territories with little need or regard for the work of the black who spoke English and was more acculturated and less manageable than newly arrived immigrants. The Republican party traded minor patronage posts for black support, which first Douglass and then Booker T. Washington delivered. "Democracy [was] something granted to Negroes on the basis of political expediency rather than as a right."[6]

As segregation took hold and the North and the South reached a *modus vivendi,* popular opinion made the Republicans afraid to support enforcement of the Fifteenth Amendment. In 1883 the Supreme Court arbitrarily declared illegal the civil rights act of 1875; liberal mugwumps, merchants and upright middle-class citizens opposed legislation such as Senator Henry Cabot Lodge's suggested bill for fair elections, which simply guaranteed the Negro his political rights; William Henry Harrison's administration abandoned him.[7] Booker T. Washington tried to bargain politically to help his people: he compromised even his conciliatory principles in an effort to persuade Teddy Roosevelt to displace lily-white Republicans and thus keep blacks in certain federal offices.[8] But the president was indifferent to such proposals.

William Howard Taft, who considered the black unfit for "higher education,"[9] reinstated Roosevelt's policy of Negro removal. There was a "downhill slide of the black politicos in [his] administration."[10] Eventually he dismissed one of Washington's favored associates, a move that seemed to be aimed at the Negro leader himself. There was no place for blacks in Roosevelt's liberal Progressive Party. And Woodrow Wilson, a southerner and a Democrat, definitively officialized segregation by extending it to the federal bureaucracy in Washington. The government (including the chief executive, who played to majority opinion and to political expedience), a hostile Supreme Court whose purpose was to convince the white public that "black . . . citizens have been given their full rights"[11] and state machinery angling for self-interest all acted in concert against the black minority, keeping it from getting to "where the power really is." In any case, says a young black Puerto Rican, "you can't trust the people with power."[12]

As disfranchisement grew and black office holding decreased, African Americans showed less interest in politics and were inclined to emphasize economic goals over political ones. Whereas before blacks had been active at the polls, they now seemed to give up a game that was stacked against them. Although this indifference was at first considered to be a temporary expedient, it was later exacerbated with the institution of all-white democracy in the South and with the mass migration of Negroes to northern cities where by subterfuge, "a spider's web of prior restraints," they were excluded from the political process.[13]

Voter registration, for instance, which was introduced with the influx of ethnics and which coincided with southern disfranchisement, was a purposeful obstacle to voting.[14] Many states instituted laws which correlated suffrage with education and income, and thus excluded the poor.[15] Political machinations, like gerrymandering, worked to neutralize large black populations crowded into the slums. Blacks had little access to municipal power when bosses turned to ghettoized immigrants and traded services for support. Confined as they were to segregated constituencies, Negro politicians found it difficult to operate on a wide sphere.[16] They were in general controlled by white political forces to which they owed their election.[17]

Party incentives were—and still are—fewer in the black ghetto.[18] There have never been the mass-media techniques to sell candidates that are used in middle-class areas.[19] The very structure of city politics and the life-style of isolated slum dwellers run counter to the bureaucratic procedures and publicity-inspired enthusiasms of middle-class campaigns.[20] And, therefore, ghetto dwellers have been politically crippled since the inception of segregation:[21] their feeling of separation from the American mainstream has produced a "sense of 'powerlessness.' "[22] Inhabitants of the slums are indeed even more apathetic[23]—perhaps with reason—than rural peasants who, as a sharecropper puts it, "aint got no political pull whatever under the sun."[24]

Segregation, the physical separation of blacks and whites, spread racist standards throughout the country. The divisions between a visible minority and the majority, even in middle American towns and urban centers, transcended those of class. From Middletown[25] to Plainville[26] to the great cities—indeed to the mafia and prison populations—the opinion prevailed that Negroes were an inferior species.

The great migrations northward, which started around 1880 and then intensified during both world wars, brought rural blacks into settled communities where their numbers caused civic disruption. Since mass black migration occurred in the twentieth century after ethnic immigration and after the institutionalization of the industrial economy, blacks found not only less room to live in, but less need for unskilled labor. In Chicago, for instance, many ethnics had amalgamated and dispersed by the time Negroes poured in. The latter inherited the slums close to vice districts at the center of the city as well as the most menial jobs. Because they were considered to be unassimilable, blacks were bound by restrictive housing covenants that *"subordinate* [as they] segregate."[27] Negroes were isolated in a "Black Metropolis" from which they could not emerge. As sociologists St. Clair Drake and Horace Cayton concluded, "The persistence of a Black Belt, whose inhabitants can neither scatter as individuals nor expand as a group, is no accident."[28] For substandard housing is one of the most nefarious effects of segregation on blacks' well-being.

Recently blacks have taken over large areas of northern cities. Black politicians, representing what are now black urban majorities with the political clout of numbers, are in control of many major metropolitan centers. This development is of course the result of segregative practices, because the white middle class fled to suburbia where it can perpetrate exclusivist housing covenants. Fearful of urban disorder, slum education and crime, whites have moved in order to avoid blacks and have imposed restrictions that seem to be aimed at Negroes. The suburbs "have . . . zoned out the poor and the nonwhites."[29]

But the "suburban exclusion of Negroes . . . limits the city in its efforts . . . to foster the integration and economic rise of the Negroes."[30] The loss of the middle class and of its tax dollars has been instrumental in bringing big cities—with large indigent populations—to financial crises to which there seems to be no solution. The "affluent suburb exploits the . . . bankrupt city," said sociologist Herbert Gans.[31] Those who live in the slums are caught in a bind that blocks their educational and job opportunities. Even "civil rights politics, which the neglect of city machines caused Negro elites . . . to adopt, had a class and status bias that prevented the black ghetto from taking on the attributes of an ethnic political subsystem."[32]

Moreover, the city, deprived of a stable middle-class base, is divided into the rich, who remain barricaded behind walls, and the poor, who are overwhelmingly more and more black. Its government must be responsible for the protection of the influential former and for the semblance of civil order. It cannot serve the interests of the disempowered and inarticulate poor. For as Cruse points out, black "voting strength has never been predicated on a political power base grounded in tangible economic, administrative, cultural or social policy issues with the visibility of forcefully influencing *public policy*."[33]

The phenomenon of new black mayors can therefore do little to increase the political clout of the black masses. Their hands are tied; they must act more or less as figureheads. Their power is limited not just by "the iron law of oligarchy,"[34] but by the mechanics of the American political game. Black politics indeed has rested on a white power base. Besides, there are really not many elected black officials: only about 1.2 percent of all the people's representatives in 1985[35] were black.

Again, as Harrington observed, immigrants "had acquired political power in an expanding economy; the black internal migrants, more often than not, won the right to allocate poverty, not wealth."[36] Their depressed situation and their practical isolation resulted, as Clark noted, in their political inexperience.[37] Officials were manipulated, if not silenced, by the party by which they were controlled. "Mayors and school boards," says sociologist Gary Orfield, ". . . in some ways . . . are like the black administrators in the Jim Crow schools in the old South: they must live on the largesse of white officials whose basic racial values they fear to challenge."[38] According to the historian Manning Marable, black mayors, whether liberal reformers or accommodationists, do not have "the actual mechanism of state power."[39] David Dinkins of New York was criticized in such magazines as *The New Yorker* and *New York* for political waffling and impotence. He lost his election. "The effective exercise of power within the urban ghetto is crippled. . . ."[40]

Segregation has served to deprive the black of an effective leadership class. It leveled all Negroes en masse—from the most to the least qualified—from university professor to illiterate peasant—from hustler to banker—and thereby perpetuated the underclass status of the group as a whole. Before the Civil War there had been class differences between blacks—not just between slaves and free men, and dark- and light-colored Negroes (the latter the product of miscegenation), but within the framework of the Jim Crow institution between craftsmen, artisans, house servants and field hands. But segregation was an attempt to equalize all blacks: it "applied to *all* Negroes."[41] It was the expression of the impersonal bureaucratization of the industrial order that overrides individual distinction in the name of efficiency. Within the black community, class difference was pronounced, but in the eyes of public law, blacks of every kind and category were imprisoned in a lower caste from which only the few could escape. The bishop of the African Methodist Episcopalian Church was thrown off a train in Florida and the Republican administration of Chester A. Arthur refused to defend his rights.[42] Booker T. Washington was assaulted by a white man in New York.[43] W.E.B. DuBois was invited to dinner by a school superintendent and seated at a separate table.[44] In New Orleans, "pushed steadily downward, the children of the free men of color had finally become Negroes."[45]

Again, since the color line obtained not only in politics but also in business, law, medicine and academia, it prevented the development of trained black leaders who could relate on a class basis to the larger society. Spokesmen for immigrant minorities identified with their groups in propelling them into the economic mainstream. They derived their power from their communities and were able to serve as mediators in their rise from the ghetto to the middle class. Segregation, however, was maliciously aimed at an entire race. As one critic observed, it is hard "for a people to work out their destiny under the hostile rule of another people."[46]

Blacks were restricted to their segregated communities, and their economic leaders could not merge into the larger society since they depended for their livelihood on their disadvantaged racial group. "In business and industry, it was only in the separate economy that a few Negroes attained leadership."[47] The anomalous position of the black bourgeoisie that on one hand was middle class in spirit and conviction and on the other outcast in civil and social status[48] reduced its efficacy and caused it to suffer from a problem of identity.[49] The black bourgeoisie had "no established tradition to define behavior"[50] so it looked to and imitated the whites who rejected it and who, at bottom, it detested. Booker T. Washington, for instance, may have idolized the "businessman, white or black," and considered him the "model citizen,"[51] but as DuBois observed, Washington had "no faith in white people . . . he . . . found out what the white man wanted him to say and . . . he said it."[52] Likewise the father of Richard Wright's character Fish in *The Long Dream,* a wealthy black community leader, hated whites but compromised with them to buy himself security.[53] Again, as Frazier pointed out, the black elite identified with upper-class whites, not with Jews and not with whites of lower strata.[54] Nevertheless, this bourgeoisie was more conscious of its place in the Negro world than of its status in the larger society. Its members "emphasize their *differentness*," although, as race leaders, they feel in principle a solidarity with " 'the Race.' "[55]

The prevailing American middle-class success ethic, which was the source of black leaders' high position, was harmful to black people as a whole: the privileged black group had "no social roots in the white community."[56] This group, therefore, could not help the race and was consequently resented by the blacks from whom it profited and to whom it owed its power and status. Since this elite was both impotent in the larger society and cut off from the Negro masses,[57] it was more or less disdained. Common blacks show a "dislike for the 'white folks' Negro,'"[58] or, as H. Rap Brown put it, for "Negro america."[59] There is no "unity of interests."[60]

In turn, the black bourgeoisie fears and dislikes the lower class. It is status-prejudiced. Langston Hughes's father "hated Negroes [and] hated himself, too, for being [one]."[61] Since Wright's entrepreneur could assume his security "only by making victims of black men, he hated the black men too."[62] Indeed, middle-class blacks were probably more isolated from whites than from their black social inferiors because their status was not clearly fixed: it did not depend on money as did every other American's. They were, said Wright, "sharing the culture that condemn[ed them]."[63] The black, writes Amiri Baraka, is "capable of identifying with the fantastic cultural ingredients of this society, but he is also, forever, outside that society. . . ."[64]

In effect, the black leader has been "at war with himself . . . with reality."[65] The system of segregation has kept him "half in and half out";[66] the white world has "threatened as much as it beckoned."[67] Claude McKay's bourgeois men and women were "without a cultural home";[68] they were misfits in a civilization that rejected them.[69] DuBois, whose whole life, he said, was bound by the one fact of race, existed in a dual personality, yearning to be free.[70] Ellison's invisible man, a striver, was a machine within a machine, drifting nameless from situation to situation.[71] The black is the only American who must reach beyond his group for identification because this group has been denied national belonging.[72] As Wright's Sam remarks to his friend Zeke in *The Long Dream*, "You ain't no American! You live Jim Crow."[73] Without power, the black man lacks choice.

Moreover, the black leader's cultural alienation from the Negro mass has led to his increased estrangement from white power sources. His success with the middle-class majority has depended on his manipulation and control of the Negro world and on his efficacious assumption of assigned roles. Since segregation limited race relations to meetings between appointed representatives of both white and black groups,[74] it was important that the latter speak effectively for their communities in order to keep civil peace or to negotiate for favors. In the

South, for instance, when whites were faced with the possibility of a massive exodus of black farmers and menials, they summoned so-called respectable blacks to participate in interracial committees;[75] they offered status compensation in exchange for pressure to keep black people at home. Obviously, this compensation depended on a leader's capacity to produce results.

Likewise, the clout of the black militants is conditioned by their ability to identify with the Negro masses. And after years of disappointment and indoctrination, people tend to be insecure and apathetic; they are weary of beating their heads against a wall. Even if, like Bigger Thomas in Wright's *Native Son*,[76] they might urgently feel the need for a real leader—a black messiah,[77] as Albert B. Cleage, Jr., the Detroit minister and Freedom Now party candidate, termed it—it is hard to find one "with power." Whenever someone exceptional does come along, it is especially difficult to keep him from being discredited by the white media or bought out, or—as too often occurs—from being jailed or, finally, assassinated.

One of the most disastrous effects of segregation with respect to black cultural autonomy has been its influence on American immigrants. As sociologist Martin Kilson points out, blacks have been deprived of the positive "quality of ethnic characterization."[78] Foreign newcomers were never segregated. Nevertheless, contemporary, mainly ethnic revisionists contend that blacks are just another, albeit lately developed, minority which is on the inevitable road to assimilation. They are, of course, ignoring the history of the black community—the most native of all and the most deliberately oppressed. Blacks are the American nation; they are the metaphor for America, as Wright put it.[79] They are the pivotal group. They are in no way "latecomers"—as neoconservative Irving Kristol[80] and sociologist Oscar Handlin pretend—for whom "equality of status and opportunity" are just "a matter of time."[81] This kind of gradualism is a liberal method of denigrating the black, for in reality ethnics owe the fact that they have integrated and succeeded to black segregation.

Immigrants who wanted to assimilate quickly adopted the most American of cultural attitudes: the idea that black people were inferior. They took up the practice of segregation and thereby also became active persecutors of blacks. Immigrant leaders imitated the rulers, who were Anglo-Saxon until after the Second World War. During the period when ethnics suffered from the stigma of low status, they even turned against their own kind. The young mocked their fathers and mothers; siblings denied one another; decent, God-fearing parents produced monsters like Sammy Glick in *What Makes Sammy Run* or, in actual fact, Lucky Luciano, the gangster. In order to survive, the dispossessed of every group are forced to emulate their social betters, or they try to become what their exploiters want to think of them. But because segregation fixed the black on the lowest rung of the order, the immigrant had a caste below which he could never sink. He could look downward as well as upward.

When, in the late nineteenth century and early twentieth century, aliens poured into the country—impoverished and illiterate—blacks might have joined with them and poor white natives in a pluralistic underclass based simply on economic criteria. Historically, however, white supremacy constituted a cultural ideology[82] to which immigrants adapted. Society singled out black people and uniquely denied them the "positive societal and cultural attributes associated with the term 'ethnic groups.' "[83] Society was explicitly oriented to the well-being of whites and it functioned by means of segregation. In fact, social norms depended on the black presence in order to exploit it both culturally and materially. Race prejudice is an attitude that transcends the mere fact of color. Black skin represented black subjugation and, by dialectical antithesis, white superiority.

The existence of the black was, therefore, essential to the white ideal of America—to its belief in its special mission on earth. And this, says Dollard, "is one of the most powerful supports of the social regulations of the South and one to which northerners or westerners respond readily."[84] Alien labor was required economically for a now fast-developing industrial order. Without the black the nation would never have reached the industrial stage in which he was not allowed directly to participate because of segregation. But the black was still indispensable to the preservation and cohesion of the white order. It seems that whites themselves recognized this fact, as they indicated when they foiled every attempt at black recolonization, which was promoted by black or white associations during the nineteenth century and even by President Lincoln. Immigrants were not as necessary to the cultural fabric of the country. When Jews, for instance, were subject to social discrimination, "the very intolerant . . . asked for [their] deportation . . . , [however] almost none . . . requested deportation of Negroes, but requested . . . that they be kept in their place."[85] Only thus could the ideal of white superiority be maintained.

Since the concept of black inferiority is an essential constituent of

American cultural attitudes, it was used as the basis for ethnic integration. Industrial development owes its success to the effect of the policy of segregation on hordes of foreigners who were imported as workers for capitalism and yet who disrupted the social order of the day. Jim Crow made possible their assimilation and the relatively peaceful transition from an ethnically homogeneous vertical class structure into a heterogeneous horizontal society which was superimposed on a subcaste and which conformed to the materialistic norms of the consumer state.

Jim Crow led to the institutionalization of white group pluralism: all the various immigrant communities were equal by contrast to one outcast minority and the prevailing but diminishing Anglo-Saxon majority. All might, therefore, affirm their own identities: they were united in their diverse nationalities because society was separated into white against black. The Negro gave them a ready-made status: the Wasp ruling class provided them with an American goal. "Around the socio-biological axis of race two social worlds have evolved—a Negro world and a white world. The white world is divided by ethnic origins and religion into Catholic, Protestant and Jewish contingents."[86] Within these schisms, avenues are open to middle-class standing. Various ethnic groups overtly utilized the black's outcast position in order to advance themselves. Jews, for instance, remarked an observer, used blacks to build "bridges to liberals with power." They made contacts with Negroes in order to "forge an alliance with the . . . Storeys . . . the Villards . . . Addams . . . Covingtons."[87]

As sociologist William Kornblum says, "The relative success of different cultural groups in American communities is . . . dependent upon their success in political negotiations and competition in political institutions."[88] Since the "personal attachments" of these groups had to "span the moral and physical frontiers of the older ethnic settlements,"[89] the cultural isolation of blacks, the fact that they were "excluded from the negotiations which brought their white contemporaries to prominence in community institutions,"[90] not only prevented their advancement, but made Anglo-Saxon natives more disposed to deal with white newcomers. Cruse writes, "As a result of [the] capitalistic evolution-revolution, every white nationality group . . . has been gathered up from the lower-class regions of the society and given an incorporated stake in the profit-sharing capitalistic club. . . . "[91] The Negro was left out.

It was segregation, therefore, that opened job opportunities for immigrants, who moved into trades that blacks had practiced and, legitimately, excluded the blacks whom they displaced. The nation *"legally"* denied the Negro "the same right to 'life, liberty and the pursuit of happiness' which it accorded Europeans as they stepped off the boat."[92] As James Boggs, the black writer, observes, it was because blacks were deprived by both bosses and workers of the chance to advance that immigrants bypassed them.[93] People who could not even speak English were able freely to vote, to work, to travel and to play. Langston Hughes commented, "The kikes and the spicks and the hunkies . . . all had it on the niggers":[94] they had jobs. An alien "could operate a store and earn a living in a neighborhood where I could not even live," said Wright.[95]

It was not just negative racism—"the stigma which attaches to black skin"[96]—that turned the immigrant away from the black. Segregation also served a positive role as it was a means of acculturation. Through it, aliens adapted to the middle-class norm and fit into the conformist mold on which the industrial state depended. Ethnics embraced the Protestant ethic and blamed the black for his low socioeconomic position, for which they, to a large extent, were responsible. If they even now are retrospectively sympathetic to the black on the subject of slavery that was practiced when they were not in America, they still refuse to accept the fact that they were instrumental in aggravating his Jim Crow status—of which they took outright advantage. "Our ancestors owned no slaves," protests a Catholic.[97] But he will not admit that he and his kind have excluded blacks from their neighborhood, their schools, their union, their politics and even their taverns[98,99]—on both materialistic and ideological grounds.[100]

Ethnics' continuing advancement is still well served by racism. The very politicization of "white neo-ethnicities"[101] works to the black's detriment. Pronounced social gain may reduce racial conflict on an individual basis, but moderate success—which is the case of the middle class—rather accentuates it. Striving ethnics are white supremacists: immigrants "think they are better people than the blacks," reports sociologist Michael Novak.[102] They resented the civil rights movement of the 1960s and complain of their "relative deprivation"[103] despite their relatively comfortable situations. They strongly disapprove of black nationalism while, at the same time, they just as strongly assert their own group identity and accept that of other ethnic communities. They do not appreciate the rising expectations of blacks on the make, which they fear might work to their disadvantage. Indeed, their very concept of ethnicity blocks blacks' efforts to affirm themselves: ethnics' denunciation of special-interest elites for trying to "save the black"[104] is a misrepresentation of fact and an evidence of their own middle-class conformity. To the extent that ethnics are thoroughly acculturated, they constitute a force for the perpetuation of racism.

The Irish, for instance—who, insists sociologist Andrew Greeley, are "less prejudiced . . . than the other groups," and who have not rioted against blacks since 1919 and who do not support racist organizations—nevertheless choose all-white neighborhoods because of crime, property values and education. They protest that they are not responsible for the plight of the blacks: they neither brought "slaves to America" nor exploited them for "hundreds of years."[105] Sociologist Thomas Sowell, however, points out that "perhaps the worst relations between any two groups in American history have been between the Irish and the Negroes."[106] Irish riots against the blacks were notorious.

As the Italians have become acculturated, their original—relative—benevolence toward blacks, in many cases their slum neighbors, has turned into antipathy. They oppose "government aid and special treatment."[107] Michael Novak studied ethnics, mainly Polish and southeastern European Catholics, who are, he claims, "less prejudiced against blacks than nativist Americans,"[108] as if this were a distinction. For, as he admits, they are racist. He excuses them because he believes they have legitimate reasons to show "economic, social and cultural anxiety about the black revolution."[109] Revolution or not, the eastern European immigrants are apparently offended by the style of black people. As Catholics, they distrust the fundamentalist Protestant moralism of blacks.[110] As parsimonious Slavs, they resent what they consider to be wild spending habits of Negroes.[111] And as suspicious ex-peasants, they fear possible aggression. They refuse to be "push[ed] . . . around."[112]

Jews indignantly reject any implications of racism. They were, it is said, involved in the campaign for racial equality long before Protestants and Catholics.[113,114] Besides, they are a persecuted people themselves. However, they tend to be paternalistic toward blacks and feel superior to a race they have outdistanced socially, materially and educationally. They look at blacks as "children in terms of power relations."[115] Moreover, Jews are defensive; they protect their own special interests. They do not favor quotas for Negroes with respect to educational and employment opportunities and they insist that blacks "meet the same criteria as the white community,"[116] when they themselves were able to benefit from open enrollment in city colleges that were closed to blacks. They also advise Negroes not to confuse natural, sometimes desirable "social segregation . . . with economic segregation,"[117] when they were vigilant in connecting exclusion from Wasp clubs with discrimination in business. In effect, they are justifying separate but equal. Their position toward the black carries neocolonial, if not racist undertones. And Jews, dedicated to the defense of world Jewry, seem paranoiacally afraid of any assertion of black nationalism.[118] "Expressive politics has always frightened the Jewish community," says a Jewish critic[119]—forgetting the military adventures of the State of Israel. Nevertheless, black power unites the Jews in a concerted counterattack on black anti-Semitism.

In general, immigrants—like Anglo-Saxon natives—resent any implication of black assertiveness, most particularly of black power. As sociologist E. Digby Baltzell says, we are "paralyzed by imagining the terrors of the journey of desegregation,"[120] so whites exclude blacks from their tax-supported neighborhoods and schools and deny them jobs or equal pay, and then denounce them for not having made good as a group. Whereas ethnics were given the chance to move out of ghettos, blacks were hemmed in both racially and economically. "Where the negro pitches his tent, he pays more than his white neighbor . . . and is a better [neighbor]," wrote Jacob Riis during the early days of immigration.[121]

In the South, native Anglo-Saxons have always been more antiblack than anti-Catholic or anti-Semitic—or even anti-Yankee. As Woodward points out, immigrants never had to face the handicap of bigotry based on skin color.[122] In the North, it is not just the old Americans; it is the whole white community that has been responsible for the policy of Jim Crow in the industrial age. Negroes have been "the most cast out of all the outcast people in America."[123] Conservatives oppose school desegregation because it denies "consensual adjustment and accommodation."[124] Liberals justify housing, school and economic separatism on the basis of laissez-faire, thereby avoiding the problem. As Harrington remarked, the difficulty of combating racist practice lies in the popularity of a liberal rhetoric that will not confront racial issues.[125] Even now, South and North, East and West, whites of all kinds and of all political persuasions will not accept the inevitable effects of discrimination, which they have instituted and which they perpetuate.[126] "The *type of status relationships controlling Negroes* and whites remains the same and continues to keep the Negro in an inferior and restricted position."[127]

Finally, segregation has been an essential factor in the development of industrial America, because as a legalized practice, it has led to the organization of the violence that necessarily went with capitalism's rise to power—including employee-employer relations and the conquest of a continental and a foreign empire. In America in particular, where class conventions have not been institutionalized, "ultimate control has always been by violence or [its] threat."[128] After the Civil War, this kind of turbulence became an arm of government and of prevailing economic interests, which it represented. While businessmen fought one another in the struggle to make money, they battled in concert against their potentially class-conscious workers.

The American idea that there is a natural law of individual rights that transcends governmental expedience permits everyone in principle to decide for himself what is good and what is bad. On the one hand, the American climate is conducive to disrespect for official law. On the other, however, the state tends to operate as a moral force, complete in itself. It becomes the absolute law even in its lawless functions.[129] Pragmatically, as Carmichael observed, "Might makes Law"[130] as it makes right. Bolstered by the license of majority opinion, state power serves as the criterion of morality. Segregative consensus politics, therefore, combines with individual disregard for legality and with sanctioned group terrorism against blacks—including lynching, mob rioting, physical assault. Segregation supposedly represented the people's will in permitting the abuse of blacks.[131]

Attacks on blacks have consequently become an aspect of state violence enacted on a community—decentralized—level by individuals. But this type of decentralization is tolerated by state organizations that do not wish to irritate constituents. The lawless, however, include almost every segment of society—from police to so-called responsible citizens to hooligans. In a class situation, "racial, economic and ethnic"[132] violence, which would have been aimed at a social proletariat, might have been chaotic and industrially disruptive. Workers—black, lower class and immigrant—are numerically powerful and able to fight back, but racial violence was able to fasten on one minority and use it as a scapegoat and as a repository for all the frustrations of an unassimilated population. Segregation permitted racial violence to transcend and progressively to swallow the aggressiveness of unorganized groups. Segregation was "*repressive*";[133] it was the "ultimate form of the tyranny of the majority."[134] As such it allowed outcast workers and ethnics to associate ideologically with the middle-class majority. In a way hostile attitudes and acts against black people served to indoctrinate these outcasts in the norms of the developing industrialized, unionized, pluralistic state.

In America, unlike Europe, organized groups have rarely used violence to challenge the legitimacy of the ruling power. State violence here is directed not against a social class but against a particular disempowered minority.[135] "Violence is accepted in america," says Rap Brown, "as long as it's white folks doing it."[136] Thus the system has never been threatened by upstarts trying "to grasp their share of wealth"[137] or by conservatives battling "to defend their property."[138] The system has not been endangered by the menace of class warfare (even during the Depression) and will not be imperiled by a potentially revolutionary black force as long as black leaders are themselves assimilated into the middle class.

Violence, of course, is never rational. The permissive aegis of segregation, however, regulated the disorder of wildcat disruptions, just as capitalist organization in conjunction with the centralization of both government and finance was able to control the anarchic rivalries of acquisitive robber barons. In the South, legalized violence actually "spread lawlessness"—but only against the Negro. Channeled as official terrorism was, it "emphasized the rule of the rich"[139] who could sit back while poor whites assaulted blacks, let these whites act out their fury and appease the worst expressions of their aggressiveness. For southern lawlessness, directed to the one end of Negro oppression, resulted in a smoother functioning of the social order than had obtained when rednecks and planters were divided along class lines. The poor and the wealthy—or relatively wealthy—were no longer openly suspicious of one another: they had a sense of social relevance. It was Jim Crow and the Bible that brought whites together against blacks: the two have always been related in southern politics.[140] Antiblack campaigns were a practical extension of the ideological faith that has sustained the concept of a white mission: they are what Ellison calls "spiritual vomiting."[141] They clear the system.

The caste structure that replaced slavery often decreased poor whites' racial animosity. As long as the upper class allowed them to erupt periodically in bloody pogroms against black individuals, they remained generally calm. Blacks were fairly easy targets. Since they were segregated in rural enclaves and in towns, they were open to mob assault. In the Atlanta riot of 1906, the "hats and caps of victims [were] hung on the iron hooks of telegraph poles" as savage whites paraded through the Negro section, attacking blacks who had respectable houses and positions.[142] Lynching in particular was an example of the type of disorganized organization that was used to oppress blacks and to provide an outlet for the brutality of frustrated whites who might otherwise have turned against the reigning powers. Lynching was supposed to be "a disciplinary device against the Negro group."[143] But it was a pathological safeguard against intraracial friction which might have troubled social harmony. The individual Negro was sacrificed with impunity to the demonism of the pack.

In the North, where segregation isolated the Negro community, violence was an arm of state and federal power. It was used to prevent contact between the races and, therefore, to ward off open conflict—or rioting—between whites and blacks. Until the Second World War, racial turbulence in northern cities and towns was always instigated by white mobs.

Police violence against blacks, for instance, was used to insulate the white middle class. It was, of course, aimed at blacks of all social strata: black professionals would be accosted if they went into white neighborhoods at night. Moreover, the police were supposed to patrol and to contain the ghetto in order to keep blacks away from whites. So-called necessary acts of oppression were fostered by the police: they were the ones to "get the blame"[144] while higher officials stayed "free of the stigma."[145]

It might have been relatively easy in the North to impose conditions of desegregation. Despite the contention that opinion cannot be legislated, "changed patterns of community behavior [do] change attitudes,"[146] which shift "from one moment and situation to another."[147] Segregation, with all its malevolent effects, was entrenched officially and irremediably when police surveillance and the threat of police violence cordoned off the black ghetto. With the increase of the extent and density of the Negro inner city, blacks have themselves erupted, although they have not yet penetrated white territory. Nevertheless, black riots have not only united the black community and frightened whites, especially liberals, but they have also threatened the functioning of the industrial machine. The riots that occurred during the 1960s "were widely considered a major threat to domestic stability."[148]

CHAPTER 3

BLACK POVERTY: THE EFFECT OF SEGREGATION

T he black civil rights movement of the sixties caused the government to initiate policies against segregation and poverty. Despite this so-called revolution and the decline of racial discrimination "on many levels," the condition of the black urban masses has not improved. "Racial ghettoization is *increasing* in certain unique and significant ways. . . ."[1] In effect, the contemporary expression of racism is directed explicitly against the poor. And these disadvantaged people are to a great extent segregated in educationally starved, jobless, crime-breeding, ill-kept slums that are for the most part black. More than one third of the black population is poor.[2] In 1966, 45 percent of Negroes were reported below the poverty line.[3] After the War on Poverty—from 1970 to 1987—"the proportion of blacks with low incomes increased by 16.7%."[4]

Since segregation has been outlawed, it is no longer federal policy. But since it exists in fact, it reproduces itself in the form of class prejudice. In keeping with the spirit of the postindustrial rational consumer state, it is based pragmatically on economic and not—in principle—on color criteria. Because a disproportionate percentage of the black population has been historically—by means of discrimination—condemned to poverty and unemployment, those American citizens who are isolated in substandard ghettos are mainly black. The white poor are not bunched together in slums. Indeed, a little more than a third of the white poor[5] and more than 60 percent of the black poor live in central cities.[6]

Since both racism—the assumption of black inferiority or of white

54

superiority—and the black's actual disadvantaged condition stem from historically entrenched cultural attitudes, the black's hereditary poverty is the effect of the arbitrary ideology on which Americanism is based. It is the outward expression of the "group mind,"[7] the foundation of national cohesiveness. Perhaps this racist ideology derived from white American rootlessness. Those who came to the country were displaced; they were confronted by a boundless territory; they were invaded abruptly by diverse ethnic nationalities; and naturally they suffered from an identity crisis. The materialistic ethnic was a substitute for a lack of self-determination or of social place: Americans sought success because they had to prove who they were on a concrete, measurable level.

The conviction that success makes right is built necessarily on the denigration of those who seem less competent. It is only by dominating others that one shows one's worth. Right depends on the imputation of wrong. A German sociologist, Peter Heinz, associated Americans' racism with their fear of failure—as he put it, "their dislike of the lower classes and their culture."[8] Inevitably, having driven nonwhite people into the lower classes, they pragmatically identified nonwhites with lowliness.

Industrialism brought with it a wave of racism that was expressed not just by segregation at home but also by interventionism abroad. Americans set out to dominate inferior, poor and/or colored peoples. "The world does not move on ideologies. . . . It moves on color," says poet Nikki Giovanni.[9] But the two are the same. The nineteenth-century program to recolonize Negroes, which represented "a monumental endorsement of the doctrine of the immutability of Negro inferiority,"[10] was followed by foreign imperialism. And the present pauperization of the black masses, which is more institutionalized than the poverty of any other group, is the effect of the new economic racism of the individual state.

Of course, economic racism is not new. The materialistic ethic has always blamed the poor for their condition. Racist morality forced dark-skinned people into subservience and total dispossession and justified their debasement by distinguishing between "Christian and heathen . . .'civil' and 'savage.' "[11] Black emancipation together with urban centralization, which went with industrial organization, subjected slaves completely deprived of capital to the machinations of the so-called open market. The principle of free competition equated poverty with failure and, if not with sin,[12] at least with unworthiness. Poverty was not simply economic in significance: it not only facilitated the exploitation of labor necessary to capitalistic progress, but it was also an antipathetic condition. As such it dialectically entrenched the ideology of the gospel of wealth, which was the focal point of the materialistic creed.

"The fact that Jim Crow discrimination and racial segregation may well be based on economic exploitation is beside the point," wrote the black militant Robert Williams.[13] In fact, it was probably the racist ideology, stemming from economic necessity, that transcended its source and became the foundation of the economic rationalization of racial injustice. Williams attributed racism to some perversion innate in the white character. Freud related the success—the very grandeur—of occidental civilization to an acquired, not inherent, dysfunction, which he identified with repression, within the psyche of western man. His interpreter Norman O. Brown observed that there was "an intrinsic connection between social organization and neurosis."[14] And it is the pattern of history that "exhibits . . . the dialectics of neurosis."[15] Indeed, if white Americans were not born with a psychic defect, it is their history that has afflicted them and that they try to ignore.

Certainly it is macabre that white Americans should still cling to a faith in ideals that they so consistently betray. Despite the fact that "a problem in political morality"[16] may bring on "a problem in the effective functioning of society,"[17] the industrial or postindustrial state in a global market has up till now maintained its power. Whether or not it has been built on perverted hate or neurosis or psychic pathology or greed, it has succeeded. And it continues, although with less clout, while it assigns the black mass to the lowly economic and social condition for which it condemns it.

During the First World War, at the time of the emergence of industrial America to the status of superpower, there was an exodus of blacks from the South. This continued through the 1920s and 1930s; it was accelerated during World War II. Blacks were driven off the land by social and economic factors during the Depression. They were lured North in a period of mobilization when jobs were available and when immigration had fallen off.

Obviously, blacks had to face problems of adjusting to an urban way of life. They, who left a "relatively static social order, in which [they had] developed . . . techniques of survival,"[18] had to adapt to industrial conditions. They settled in the ghettos of the northern cities, many of which—Chicago, for example—were being vacated by newly assimilated immigrants. But blacks were able to survive. H. L. Mencken observed that Negroes in the North progressed culturally faster than the masses of whites—particularly southern whites—who emigrated.[19]

At this time segregation governed the ecology of American cities. In Chicago, blocks of immigrants left the slums, moved up from menial jobs and were replaced by Negroes. The city was "split into three large economic groups, predominantly white American: the wealthy few, a growing new middle class and the poorer wage-earners [among whom were] more than a third of a million [poverty-stricken, segregated] Negroes."[20] Hampered by job discrimination, restrictive housing covenants, inadequate schooling, "white acts of persecution and violence"[21] including white-instigated race riots and even the disappropriation of already-established Negro bourgeois, the black ghetto was never absorbed as had been immigrant ones. In effect, the black slum got bigger: an intentional development, as Drake and Cayton observed.[22]

The 1920s, the decade of the first postwar boom, brought the illusion of good times to black communities in the North. Negroes established a structural solidarity in their segregated neighborhoods and imbibed the prevailing mood of optimism. A new black middle class with economic roots in the community rose to take the place of the more white-oriented old guard. A "deep feeling of race is at present the mainstream of Negro life," wrote Alain Locke.[23] This was the era of the so-called "New Negro."[24] Of course, in the South, the economic situation was depressing. Opportunities had been blocked with the signing of the peace treaty, and the agricultural market declined. Soldiers came home to find themselves relegated to peonage. In the South, black poverty was accentuated during the 1920s.

In the North, despite the appearance of gaiety, optimism and, superficially, racial progress, the decade of the 1920s did little to advance the cause and the condition of the Negro. Virulent racism spread in the form of the Ku Klux Klan, which went North to assume the dimensions of a national movement.[25] Second- and third-generation ethnics, even or perhaps especially those who were objects themselves of discriminatory practices, adopted middle-class nativist attitudes. Blacks were subject to a generalized pattern of prejudice. In postwar Cleveland, for instance, remarked Langston Hughes, "the color line began to be drawn tighter and tighter."[26]

Harlem, which had been the golden Mecca to young progressive blacks and liberal whites, found that its veneer of prosperity—and of social equality—was "so little and so thin."[27] Segregated attitudes underlay integration initiatives. Harlem's big jazz clubs banned black clients; smaller ones went under. Its cultural Renaissance, like its interracialism—which did not affect the lives of the Negro ghetto masses—was stifled by its dependence on the largesse of white patrons and publishers[28] and on the paternalism of young thrill-seeking whites who were "doing" Negroes. "It was the period when the Negro was in vogue," wrote Langston Hughes. But "the ordinary Negroes hadn't heard of the Negro Renaissance. And if they had, it hadn't raised their wages any."[29]

The Harlem Renaissance, as historian Jeanne Noble points out, was "sucked of its vitality by whites who either co-opted its ideas and style . . . or . . . repressed [it]."[30] They took over blacks' original creations and used them for themselves. Moreover, the movement was elitist: the "fate [of the middle classes] was no longer bound to poorer classes."[31] They divorced themselves from the common people. Besides, the non-intellectual Negro business and middle class did not support the Renaissance, and established leaders like DuBois were suspicious of it. He actually considered it a failure because it was "a transplanted and exotic thing" aimed at whites.[32]

It was, of course, the Depression that laid bare the extent of black penury and destroyed the hopes of the young intellectual optimists. It definitively exposed "the general economic insecurity of the Negro masses."[33] In effect, black employment gains had lasted only about fifteen years—from 1914 to 1929.[34] From Middletown, where blacks were the most marginal group,[35] to New York City, where "the exploiting group [gave] no sops,"[36] the black minority was the most affected by the economic disaster of all ethnic, class and age sectors of the population.[37] Black America "almost fell apart."[38] The small but solid upper middle class was weakened and the middle middle class practically went under. Those who had jobs were paid 30 percent less than whites,[39] and only the few held white-collar or bureaucratic positions. Negroes were on the periphery of the economy, the last hired and the first to be laid off. Unemployment was "two to three times as high as that of whites";[40] one fourth of the Negro population was on relief. As Langston Hughes ruefully understated, "We were no longer in vogue . . . we Negroes."[41]

Inevitably the segregated ghetto became more and more run down. Unemployment meant no rent money and no payment for merchandise, usually purchased on the installment plan. So slum landlords sought profits through the deterioration of their properties whose upkeep they disregarded,[42] and dealers gouged their clients by high interest rates. The Depression also uprooted the family, which had been a psychological and cultural means of survival in the South. There was "notorious and widespread wandering"[43] as males migrated everywhere in their quest for jobs. The onus of poverty was falling on the shoulders of women,[44] who found it easier than men to get work[45]—generally in domestic service, for which they were scandalously underpaid—and who could adapt to the pattern of extended family life. The female-run household was a cultural development that seemingly destabilized the black community. As Cruse observes, *"The black populations, then newly arrived in the northern urban centers, would never fully recover from the sociological shock treatment experienced during the Great Depression even into the late 1980s. . . . Additional migratory waves would only aggravate the . . . existing urban pathologies introduced in 1929."*[46]

There was no New Deal for black people. Certain material benefits did result in the consolidation of a limited black elite[47] and in what has been called a "new climate of opinion,"[48] but these gains were less than relevant to general black welfare. As the New Deal brought formerly excluded ethnic groups into the middle-class mainstream—because they were politically significant—the process of horizontal leveling exposed the black (who was politically, socially and economically isolated by segregation) as the one nonassimilable minority. "Share-croppers, slum dwellers, most Negroes [were left] outside of the new equilibrium."[49]

In the South, New Deal reformism benefited the white and not the black farmer. It squeezed the latter off the land, and it forced out the poorest sharecroppers, who were politically inarticulate and legally impotent, thereby depriving them of their living. Since farmers cut down on their acreage to limit production, they got rid of their tenants, who were mainly Negro. The process of displacing black people who were accustomed to old ways of raising crops was expedited by the mechanization that went with scientific agriculture.[50]

Moreover, as the South, a particularly disadvantaged area, received a large share of social welfare, it distributed its bounty in the form of outright grants and educational subsidies to whites over blacks.[51] And, of course, politicians were able to manipulate funds for their own use. Indeed, during the Depression, when regional cohesion was disintegrating, the practice of discrimination against the black was the one unifying force that remained.[52]

"Race relations in 1934 . . . were not notably different from those in 1900," said a Negro editor.[53] Franklin Roosevelt, for instance, was personally unsympathetic to the black cause. He did not come out strongly against lynching;[54] he would not antagonize southern Democrats. He was a pragmatist who accepted, if not sanctioned, existing segregation. Despite her liberal inclinations and her much publicized friendship with Mary McLeod Bethune, Eleanor Roosevelt had what Ralph Bunche called a primitive attitude to non-occidentals—he was referring to her treatment of Arabs.[55] She was a visionary idealist who criticized Negroes for their lack of self-reliance, and remained attached to materialistic principles of laissez-faire—as was Bethune herself, the self-made daughter of a slave, schooled in the ethic of Booker T. Washington. Nevertheless, as Washington had manipulated Eleanor Roosevelt's uncle with some but little success, so did Bethune manipulate the niece for some black economic advantages.[56]

A combination of economic, social and technological circumstances have increased and entrenched the incidence of poverty in industrial America. The fact remains, however, that a "large number of the total number of poor people are black,"[57] and a disproportionate percentage are on welfare. At the same time that blacks made civil and economic advances after the 1960s, there developed "a large ingrowing underclass . . . principally made up of blacks and Hispanics in the central cities [who] are more economically isolated, more socially alienated than . . . before." Sociologists Fred Harris and Roger Wilkins concluded: "Poverty is worse now than it was twenty years ago. More people are poor . . . those who are poor are poorer. Escape from poverty is harder. Overall unemployment for blacks is . . . twice what it is for whites."[58]

Whether poverty is a culture, an effect of external circumstance, a vicious circle or the result of social isolation is an argument for social analysts. The fact is that it implies concrete disadvantages in life, including inadequate housing conditions, educational deficiency and sub- or nonemployment. Not only does poverty reproduce itself but it also breeds antisocial behavior such as crime, delinquency, instability, broken family life and apathy—or a feeling of total powerlessness. And it does all this without drawing racial lines. Most deprived groups, ethnic or native, have manifested dysfunctional social characteristics. The transition from a rural to an urban environment produced the Irish slum with its incidence of brutality, drunkenness and family disorganization, reported Daniel Patrick Moynihan[59]—who was seconded by sociologist Laura Carper.[60] Jews in European shtetls suffered from fatherless households, as did Puerto Ricans whom sociologist Oscar Lewis studied.[61] Poor people are, in effect, not middle class, even if they might have the same cultural designations. Poverty, sociologist Charles Valentine observes, is a socioeconomic stratum and not an ethnic or racial categorization. Its "essence . . . is inequality."[62]

In America, however, poverty amounts to a new form of segregation of blacks. Since they have been historically consigned to unequal status by deliberate racial deprivation, they have been made to be poor. Their struggle has been the most difficult of all minorities.[63] Whereas, Kenneth Clark remarks, the white poor have had "the advantage of . . . the belief that they can rise economically and escape from the slums,"[64] the Negro has been absolutely confined by segregation to poverty areas. Because whites refuse to live next to him, he has been consistently isolated. The opposition of organized community groups to public housing in their neighborhoods "led to massive, segregated housing projects, which became ghettos for minorities and the economically disadvantaged."[65]

Enclosed in poverty, which produces asocial characteristics, the black minority is the group in America that is most identified with all its pejorative connotations. Thernstrom suggests that "in talking about poverty we really have in mind the problem of the Negro,"[66] a statement which he repeats.[67] Zahova Blum and Peter Ross, also sociologists, call the poor and the Negro "largely coterminous,"[68] and Thomas Gladwin considers poverty "essentially a Negro problem."[69]

As the social analyst William Julius Wilson points out, "The social problems of urban life . . . are . . . the problems of racial inequality."[70] The inequality of poverty, which stems "largely not from the legacy of poverty, but from the legacy of race,"[71] has served pragmatically to exonerate whites not only from the onus of undemocratic racism, but also from their responsibility, as the Kerner Commission reported, for having created, maintained and thus condoned the ghetto.[72]

At bottom, the inequality of American poverty is racist. Indeed, there has risen a "concept of a specifically Negro culture of poverty."[73] As historian Lerone Bennett writes, to the racist "there is a Negro and a white way of being poor . . . of being immoral. . . . White people and black people are criminals in different ways."[74] The notion that poverty constitutes a "whole"—a culture in itself which is practically irremediable and ideologically distinct from the prevailing one—tends not merely to justify its existence but to relieve white society of any responsibility for it. If, as Oscar Lewis supposes, poverty is a way of life that is handed down from generation to generation and that inspires people to reject the constraints of middle-class standards, then poverty transcends the sordid fact of being poor. It is probably incurable. The poor are not only not middle class; they also do not want to be. In America, where norms are materialistic, they would not care about consumer power.

As the black is associated with poverty—or poverty with the black—the poverty cultists identify the quality of being poor—with all its social characteristics from crime to sexual promiscuity to instability—with the quality of being black. Moynihan accepted this fallacy when he fastened on the female-headed family as "the fundamental problem"[75] which was "at the heart of the deterioration of the fabric of Negro society."[76] The idea that blacks have a distinct psychology "characterizes the ideology of . . . [Moynihan's] *Report on the Negro Family*," says Carper.[77]

Other critics challenged what has been called "the habit of analyzing data by color rather than by income [which] encourages the tendency to attribute to race-related factors differences that may in fact be due to income level."[78] The Moynihan Report, said James Farmer, formerly of CORE, served as a "basis for several new brands of bigotry."[79] Neoconservatives went even further than Moynihan: not as benignly as he, they made a correlation between blackness and instances of corruption and vice.[80]

Particularly after the black liberation movement, liberals began to suggest "that many of the poor were lazy, dissolute and prone to the breeding of large numbers of children for . . . welfare allowance."[81] Recently they have blamed the poor black's condition on circumstances beyond his control and thereby have caught him in an irremediable bind. According to Harrington, a critic composed a paradigm after Moynihan that went from poverty to cultural deprivation, to inadequate education and low motivation, to substandard wages, back to poverty.[82] Harrington's own paradigm, which started out with corporate monopolization of resources, led through political and economic exploitation to the process of facilitating corporate monopolization of resources. Again, as Valentine remarks, other analysts have defined the poor as an oppressed subsociety in an exploited subculture. In all cases, the "cult of cultural deprivation"[83] tends to entrench poor people in a vicious circle from which there is no issue. Moynihan fell into this trap when he traced the broken Negro family back to conditions that obtained in the days of slavery, implying consequently that such social dysfunction was peculiar to Negro culture alone. As historian Herbert Aptheker observed with respect to the vicious-circle theory, as expressed by Myrdal, "The natural inferiority of the black is taken to be unproven . . . but his socially induced inferiority is held to be a palpable fact."[84] Novelist William Styron's "psychosocial experimentalism" deprecates blacks.[85] The presentation of "data on the oppression of the Negro People" can serve as an "excuse for that very oppression."[86]

As Clark explains, the Negro child whose pitiful school record, for example, is rationalized by a "cultural deprivation approach" is not expected to achieve.[87] "Children who are treated as if they are uneducable almost invariably become uneducable."[88] Moreover, teachers presented with children who are considered uneducable seldom make a strong effort to educate them. The same is true for street kids who, because they are regarded as crooks, often become crooks. Innocent or not, they are many times gratuitously booked. And if they feel that society is against them in any case, they find no advantages in following its laws.

To explain slum behavior, therefore, is to assume that it is anomalous and, dialectically, that middle-class standards are the absolute criteria of decency and aberration. To rationalize slum behavior is to colonize the poor and to further reduce them to cultural isolation. The middle class, for instance, was appalled by the riots of the 1960s, but the lawbreaker at that time was in many instances an upwardly mobile marginal whose lawlessness was protest. The black bourgeoisie which realized this—to the dismay of whites—often considered the riots "legitimate protests about . . . abysmal conditions"[89] that were designed to move the white community to action. New poverty, however, has been more and more divorced from mainstream comportment, to the point that there is little area for contact between the down-and-out and the comfortable. "A truly hopeless group makes no demands and . . . does not insist upon stark social confrontations."[90] The untrained, practically illiterate, unemployed and designated unemployable, young slum black whose livelihood is based on huckstering, stealing, crack dealing—within the confines of his own black community—exists for the moment. Perhaps he is at heart a rebel, but he has no outlet. Quite naturally he prefers drug trafficking to washing dishes. Not only does it bring him the "material trappings of success"[91] that are socially approved—for he does adhere to the standards of consumer culture—but, as a high-risk occupation, it is also as interesting as capitalistic speculation. Claude Brown, for instance, enjoyed his way of life as a delinquent.[92] But, of course, he was subject to forces beyond his control. As Rap Brown described one of his most talented friends, who was deprived by his education and his segregated environment of a chance to express himself and was sentenced to life imprisonment at eighteen years old, "He was rebelling against the way the cards were stacked against him and even his rebellion was a stacked deck. . . . What was legal in our world wasn't legal in the white world and . . . he went down."[93]

Nowadays in many ways the black underclass suffers from poverty discrimination perhaps more than from segregation—although the two are very closely related. Poverty breeds poverty; it ensconces the poor person progressively deeper in miserable conditions. The two separate Americas that the Kerner Report foresaw are those of the black poor and the middle-class majority. Not only are the former divorced from those members of their race who have made it, but they are also blamed for their state. Since segregation has been outlawed, blacks no longer have a crutch on which they can racially rely to excuse their lack of opportunity.

The government has in principle reversed its position and condemned discrimination in housing, labor unions and schools. Of course, the fair-housing law passed in 1968 was so weak that it lent itself to nonenforcement. Segregation in this area is not the result of income levels: discrimination, which is "subtle, covert and sophisticated,"[94] is pervasive enough to restrict black people from healthier suburbs and to enclose the poorest of them in ghettos where "poor non-Hispanic whites were six times less likely . . . to live."[95] Obviously, school desegregation has not worked and black unemployment is more than double that of whites.[96]

Nevertheless, the law stands and the black is deemed responsible for his low socioeconomic status and for his growing and disproportionate dependence on welfare. "What we have had," reports the National Urban League, "is an administration saying that we are now a color-blind society with no racial problems."[97] Likewise after emancipation, the totally decapitalized ex-slave was reproached for his inability to compete with whites in an open market. It is as if the immediacy of an act can wipe out a historical tradition. As Wright observed, "The philosophies of . . . all the pragmatists . . . are but . . . adjurations to the white men of the West to . . . live within the . . . moment and let the meaning of that moment suffice as a rationale for life and death."[98] Whatever is, is right.

It was Lyndon Johnson's War on Poverty, his response to the so-called black revolution, that was instrumental in institutionalizing the correlation between black and poor. Despite, or perhaps because of, its good intentions, despite its very significant gains, the War on Poverty initiated the contemporary phase of segregation or social isolation: the discrimination that is aimed at the poor. It not only established a connection between the poor and discrimination, but, operating as it did "in the shadow of the civil rights movement and of the black urban riots,"[99] it also pretended to favor the black over other poor minorities. Moynihan, for instance, went so far as to blame its questionable achievements on "the transformation of the war on poverty from a program concerned generally with the poor, to one understood to be primarily for Negroes." It was, he continued, "a device that enabled the . . . government to launch . . . programs designed primarily to aid Negro Americans."[100]

The poverty war necessarily failed to vanquish poverty. All such projects, including those of urban renewal, are unrealistic if they do not attack the structural causes of economic dislocations. They would solve a fundamental cultural problem by enlarging privileges and, in effect, covering over the inequities that are at its source. They would not try to relate poverty to the industrial operation as a whole and thus suggest a solution that might affect the material status quo of sectors of the population that are more politically influential than poor groups.

The poverty war conflicted with the "reality of Lyndon Johnson's Great Society": it exposed the "substantial unemployment, particularly of blacks, in the midst of general prosperity."[101] Actually, it was a temporary expedient: Johnson wanted to outflank black protest while remaining within the framework of the traditional middle-class ethic. He offered not specific jobs, but opportunities "to *learn* to 'want to earn' in the American way."[102] He would, in other words, middle-classify the poor. But, as a critic remarked, "the pronounced program of the Great Society and Negro freedom, cannot be won within the context of the existing political-economic system."[103] Rather, "the introduction of a program aimed at the radical goal of eliminating poverty, ultimately sustains the system and ideology responsible for that poverty."[104]

Poverty projects were also inadequate on a practical level. They often created power positions for functionaries—white and black—who launched and controlled local self-help associations. The poor benefited less than civil service overseers. Besides, "community participation" campaigns ran up against and were undermined by "massive bureaucratic resistance to . . . decentralization."[105] Professionals quite naturally resented amateurs' initiatives: they disliked the confusion and the disorder. Moreover, with the institutionalization of decentralization, poverty programs met the opposition of ensconced local leaders, who were often white ethnics. Paradoxically, in the end, the ghetto walls were reinforced by the stratified social planning. Class and race combined to solidify a poverty dividing line.

On a political level, the War on Poverty victimized the poor. It set out to "redefine the racial conflict as [one] between the 'haves' and the 'have-nots' " and so to universalize and domesticate it. Yet since it identified the have-nots as blacks, this political "transmutation of the Civil Rights movement," as sociologist Elinor Graham observed, "secured the threatened power position of whites as whites"[106] or as haves. Indeed, it put the paternalistic state—in this case Democratic—back firmly in control. Johnson represented the liberal authority dispensing benevolence to his most disfavored, but theoretically not least loved, constituents. As Graham continued, "The poverty program redefin[ed] civil rights in a manner that secured the power positions of white public leaders. . . ."[107]

Nevertheless, the poverty program did result in real economic and educational gains for black people. Its "green (dollar) power," which was never very pronounced, may not have bought them off, as Rap Brown ironized,[108] but it did allow them to advance. It was, of course, aborted by circumstances that had little to do with the poor. It was stifled mainly by the escalation of the war in Vietnam and incidentally by the economic recessions of the 1970s and early 1980s. But the fact that the poverty program failed after it had been oversold—after it had promised with much media fanfare to eradicate poverty, which it identified with the Negro—served to discredit him.

Since the poverty war was also connected with a mission to exonerate the white middle class by assuring it that it was spending huge sums and engaging in an all-out campaign to uplift the black, it encouraged the conclusion that the latter was irremediably substandard. The poverty war was underfinanced because of Vietnam:[109] "There never was a gigantic program of handouts to the poor and to the minority poor in particular. . . ."[110] But because the poverty project publicized its largesse, because it would not admit its limitations, it implicitly shifted the onus of its failure onto the shoulders of the black poor. In keeping with the methodology of the industrial state—as well as with the president's own materialistic value system—the Great Society amounted to a pragmatic justification of racism. Not only did it institutionalize the black's association with subnormal poverty—which is traditionally reprehensible—but it also laid the burden of asocial comportment on the back of the black whom it had desegregated in principle and launched a total war to redeem.

As the War on Poverty died out with falling prosperity, the black masses were relegated again to poverty and entrapped in a synthesis of class and race inequality. Poverty is the dividing line—the "threshold of deprivation"—the boundary that separates America.[111] However, poverty makes it easy for middle America to cover over caste racism through class differentials: it disqualifies the poor from proper schooling, housing and jobs. As Cruse observes, "When civil rights programs fail to deliver economic parity, then the onus for black economic deprivation is shifted back to the blacks themselves."[112]

White America could justify its rejection of the poor on the grounds not simply of the capitalistic ethic of equal opportunity but of its own tax output. White America was under the illusion that it was exonerated of any obligation to poor people because it paid for poverty. In fact, blacks, of whom a disproportionate percentage were on relief, became intimately identified with the welfare state. Aid to Families with Dependent Children in particular has been associated with the children of the black slums.[113] And since the middle and working classes—including blacks who have advanced to this stratum—resent handouts and rail against "welfare cheats,"[114] they were inclined to turn not just against the black poor, but against the black cause for equality. "Civil rights has been a very low priority for whites since the mid-1960s. . . ."[115] Whites blamed welfare for the stagflation and recession of the 1970s;[116] they related it to illegitimacy, crime and unemployment. They practiced their new form of discrimination that identifies blacks with low class and which, during the Reagan administration, resulted in "deeper race and class divisions."[117]

The poor black was dissociated racially from whites of all minorities and classes. There was the majority and there was the outcast black. The feeling of separation, racially founded, was expressed in whites' uncompromising hostility to welfare. "The only persistent element of cleavage [with respect to national opinion on welfare] is the difference between whites and blacks, which has grown dramatically. . . . "[118] White America has, in effect, abandoned the black masses, as it did after Reconstruction. And because welfare is financed by taxes—which are actually inadequate, amounting to less than "one percent of the nation's personal income"[119]—white America is able to justify its neglect of the poor. Many reproach the victim, "the lazy native-born poor, for not being as hard-working as the immigrants and the undocumented," said Harrington.[120] "The welfare system is the price that the white majority pays in order to exclude the black minority from the general society . . ." writes Gore Vidal.[121] And the white majority begrudges this price.

Since the demise of the Great Society's project for social equality, white America has settled back into inegalitarianism. "Racial inequality in economic life is . . . the norm . . . ," says sociologist David Swinton.[122] The magnitude of the parity gap is striking on all levels of the economy: "the disparities have been worsening in most dimensions for at least . . . ten years."[123] Not only has black America remained "mired in recession,"[124] but the black poor have also coalesced into what appears to be a permanent underclass. Their poverty is labeled "persistent."[125]

Meanwhile, a certain, although relatively small, sector of the black population has benefited racially and economically both from the black liberation movement and the War on Poverty. Of course, as sociologist Bart Landry points out, "black middle-class families continue to be less successful than whites"—to the point that "the average net worth of middle-class whites in 1976 was two hundred and fifty times that of blacks."[126] Blacks suffer from discriminatory practices in pay and job status, in housing and education. Of the 21 percent who seek higher degrees, almost half are enrolled in community colleges. Nevertheless, they have moved up on the socioeconomic scale. Twenty-three percent of blacks are "middle income"—as compared to 46 percent of white families.[127] An analyst rates the black social world as 10 percent upper, 40 percent middle and 50 percent lower class.[128] According to Landry, one out of four black workers was able to rise into the American mainstream in the years between 1960 and 1970.[129] Sociologist Alphonso Pinkney likewise claims that 20 to 25 percent of blacks are, properly speaking, middle class.[130]

Still, as William Julius Wilson writes, "While the socio-economic status of the most disadvantaged members of the minority population has deteriorated rapidly since 1970, that of the advantaged members has significantly improved."[131] There are "two *black* Americas," said Harrington.[132] Qualified, educated blacks profited from race-specific initiatives—from civil and voting rights programs to poverty projects to affirmative action policies—which were supposed to be a "solution to the problems of all blacks regardless of economic class."[133] So while the many retrogressed, the few went forward. Groupwise, observes Cruse, "the equal opportunity legislation catapulted at least one third of the black minority into the middle-class economic range, while the remainder experienced a descending level of economic impoverishment."[134]

Quite naturally the aims and goals of this middle-class black minority are those of the American majority. They are in many ways totally accepted by the latter. For whites use class differentiation both negatively and positively to sanction their racially inspired rejection of blacks in general. Because they are inhibited by the American creed from thinking constructively along segregation lines, they maintain their illusions of democratic America by supporting the idea of equal opportunity for all blacks. So they are disposed, in principle, to welcome the new black middle class into their midst. On the one hand, having associated underclass with black and emphasized measures like welfare—of which they disapprove—to keep poverty within limits, they feel that they are right in condemning the aberrant American element. If the black has been given access to the middle class and still remains poor, then he is inferior or lazy and his dole should be curtailed. They can feed their racist inclinations on this rationale.

On the other hand, having restricted black achievers in their offices, schools, playing fields and sometimes neighborhoods, whites are confirmed in their rejection of the out-group by their acceptance of the in. They can convince themselves that they are not racist—even though they still refuse to live near poor black people.[135] It is easy to be integrative in spirit with the successful minority of a minority whose numbers pose no competitive threat and when prejudice can be covered over by rationalization. As a critic remarks, there is a discrepancy between whites' acts and their defense of their tolerance. Now they tend to discriminate by calling blacks "uppity or pushy . . . benefiting from preferential treatment."[136] And besides, as Pinkney emphasizes, "so few black families have reached a parity with white families that it can hardly be considered a trend."[137] Indeed, certain observers insist that race has little to do with urban discrimination. "Much of what appears . . . as race prejudice is really *class* prejudice or . . . class antipathy," says one. But since "much of what appears . . . as 'Negro' behavior is really lower class behavior,"[138] race prejudice can be rationalized as class bias.

With the black minority's entrance into the middle class it has become socially and economically separated from the black mass. There is an increasing gap between high- and low-income blacks.[139] "The socio-economic position of middle-strata blacks . . . improved much more dramatically than the black 'under class.' "[140] Culturally the two sectors have been separated to the point that the black middle class has abandoned the poor with which it enjoyed a certain solidarity during the black liberation movement and the black urban riots—when it had a common cause, sustained by violence. According to Cruse, the new black middle class is *"less nationalistic"* even than DuBois's Negro " 'upper-class' . . . of the 1930s."[141] It is materialistically oriented, but it lacks a sense of social responsibility and of its failure in this respect, which was a weakness that troubled Frazier's "black bourgeoisie." It is, continues Cruse, "an *empty class* that has flowered into social prominence *without a clearly defined social mission* in the United States."[142] Like immigrants who have been assimilated, its members pride themselves on making good, and tend to blame the poor for their dirt, their crime and their illegitimate children.

Naturally, as Wilson says, the black bourgeoisie's desertion of the black underclass has contributed to the latter's growth and spread. The exodus of the working and middle classes from the ghettos made it hard to maintain the institutions—such as schools, churches, lodges—that might have preserved social discipline, if not upheld positive social standards.[143] The better black students, for instance, left slum schools as soon as they could, thus abandoning a subgroup of untrained young people who had nobody to look up to.

The exodus of the black middle class removed "an important 'social buffer' that could deflect the full impact of . . . prolonged and increasing joblessness," says Wilson.[144] It left disadvantaged and uneducated blacks in social isolation to cope for themselves against the malevolent indifference of outside society and against the dearth of opportunity within. If the poor do have the same cultural orientation—including the same values and aspirations—as most materialistic Americans,[145] if they are unhappy with their status, then their deliberate ostracism would be a factor in intensifying the antisocial behavior to which they are subject by their poverty.

Wilson thinks that "economic shifts" have been responsible for the growth of the black underclass. The emphasis on services over goods, the movement of industry away from the central cities, the decline of low-skilled blue-collar jobs and the postindustrial stress on "knowledge-intensive" employment, all have led to the loss of opportunity in the ghetto.[146] There have also been cuts in programs to help the poor. Consequently, from 1970 to 1980 poverty rose by 12 percent in America's fifty largest cities and by 22 percent in its five largest. Since inner-city schools train the young in such a way that they are qualified only for low-wage jobs,[147] they seem to be shunted outside the economy. Indeed, the existing "social and educational systems work to eliminate the majority of [children in school],"[148] leaving them totally unprepared for any but the most automatic of productive work. "Black and Hispanic schools remain extremely different from white schools in ways that are decisive for the preparation of students for work and culture," says a critic.[149] And since "the community and the school are inseparable,"[150] since if one declines the other does also, "the problem of education is the problem of segregation."[151]

With the failure of busing, moreover, slum schools are more than ever segregated and unable to train the young. It is the poor, therefore, on whom the burden of unemployment persistently falls. Only 58 percent of all young adult males of the ghetto had jobs in 1984.[152] And this group, a potential staple of a viable social structure, has been so irreparably put outside the economic mainstream that an alarming proportion is a part of the prison population. The entire black social fabric is affected. Because there has been a "rapid contraction of the black 'male marriageable poor,' " as Wilson puts it,[153] there are fewer marriages and more teenage illegitimate births and more dependent children.

It is not just external economic factors that have led to the emergence of a black underclass. It is because the black has historically been penalized by segregation that he is more susceptible to economic transformations than members of other minorities. "A racial division of labor has been created due to . . . centuries of discrimination, and . . . because those in the low wage sector of the economy are more adversely affected by economic shifts . . . the racial division of labor is reinforced."[154] The white has not been irreparably consigned to the ghetto, that ecological organization by which poverty was associated with race. Since the days when blacks had to pay higher rents than newly arrived and destitute aliens[155] to modern times when housing in an anachronistic urban structure segregates by income, blacks have been crowded into districts with eroding tax bases.[156]

Also, the government tends to tolerate, if not encourage, some unemployment: "an overheated economy can be cooled by creating unemployment," says sociologist Bruno Stein.[157] The " 'inflation threshold unemployment rate' "[158] to which Harrington referred amounts to the acceptance of joblessness and, in view of obtaining conditions, of joblessness in the black slums. Indeed, government seems to view a reasonable proportion of unemployment as relatively healthy—particularly as it falls on the backs of an increasingly unpopular and politically impotent segment of the population. The entire middle class, both black and white, looks with growing disapprobation on black slums and their incidence of violence, delinquency and drug activity as an *a posteriori,* or pragmatic, proof of black civil incompetence. It is blacks who are deemed responsible for urban insecurity. Since their poor have been disproportionately represented in the welfare, drop-out and criminal populations, they are branded as undesirable—which, in effect, many of them are. Therefore, the "racial discrimination [that] is deeply rooted in the structure of American institutions"[159] persists whether it is rationalized as class or race bigotry.

The economic rationalization of racism has been described by Kovel as "metaracism": an official attitude that eliminates racial bias expediently, but "reduces people to its own ends."[160] Metaracists support the prevailing system that not only denigrates the black poor, but also mires them in their poverty. Metaracists acquiesce to the larger cultural order that continues the work of racism. Since some kind of poverty—like some degree of unemployment—is necessary, if not advisable, and since blacks, blocked by racism, are already poor, it is easier to let them continue as such than to risk afflicting other, more vocal segments of the population and arousing reactions that are not channeled by anti-black racism.

In the long run, historically entrenched racism still seems to contribute to the success of the postindustrial state. Had blacks' exploitation not been cultural—had it been merely economic, as certain of the founding fathers pretended when they called slavery a necessary evil—blacks would have been, Ellison wrote, "by all historic logic . . . rationalized out of existence."[161] But racism is essential to national viability on noneconomic as well as economic levels.

It has been said that blacks would be irrelevant to a postindustrial culture. "In 1850 American Negroes were integral to the industrial revolution by institutions of segregation, disfranchisement, and proscription."[162] And in 1900 they were disqualified by their poverty and its effects. Blacks were unnecessary. DuBois remarked that "American Negroes have always feared . . . their eventual expulsion from America. . . ."[163] Now with cybernetics and advanced technology that preclude the functional demand for unschooled labor, blacks are no longer needed in the structure, as James Boggs put it.[164] Soledad Brother George Jackson, who witnessed the entrapment and assassination of his fellow militants, went so far as to mention "genocide."[165] He believed that "blacks and other Third World peoples have the very imminent prospect of genocide tactics to contend with."[166]

According to sociologists Edwin Powell and Sidney Wilhelm, whites no longer have to exploit the Negro and so he "is not needed . . . not so much oppressed as unwanted, not so much unwanted as unnecessary, not so much abused as ignored."[167] In effect, not to want is to oppress; to ignore is to abuse, especially when material deprivation is the result of indifference. The fact that blacks "are no longer a source of wealth,"[168] as James Baldwin put it, seems to pose an insoluble problem to self-interested middle-class America. Of course, as social analyst Eric Lincoln speculated, it would not eliminate blacks. Nevertheless, certain thinkers have associated this policy with the introduction of drug traffic into the ghetto. "Substance abuse" can be judged "at worse, an instrument of genocide in the African-American community," write sociologists Wade Nobles and Lawford Goddard. "It is highly likely that through acts of commission and/or omission the command mechanism of government has allowed the drug problem to go unchecked and consequently, those communities with the least ability to resist the inevitable destruction are being systematically destroyed."[169] Dope addiction, says one of writer George Cain's characters, is "part of the Man's scheme, a way to keep a large part of the people helpless, an excuse for jailing and abusing them."[170] Cain's girl tells him, "They must want you this way . . . sick, stealing and robbing, acting like you crazy."[171]

But the poor black population with its high birth rate and its survival techniques—including drug dealing and other methods of adjusting to slums—promises to grow, not to die out. It has been projected that by the year 2000, 25 percent of the American population will be nonwhite, and ill educated, ill housed and ill employed. The enlarged ghetto will present a threat to the stability of the middle-class society. At some point in the twenty-first century, according to sociologist Price Cobbs, whites will constitute a minority. The question of racism as of genocide will be irrelevant to the continuance of America.[172]

PART II

BLACK DEFENSE STRATEGIES

CHAPTER 4

SELF-HELP AND COMMUNITY

In reacting to the policy of post–Civil War racism, which culminated in legalized segregation, the black has utilized two apparently conflicting but parallel strategies. He has fought for integration in American middle-class society and he has struggled for autonomy in his separate community, which would entail economic and political self-determination. The prevailing order, however, has consistently denied him access to both those goals. Segregation, an ideological white position, made integration impossible and held the black in a subequal status. Political and economic colonization, which was inherent in the pragmatic methodology of the industrial machine, kept him dependent on its operation.

In effect, blacks have found it difficult to maintain a coherent policy either of integration or of separatism. The black suffers from this dual identity in his relations with his country—which denies him his rights—and with his own group. Frederick Douglass, the great ex-slave abolitionist, stressed self-help, racial solidarity and economic self-determination[1] while at the same time he "always opposed racial separation."[2] He was a humanitarian optimist in the sense that he was an integrationist: he sought "assimilation in the body politic,"[3] and called race pride "a positive evil."[4] He rejoiced, he was quoted, "to be like white folks";[5] he even married one. Nevertheless, he was increasingly suspicious not simply of the victorious Republican party—to which he loyally delivered the votes of freed Negroes[6]—but also of its leaders who sought his support. By the 1870s, according to historian Benjamin Quarles, Douglass realized that "the cause of the Negro seemed . . . to have reached a stalemate."[7]

He was, however, unprepared to deal with the problems of burgeoning capitalism. As an ex-slave, Douglass was from the agricultural upper South (below the Mason-Dixon Line) and had come north to agitate on principles. Indeed, he adhered to the nineteenth-century ethic of self-reliance and laissez-faire: like militants such as Henry David Thoreau, he believed that "the man who is right is a majority."[8] Although he realized that the Civil War had been fought in part for economic interest—that, as he put it, slavery had been destroyed "not from principle, but from policy"[9]—he preferred to think of the war as a moral struggle. He had faith that freed Negroes would be recognized as citizens, that black people would be able to assimilate in the social order on the same terms as whites. "What I ask for the Negro . . . is . . . simple justice . . ." he said. "Do nothing with us!"[10] Politicians, businessmen and fellow Americans did exactly that: they left blacks to the South.

After Douglass the concept of black nationalism seemed to gain ground slowly but progressively. It was a pessimistic philosophy as it was based on the assumption that a white-controlled system would never grant full equality to the black. Booker T. Washington was probably the first influential advocate of economic nationalism and of race pride—although Martin Delany, a free black, had preached "usefulness and business" for Negroes.[11] But Washington was the leader of the emancipated blacks during the post-Reconstruction period when they were systematically being deprived of their rights. He was faced with the problem of constructing some kind of power base on foundations that were deliberately being eroded. Moreover, Washington was equipped with a precorporate capitalistic ethic in an age of increasing massive exploitation and centralization. Inevitably, he was caught in a bind.

Washington could counter the offensive pragmatism of the growing industrial state, which looked only to success, with a kind of defensive pragmatism of his own. In teaching his students "to meet conditions as they exist *now*"[12] he was, despite himself, preparing them for a subservient role in the order. He clung to the myths and symbols that inspired middle-class whites, who were themselves being displaced. He was a Horatio Alger figure who had really risen up from slavery but without the advantage from which Alger's heroes profited: that of marrying the master's daughter. He believed in the materialistic ethic; he admired businessmen, both white and black; he prized individual excellence, laissez-faire and the utilitarian virtues that had first been expounded by Benjamin Franklin's Poor Richard.

The clean, industrious, polite and punctual young man was sure to make good. DuBois said that Washington's tenets were "Thrift, Patience, Industrial Training."[13]

As Washington had little faith in socially humanitarian solutions to the black's deprived condition, he advocated the doctrine of economic self-help. "Freedom can never be given," he insisted. "It must be purchased."[14] He was a capitalist in the old Puritan sense of the word and, like Douglass, disapproved of labor unions.[15] But he had practical reasons for his hostility to them that outweighed those of the ordinary white businessman: almost without exception, unions excluded Negroes.

As president of the Tuskegee Institute, Washington used the institution to help black farmers, black merchants and black professionals.[16] They would be the advance guard of a still-backward peasant people. Indeed, he assumed that his educational center would serve the interests of all blacks, just as all Negroes must build on the foundation of agriculture. The failure of Tuskegee "would cause people . . . to lose faith in the ability of the entire race."[17] Only the gospel of work could solve the issue of racism, he preached. Prejudice would fall to the power of the dollar and to the force of achievement. The "pillar of fire by night and pillar of cloud by day shall be property, economy, education and Christian character," he wrote.[18] All else was chaff. The leaders whom he sought to train would thus have a "constituency or . . . foundation from which to draw support."[19]

By stressing industrial education and self-help, Washington hoped to keep black people more or less separate from the white job market. They would, therefore, avoid the antagonism of white workers and they would be removed from competition with immigrants, whom he distrusted,[20] and—more significant—they would "buy Southern good will and Northern philanthropy,"[21] the conditions of black group survival. Blacks should remain in the South under the protection of their old masters and look to the North for charity. Nevertheless, it was through the Tuskegee principles of race uplift and implicitly of race pride that are found, as Cruse points out, the origins of the feeling of black community solidarity.[22] "We are a nation within a nation," wrote Washington.[23] He has been echoed by blacks from Garveyites to Muslims to Panthers.

Washington was also a skilled manipulator. He was a child of his day: his singleness of vision, his total immersion in his task were marks of the practical "successful man,"[24] as DuBois called him. He was, in

effect, a remarkable success. He built the Tuskegee Institute into a machine as powerful as that of any northern boss.[25] He was "a politician
. . . a man who believed that we should get what we could get," said
DuBois; "he . . . had the idea: 'Now what's your racket?' "[26] A New
York newspaper commented on Washington's place as the "political
boss of his race."[27] In his goal to effect a "triple alliance between
Northern capitalists, the . . . Southern white leadership class, and
blacks,"[28] he used, cajoled and catered to the former two—whom he
disarmed despite his distrust[29]—and demanded absolute loyalty from
the latter to the point that he often resorted—like every boss—to
strong-arm methods to keep his troops in line.

He enjoyed a prestigious reputation with his people and cultivated
faithful protégés. Often, in exchange for federal posts, Washington enlisted the support of influential black leaders, from Louisiana governor
Pinckney B. S. Pinchback to liberal philanthropists Robert and Mary
Terrell to publisher Thomas Fortune. On the other hand, he used any
means to silence his critics. When he was heckled in Boston by educated
young black radicals, led by Monroe Trotter of the Boston *Guardian,*
he tried to quash press coverage of the incident.[30] His control over black
newspapers was so tight that he could persuade them to underplay—
even to ignore—the Niagara movement[31] led by DuBois and the precursor of the National Association for the Advancement of Colored
People (NAACP)—which was an open challenge to his leadership role
in the black community. He even covertly took over Fortune's newspaper *Age.*[32]

Washington attacked the Negro church[33] in order to clear away any
obstacle to the attainment of his goals. He wanted not just to prevail
over, but "to humiliate" his rival, DuBois,[34] whom Washington discredited with his white patrons. He was an anti-intellectual pragmatist
who resented his elitist opponents: they were not realists, he argued;
they understood theories, not things. He went to all lengths to carry
through his program for the uplift of black people. He hoped to create
what he called a "New Negro for a new century"[35] whose thrust would
be based on "race pride, group solidarity and self-dependence."[36] These
were noble goals.

But in his day black people could not prosper on these terms. They
had to function in a climate of deprivation. Indeed, it was precisely
because they represented a nation within a colonizing nation that Washington's project could not succeed. To "cast down your bucket where
you are"[37] meant—for an already disadvantaged and disempowered mi-

nority—to accept a condition of lower political, economic and educational status. It was hard to fight pragmatism with pragmatism when the adversary controlled the necessary arms. Ironically, Washington personally succeeded, at least on the surface, through the very tactics that seemed to penalize his race. His doctrine was enthusiastically embraced by northern and southern racists and northern and southern paternalists. For the practice of segregation—which was already installed—perverted his teachings into a justification of black inequality, while it gave him international prestige as the black leader who knew his place.

As blacks were progressively disfranchised throughout the South, Washington's political objectives were defeated. Despite his influence and reputation, in 1901 his own county was deprived of the vote: the administrators and faculty of the Tuskegee Institute were refused at the polls.[38] They resisted by launching a boycott, but the whites were obdurate. Merchants preferred to lose money rather than surrender their political power. Washington himself was inclined to forgo militancy: he did not agitate for the reduction of the South's national representation after black disfranchisement and thereby incurred the animosity of young radicals like Trotter.[39] "What man," wrote the latter, "is a worse enemy to a race than a leader who looks with equanimity on the disfranchisement of his race in a country where other races have universal suffrage. . . ."[40] As Washington's biographer, Louis Harlan, remarks, "Considering the time and energy that [he] . . . and [his] . . . lieutenants were devoting to politics, its rewards were small."[41]

His economic program was obsolete in a world now dominated by rising industrial capitalism. He was playing to the farmer and the small businessman in an agrarian system in which blacks were trapped. In his day, as he noted, "eighty-five percent of the colored people in the Gulf States depended upon agriculture for their living."[42] As a southerner, he believed with Thomas Jefferson that people "are at their best when living in the country, engaged in agricultural pursuits."[43] And he realized that the vast majority of blacks were caught in such an environment and were qualified only for such employment. But individual skill, craftsmanship, hard work and independent research—within the climate of white-directed laissez-faire—were irrelevant at a time when capital and technology were being adapted to the early stages of agribusiness. One cannot develop an enterprise, as DuBois observed, when the small grocery store cannot compete with a large one.[44]

The all-Negro town of Mound Bayou, Mississippi, for instance, a self-help enterprise capitalized by northern moneys, could not fulfill

Washington's expectations, despite the efforts of its founder, Isaiah Montgomery.[45] Not only was it set in a national urbanizing economy in which it, like all Negro projects, as Frazier pointed out, had to depend "economically upon the economic institutions of the American community,"[46] Mound Bayou also was situated in the segregated South and had to deal with the jealousy of neighboring racists who "white-capped" it:[47] they drove upwardly mobile blacks out of town. Even in Durham, North Carolina, where black businessmen did succeed, they had to manage their affairs surreptitiously. John Merrick, a contractor, insurance agent and real-estate investor, was refused service in a store in one of the buildings he owned.

Moreover, Washington misjudged the industrial current of the times. It was not self-reliance but bureaucratic organization, capitalization and financial management that would prevail. Washington's single-mindedness led him to concentrate on manual arts and vocational instruction for Negroes as an end in itself. DuBois accused him of changing the program of industrial education "from a by-path into a veritable Way of Life."[48] He tended to deny that there were alternative possibilities for blacks and so deprived them of the means of developing an independent economic base.

Socially, Washington was compelled by circumstance to accept segregation as there was little he could do to combat it. But in order to appease southern racists and to avoid antagonizing northern philanthropists, he denounced blacks' aspirations for immediate social equality as "the extremist folly."[49] Indeed, after 1895 he did not come out in public against segregation. His attitude was rather conciliatory, although he tried to rationalize his policy by distinguishing between segregation and subordination.[50] Nevertheless, he knew that African Americans were being subjected to unjust practices, particularly in the field of education through which he wanted to uplift the race. His appointment as a nonfunctioning member of the—obviously white— Southern Education Board (which oversaw the distribution of tax money to schools) was a ploy to quiet his people while the board "did its work of promoting white education" by seizing the school funds of disfranchised Negroes.[51]

Washington's policy of conciliation did little to improve the condition of blacks, who continued relentlessly to lose the erstwhile benefits of Reconstruction's military occupation. And yet that policy attracted the attention of northern capitalists, who helped Washington financially because they—like southerners—preferred that Negroes be humble and lowly. But Washington lost the support of many black leaders—including Fortune—when it became evident he had less and less significant influence with white officialdom. Teddy Roosevelt, for instance, ignored Washington's muted objections and callously dismissed black troops in Brownsville, Texas, after a white-incited riot. Washington's control over patronage posts decreased and Negro opposition to him mounted; he was progressively deprived of what he had considered to be his power base. After he was savagely beaten up in New York, Washington realized—says Harlan—"that in the atmosphere of American racism even Booker T. Washington was lynchable."[52]

At heart Washington was, of course, opposed to segregation and disfranchisement. Vocational training and small-business enterprise were valuable as means by which a marginally employed and industrially undeveloped peasant minority could survive in a racially hostile environment. Blacks who were dispossessed had to depend on outside aid, and northern paternalists had money to offer. As even DuBois realized, Washington was in a situation in which he had to accept the prevailing order and make up to white people in strategic positions. What Harlan calls his "artful dodging"[53] was Washington's way of getting along with them—even of manipulating them. Whites liked him because he played to what they wanted, as DuBois observed.[54] "The young Negro of the South . . . must flatter and be pleasant, endure petty insults with a smile, shut his eyes to wrong; in too many cases he sees positive personal advantage in deception and lying. His real thoughts, his real aspirations, must be guarded in whispers."[55] Inevitably, Washington became entrapped in his own methodology. He was, concluded DuBois, "an opportunist, slow but keen-witted with high ideals," who "had not the slightest doubt that the current organization of industry in the United States was normal and right."[56] And he loved the country that did in his race: he was a chauvinist who believed in America.

His work in any case was not lost. It was Booker T. Washington who revived and popularized the ideal of race solidarity. As the black community was forced to withdraw into itself, it spawned a rising class of businessmen and professionals—Frazier's black bourgeoisie—that actually profited from segregation,[57] in which it had a vested interest.[58] This new elite displaced the older upper stratum of Negroes who were subsidized by whites[59] and who consequently owed their loyalty to them.[60] The "*status* group," as Landry calls it, had been made up of free blacks or mulattoes whose prestige in the black community derived from their direct blood relation to members of the white upper class, by whom they were often subsidized.[61] They were the snobs who blamed race prejudice on poor whites or on poor Negroes: they engaged in service occupations and tended to reject any implication of black nationalism. Many of them passed as white.

But they lost their ties to the white upper class through the effects of segregation and northern migration,[62] and as they did, their status declined. The new bourgeoisie, on the other hand, earned its living from the black community, although it often tried to sever connections with the Negro masses. This black bourgeoisie was separated from direct competition with the white middle class because it was enclosed behind the walls of the black ghetto.[63] It was composed of the merchants and professionals with whom black people dealt.[64]

Segregated schooling, for instance, required Negro teachers, whom the black community treated with the respect that Europeans bestowed on educators.[65] Blacks prized learning as much as Jews, although, unlike Jews, blacks were denied entry into America's most reputable institutions. Black doctors and dentists and undertakers were supported by black folk who could not be treated or laid out by whites. In the beginning of segregation, there were only a few black lawyers and they were excluded from the American Bar Association. But as the NAACP gained strength, there was more and more demand for competent African American attorneys.[66] Black ministers preached to black congregations as during slavery; black real-estate and insurance agents struggled to build up black businesses.

But the black community lacked a solid economic base. It was a colony that ultimately depended on downtown forces. Since black businessmen and professionals were denied access to centers of power and could not succeed on a large scale, they tended to be social opportunists.[67] They were oriented to the economic mainstream and they seized every chance they could, even if this involved toadying to their colonizers and profiting from their fellow blacks. DuBois accused many black entrepreneurs of "aping American acquisitive society" and of exploiting their brethren instead of assuming "the uplift of their . . . proletariat."[68] Jean Toomer, poet and grandson of Governor Pinchback, mercilessly attacked the materialism and hypocrisy of the Negro middle class.[69]

In many ways Frazier's black bourgeoisie led the empty existence of which he accused it. But it was instrumental not only in consolidating the black racial group but also in stabilizing it. As Landry says, it "achieved its greatest success in creating parallel institutions for the growth and development of the black community." It "developed a life style largely centered around home and clubs."[70] And since these insti-tutions—and others, including the church—were not based uniquely on economic criteria, the black environment had a character of its own which differed from that of whites. The stress on self-cultivation and self-help, which seemed outdated in an industrial urban culture, was an element in an idealism that fastened on concrete goals and which in many ways reflected the defunct Puritan tradition. Blacks, writes Ralph Ellison, have abstracted desirable qualities from their enemies not sim-ply to survive, but to construct a point of reference for moral realism.[71] This ethic exists to this day. Most black leaders—from Malcolm X to Martin Luther King, Jr., to Huey P. Newton—have leaned on it.

The black church has also been a positive source of black nation-alism. It was the oldest indigenous black cultural institution that for centuries served to preserve the black historical experience. It was "the first distinctly Negro-American social institution," wrote DuBois, who did not consider it a branch of orthodox Protestant Christianity, but a "mere adaptation of . . . heathen rites."[72] It was the only Negro organ-ization "which started in the African forest and survived slavery."[73] Frazier also related the black church to its African heritage. "One might reasonably assume," he said, "that among the Negroes who received the 'call to preach' there were some who had been influenced by African traditions and that others cherishing memories of their African back-ground found in . . . emotionalism an opportunity for self-expression."[74]

The church, however, was subject to the contradictions that plagued the black experience in America and, as a result, served a double func-tion. On the one hand, it preached submission to authority and rec-ompense in the afterlife, while on the other it promoted a desire for freedom, if not for revolution; it was subversive. Church meetings had a dual purpose, wrote Margaret Walker in *Jubilee*.[75] The church was an organizer[76] and "tended both to play an accommodating role and to stimulate the sentiment of racial solidarity."[77] It was the solace and the outlet of the Negro masses[78] and, says writer Charles Hamilton, the only association black people "belong to which is decidedly and exclu-sively theirs."[79] It was, even in the North, a "Race Institution" whose ministers "display a lively interest in 'advancing the Race.' "[80] And the church was instrumental in the difficult adjustment of a rural peasant folk to an urban environment. In Rudolph Fisher's story "Vestiges," an old preacher, displaced in the city, attends the services of an ex-gambler and meets his former congregation and everyone rediscovers his roots. As Fisher's Luke, a tough street kid, remarks of a revival meeting, "It just sorter gets me."[81] Similarly, writer Maya Angelou escapes her white husband by sneaking off to church to hear the songs that are "sweeter than sugar" and to feel black again.[82]

"The Black Church," writes the Reverend Albert B. Cleage, Jr., "has not always been revolutionary, but it has always been relevant to the everyday needs of black people."[83] Frazier thought that because Negroes were eliminated "from the political life of the American community," the church became "the arena of their political activities."[84] Certainly many of the most influential black leaders of the twentieth century have used it as a power base from which to launch their political careers, from Marcus Garvey to Adam Clayton Powell, Jr., to Martin Luther King, Jr., to Jesse Jackson. During the 1960s the ideology of black nationalism inspired a call for a new black theology that would be related "to black consciousness and black liberation" and which would reject the principles of racist white religion.[85] Cleage unveiled a black Madonna on Easter Sunday and preached "the stabilizing influence of the religion of the Black Messiah, Jesus Christ," as a positive factor in "the Black Revolution."[86]

The new black theology is not new. Blacks have always adapted white religion to their needs. To Garvey the Virgin Mary was black.[87] DuBois questioned the concept of a white God: "Surely, Thou too art not white, O Lord, a pale, bloodless, heartless thing?" he wrote.[88] Daisy Bates, the Little Rock activist, felt as a little girl that "if Jesus is like the white people, I don't want any part of Him."[89]

Since it was the segregated black church that preserved and incarnated the black experience in America, it was essentially the source of black creative expression. In fact, black music, America's one significant artistic contribution to world culture, evolved from early church spirituals. No matter how irrelevant the black church seems to be in urban America, no matter how opportunist many of its ministers and how tacky and commercialized their message, the church represented black communality in its noblest and most profound sense. And it could be revived.

The lodge was the secularized version of the church for the black middle class. It was fraternal, convivial, implicitly nationalistic, and above all it was ethical in orientation. Its purpose was not simply to promote a feeling of black brotherhood, but to uplift the black community as a whole. Indeed, it would raise the Negro masses to the level of responsible citizenship.

But the lodge was elitist. The fraternity and the sorority were exclusivist, if not snobbish. These groups wanted to uphold high educational and moral standards for their members, not simply to warrant the respect of society at large, but to assure their status in the Negro world. They were, however, following the directives of such black leaders as W.E.B. DuBois and Mary Church Terrell. While DuBois advocated the development of a talented Negro leadership, Mary Church Terrell urged black women to go in the interest of "self-preservation . . . among the lowly, illiterate and even the vicious, to whom they are bound by ties of race and sex . . . to reclaim them."[90] Middle-class organizations, suggests writer Paula Giddings, were affirmatively race conscious: "The sisterhood was the cohesive glue. . . ."[91]

CHAPTER 5

AGITATION FOR
CIVIC EQUALITY

I f black nationalism is a means to black solidarity and to the autonomy of the race in implicit defiance of white neocolonialism,
then integrationism seems on the surface to represent its opposite.
As the traditional solution to segregation, the latter has been middle
class, reformist and even leftist in spirit. Moreover, it has rejected the
premise on which the black sense of community was based by affirming
the value of white norms. To make it, to join the white world, was to
affirm the prevalence of white criteria. Integrationism suggested, said
writer Larry Neal, "an uncritical acceptance of a white value system."[1]

Indeed, the very principle of integration denied the culture of blackness much as the idea of the melting pot had degraded ethnicity. As
Stokely Carmichael observed, the integrationist would not accept black
group identity as "a functional and honorable segment of . . . society."[2]
The white middle-class norm is built on the hypothesis that there is but
one right and that everyone must conform to given standards. French
philosopher Roland Barthes, for instance, has noted that the pre- and
postrevolutionary European bourgeoisie developed an essentialist—a
universalist—mythology of mankind.[3] Even a sociologist like Gunnar
Myrdal, an apparently unbiased scientist, was blocked by his assumption that integration was the solution to the American dilemma. His
study of race relations was limited because, implicitly, he looked at the
United States as a European (that is, white) country. The *"Negro problem"*[4] was a distorted part of the complex of "the general American
culture":[5] the black was a white in blackface with a caricatural structure
that corresponded to that of his white peer. In other words, the black
did not have a cultural tradition of his own. Ellison has called Myrdal's
thesis little more than *"a blueprint for a more effective exploitation of*

the South's natural industrial and human resources."[6] In fact, the contemporary relaxation of segregation and the stress on integration in the
South led to a mobilization of the southern work force and has facilitated the establishment of corporate enterprise in the region.

As has been pointed out, integration without power is meaningless.[7]
It would siphon off "acceptable Negroes into the . . . middle-class white
community"[8]—as it has done—and force the ordinary black to deny his
heritage in order to identify with those blacks who have made it "against
the odds of racism."[9] Integration would benefit the individual striver at
the expense of an industrially rejected "lumpen population," which, says
Saul Bellow's Dean Corde, "we do not know how to approach." In accordance with prevailing materialistic norms, he concludes, "those that
can be advanced into the middle class, let them be advanced." As for the
rest, he suggests that they be left alone. "They kill some of us. Mostly
they kill themselves. . . ."[10] Integrationism in the postindustrial system is,
in effect, a form of colonization. "No sane black man really believes that
the white man will give the black man anything more than token integration . . ." said Malcolm X, who wanted blacks to separate from a corrupt
and decaying society.[11] Indeed, only one third of the black population today has been able—or willing—to integrate.

Yet in the sense that integration implies group recognition in a pluralistic society, it is not theoretically antithetical to the concept of black
nationalism. In principle integration represents an ideal while black nationalism seems to be a methodology. Hamilton and Carmichael have
treated black power as a means of assimilation. *"Before a group can
enter the open society,"* they write, *"it must first close ranks."*[12] Malcolm X says, "There can be no black-white unity until there is first
some black unity."[13] And Cruse considers black nationalism as "a strategic retreat for a purpose . . . to change . . . the black world . . . by re-
forming it into something else politically and economically."[14] He
advocates plurality with equality: in a society dominated by potent interest groups that compete for privilege within a materialistic middle-
class framework, the black community would have to assert itself in
unison and with force to claim the equal treatment it demands.[15]

Throughout the twentieth century, however, integrationism and
black nationalism were not just conterposed but oversimplified and abstracted into antitheses. This was relatively easy to do: Booker T. Washington, who theoretically represents the idea of black autonomy and
black separatism, was in fact opposed by W.E.B. DuBois, who, again
theoretically, was supposed to be an assimilationist. But as DuBois ex-

plained, "I believed in the higher education of a talented tenth who through their knowledge of modern culture could guide the American Negro into a higher civilization. . . . Mr. Washington . . . believed that the Negro as an efficient worker could gain wealth and that eventually through his ownership of capital he would be able to achieve a recognized place in American culture and could then educate his children as he might wish and develop their possibilities. . . . These two theories of Negro progress were not absolutely contradictory."[16] Washington suggested that his concept of material self-improvement was a means. "If this generation will lay the material foundation, it will be the quickest and surest way for the succeeding generation to succeed in the cultivation of the fine arts . . ." he wrote.[17]

Washington's and DuBois's struggles were obviously ambivalent. Washington, who distrusted but deferred to whites and was popular with them, took pride in his country and hoped eventually for the full integration of his people in its values and norms. DuBois, perfectly able to fraternize with individual whites on an equal basis, declared that "the Negro has . . . come to consider that whatever is for the benefit of the white man is for his detriment."[18] He was detested by white political and business leaders, including Theodore Roosevelt.[19] As Washington accepted segregation and contended that the Negro gained "a strength, a confidence" from the harshness of his battle to survive,[20] so DuBois spoke at times for segregation. "I was fighting segregation but simultaneously advocating such segregation as would prepare my people for the struggle they were making," he said.[21] Indeed, he was not against separation if blacks were treated with equity. He was definitely for Negro cooperation. We must "organize our economic and social power, no matter how much segregation it involves," he wrote.[22]

Washington was deeply attached to the cause of his people. DuBois had a profound emotional—even spiritual—bond with his folk, whom he thought of as qualitatively distinguished over other groups and for whom he dreamed of "a Negro self-sufficient culture even in America."[23] The Negro, he wrote, is "essentially an artistic being";[24] he had not only "brought to America a sense of meekness and humility which America has never recognized and perhaps never will,"[25] but he had also by his suffering achieved a nobility of spirit which white America was too callous to appreciate, much less itself to share. Blacks were the "sole oasis of simple faith and reverence in a dusty desert of dollars and smartness."[26] Blacks had a feeling of community or of collective consciousness that had "sprung from common joy and grief . . . from a common hardship in poverty, poor land and low wages; and, above all, from the sight of the Veil that hung between us and opportunity."[27] It was not biological racial similarity but "common suffering" that was the "important factor uniting the Negro,"[28] giving him his cultural depth and his "idea of community, of brotherhood."[29]

Whereas Washington had risen from slavery—from destitution and from an entrenched tradition of racist persecution—DuBois was far removed from that institution. He came from a line of free, upright, practically (that is, on the surface) integrated blacks. As a boy, he later admitted, he was "long unconscious of color discrimination in any obvious and specific way."[30] His grandfather, he said, "was not a 'Negro'; he was a man."[31] DuBois grew up in Great Barrington, a small, relatively classless Massachusetts town where "the contrast between the well-to-do and the poor was not great."[32] The lower-class Yankees and Irish immigrants were more slovenly and disordered than the blacks. DuBois also was highly educated. He graduated from public school, where he was an outstanding student, and went from Harvard to post-graduate work at the University of Berlin in Germany.

Consequently, as biographer Arnold Rampersad observes, "DuBois's youth prepared him to champion an ideal: Booker T. Washington's youth prepared him for a life defined by the reality of oppression."[33] DuBois was open and volatile; he was a cultural pluralist who believed "in an aristocracy of intelligence and morality that knew neither race nor color, and in ultimate ideals beyond the distinctions of cultural relativism."[34] Washington, however, was "wary and silent";[35] he was secretive and suspicious of people in general; and through no fault of his own was engaged in a never-ending war with the world. Pragmatically speaking, he accepted the inexorable weight of race prejudice in the same way he accepted the fact that most blacks lacked the qualifications for political and economic advancement in an industrial order. DuBois fought for equality of opportunity: as he put it, he "was fighting to let the Negroes fight" for their full social, political and economic equality.[36] He thought "that if once we could bring the facts of our desert and suffering before influential portions of the American public . . . we would receive enough cooperation and sympathy to break down the main lines of segregation."[37] Booker T. Washington, like Marcus Garvey, had no such optimistic expectations with respect to whites.

DuBois was forced to suffer the trauma of racism in America. "In early youth a great bitterness entered my life and kindled a great ambition," he wrote.[38] From then on, he was acutely conscious of "the

Veil, the Veil of Color."[39] He might have escaped it—in Europe or elsewhere—but he went South to affirm his essential identity. "A new loyalty and allegiance replaced my Americanism: henceforth I was a Negro," he proclaimed.[40] He then dedicated himself to a mission to make the American black the vanguard of all the colored races of the world and, therefore, of humanity in general.[41] His teaching, writing and editing, his sociological studies of black folk, his pan-African militance and his socialist politics were all aspects of his cause.

As long as blacks were segregated rejects of white society, consigned to a condition that depended on white paternalism or on what DuBois called "alms-giving"[42] and thus on white control, they could not advance as a race. Because racism had deprived them of a chance to compete in an open market, they lacked "training and understanding"; they were reluctant "to venture into unknown surroundings" and afraid "of a land still strange to family mores."[43] DuBois, who acknowledged what he called "the fact of human inequality and difference of capacity,"[44] wanted to develop a black elite, educated in the humanities—"a class civilized in the nineteenth century meaning of the term."[45] To this end, he encouraged Negro leaders to teach and inspire Negro youth. He wanted educators to analyze the situation of the Negro in America and to uplift the Negro people. The economic and social condition of the Negro is a fit subject of study, he insisted.

In many ways, DuBois was as much a cultural—and economic—nationalist as Washington. "We must strive by race organization, by race solidarity, by race unity for the realization of . . . broader humanity," he urged.[46] He was simply against Washington's policy of conciliation with respect to segregation and disfranchisement, a policy that did not seem pragmatically to work. Inevitably, he ran up against white—and black—opposition both in the NAACP, which he helped institute and which he felt whites were tending to control, and in his career as a professor of sociology and as an educational and civil rights consultant. His project to develop a talented tenth of exceptional leaders was stymied by forces of entrenched segregation. His inclination toward socialism brought him into conflict with the federal government and as an old man he was indicted "for not registering as an agent of a foreign power in the peace movement."[47] He won his trial, but, he warned, "The American Negro must realize that the attack on me for socialism is but the cloaked effort of Southern whites to deprive Negroes of leadership in my and other cases."[48] The cause of black autonomy, or black uplift—whatever the means to achieve it—contradicted the goals of the industrial state.

CHAPTER 6

BLACK COMMUNALITY AND BLACK URBAN MILITANCE

Despite Washington's influence with northern newspapers and DuBois's experience with the New York NAACP and his sociological studies on urban Negroes in Philadelphia, both leaders operated mainly in the South. With black migration to the cities, which began in force during the First World War, the focus of black existence shifted to the large urban centers of the North. "The race crisis" became "a city crisis."[1] The intensification of black segregation and black poverty in metropolitan slums brought about a new spirit of black nationalism. "The urban ghetto was at one time and the same time the force that constricted Negro life and aspirations and yet formed the base for black political power and the activities of civil-rights organizations."[2] As DuBois wrote, "The upper class Negro has almost never been nationalistic. This solution has always been a thought upsurging from the mass. . . ."[3]

Sometimes poverty and isolation have positive cultural implications: they inspire a sense of solidarity and make for a feeling of *we* against *them*. The Negro could not ever become white and that was his strength, writes Amiri Baraka.[4] Blacks were united by a visible racial difference that went beyond intragroup class distinction. They shared their "precarious . . . and painful relation to the white world," said James Baldwin.[5] They were "bound together by the animus of the white man," agreed Louis Lomax.[6] And from this negative condition, blacks developed a positive viewpoint. Even in adapting to often miserable conditions, they learned skills and attitudes that made for a special

93

black way of life. It was blacks' "remarkable racial gift of adaptability," observed writer James Weldon Johnson, that enabled them to "create something artistic and original, which . . . possesses the note of universal appeal."[7]

In effect, as Clark remarks, "the *facts* of the ghetto are not necessarily synonymous with the *truth* of the ghetto."[8] There arose a vitality—deriving from a sense of community—in the slums that transcended the degradation of their reality. "Segregation helped make Harlem alive."[9] As Langston Hughes pointed out, "I came to this vile street / and found Life stepping on my feet."[10]

The lower classes are the most potentially disruptive of all segments of a population because they defy the moral and social taboos by which the order functions. In Chicago, for instance, it was they who were the most attracted by leftist and race movements before World War II.[11] Recently, it was the "Black working class" that generated the strongest support for Harold Washington, the former black mayor of Chicago.[12] In New York in the 1920s, Garvey's followers, like those of Malcolm X, were chiefly the black masses. According to Frazier, as the lower class adjusted to its inferior status, it had less to lose with respect to the larger society. It was more prone to violence against whites and more conscious of race solidarity and resented the fact that "Negroes do not stick together."[13]

The pejorative view of a poverty culture that stems from an ethic based on materialistic norms has provoked on the part of the larger society indifference at best, and at worst, hostility—attitudes that reinforce the solidarity of the black poor in their consciousness of rejection. Whites, of course, stress the asocial behavior of the underprivileged in order to control them or at least to justify their ghettoization. Sociologists have treated slum Negroes as if they were either environmentally or inherently incapable of assimilation into the middle class and have thus condemned them to outcast status. Most often these blacks have turned their aggressive instincts against themselves and become their own chief victims.

The fact is that poor blacks have manifested antisocial behavior.[14] They have been gamblers, drunkards, junkies, pimps, prostitutes, dropouts, drifters; they have robbed, cheated, killed; and they make up a disproportionate percentage of the jail population. They have been casual lovers; they have illegitimate children for whom they have not provided; and their matriarchal family patterns, on which DuBois first commented with respect to Philadelphia Negroes, stand in glaring contrast to the nuclear patriarchy on which the white bourgeois order was founded. The fact also is that neglected poverty has increasingly ensconced poor blacks in a vicious circle of illiteracy, misery and the slum situation of today. Given the disparities between ghetto and middle-class America, as David Swinton remarks, "The capacity of the black community to develop using strictly or mainly internal resources is clearly limited."[15]

Moreover, the black nationalist potential has suffered because of the class divisiveness that was inherent in the black community and that was accentuated after the collapse of the black movement of the 1960s. The black poor have not been able to translate their discontent into affirmative race action. Black solidarity was disrupted by intragroup disharmony. On the one hand, as Martin Luther King, Jr., discovered in Chicago, the poor were too apathetic, if not defeatist, to support his positive social program.[16] "They're beaten down psychologically," said his associate Hosea Williams.[17] On the other hand, they lack direction: no one has emerged recently to develop a project that might mobilize them as did Malcolm X, for instance, or the Black Panthers.

James Baldwin illustrated the confusion of the black intellectual—the middle-class black—with respect to the black poor and the black criminal when he criticized Richard Wright's Bigger Thomas in *Native Son* for being a stereotype, a phantom, of Negro manhood. Bigger was "only one part of a larger reality."[18] His "isolation . . . within his own group," said Baldwin, his ensuing monstrous, apparently gratuitous, violence, gave the impression that there was no Negro tradition.[19] Yet, in his turn, Baldwin painted a similar portrait of the introverted and isolated urban black man in his characterization of Rufus in *Another Country*. Rufus's rage and "murderous impulses" made him "turn back upon himself" and drove him to suicide.[20]

Perhaps it was the asociability of the outcast black that intensified his sense of black community. Drug dealing, violence, robbery and sexual license have been used as means by which deprived black youth has increasingly created its own subsocial life-style, which is not, but could be, affirmative. President Lyndon Johnson, spurred by Daniel Patrick Moynihan, worried that the disintegration of the male-led family—"the cornerstone of our society"—would bring on the chaos.[21] But the question really is, as sociologist Herbert Gans wondered, whether the matriarchal family and widespread illegitimacy are, in fact, indications of the pathology of the black community. They might be healthy forms of nonwhite, non-middle-class cultural behavior.[22]

Once freed of the restrictions and demands that go with patriarchal or revolutionary sex patterns, which subordinate the woman, lovemaking can quite obviously be a real source of enjoyment. The matriarchal family is an extended one, embracing different generations from grandmothers to aunts to cousins. And such an arrangement tends to accentuate a sense of community. In any case, children, illegitimate or not, assure the continuity of the race.

Drug dealing, of course, is a nefarious traffic that has preyed on black people. It is, however, the only means of survival for many blacks who have been put outside the job market and have no alternative but to resort to it. Its rewards are almost higher than its risks. Besides, drug dealing has perhaps been deliberately imposed on the black poor by the industrial order: according to a 1989 Urban League report, it is at worst "an instrument of genocide in the African-American community."[23] Other observers, including writers like Nikki Giovanni, have suspected that something is wrong. "I can't say that they're putting poison in [the stuff]," she remarked, but she had her suspicions.[24]

Criminal activity in the black community has increased to the extent that more than one fourth of all young blacks have been or are in prison, and most convicts are from the disadvantaged ghetto. As actress Ethel Waters wrote of her own era, for the poor "vice was the most important business."[25] Clark has pointed out that crime "may ... reflect the individual's responsiveness to and socialization within an oppressive ... anti-social system."[26] According to sociologists Lee Rainwater and William Yancey, "Some of the behaviors that appear pathological ... are functional in terms of the ability to make as gratifying a life as possible in a ghetto milieu."[27]

Certainly many black criminals—and subsequent leaders—thought of themselves as victims of a vicious conspiracy that turned right into wrong. In many cases, said Huey Newton, "they have learned to see themselves as political prisoners in the classic, colonial sense."[28] According to Elijah Muhammad, as Malcolm X reported, "The black prisoner ... symbolized white society's crime of keeping black men oppressed and deprived and ignorant, and unable to get decent jobs, turning them into criminals."[29] Muslims were able to rehabilitate many convicts by teaching them that the enemy was the white man: Muslims were preconditioned to hear that the white was the devil, wrote Malcolm X.[30] George Jackson observed that "black men born in the United States and fortunate enough to live past the age of eighteen are conditioned to accept the inevitability of prison."[31] Very few "feel that they are really guilty."[32] Although Eldridge Cleaver realized that his crime motivations were "often of . . . a bloody, hateful, bitter, and malignant nature," nevertheless, the fact that he was an outlaw had an affirmative effect on his attitude. He became a Black Panther who considered that "the struggle of his life is for the emancipation of his mind."[33] As social analyst Charles Reich put it, one cannot "achieve an independent consciousness unless he cultivates the feeling of being an *outsider*."[34] And Jackson concluded, "When this standard [of personal financial success], this criterion for the measurement of individual merit and worth in this society is applied to us . . . we cannot help but come out with a very low opinion of ourselves."[35]

Jackson was driven by his consciousness of being an outcast into crime and incarceration, from which he joined the black movement for liberation. He "became politicized by his prison experience," says his editor.[36] He wrote that he "attempted to transform the black criminal mentality into a black revolutionary mentality."[37] He was killed while he was still in jail because he was a militant, as his friend Angela Davis observed. She herself under prosecution wanted "to reevaluate the traditional definition of 'political prisoner' as a result of the intensification of racism."[38]

Historically, the black has been driven to crime before he committed one: "The first step for the ghetto youth is the pure and simple rejection of the law."[39] Writer Etheridge Knight felt that he was in prison "first because he is black and then because he broke the law, [and] that he breaks the law because being black signifies being outside the law."[40] Anne Petrie's Lutie in *The Street,* for instance, was inexorably compelled to murder her black lover because she was caught in a self-defeating struggle with an implacable, impenetrable world. Bigger Thomas—whom urban migration pulled out of a segregated communal society into one that was individualistic, impersonal and segregated—was guilty before he committed his crime. He had to create himself out of his fear, rootlessness and defenselessness before a powerful white order which knew all about him and which stood over him like "a sort of great natural force."[41] He could not escape; nothing could protect him. So he lashed out and killed brutally and senselessly, not because he was crippled by his environment (although Max, his liberal lawyer, tried to excuse him on these grounds), but because he was hemmed in and sought existential liberation. He discovered through the act of killing that he had a self and that whites had limits. They were mortal like him.

Black consciousness of self linked with group identification has always, necessarily, involved hostility to white overlords. Black militance depends on a sense of aggressiveness. "I am proud that they respond," said Nikki Giovanni with respect to black activists. "I am existential enough to say we cannot have reconciliation until *all* the killing is done. . . ."[42] And Baldwin admitted, "No American Negro exists who does not have his private Bigger Thomas living in the skull. . . ."[43] The negative dialectically has led to the positive: in fastening on the white adversary, the black finds himself, because "Negroes hate white people far more actively than white people hate Negroes," as novelist Chester Himes realized.[44] J. Saunders Redding's grandmother "hated white people,"[45] as did he, a respected and successful bourgeois intellectual Negro. Alice Walker's Sofia in *The Color Purple* wants to kill them all off.[46]

Hate, of course, is a means to black solidarity: it is "a culture, a creed, a religion," said Richard Wright.[47] It fortified the sense of black community. It was also a way to defend oneself against the intrusions of the white world: "When you recognize *who* your enemy is, he can no longer brainwash you," Malcolm X explained.[48] Historically, hate of the white man led the black urban poor to a series of riots that unified the people—often even the Negro middle class—against the white oppressor.

Actually, poverty itself—even as it might serve methodically to maintain a kind of economic equilibrium—is a negation of the nationalistic principles of postindustrial culture. Built on a balance of work and consumption, it also brings with it severe class implications. Poverty is an automatic obstruction to the functioning of the consumer market: to buy things is to qualify for membership in the dominant middle class. No matter how much a poor person wants products, he cannot legitimately procure them. The struggle to do without and to survive, as William Faulkner put it, is a threat to the white economy of waste and, therefore, to whites themselves.[49] The increasing incidence of thievery disturbs production planning, not to mention insurance coverage.

If the black did get his hands on something he wanted, he used it or squandered it or wantonly displayed it. He did not prize it as an end in itself; the product was not king in the way it was to the middle-class industrial consumer. Poverty has led to hedonism and cynicism with respect to material acquisitions, both of which are considered to be antisocial attitudes. The poor person looks at things in terms of easy come, easy go; the bourgeois prizes his possessions. Langston Hughes's mother and stepfather desired money to spend, not to keep; his middle-class father, on the other hand, craved to accumulate it. Often, the black bourgeoisie seemed to link "true culture and character"[50] with money in its attempt to uplift the black masses out of "ignorance and immorality."[51] The black bourgeoisie embraced the principles of materialistic culture.

Because the deprived black had a cynical attitude toward the material goods that were beyond his legitimate reach, and because he was the dispossessed outsider who felt free to take whatever he could get by any means, he filled the proverbial role of the con man. This is, of course, a traditional, even classic American type portrayed in the writings of novelists from Herman Melville to Mark Twain to Ralph Ellison to Ishmael Reed. The black historically has been the trickster. In the South, as writer Zora Neale Hurston recorded, he was John, the clever slave, who was "too smart for Ole Massa."[52] He was Old Nick, the devil purged of his terror; he was Brer Rabbit, who outwitted his animal and human adversaries.[53] In the North, he was the ghetto hustler, a potential danger for white society, said Malcolm X, because he "has less respect for the white power structure than any other Negro in North America. . . . [He is] restrained by nothing . . . no religion, no . . . morality . . . no fear. . . ."[54]

With his contempt for conventional standards and rules, the hustler was a model for disadvantaged, discontented young people of the slums who saw in his exhibitionism a defiance of the white world. But in the sense that he—like the thief and the drug dealer—is gratifying his immediate needs, he is adapting to the norms of the industrial ethic.[55] He is not offering an alternative that might affirmatively serve the black world. His careless, even debonair cynicism has given zest to his often sordid achievements: he has been the nonmaterialistic materialist who takes what he can from consumer society for his own supremely selfish purposes. It has not been in his interest to overthrow the oppressor's machinery or the oppressor, but to make both work for his individual ends. He has been a parasite of the reigning order. As a black convict wrote, "I'm against this system, but I still like Cadillacs."[56]

In a larger sense, however, it is the trickster "with his 'filthy' tricks" who, according to Norman O. Brown, is "a great Culture-hero, the source of man's material culture." It is he who brings out into the open the avaricious, even morbid roots of the money complex—itself a "social derivative of the anal complex—roots which are not a manifestation of Eros . . . but . . . of the death instinct." The trickster plays harshly, even brutally, with conditions as he finds them, but he does so in order to rephrase them in another context than the one in which they are accepted. Unlike the successful white capitalists to whom Freudians like Brown attribute "quantifying rationality,"[57] which is associated with infantile, repressed anality and death, the black trickster is historically a joker. He is life-centered: the black, as a study called "Psychodynamic Inventory" reported, does not have an anal complex.[58] Because he was systematically excluded from the money culture—which he would loot and pillage—he was relatively free of the introverted guilt by which it was instigated and sustained.

After the First World War, black antiwhite riots erupted in northern ghettos. These were launched spontaneously in retaliation for "white acts of persecution and violence." The Ku Klux Klan spread throughout the North; white mobs, incensed by what they imagined to be a black "take-over," went on the prowl through Negro districts looking for victims.[59] At that time, during the 1920s, a group of black intellectuals developed the theory of the "New Negro," a concept that Booker T. Washington had, in fact, introduced in his day in his own context. On this theme, the so-called Harlem Renaissance was launched.[60]

Philosopher Alain Locke was the most articulate theoretician of the New Negro movement. He wanted to convert a negative identity, imposed by white oppressors, into a cultural affirmation. He would "repair a damaged group psychology and reshape a warped social perspective";[61] in effect, Locke was advancing the theme of black nationalism. The New Negro was a product of the urban North; the old Negro was a "stock figure," a "fiction" buried in white myth. The New Negro took pride in his race: he promoted "self-respect and self-reliance" and, naturally, "race co-operation."[62]

According to Locke, the "deep feeling of race is at present the mainstream of Negro life."[63] He insisted that the black possessed a distinct character that derived not uniquely from his racial heritage but from his conditioning. His particular traits, "his naïvete, his sentimentalism, his exuberance and his improvising spontaneity are [not] African," wrote Locke. "They are the result of his peculiar experience in America and the emotional upheaval of its trials and ordeals."[64] As DuBois had urged black intellectuals to focus on Negro studies, so Locke encouraged them to use art forms that were expressive of Negro folkways. "The young Negro writers dig deep into racy peasant undersoil of the race life," he said.[65]

Locke was a philosophic pluralist whose version of black nationalism was aesthetic and not separatist, as he made clear. But as Cruse quotes Frazier, who wrote an article for Locke on the successful business ventures in Durham, North Carolina,[66] the new movement " 'is divorced from any program of economic reconstruction.' " It " 'functions in the third dimension of culture; but so far it knows nothing of the other two dimensions—Work and Wealth.' "[67]

And, therefore, with no practical program, the new movement was cut off from the concerns of black masses on whose traditions it drew, as well as from the black middle class, which rejected its self-conscious romanticization of black folkways. It was, in effect, restricted to Negro intellectuals and to liberal white sponsors who patronized it and often absconded with its creative materials. Because the New Negroes were isolated in the black community, they tended, as Cruse points out, "toward total acceptance of racial integrationist premises" and "allowed a *bona fide* cultural movement . . . to degenerate into a pampered and paternalized vogue."[68] And Ellison, according to critic George Kent, is even more severe in his judgment of it. He thinks the Harlem Renaissance itself "represented . . . a literature that was still a bawling infant choosing decadence as its model for expression."[69]

Both Cruse and Ellison are perhaps too harsh. The movement did lay the groundwork for a cultural revival to come. It was, however, never able to flower. Although the Renaissance projected a social as well as an artistic goal, it was too separated from the roots with which it was trying to identify and which in principle it would bring to the forefront of black aesthetics to flourish in its time. The New Negro himself became "a stereotype" and consequently writers felt "betrayed and bitter."[70]

Coincident with the New Negro's promotion of black nationalism was the movement that was started by Marcus Garvey. His Universal Negro Improvement Association represented an internationalist mission to unite the entire black race against its enslavers and colonizers. Garvey was from the British West Indies and he had a global point of view. "The U.N.I.A.," as he explained it, "is an organization among Negroes that is seeking to improve the condition of the race, in the view of establishing a nation in Africa. . . ." It was not, he insisted, narrowly nationalistic: it "believes in the rights of all men, yellow, white and black."[71]

Garvey, who was from the working class, directed his appeal chiefly to the Negro masses. He disliked intellectuals—of whom he was perhaps jealous—as much as he distrusted mulattoes, whom he associated with the bourgeoisie. In fact, he seemed to equate the two—as in the cases of both DuBois and writer George Schuyler. Garvey was against integration, which he thought the colored middle class promoted. His movement, unlike most in America, which "sought to teach the Negro to aspire to social equality with the whites," preached "pride and purity of race."[72] DuBois, on the other hand, "prefers to fight and agitate for the privilege of dancing with a white lady at a ball at the Biltmore or at the Astoria."[73]

Quite naturally, Garvey's antipathy for middle-class blacks was reciprocated. Locke, who belittled "the transient . . . phenomenon"[74] of Garveyism, made only a passing reference to it in his book on the New Negro.[75] A. Philip Randolph of *The Messenger,* originally an independent socialist, opposed Garvey's idea of a black empire, as well as his hostility to unions.[76] James Weldon Johnson, the black writer, blamed Garvey—a foreigner from Jamaica—for "ignoring . . . the techniques of the American Negro in dealing with his problems of race."[77] Claude McKay referred to Garvey as a "West Indian charlatan,"[78] and although DuBois called him a "sincere and hard-working idealist," he deplored his "bombastic, wasteful, illogical and almost illegal" methods.[79] In general, high-strata Negroes—with whom intellectuals were socially if not philosophically associated—were suspicious of any mass movement.

Nevertheless, it was Marcus Garvey who most successfully popularized the ideology of black nationalism throughout the black world. If eventually he was defeated, his message had, and still has, a profound impact. As Malcolm X (whose father, a Garvey admirer, had been murdered for his race pride) said, "Garvey never failed. Garvey planted the seed which has popped up in Africa—everywhere you look."[80]

At the summit of Garvey's popularity, his movement posed more of a threat to the white social order than did Communist agitation. Garvey had contempt for the left, which was, of course, white led. He refused to have "anything to do with socialism and communism," and considered their organizations to be "inherently prejudiced against the black race, since they were dominated by whites."[81] He also distrusted trade unions: as a young man he had been busted in a strike in which a union comrade absconded with the funds.[82]

As a nationalist, Garvey had been influenced by Booker T. Washington's book *Up from Slavery.*[83] He agreed with Washington on race self-improvement, race capitalism and race self-sufficiency. In a subdued way, he was even encouraged by Washington, who did wish him success and who looked on UNIA as a variation of the Negro Business League.

Washington's favored lieutenant, Emmett Scott, however, was a fervent Garvey supporter.[84]

Garvey had a talent both for management and publicity. Not only did he organize successful mass meetings, parades and celebrations, but he also embarked on a commercial business venture. His Black Star Line, a projected fleet of ships, was launched not so much at first to carry blacks back to Africa as to make money and build goodwill for his mission. The enterprise was modeled on the pattern of fraternal societies—"its active membership was entitled to draw sickness and death benefits from [it]."[85] Unfortunately, the business failed, because of the corruption of subordinates, the misuse of postal service and faulty bookkeeping—for which Garvey went to jail—and mainly because his company, like those of other economic nationalists, was a small under-capitalized outfit in a large competitive industry. It really had no chance of succeeding. As Cruse says, "The chief flaw of Garveyism was its capitalist economics."[86]

Garvey did not give up. He organized the Black Cross Navigation and Trading Company, which proposed to carry disadvantaged blacks back to Africa. In keeping with former colonization projects of black nationalists, Garvey enlisted American Negroes in a project to rehabilitate the continent from which they had come and thereby to unite black Americans.[87] "I call upon you four hundred million Blacks to give the blood you have shed for the white man to make Africa a republic for the Negro," he proclaimed.[88] As Alain Locke commented despite his coolness to Garvey's movement, "The possible role of the American Negro in the future development of Africa is one of the most constructive and universally helpful missions that any modern people can lay claim to."[89]

It was perhaps this aspect of Garvey's campaign that mobilized white American and European opposition to him: conservative, capitalistic and consequently controllable as he was in economics, he was dangerous as a cultural radical. American officialism rejected his back-to-Africa movement, liberals ridiculed his flamboyant messianism and he was denounced as a demagogue, a "chauvinist and . . . charlatan."[90] The American left, including influential Jewish intellectuals who were prominent in socialist and labor organizations, refused to accept his kind of black Zionism. Reformers feared the appeal of black nationalism to the lower classes. White Americans, said Kelly Miller, president of Howard University, were afraid of him because his Negro improvement program was "calculated to give the Negro a sense of self-respect in his own personality."[91] Garvey, imprisoned for fraud, was deported and immobilized: he died in London separated from his people.

It was Garvey's racial nationalism, however, that stimulated a profound emotional response among American blacks. As whites had banded together against him because of it, so blacks reacted with an eagerness that bore witness not only to their dissatisfaction with their condition in the white order, but also to their positive feelings of communal identity. Even Garvey's middle-class Negro adversaries were—despite themselves—impressed and attracted by his message. "In a world where black is despised, he taught [the masses] that black is beautiful," wrote an editor of *The Amsterdam News*.[92]

Moreover, his nationalism was founded on positive themes. His historicization of the black's relation to and possible role in Africa, the cradle of human civilization, gave black people a heritage that, symbolic or even messianic as it might have seemed, bolstered their sense of racial pride. He rejected the white God and introduced a black Madonna, preserving and rephrasing the spiritual tradition of black folk. Garvey spoke for race purity and race solidarity in a society whose norms were based on white values: he turned the social standard upside down. He worked on the assumption that blacks would never find justice and opportunity in a world controlled by whites—and that self-determination in another environment was their only hope.

But his project was defeated: he had to operate in a capitalistic world that had been preempted by white forces. Cruse considers Garvey an economic reformist, not a revolutionary. Also, his "nationalism failed on the cultural plane in terms of program and methodology": it had "no real, functional cultural program."[93] As Locke wrote, "The Negro is radical on race matters, conservative on others . . . a social protestant rather than a genuine radical."[94] Nevertheless, the movement remained—as have similar black nationalistic projects throughout the history of the black experience—ready to be revived and adapted to the changing times. Garvey's mission was based dialectically on the black's consciousness of his unfavorable situation in America and on his inherently human affirmation of himself and his kind. "Garvey's very success in selling an unrealistic escapist program of racial chauvinism to American Negroes," says his biographer E. David Cronan, "throws into sharp relief the burning discontent and bitter disillusionment . . . he found in the Negro world. . . ."[95]

A. Philip Randolph—although an integration-oriented socialist—founded an all-black labor organization after the First World War. It might have been based more on social themes than on racial ones, but in its effect it was nationalistic. As a conscientious leftist, Randolph followed official policy in opposing the war—unlike many of his white leftist peers. He had started a magazine, *The Messenger,* which was connected with the New Negro movement. But he was disillusioned by the implantation of Communists in Negro associations and by their relegation of blacks to subordinate roles. Because they were trying to turn the National Negro Congress into a Communist front organization which would subject blacks to white direction, he resigned from it.[96]

Randolph became implicitly more and more nationalistic in spirit. He formed the Brotherhood of Sleeping Car Porters in spite of the Communists. He criticized the NAACP because it was led and controlled by whites, by a group, he said, "who are neither Negroes nor working people."[97] He argued that "the National Negro Congress should be dependent on resources supplied by Negro people alone. . . . History shows that where you get your money you also get your ideas and control."[98] And when he mobilized his black brotherhood in collaboration with Negro labor throughout the country for a march on Washington, he frightened President Franklin Roosevelt into issuing an executive order against job discrimination along racial lines. It was the threat of agitation by an all-black body that made the president act.

Randolph was not a radical and his nationalism was not extreme. He was "leery of overt nationalism," says Cruse,[99] as were most black intellectuals. He was careful to stress nonviolent civil disobedience and to insist that his movement was "not anti-white." But the very fact that his proposed march was "all-Negro, and pro-Negro,"[100] turned him into a fearsome force—possibly against the administration. He was considered the "most dangerous Negro in America."[101]

Randolph also emphasized two aspects of the ideology of black nationalism that would influence its future methodology. In the first place he grounded it on an implicitly political power base: only through the solidarity of the mass—in his case, black workers—could black people hope to achieve their objectives. "Only power can effect the enforcement and adoption of a given policy . . ." he said. "Power is the active principle of only the organized masses. . . ."[102] Actually, his proposed march captured the imagination of blacks of all classes—from lower class to higher.[103] And it served as "the organizational ground from which the Civil Rights movement was later to develop," as a critic points out.[104]

Second, Randolph transformed black people's emotional attachment to their African roots—which through the efforts of DuBois, Garvey and many others had led to their positive affirmation of their historical identity—into a realistic denunciation of American foreign policy. As he had come out against the First World War on socialist anti-imperialistic grounds, so, backed by millions of African Americans, he opposed the Second World War on black nationalistic principles. This was not a war for freedom, democracy and the common man, he wrote; it was "commercial."[105] "It is a war to maintain the old imperialist systems" and "to continue 'white supremacy.' "[106] The Roosevelt administration would "insult the Negro people by . . . asking us to support this war in order that we may further enslave ourselves and oppressed peoples throughout the world."[107] Because the black was "not equal"[108] he was not free, and there was no point in his risking his life and his livelihood to battle foreign racists when domestic ones, including leaders of the federal government, were depriving him of both. The black would do better fighting the Hitlers at home than joining a combat on the side of colonial nations abroad.

Many blacks took advantage of war propaganda to claim a fifth freedom for themselves. When America first entered World War II, some African Americans identified with her colored enemies, the Japanese.[109] Naturally, Roosevelt felt threatened by such attitudes. It did not matter whether Randolph's march for fair employment would have brought out the black population en masse or not; its very prospect was enough to compel the administration to do something.

So-called integrationist institutions—such as the Urban League and the NAACP, which depended on outside financing and, therefore, on white subvention—were supported by the black middle class. The NAACP was rationally and morally oriented and worked within the context of the prevailing white ethic: it focused primarily on legal action and sought *"to reach the conscience of America."*[110] DuBois went back to work for it as a titular consultant—to his dismay under the direction of its conservative leader Walter White.[111] However, according to Manning Marable, DuBois "recognized the trend toward accommodation within the NAACP and the Negro elite . . . and attempted to combat it."[112]

There were messianic as well as secular black movements during the Depression, which were inspired mostly by clergymen and centered mostly in the ghetto. Father Divine, for instance, attracted a mass following. He capitalized on the traditional spirituality of black people by assuming the role of a messiah and asserting what has been denounced as "a new kind of chauvinism."[113] He might have denied the relevance of color and welcomed believers of all races of mankind, but in preaching his own divinity as a black man, implicitly he was proclaiming the superiority of blacks in particular. Naturally, African Americans made up the largest proportion of his flock.

Educated black activists such as Dr. John Johnson, an Episcopalian minister, organized the Citizens' League for Fair Play (which was denounced by the Communists) and even started a black boycott under the slogan "Don't-Buy-Where-You-Can't-Work."[114] Adam Clayton Powell, Jr., the black congressman-clergyman, was involved in similar protest demonstrations based on mass black participation and on what has been called a "petit bourgeois black business philosophy."[115] The integrationist methodology, spiked here and there with black nationalist techniques, seemed to be focused on nonviolent direct action—or reformism. Basically, however, because it was founded on moral and rational premises, it was confined to a context that was directed by the white industrial state, which itself promoted the moralistic and nationalistic principle it violated.

With the Second World War came an upsurge of new black movements. CORE (the Congress of Racial Equality) was an offshoot of a white pacifist group that was made up of young middle-class intellectuals.[116] It started as a nonviolent association to end racial discrimination[117] but eventually, to be in tune with the times, shifted to a black nationalist position and focused on activist protest.

James Baldwin suggested that perhaps the Second World War was the turning point in the attitudes of the Negro community.[118] The war led to the spread of black nationalism from the lower to the middle class. Before the 1940s, blacks had remained segregated and downtrodden, had suffered miserably during the Depression and had been divided regionally, socially and ideologically. As a white critic remarked, blacks were considered neither "a threat nor a problem for the white nation. . . . [They were] unobtrusive, apparently uncomplaining, and virtually invisible. . . ."[119] According to literary critic Alfred Kazin, a child of recent immigrants, "Negroes were the Schvartze, the blacks. We just did not think about them."[120]

But World War II, with new migrants from the South, provided jobs in military and defense industries and relief from the Depression. Yet it offered blacks less of a chance to rise in relation to their ambitions and abilities and in comparison with other minorities than the First World War. Around 1917, "masses of illiterate cotton-field hands"[121] with the fixed cultural status and tradition of peasants had poured into northern ghettos to take advantage of an unaccustomed, though restricted, "freedom to come and go."[122] They had been impressed. By the Second World War, however, blacks had become worldly wise, disillusioned and bitter. Even "rural Southern Negroes were different this time."[123] The black population was now ready for a new spirit of nationalism.

The urban black bourgeoisie had long been established in the North. Poor blacks had had to contend with police brutality, bad housing, job discrimination and racial discrimination in general and everywhere. Their children, returning home from segregated military service to segregated communities, were disgusted with a society that required them to risk their lives for a liberty which it denied them. Baldwin commented, "A certain hope died, a certain respect for White America faded."[124] The army, wrote novelist John Killens, "brutally raped [his protagonist Solly in *And Then We Heard the Thunder*] of his youth, his faith, his idealism. His great ambition."[125] For it was the Janus-faced American attitude to war, which promised the power of justice on one side while on the other it violated the dignity of its citizens, that focused the attention of most Negroes on their irremediably unequal status. They began vocally and aggressively to repudiate what was to them the "American nightmare."[126]

The growth of the Black Muslim movement, which whites had originally dismissed as just another expression of black evangelical emotionalism, reflected the increasing spirit of black nationalism among the lower classes of the urban slums. Elijah Muhammad—inspired by Noble Drew Ali, a self-proclaimed Muslim prophet incarnated in the person of W. D. Fard, and Marcus Garvey—established a temple in Detroit in about 1932. "It is said," writes critic E. U. Essien-Udom, "that [Elijah Muhammad's] first followers were his mother, his wife, and his six children."[127] He based his teaching on three nationalistic principles: first, that the white was ineluctably the enemy of the black and that, therefore, the latter must separate from him; second, that the blacks, who would be racially fulfilled though the prophecy of Allah as represented by his messenger, Elijah Muhammad, must uplift themselves; and third, that their true home was among their true people in Africa or in the Near East. Elijah Muhammad's Muslimism, like Judaism, represented both religious faith and nationalistic patriotism. It was a paradox in both senses, as Essien-Udom and Eric Lincoln have pointed out. As a religion, Black Muslimism is an Islamic sect.[128] But it takes its teaching from the Christian Bible and rejects "the cardinal Moslem doctrines ... of pan-racial brotherhood and the unique divinity of Allah."[129] It promises no afterlife in any kind of heaven, Christian or Muslim, but the destruction of the white devil and of his religion, and the fulfillment of the black race on earth and its reestablishment in its original homeland.[130] It promoted the idea of a black God but, even as it denounced Christianity, upheld its moral doctrine. It is in its celebration of the black that it expresses black nationalism.

First, Black Muslimism was separatist. Elijah Muhammad preached that blacks would never be accepted on a plane of equality in white America in any case, and his followers did not want to be so assimilated. White America was a doomed society with false moral values and he refused to integrate into it. He would not send his children to public school and he incited Muslims to resist the draft.[131] Both policies occasioned his arrest. Elijah Muhammad also asked for independence from the U.S. government and for appropriate property to compensate black people for centuries of unpaid labor, but was summarily ignored.

Second, Elijah Muhammad assumed that black separatism entailed black uplift. Until the time when black Americans would be redeemed or receive a territory in which they might settle, they must coexist—"a nation within a nation,"[132] to echo Booker T. Washington—peaceably and fruitfully under the actual white hegemony. They were to adapt to the laws and conventions of the state in which they were temporarily condemned to live and, in general, they did. Muslim workers were hardworking and served their white employers conscientiously.

Meanwhile, blacks must uplift themselves in their community. Elijah Muhammad preached black self-improvement, black solidarity and black self-sufficiency.[133] Muslim teachers were encouraged "to re-educate the so-called Negro who has been the victim of centuries of mis-education . . . to attain his rightful place in the sun as a Black Man [and] to give the students a feeling of dignity and appreciation of their own kind."[134] To this end, two universities of Islam were instituted: one under Fard in Detroit in the early 1930s and another under Elijah Muhammad in Chicago. Muslim entrepreneurs were urged to launch their own companies, in which they enjoyed moderate success. As a rule, Muslims were taught to be exemplary citizens while they struggled to make a living.[135] They were to obey their leader in all respects; they were to observe strict dietary laws; they were not to drink or smoke or use drugs; and they were to be clean, polite and respectful of others—whites as well as blacks. The black nationalism that they practiced made for communality, the pooling of resources, fraternal and familial loyalties and pride in work.

Last, Elijah Muhammad preached that the true place of the African American was in the Near East or in Africa. Although he established contact with certain Arab representatives of Islam, he treated the idea of a black homeland as an eschatological ideal. It had little existential bearing on his practical doctrine. Elijah Muhammad looked to destiny to accomplish his mission.

By identifying the white man as the black's basic enemy, Elijah Muhammad was able to make clear and comprehensible the fundamental cause of black people's disadvantaged condition. "Negroes," says Essien-Udom, "tend to perceive white society as a monolith united in opposition to their advancement. . . ."[136] Elijah Muhammad showed them that they had a good historical reason for such a perception. But since God was on their side—both morally and spiritually—membership in the nation gave them strength to rise above a constantly threatening adversary and to discover their fellowship with one another.

At first whites contemptuously dismissed the Black Muslim movement. Then, as it grew, they viewed it with suspicion, and still later with fear. It was "directed at the whole structure of the white Christian society," said Eric Lincoln: it rejected the very American creed.[137] It was "*building on hate*," wrote Saul Bellow disapprovingly,[138] but its accomplishments were spectacular, particularly among the ghetto masses. It reformed apparently hopeless criminals and cured drug addicts and turned hustlers into doctrinaire family patriarchs.[139] It gave its people a sense of pride and purpose by which they could transcend the apathy and emptiness and drifting and drudgery that made up the pathology of slum existence. A mass movement "is a desire for a personal rebirth," explained Lincoln.[140] As philosopher William James had put it, "To be converted, to be regenerated, to receive grace . . . are so many phrases which denote the process . . . by which a self hitherto divided . . . becomes unified and consciously right superior and happy. . . ."[141]

The contradictions inherent in the Muslim movement were, however, implicit in the condition of being a nation within a nation. Economic self-capitalization was inadequate in an advanced oligopolistic industrial state. Muslim businessmen could not seriously compete in the corporate market, as they lacked both "the capital for a large-scale industrial venture" and "skilled and experienced personnel."[142] Social self-determination, such as educational training and job qualifications, was dependent upon resources already controlled by the existing order. Politically, the Nation of Islam was condemned to noninvolvement since it rejected the workings of a government from which it would be separate and to which it did not in any case belong. The dichotomy between practical methods and esoteric ends led to a lack of interest in political particulars.[143] The messianism of Elijah Muhammad, like that of many frustrated black leaders, forced him blindly to rely on an eschatology that had little relation to the current situation in which blacks were ensconced. Marcus Garvey, too, had looked to destiny, and black preachers had put their faith in heaven to right existing wrong. The black, said Albert Cleage, is always hoping for a Black Messiah.[144]

CHAPTER 7

THE BLACK MOVEMENT
OF THE SIXTIES

T he nationalism of the Black Muslim movement had a significant influence on black leaders, particularly after Malcolm X became its minister. The black so-called revolution of the sixties was based neither on progressivism nor on Marxism—in the general liberal American tradition—but on a feeling of racial pride. Its roots were middle class: it had "middle-class goals"[1] and its activists were often the sons and daughters of the black bourgeoisie.[2] Although it represented seemingly antithetical methodologies, it stood implicitly against the prevalent white social norm and the liberal rhetoric that went with it. Blacks might have been considered "an ascending group" during the 1960s, but their position differed profoundly "from that of the new middle class,"[3] which was made up of a compound of acceptable ethnics.

Since black nationalism was based on a collective experience that was historical as well as existential, it was the expression of a profound American reality. It was a search for meaning that transcended what Ralph Ellison called the effort of the imagination to "overcome the frustrations of social discrimination"[4]—an effort that every immigrant group had exerted in its process of Americanization. Therefore, black nationalism was the ground on which a positive ideology could be built as an alternative to that of the postindustrial state. The thrust of ethnic minorities, on the other hand, was lost in the materialistic standards that governed industrial culture: it could not reach beyond existing social and political structures.

In effect, it was the need to go beyond negativity—the will to turn self-belittlement into self-affirmation—that gave black dialectics its moral and universal impact. "The positive is contained in the negative

112

formulation."[5] For this reason and to the disgust of the dominant middle class, the black movement attracted, at least for a time, the support of young whites. But these whites—students, assorted ethnics, rebels against the middle class—lacked a sense of community. They could found their protest only on their opposition to existing norms. In a way, they constituted an inhibitory force: they represented "counterculture" as an end in itself. Indeed, they tended not only to stress the purely negative, asocial aspects of revolt (including criminality, drug consumption and sexual promiscuity) but also to associate these gratuitous sensations with black consciousness. Their disapproving white elders picked up this feature of their dissent. One went so far as to accuse white youth of imitating blacks in everything: "in their speech, their ghetto separation, their music, and even their vice."[6] As this critic continued, "Since blacks smoked marijuana it had to be a good thing. Heroin addiction became a sort of secret cult."[7]

Whites of all kinds, young and old, hedonistic and moralistic, seemed unable to understand that the black movement of the sixties had profound roots. Militant groups, many of whose black adherents were, like young whites, simply reacting to bourgeois taboos, had to struggle to maintain a clear distinction between disciplined revolution and disorganized libertarianism. "From its very beginning," wrote activist Bobby Seale, "the Black Panther Party has had problems with . . . people who come in and use the Party as a base for criminal activity which the party never endorsed or had anything to do with."[8] The Black Panther Party expressly forbade all illegal practices, including the consumption of drugs on the job. Black leader James Forman associated pot smoking with middle-class individualism and admitted that it was an obstacle to the execution of the program of the Student Nonviolent Coordinating Committee (SNCC).[9] Hosea Williams, an associate of Martin Luther King, Jr., regretted that Chicago staff members of the Southern Christian Leadership Conference appeared to lose their dynamism and were "doing little more than lying around their rooms all day, playing cards, drinking and smoking pot."[10]

But this problem has been common to all political uprisings. The French communards, for instance, lost much of their revolutionary fervor in an orgy of dancing, wine drinking and lovemaking on the boulevards of Paris. Fundamentally, it was the historical implications of the black movement of the sixties that made it so culturally significant. To the extent to which a philosophic project is *"ideological,* it takes on the characteristics of a *historical* project," wrote the neo-Marxist Herbert

Marcuse.[11] "The truth of metaphysical propositions is determined by their historical content. . . ."[12] Marcuse and others considered blacks the only existing group with enough historical consciousness to reconstruct American society, economically, politically and socially[13]—in effect, culturally—and to convert it into a realm of freedom and equality for all.[14] Sociologist Anton Zijderveld gave them the role of the former class proletariat.[15] "Only the black militant could be construed as serious . . ." agreed writer Joan Didion.[16]

The black movement was launched in the 1960s, a decade of prosperity. Even blacks, as King pointed out, had made economic gains.[17] It was a collective campaign that succeeded for a while in bringing together all kinds of disparate segments of the black population—North and South, ghetto and rural, refined and uncouth. It had the ideological power to appeal to the youth of the entire country. It produced leaders of exceptional quality. Its middle-class activists, motivated chiefly by the morality of the cause, turned back to the ideas of their grandfathers and grandmothers, who—as Paula Giddings points out—had played an essential economic role in the rise of the black bourgeoisie.[18] King's father, Martin Luther Sr., was the son of a downtrodden sharecropper who came to Atlanta, educated himself, married the daughter of a respected minister and enjoyed the comfortable life of a middle-class Negro. But, surprisingly, the black revolution bred an increasing number of responsible leaders from the slums—often poor and uneducated. It was indeed one of the few revolutions of the era of bourgeois hegemony to have done so. "We fabricated our heroes and ideals catch-as-catch-can, and with an outrageous and irreverent sense of freedom . . . in complete disregard for ideas of respectability," said Ellison of his growing up.[19] Black student rebels, themselves part of "the Negro situation"—unlike their white peers—were, in general, supported by the adult community as a whole. They "enjoyed a kind of freedom from reprisal and a tolerance,"[20] for they were expressing the cultural attitudes of an entire historical people whose divergences did not seem to matter. Their movement had deep roots.

Although united in spirit, the black movement of the sixties was divided into two wings, which were not only regionally but apparently ideologically and, in fact, methodologically opposed. That of the South was led by established and educated bourgeois who preached the ideal and practiced the strategy of nonviolence. They were both moral humanists and pragmatists, and their case was founded on their faith in the natural good of man and universal reason. In theory they were integrationist: as middle-class blacks who had made good, they were inclined to accept the values of the prevailing industrial ethic. The northern wing, which was based more or less in the cities, sought the support of the urban masses. It was ideological in orientation and militant in action. It was nationalistic, and championed separatism and black self-sufficiency. Northern blacks were neither universally humanistic nor optimistic: they had neither trust nor hope in the white man's justice, reason or charity.

As writer Thomas Brooks points out, the black revolution of the sixties was made possible by the increasing migration of blacks to the North and by—perhaps more significant—"the crippling impotence of the segregated South to the industrial urban North."[21] Postindustrial society did not have any vital interest in the open social and political repression of southern blacks. Not only did society have to deal with an increasingly sensitive world opinion within the context of the cold war, not only were liberal attitudes at home affronted by the discrepancy between American principles and propaganda and American acts, but also industrial expansion in the South was obstructed by the irrationalities of segregation. The bureaucratically organized work force, on which the corporate operation depended, could not function smoothly in an atmosphere in which meritocracy had no place. Martin Luther King, Jr., used this argument when he warned that "new industry will not come where dying customs create social tensions, second-rate education and cities without the cultural institutions required for the technical personnel of modern industry."[22]

Segregation, in other words, no longer served the interest of an industrial state competing both economically and ideologically in a world market. It was inevitable that the legal bastions of Jim Crow would fall—particularly as the postindustrial culture could maintain blacks' lower status by the economic, and rational, device of entrenching most of them in a condition of poverty. In 1952—as Europe and Japan were recovering and the cold war was intensifying—the Supreme Court ruled that "compulsory racial segregation is itself an unconstitutional discrimination."[23] In 1954, Chief Justice Earl Warren wrote that "separate educational facilities are inherently unequal."[24] And in December 1955, Mrs. Rosa Parks, a black middle-class tailor's assistant at a Montgomery, Alabama, department store, on her own initiative tested the law of Jim Crow on a public bus. Immediately, a mass organization of supportive blacks rushed to her assistance and the civil rights movement was launched.

Since the southern wing of the movement was pragmatic in its approach, it fed on events. King was thrust into a leadership role when the Reverend Ralph Abernathy chose his church as a meeting place for the committee to defend the then-arrested Mrs. Parks and King was chosen president of the new group. He was probably elected because other eligibles, who were natives of Montgomery, did not want to expose themselves before the white population as activists in an upstart association. Certainly King had never been known for his militance. "I just happened to be here," he confessed later.[25] As, according to him, Mrs. Parks was "tracked down by the *Zeitgeist* . . . of the times,"[26] so he admitted that "it was not until I became a part of the leadership of the Montgomery bus protest that I was actually confronted with the trials of life."[27]

Until that time King had been a rather passive spectator of events. He seemed to withdraw into the relative comfort, if noncommitment, of middle-class southern Negro life. He had distinguished himself as a student in southern and northern institutions; he had a reflective, not an activist, mind; he was a trained theologian who, having disdained the emotionalism of the low black church[28] and the inadequate preparation of many of its pastors, had finally decided to follow his father's calling to be a Baptist minister. King had been, as his future wife remarked, a clothes horse who liked a good time.

Consequently, he seemed hardly qualified for the role he was to fill. He had few grounds for contention with the world at large; he had no mission. As Lerone Bennett wrote, King "didn't seek leadership . . . ; leadership sought him. He didn't choose nonviolence; nonviolence chose him. . . ."[29] Perhaps it was his father's and his grandfather's stubborn refusal to accept the conditions of segregation and to gloss over them before their congregations[30]—as Negro leaders were supposed to do— that gave King a moral foundation from which he could draw both assurance and inspiration. Because King believed segregation was "immoral, a mortal sin, a violation of divine law,"[31] he assumed that there was a rational and moral nature or godly order of the universe that could not be transgressed with impunity. And this "strong sense of fate,"[32] this feeling not simply that he was "a part of world history and human destiny,"[33] but that he could work through both, this idea that God operates "through history,"[34] gave him a dedication and a purpose that served him and his cause throughout his career. This religious and moral conviction united the black community under his direction and unleashed a national movement that attracted whites as well as blacks.

King was young and dynamic and totally devoted to the morality of his mission. His leadership of the Montgomery Improvement Association—which succeeded in integrating the public bus system—propelled him to national prominence. Blacks all over the country were inspired by the Montgomery community's performance. In 1956, wrote James Forman, people said "black folks . . . can't stick together."[35] In Montgomery, not only did they unite in a long and dreary boycott, they also used the media to publicize their communal solidarity against vicious forces of oppression. King's Southern Christian Leadership Conference rose out of the Montgomery crisis.[36]

One of King's greatest strengths was his moral rationalism. He was a logician who was able to evolve a plausible and complete theory for his program. Indeed, he used the European structure of dialectical argument in order not just to enlist white aid but to validate his action on a universal plane. Nonviolence, which had been suggested as a tactic by a white female observer, served King's strategic and idealistic requirements. He developed it thematically until it represented both a methodology and an ideology on which he could build a positive movement. "Ends and means must cohere," he insisted,[37] doggedly sticking to his ethical premises. If the mobilization of black America had depended on various social, economic and political factors—such as the Supreme Court decision against school segregation, northern Negro migration, the Negro middle class's relative economic and education gains, and the emergence of new, colored third-world nations[38]—nevertheless, the movement had come into being because "there is something in the universe that unfolds for justice."[39] The fact that segregation was an unjust law granted a license—indeed a duty—to all blacks and to conscientious whites to break it. Conversely, since "a just law . . . squares with moral law,"[40] the principle of nonviolence—which answered active evil with passive good—served not just as a strategy but as a truth.[41] As King put it, it was "the most practical technique to be used in a social situation [and] as a way of life."[42] It was a philosophic means as an end in itself.

King was a missionary pragmatist. Nonviolence would dramatize social evils "in such a way that pressure is brought to bear against these evils by . . . forces of good will . . . and change is produced."[43] Nonviolence was valid, he explained, because it was in tune with the Negro religion,[44] on whose emotionalism King now capitalized in order to mobilize his people, because it excluded vengeance, because it was inspirational, because it contained an inherent check on discord and because it was aimed at the white man's conscience. The Montgomery campaign succeeded not just because it was founded on the ideal of nonviolence, but also because its objective was pragmatic; it was limited to integration of city buses.

But if King's moral rationalism was a great strength, it was also a weakness. He was caught in the limitations of the same thought structure that he expounded: he, like all pragmatists, could not imagine an alternative to the world in which he found himself. When he made a speech to his Montgomery followers, he wanted it to be "militant enough to keep my people aroused to positive action and yet moderate enough to keep this fervor within controllable and Christian bounds."[45] King accepted the premises on which the white order was built: "The Negro revolution is seeking for integration, not independence," he wrote.[46] He was, in fact, a reformer, a "conservative militant,"[47] and not a revolutionary; he worked conscientiously within the context of the existing system. He stood "for the liberal tradition";[48] he played the orthodox black middle-class role of friend to the white man and counted on God, religion and white guilt to bring his by now excessively violent adversaries to their right mind. In so doing King was disregarding the irrational and certainly immoral force of white self-interest as well as being subject in his methodology to the innate contradiction of his mission. His campaign succeeded, whenever it did so, not because of the power of nonviolence, but because of the much-publicized spectacle of white aggressivity that he elicited.[49]

As King attracted national and world attention and inspired blacks in the North as well as in the South, other acts of repression—such as the exclusion of qualified blacks at colleges—fed popular indignation. There seemed, however, to be more crises than he could handle. Often unorganized, spontaneous acts of protest followed one another throughout the South while CORE-initiated sit-ins and freedom rides took place. King usually supported these affairs that he had not "instigated or planned [nor] was eager to be involved in."[50] He was thrust against his will into the movement to challenge segregation in Albany, Georgia, which, he claimed, instilled a feeling of self-confidence in the Negro community. It produced few gains, however; it did not induce government intervention as had been hoped. As one critic remarked, it was "successful only if the goal was to go to jail."[51]

King and his organizers were much more successful in soliciting funds from liberal white and black benefactors, who were impressed by the theme of nonviolence and moved by King's appeal to morality. But he had to deal with duplicitous government administrations that, for political expedience, were trying to hush up the turmoil in the South. They lacked the aggressive leadership for which he called and refused to assert the executive power with which they were endowed.[52] The Kennedys "sought to contain and manipulate Civil Rights agitation"[53] as well as King himself. They wanted to settle for token concessions. They hoped to enlist King's black supporters in a Democratic coalition and made overtures to the white South in order to keep the antisegregation campaign "under wraps."[54] Lyndon Johnson refused to implement anti–Jim Crow laws that had already passed Congress.[55] But with media exposure and liberal sympathy, King, despite his natural reticence and even timidity, was able to use certain federal agencies to his advantage.

In spite of the fact that King openly championed the liberal ethic of integrationism and advised against even the use of the slogan "Black Power"—an ideology he thought had to be tempered by Christian charity or love—his entire thrust was underscored by a tone of black nationalism. In the first place, he was a minister of the black—implicitly nationalistic—church; he was a southern Baptist with fundamentalist congregations; and his melodic oratory reflected his black cultural roots—particularly as he played on the emotionalism of his audience. The black church is essentially "a black institution"; it is "an economic, political, social and moral power base."[56] In working through the church—particularly in the South—King was expressing the basic communality of his people. His "peculiar genius," says Lincoln, ". . . is that he was able to translate religious fervor into social action, thereby creating political leadership under the rubric of his religious ministry at an extraordinary level of involvement and commitment."[57]

Second, his faith in the redemptive powers of "unearned suffering"[58] and Christian love (*agape*)—both features of the black communal experience—did more than appeal just to a liberal white community. Those features reflected what Ralph Bunche called the paradoxically "optimistic fatalism"[59] of black people, an attitude that King also shared. They were perhaps unconsciously his articulation of black people's cultural destiny in America.

And third, King was always, maybe despite himself, aware of the limitations of the integrationist approach. He recognized the futility of ethical persuasion in a system that functioned on pragmatic principles: whatever was, was right. Liberal theology and the social gospel, as he remarked early in his career, confuse "the ideal . . . with the realistic means which must be employed to coerce society into an approximation of that ideal. . . . Men are controlled by power, not mind alone."[60] The oppressor, he realized, as had Booker T. Washington, "never voluntarily gives freedom. . . . Freedom comes only through persistent revolt. . . ."[61]

King grew in his role as an activist black leader. As he struggled, in and out of jail, to gain lawful black rights, he began—subtly, almost as if he were fighting against himself—to surrender the principle of nonviolence as an end in itself. "The Negro in the South can now be nonviolent as a stratagem, but he can't include loving the white man . . ." he conceded. "Nonviolence has become a military tactic approach. . . ."[62] It was the alternative to black extinction, because revolution could never succeed. Moreover, he started to look to the North in order to work for the consolidation of the black urban population—which had not been openly active in his movement. "There is more power in socially organized masses on the march than there is in guns in the hands of a few desperate men . . ." he argued.[63] He moved into the ghetto to "gain identity with [its] dwellers."[64]

At the same time as he was leaning increasingly toward a feeling of black nationalism, King became more aware of events on the international front. He projected his humanitarian idealism onto a universalist view of world politics. He broadened his approach, he no longer restricted his operations to the confines of American affairs, and he attacked his government for its intervention in Vietnam—and despite ferocious opposition, he held to his principle. Malcolm X also extended his own combat to a world arena.[65] Both leaders, while contending with the redoubled hostility of their government, transcended "civil rights" by appealing to "human rights"[66] and specifically to communal relationships among Africans, Asians and black Americans.

As King's efforts were more and more frustrated, he felt more and more deceived. He turned increasingly radical in an economic sense and he lost his liberal following. He had been disillusioned by the response of clergymen and moralists on whom he had counted and who seemed to desert him when the situation worsened. Reporters accused him of using "the rhetoric of power"[67] and the media in general appeared to have tired of him. But King realized to the dismay of many of his white supporters that the American system would have to be basically altered in order for him to obtain even moderate objectives. Authentic integration involved a shift in the power structure: it entailed shared power, "a radical redistribution of economic and political power."[68] As King explained, "I think you've got to have a reconstruction of the entire society, a revolution of values."[69] At bottom, "most Americans . . . are unconscious racists"[70] who would not docilely concede the advantages they possessed. Therefore, he was able to understand that "the evils of racism . . . materialism and militarism"[71] were all tied together. White America in general "never did intend to . . . be fair with Negroes"[72] in housing, schooling and employment. He began, although secretly, to refer to "a democratic form of socialism."[73]

With the extension of his program, King had, of course, to confront growing opposition, including that of his own people, particularly in the North. Black rivals and associates carped at him: he was accused of cowardice. It was true that he had been timid: he refused to give up the strategy of nonviolence. He stuck to it although it seemed to question the courage of black America and although it had not produced enough victories to confirm it as an effective methodology. It was unhealthy if not impossible to constantly forgive one's oppressors, contended Kenneth Clark. King's formula reflected "unrealistic, if not pathological" tendencies.[74]

King's first march on Washington, although a huge demonstration of black support and potential power, involved a capitulation to the white representatives of officialdom. As Forman pointed out, President Kennedy used the black presence to elicit support for his civil rights bill and, therefore, manipulated King—who, in conjunction with other Negro leaders, censured SNCC's criticism of administration policy.[75] Malcolm X, consequently, called the march a "Farce on Washington,"[76] and Forman, because of this and other incidents, accused King, the so-called mighty leader, of having a "Messiah complex" as well as "heavy feet of clay."[77] Eventually, King's apparent failure to bring about practical results in the communities in which he operated caused workers in his own ranks to suspect his motives. Local followers, said Hosea Williams, were inclined to believe that "people are secondary to our primary objectives—building images, getting publicity and raising funds."[78]

King made no headway in the North: conditions there, as he admitted, had retrogressed. Local leaders resented his intervention in Harlem; he was outmaneuvered by Mayor Richard Daley in a fruitless Chicago campaign[79]—although he did unknowingly pave the way for a more streetwise follower, the Reverend Jesse Jackson. He was attacked by white and black politicians for his stand on Vietnam; he was pursued and investigated and harassed by government agencies, particularly the FBI. He was abandoned by liberals who tired of his appeals for money and to conscience and tired, too, of his demonstrations.[80] Slum dwellers ridiculed his moralism and his call for Negro uplift. And as the pressure mounted, King was assailed by a self-doubt that led to extreme emotional fatigue. He was caught in contradictions he could not resolve. Unlike the white pragmatist who assumes his rights and uses rational means to enforce them, King still sought the coherence of nonviolence as a tactic and as a good in itself. He maintained it even when he must have known it would not work, and even when he must have realized that its greatest success depended on its capacity to produce white brutality in response to it—it was, in a dialectical context, the affirmation of violence. Inevitably, King began to suffer from what an associate called a "weariness" of the spirit: a chronic emotional despondency that some, including his friend the black leader Bayard Rustin, likened to a "death wish."[81] Nevertheless, he carried on in a still more radical vein. He embarked on a mission to lead a prolonged poor people's march on Washington, which would alarm the government and, subsequently, call into question his ability to lead a nonviolent protest and would precipitate his assassination. He was murdered before he started.

Criticized and harangued as he was, even denounced by many of his own people, Martin Luther King, Jr., the ever-idealistic black preacher, represented the spirit of the black tradition, which has been associated with black nationalism. He might have served merely a symbolic role in which his power did not match his prestige—as August Meier claims.[82] It was this symbol that inspired his people more than aborted results could ever have done. Indeed, his figure took on mythical dimensions which in a way evoked a reality outside of fact and which moved and has continued to move the black population to this day. "It was [his] symbolism which blacks responded to and loved," writes commentator Julius Lester.[83] "Despite all the militant and revolutionary slogans . . . espoused by a Robert F. Williams, a Stokely Carmichael, a Rap Brown, a Malcolm X, and no matter how radical the *Zeitgeist* of the sixties generation who could not abide King's nonviolence, none of them could compete with King for the 'soul' of black America," says Cruse.[84]

King's SCLC, which in principle renounced neither its tactic of nonviolence nor its goal of integration—despite a series of strategic defeats—was the conservative middle-class organization in the civil rights movement. The Student Nonviolent Coordinating Committee of James

Forman and Robert Moses—both of whom, well-educated bourgeois activists, came from the North to the South—was made up of young and often lower-class black militants. Although SNCC worked alongside the SCLC, it refused to become an arm of the more financially viable liberal group.[85] Moreover, it developed its own plan, to the point that it began to reject many of the SCLC's principles: it adopted the policy of nonviolence only as a tactic and not as an end. As Forman explained, "I did not believe in [it] as a way of life. . . ."[86] But by preaching nonviolence, he and his workers subjected the movement to a contradiction of ethics and methodology—ends and means.[87]

SNCC also rejected the cult of personality that seemed to dominate the black thrust for equality. It was explicitly a decentralized noninstitution that was non–leader oriented. Forman even tried to set "a wage-scale that would make it impossible for anyone to develop a vested interest in the survival of the organization."[88] Ideally SNCC was "a people's movement";[89] it denounced the American materialistic success ethic; it would advance the cause of the poor for which it demanded a structural revolution of the American system. It was expressly activist, if not militant.

SNCC's two campaigns, one of which was involved in direct action and the other in voter registration, converged under the united attack of southern racists. SNCC workers were not only arbitrarily sent to jail, but also battered and beaten, and even murdered. "The white supremacists who kept Negroes from voting did so by methods so cruel, so inhuman, so patently unlawful that they can only be called cynical," writes journalist Anthony Lewis.[90] SNCC activists were also inadequately defended by federal agencies; in fact, they were harassed. As Bobby Kennedy did not come to the aid of civil rights workers,[91] as officials such as Arthur Schlesinger, Jr., tried to rationalize the government's neglect of its wronged citizens by accusing them of "unpardonable" association with alleged Communists,[92] so the FBI pursued and persecuted them. Rap Brown was falsely indicted for arson in Cambridge, Maryland; four SNCC militants were framed in Philadelphia, an incident that "proved" to Forman "that the total power structure of the United States—with the press as its working tool—was out to destroy SNCC."[93] And Rap Brown asked, "Which side is the federal government on," that of the law or that of the lawbreakers? He obviously concluded that it was on the side of the latter.[94]

At the 1964 Democratic convention, the Mississippi Freedom Democratic party, which had been developed through SNCC's voter registration drive, was traduced by what Forman called "the white liberal-labor syndrome and its black sell-outs."[95] Under relentless pressure the organization as a whole lost momentum after the campaign in Selma, Alabama.[96] Its black center was fragmented; it was infiltrated by whites who undermined its activism; and it was denounced particularly by Jewish groups, former contributors who abandoned it after it identified with the cause of the Arabs in the Near East during the Israeli-Arab conflict.[97] Rap Brown was put away and subsequently broken: someone squealed on him, said Nikki Giovanni.[98] SNCC expelled militants like Stokely Carmichael, who was accused of violating organizational discipline as well as taboos against the cult of personality.[99]

Forman blamed SNCC's disintegration on organizational and ideological contradictions. Although it was for the cause of the poor, it was supported chiefly by middle-class reformers who tended to patronize and romanticize those lower in status than they. They had "local peopleitis," as Forman put it.[100] Since the organization was interracial, it had to depend on inadequately motivated white students, including some who wanted to control it and others who could not keep up the pace when ceaselessly confronted with conflict. Many of them, as writer David Halberstam pointed out, had "moved into the civil rights thing because it was the most tangible way to express their discontent."[101] Because they were trying to resolve their own emotional or intellectual problems, they could not last; they were not serious. Many workers, both black and white, resented the discipline: they were inclined to voluntaristic dissent and disobedience; they hung around smoking pot and making casual but emotionally disturbing love to one another. Also, perhaps most significant, the strategy of nonviolence was misleading, as Forman realized. "I believe it was a great mistake not to organize . . . a cadre for the inevitable period of armed struggle," he concluded.[102]

Nevertheless, SNCC—together with the Mississippi Freedom Democratic party—did succeed on a practical plane. It helped register black people who had been deprived of the vote for more than seventy years and it served as an inspiration for other black associations that were based in the ghettos of urban centers. Tactically it was able to develop a coherent activist program grounded on the communal group—or on what Carmichael called a politically modernized "sense of community,"[103] what Rap Brown called "political"[104] blackness and what Forman called black nationalism.[105] Black politicization, of course, had to be founded on some kind of concept of black power—or on the mobilization of the black masses—as Forman realized. King had tied civil rights to political involvement[106] and to direct action.[107] The "black movement . . . must derive strength through politics," says Martin Kilson.[108] It was the organization of black America along political lines that "could strike terror into the hearts of the white majority," as critic Lewis M. Killian writes,[109] and as CORE, the SCLC, SNCC and the Black Muslims demonstrated.

It was SNCC that perhaps first effected the liaison between the southern and the northern wings of the black movement. Since many of its workers were northern middle-class students on an ideological binge, some returned to the North to proselytize. The term "black power" and the symbol "Black Panther" both originated in the process of SNCC activism in the South. One was the invention of a SNCC member, Willie Ricks; the other was the emblem of Carmichael's campaign in Lowndes County, Alabama.[110] As Angela Davis remarked, "In spite of the absence of a homogeneous ideology," the civil rights movement engendered a feeling of "the heights of brotherhood and sisterhood."[111] It succeeded in bringing black people together.

As often occurs in ideological middle-class movements for the people, the black population, North and South, seemed to derive few concrete benefits from the black revolution. "We failed to define or to bring about identifiable change . . ." wrote Hosea Williams to King.[112] CORE with its freedom rides, SNCC with its courageous militance and other organizations were unable to produce significant gains for the black masses. Most of them were too poor to have reached a stage where color was the only criterion of discrimination; they were so underprivileged that they could not take advantage of the social uplift of civil rights.[113] Only the spontaneous riots in the northern urban centers had the power to compel the federal government to take positive action. These not only disturbed the complacent white majority but also moved President Johnson to adopt measures, inadequate though they were. The riots were wildcat manifestations of black nationalistic violence, and they were taken by whites to be the concerted expression of what one called "the hostility toward 'whitey' felt by most, if not all black Americans."[114] They were frightening, and the white conscience turned paranoid.

Radicals saw in black violence—in the act of slum dwellers burning down supermarkets, for instance—"a spontaneous and instinctual revolt with reference to capitalism [which took] the form of a refusal of merchandise."[115] Since industrial society was based on consumer power (on the production and sales of goods through the medium of money, "the universal condensed precipitate of property"[116]), black destruction of products represented an assault on the system. Marcuse, who sympathized with black rebels, was perhaps overly optimistic, if not dialectically romantic, with respect to the revolutionary motivation and potential of black riots.[117] But he realized that revolt could not be founded on marginals, streetfighters or robbers. Even the proletariat, which was undirected and chaotic in its reactions, was incapable without leadership of concerted organization. The lower class might be "the most revolutionary class"—as George Jackson contended—but it cannot carry through a revolution by itself.[118] In a sense black looters were not acting against the capitalistic order: they were trying to claim the symbols of middle-class comfort for themselves. They were at heart materialistic integrationists and their violence, consequently, was not sustained.

There were various organized black movements in the cities which tried to mobilize the poor in a political bid for power based on black communal solidarity. The Reverend Albert Cleage, Jr., of the Freedom Now party, enlisted followers on the principle that "we are a Black Nation in a white man's world."[119] He was explicitly nationalistic: he used his church as the cornerstone from which he launched his drive. He preached Jesus, the Black Messiah, born of a black Madonna— whom he unveiled at Easter—and he followed the doctrine of Booker T. Washington and Malcolm X; he was, he admitted, not "for racial peace."[120] He was particularly sympathetic to the workers of SNCC who had suffered the brutality of white opposition. He wanted to ordain them to protect them from jail and from a draft that would send them to be killed in Vietnam. "God help H. Rap Brown," he prayed.[121]

Despite an active branch in New York City, the support of various black celebrities and the tacit approval of Malcolm X, the Freedom Now party had little impact on the black community as a whole. It was contested by leaders like Martin Luther King, Jr., and Adam Clayton Powell. The idea of a third and independent black political party did not appeal to professionals who had been limited to maneuvering within the Democratic or Republican organization. Indeed, it seemed to be less influential than several black cultural movements in urban ghettos.

LeRoi Jones—Amiri Baraka—for instance, was a middle-class intellectual who Africanized his name, divorced himself from white society (including his white wife and his liberal, left-wing friends) and turned militant in order to wage war on white society. He had been a much-respected poet, playwright, essayist and university instructor; he had also led a cultural movement in Harlem. But progressively he assumed a more and more revolutionary stance based on hostility to whites. He shared the pessimistic position of earlier black nationalists and maintained that "there is *no* chance that the American white man will change."[122] Baraka settled in Newark, New Jersey, founded a society called the "Spirit House Movers"[123] and initiated a movement to politicize blacks. He was criticized by the Black Panthers for inverse racism and by black women—such as Angela Davis—for demanding "the total submission of the Black female as rectification of the century-long wrongs she has done the Black Male."[124] Nikki Giovanni objected to Baraka's political strategy of militarism and of politicking with whites in power.[125] He also—perhaps despite himself—experienced the paradox of attracting whites' attention: the more he attacked them, the more they deferred to him—or "patronized him," as a critic put it— and the more white officialdom harassed him.[126] As Cruse remarked about Baraka's earlier aesthetic drive, "Even a LeRoi Jones can be absorbed and tolerated for the sake of being abused as a threat."[127]

Baraka shifted his emphasis during the 1970s. "We were not guided by revolutionary science," he explained. "We attacked all whites. . . ."[128] His movement had been "based on narrow experience, without the benefit of summed-up experience of the working class in the struggle for power all over the world." He concluded that revolution had to have an economic perspective, and so he turned socialist. "Skin-color is no indicator of one's political line . . ."[129] he decided. But he was still careful to relate his cause to that of the black community. He had learned during the Newark riots, he claimed, that the "rebellions [which] took place in over 100 major American cities . . . were not carried out, as the . . . media would have us believe, by pimps and prostitutes [but] by black workers rising up against their double oppression by monopoly capitalism."[130]

Ron Karenga was another so-called cultural nationalist of the 1960s who organized his group, US, on antiwhite principles and incurred the hostility of other black associations. Karenga's followers were excessively militant: they would build black pride by exposing the enemy; they indulged in shootouts with rivals and were accused of collaborating with the white "power structure" in order to eliminate Black Panthers.[131] "We called Jones and Ron Karenga the high priests of cultural nationalism because they didn't really produce anything except fanatics," wrote Bobby Seale.[132] As Angela Davis explained, "Because the

masses of white people harbor racist attitudes, our people tend to see
them as villains and not the institutionalized forms of racism. . . . When
white people are indiscriminately viewed as the enemy, it is virtually
impossible to develop a political solution."[133]

Meanwhile, in Chicago the Reverend Jesse Jackson was mobilizing
a deliberately political movement in the wake of King's failure to arouse
the ghetto masses. Jackson preached black moral rectitude, black self-
help and black education, perhaps even more than his mentor. "If we
are going to close the gap and catch up, we must do so by disciplining
our appetites, engaging in ethical conduct and developing our minds,"
he said.[134] But he was explicitly pragmatic. As poet Gwendolyn Brooks
reported, Jackson insisted that "the church was our salvation . . . holding the People, keeping them away from suicide until 'we' could come
to them and help redirect them."[135] Indeed, he seemed to mistrust the
messianism that appeared to be implicit in black causes. When Brooks
asked why he did not appeal positively to Africa, he replied that it was
not intimately involved with black objectives in America. If African
coffee producers had interests in Watts or Detroit, he explained, and if
whites were to do something to American blacks that might "threaten
those coffee interests, THEN they would 'feel our grief,' and would
. . . move to help us [and themselves]."[136] Jackson was a realist.

Jackson's "Operation Breadbasket"—a boycott of white enterprises
that did not hire blacks—was a definite, if limited, success. Jackson had
a talent for raising funds from foundations as well as from the government, and he enlisted sponsors in his cause. He organized PUSH (People
United to Save Humanity), a program for economic self-help. He also
launched EXCEL, an educational project for black youth. He was, however, accused of opportunism, of abandoning every new movement he
started and—by one of his black critics—of obscuring "the need for
black power, for the collective force of the black community."[137] Jackson was building a political base, and since it was grounded in the black
ghetto, it was—by the very circumstance of segregation—oriented to a
sense of black nationalism. He was not simply struggling negatively for
survival: he was appealing from his black base to allies from any group
that he could reach. He wanted to form a rainbow coalition of all colors
of the human species.

The Black Panthers also recognized the necessity of cultivating allies
from the outside. Since they, too, functioned from their base in a black
ghetto and since their membership was exclusively black, they did not
fear that they would compromise the principles of black community

solidarity on which they operated. They separated from a black nation-alist faction that would incite the masses to revolution in order to form their own movement in Oakland, California. Led by Huey Newton and Bobby Seale, the Black Panthers worked on the assumption that they, like all slum dwellers, were racial outcasts in American society. Their members were all young, indeed very young, and dedicated to their cause: they were "bad" black hustlers who had disturbing courage and effrontery. In fact, it was their so-called badness that made them for-midable to the opposition and admirable to their fellows in an order in which values were turned upside down and good was evil, and vice versa. Eldridge Cleaver once complimented Huey Newton as the "bad-dest mother fucker ever to set foot in history."[138] According to Bobby Seale, "Malcolm X was a bad nigger."[139]

Because the movement was rooted in the ghetto, it fastened on con-crete objectives. The Panthers stressed self-defense and threatened to teach black people how to resist institutional assaults on their rights by the use of arms. This tactic was a means of encouraging a feeling not just of community solidarity against an ever-present invader, but of black pride. Arms were easily obtainable in California. Although the Panthers were anti-middle-class and anti-intellectual—for intellectual-ism implied class differentiation—as autodidacts, they were well edu-cated: they had a metaphysical bent. Huey Newton, a self-confessed "functional illiterate" at the end of his public school career, taught him-self law, economics and social history.[140] He separated from cultural nationalists such as Ron Karenga—formerly Ron Everett—whom he accused of treacherously assassinating two Panthers.[141]

The stress on self-defense—in contrast to nonviolence—perhaps contributed most to the notoriety of the Black Panther Party. The thought of blacks with legally procured guns seemed to terrorize white America. But the Panthers' ten-point program, which Newton called one of "survival,"[142] was a moderate project: it included practical pro-posals for fair housing, schooling and employment, as well as broad appeals for freedom and self-determination. "We want land, bread, housing, education, clothing, justice and peace," it proclaimed.[143] At one point, Panthers agitated in collaboration with official poverty work-ers for a traffic light at a dangerous intersection.[144] They later initiated a children's breakfast project for which they solicited—and were ac-cused by authorities of extorting—funds from neighborhood merchants. They were also political in orientation: since many of them had been institutionalized for delinquency, if not outright crime, the Panthers considered themselves to be politically victimized. They were militants, who bravely faced police brutality; they withstood raids on their meeting places and false incriminations and assassinations.[145]

The Panthers worked under the principle that they were representing the "laboring-class people."[146] They announced that they wanted to focus on "what the people want and not what some intellectual personally wants or some cultural nationalist or some jive-ass underground RAM motherfucker wants."[147] For this reason, insofar as whites could assist them in their community or general black help program—with money or legal or moral support—they accepted the possibility of race collaboration. But the Panthers remained wary: they were "down on bohemians and white radicals," according to Newton.[148] They were also careful to use self-defense only as a tactic and not as an end. "Huey . . . always had the revolutionary tactics and the revolutionary means in mind as to how the people must go about getting . . . basic desires and needs," said Seale.[149] He and Newton instructed the black masses in the use of guns because "self-defense was politically related to their survival and their liberation."[150] This instruction entailed a close observance of the law: "the Black Panthers were and are always required to keep their activities within legal bounds," wrote Newton.[151]

Although the Panthers' program stressed concrete goals and was aimed at specific community needs, their inspiration was based on idealism. "Our ideology," said Newton, ". . . is the most important part of our thinking."[152] White liberals were quick to fasten pejoratively on this feature of the Panther campaign. One critic referred to the madness and despair of the Panthers.[153] Another remarked that most of them, whose guns represented "the regained phallus of emasculated men,"[154] were "naive malleable ghetto kids, angry and despairing, but not . . . vicious or mean spirited . . . warmed by . . . feelings of fraternity and solidarity that . . . accompany . . . quasi military discipline," and that "Hitler's Brown Shirts" and the armies of Mao, the Bolsheviks and the Vietcong must have felt.[155] Yet another critic observed that the black movement in general had been transformed from pragmatic to ideological—even mystical—leadership.[156] But after even its most moderate spokesmen were killed or silenced, quite naturally blacks everywhere began to seek ideological confirmation for their activities. As Julius Lester wrote after the death of King, "We learned, beyond a doubt, that if he, who offered nothing but love, could be murdered . . . the lives of us lesser blacks were that much more precarious."[157] Perhaps the fact that black lives were so precarious made Huey Newton and his young street brothers able not just to stand up to official armed violence against them, but, on the strength of their conviction of right, to develop a cause for which they were willing to die. Ideology scares middle-class America.

From the very beginning, ideology was implicit in the Panther movement, which was made up of a small cadre of ghetto blacks fighting for the economic and political liberty of their people and prepared to use arms against their active aggressors. It was the cause that inspired them to provoke, defy and insult police oppressors. "By wearing and displaying weapons [and patrolling the cops and calling them pigs] the street brothers would relate to [an] example of leadership," wrote Newton.[158] Self-defense was a form of political expression: "Politics is war without bloodshed, and war is politics with bloodshed . . ." he concluded.[159]

As the Panthers related racism to the capitalistic order, they used Marxist dialectical materialism as the basis of their ideological viewpoint. "Although the Black Panther Party believes in black nationalism and black culture," wrote Seale's editor, "it does not believe that either will lead to black liberation or the overthrow of the capitalist system. . . ."[160] Newton, who announced that he was a *"dialectical materialist,"*[161] explained that the Panthers started out as "revolutionary nationalists . . . who want revolutionary changes in everything, including the economic system the oppressor inflicts upon us." Since the Panthers recognized their common cause with other revolutionary peoples of the world, they called themselves "internationalists."[162]

Within the dialectical context of materialistic determinism, Black Panthers seemed to feel that Marxism had been transcended. They were not Communists. Newton, said George Jackson, attacked the strategy of the American Communist party and the liberal left revisionists for not taking racism into account.[163] Newton was "never convinced that destroying capitalism would automatically destroy racism," although he thought "that we could not destroy racism without wiping out its economic foundation."[164] He would improvise his own ideological solution: since the world was actually "a dispersed collection of communities" that wanted to control their own destinies, and since their aims were being obstructed by the powerful technological and industrial empire of America, Newton proposed a "revolutionary intercommunalism"[165]—an idea to which George Jackson subscribed[166] and which corresponds to writer Ishmael Reed's "policulturalism"—to overthrow the negative, concentrated force of oppression. Newton considered

American blacks "the vanguard of the revolution of this country"[167] and he counted on them—most specifically the lumpenproletariat, the "unemployables,"[168] in collaboration with all poor people and third-world outcasts—to provide the necessary thrust. He was not ideally a racist: he looked eventually for "universal identity," or, he warned, "we will have . . . the kind of ethnocentrism we have now."[169]

But it was positive black consciousness, the ideological negation of inflicted black racism, that was the cornerstone of Newton's mission. And, of course, he and his followers had been profoundly influenced by Malcolm X. "We . . . believe that the Black Panther Party exists in the spirit of Malcolm," said Newton.[170] It was Malcolm's badness that attracted Bobby Seale.[171] Eldridge Cleaver also "loved Malcolm X."[172] The Panthers also sought links with other black organizations: Newton wanted to draft the leaders of SNCC, including Carmichael, Forman and Rap Brown, because he respected their disciplinary and administrative skills. "We hoped to create a merger," Newton remarked, ". . . since it seemed that only by merging could we produce the strong leadership we need."[173]

The party and its reputation grew over a very short period. Blacks were impressed by the Panthers' courage; whites, particularly the radical chic who were seeking, as writer Tom Wolfe recorded, "the primitive, exotic, and romantic,"[174] began to patronize them. To confront the power structure was in itself a heroic exploit, although perhaps one without an issue. In fact, Newton referred to his course as one of revolutionary—as contrasted to reactionary—suicide. Since he did "not think that life will change for the better without an assault on the establishment,"[175] he concluded that it was necessary "to oppose the forces that would drive me to self-murder."[176] Tragically for him, he did not die in the struggle as so many of his comrades did. He was beaten down remorselessly by pressures outside and inside his movement: he succumbed unheroically.

Expansion, collaboration, assassination and the forced exile by imprisonment of Newton and other black leaders brought conflict and confusion to the Panther program. As a community enterprise, the party was decentralized; it had no concrete long-range program to hold it together. James Forman commented that he could not join the Panthers because they had no security, no discipline, no structure.[177] They did not relate to the black middle class: they had no "buffer," remarked critic Reginald Major,[178] no "substantial, sympathetic base within the ranks of established black leadership."[179] Although it was said that "if the middle class could not be forced to serve mass interests, mass activity would . . . serve middle-class interests,"[180] in reality it was difficult to coordinate the mass.

The authorities coalesced in reinforced concerted opposition to the Panthers. Within three years, "the Black Panther Party . . . succeeded in aligning against it all the forces of reaction."[181] A California legislator introduced what was called the Panther bill to outlaw the right to bear arms. The police, who had at first been "frightened and confused"[182] by the defiance of blacks with guns, began to react with fury. They entrapped Panthers, staged arrests, provoked shootouts and framed and successively killed off leaders from Bobby Hutton, Fred Hampton and Mark Clark to Alprentice Carter and George Jackson. They attacked Cleaver and revoked his bail, forcing him to flee the country. They wounded Huey Newton and jailed him.[183] They accused both him and Bobby Seale of murder. And the Panthers' national expansion exacerbated the antipathy of the FBI, which could now pursue the party relentlessly. "Panther plots were discovered all over the country."[184]

Quite naturally the media turned on the Panthers. Whites, including federal spies, infiltrated the movement—and encouraged intra- and rival-group dissension. Not-yet-politicized black delinquents used guns and revolutionary rhetoric to justify self-interested criminal activity. Using the name of the Panthers, they alienated the Negro middle and working classes. Civil rights organizations attacked the Panthers. White radicals balked at their subordinate role in the movement. Former leaders, like Eldridge Cleaver, defected and broke with Newton. Increasingly, members became suspicious of one another and paranoid with respect to the authorities—as they had good reason to be. They were obsessed by their fear of genocide, which, says Major, "accompanies a belief that . . . Negroes are controlled by the police."[185] Eventually, the Panthers succumbed; they were overpowered. "Few people can reasonably be expected to engage in warfare with police."[186] In effect, they were cruelly wiped out. As Cruse wrote, when the Panthers "left their natural environment of California on the assumption that they could become a national organization [they] encountered the brutal, repressive reality of Chicago and New York, and [were] destroyed."[187]

There were other nationalistic groups during the 1960s that seemed to rival one another in militance. RAM (the Revolutionary Action Movement) worked for organized violence under the rubric of "revolutionary nationalism, black nationalism or just plain blackism."[188] Its leader, Max Stanford, who was jailed in 1968, believed that it was "too late to save America."[189] Milton Henry—or Brother Gaidi—of the proposed Republic of New Africa, gave up on white America and tried to claim territory, including five states, in the Deep South for the blacks. He made an appeal for aid from Red China.[190] Detroit automobile workers, disgusted by a racist union that pretended to represent them and a racist management that exploited them, started the Dodge Revolutionary Union Movement.[191] They were nationalistic in their membership as well as in their objectives. None of these groups had much effect; they were, nevertheless, indications of the profound frustration that had affected the entire black population.

It was Malcolm X's movement that seemed most to have influenced the course of black nationalism. Of all the militant campaigns of the 1960s, it had the most impact on black thinking. Its weakness, however, lay in its almost total dependence on Malcolm X, both as a charismatic leader and as an organizational genius. He was irreplaceable and, therefore, his Organization of Afro-American Unity could be stamped out in the single act of murdering him. He was the last great black hero: his very assassination proved that he posed such a threat to the industrial order that he had to be eliminated. As sociologist Eugene Victor Wolfenstein writes, "The substantive elements of black revolutionary consciousness were Afro-American Unity, Black Power, and Black Pride. More than any other individual, Malcolm X was responsible for the development of these interrelated concepts."[192]

Unlike the positive pragmatist whose means are based on hypotheses that imply the acceptance of things as they are, Malcolm's assumptions were founded on negative realities—on the idea of a reverse order of what was. He developed his ideology from his experience of the antithesis of what should be, and in this way reflected the black's approach to life in America: "Even though the black man's present condition is that of spiritual death," writes biographer Harry B. Shaw, "he inherits a strong racial sense of having fallen from a past glory. . . ."[193] Therefore, he claims a higher morality than that which exists—as Malcolm X illustrated.

Malcolm X was a dialectician: he was the pragmatic antipragmatist who unflinchingly sought the realization of the black man's truth. As he existed in the present, he was the devil's "bad nigger";[194] when he was in jail he was actually called Satan by his fellow prisoners.[195] Because he had to survive in a system where his people were deprived, reduced by poverty to servitude, jailed and killed, he believed "that men lived by the law of the jungle and the law of history: by conflict and retribution."[196] As he himself put it, "I had a jungle mind, I was living in a jungle. . . ."[197] Cruelty and violence governed the actions of those in control of the system. Yet by a peculiar leap of faith, Malcolm X was able to intuit that there was a real realm of justice, freedom and peace: in essence, he saw society reflected upside down.

Fundamentally, Malcolm X was a deeply spiritual man. His conversion to the Nation of Islam filled a need in his soul and he felt as if it had been preordained. "I've so often thought that Allah was watching over me," he confessed.[198] Not only did he find personal strength and security in his "submission and obedience to the will of Allah" and to Elijah Muhammad, his "divine leader and teacher . . . in America,"[199] he said, but he also discovered he had a positive role in life in serving God's people. Allah had made "His choice from among the lowly, uneducated, downtrodden, oppressed masses, from among the lowest elements of America's twenty million ex-slaves."[200] To uplift black people both economically and morally was to carry out the purpose of God. Malcolm X was not a Marxist materialist: he was a Platonic idealist.

Malcolm sought to advance the cause of the forgotten black masses. He saw very well that with proper direction they alone could be the source of revolutionary action. "The aroused black man can create a turmoil in white America's vitals—not to mention America's international image," he wrote.[201] Moreover, he felt a spiritual relationship with his people. He had been poor himself; his father had been murdered by whites; his family—his sisters and brothers and widowed mother—had been on welfare, a condition he bitterly resented for he had suffered the debilitating paternalism of the white world. He blamed the welfare people—to whom "we were just *things*, that was all"[202]— for acting as if they owned his family and thus for destroying its pride and solidarity. He had had to endure the patronage of the white couple who took him under its wing, treated him kindly like "a pet canary," and "never really did see *me*."[203] He had had to undergo disillusion when a favorite white teacher encouraged him and then stifled his ambition by advising him that the legal profession, which Malcolm X had chosen as a career, was "no realistic goal for a nigger."[204] He had many reasons to distrust whites.

Like so many street blacks, Malcolm X had been a hustler, a hoodlum and a pimp. He was the secret lover of a white middle-class adventuress, a drug dealer, a convicted thief. He had profound ties with the rootless, luckless black folk of the ghetto. He felt an inherent solidarity with them and was "relaxed among Negroes who were being their natural selves."[205] He seemed to have enjoyed the company of the small-time crooks who were, like him, "victims of the white man's American social system" and who "huddled in [Small's Paradise Bar] bonded together in seeking security and warmth and comfort from each other."[206]

In general, Malcolm X came to identify wholly with his race and to avoid the quality that had plagued the black spirit under white rule. He admired his father and his half sister, Ella, both of whom were black in color, proud and assertive. Ella might have risen to bourgeoisie status, but her allegiance to her kind and to her family made her tolerate Malcolm X's delinquency. He felt that she "admired my rebellion against the world."[207] He had loved but defied his mother, who was white in appearance and who had been unable to cope with the poverty that ravaged her family and tore her children away from her: she went mad. She was ashamed of the white man who had forcibly fathered her, and Malcolm X "learned to hate every drop of that white rapist's blood that is in me."[208] He also regretted his school career, which was aborted early on because he had been "trying so hard, in every way I could, to be white."[209] It was not just that the "white man is the black man's enemy"[210] in the sense that he imposed his economic and political pressure from the outside. It was also that the white seemed insidiously to penetrate the black psyche and deprive it of its positive force.

Malcolm X underwent his conversion when he was a prisoner. His integrity was based on moral tenets that he seemed unable to traduce no matter what role he assumed. As a boy, he had never been a "hypocrite,"[211] remarked one churchgoing woman. As a hustler, he kept to the code of the street, at the risk of his life. And as a convict, he maintained his early principle that "right is right, and wrong is wrong."[212] So when, after much soul-searching, he embraced Islam, he was free to uphold positively the values that he had never essentially forsaken while at the same time he gained a new perspective on himself.

With this new perspective, Malcolm was freed of guilt for his admittedly "depraved"[213] life. "Only guilt admitted accepts truth,"[214] he wrote. He knew he was not responsible for his crime; it was America that was the criminal. The white man, not Malcolm X—known as Satan—was the devil. The objective reader, he said, "may see how in the society to which I was exposed as a black youth . . . for me to wind up in a prison was . . . just about inevitable."[215] By dialectical inversion, it was the prisoner who was the potential spokesman for moral right against an immoral order. "Uncle Sam has no conscience," he observed later. "They don't know what morals are."[216] But he did repent that he individually had played not only gigolo to a white playgirl—whom he did not respect[217]—but small-time "depraved parasitical hustler"[218] to a structure of big-time criminality. He had been "*living* like an animal; *thinking* like an animal,"[219] implicitly accepting the white man's denigration of him.

Malcolm X, as chief promoter of the Nation of Islam, was able in less than a decade to multiply its membership a hundred times.[220] He learned the strategic value of black nationalism as an ideology and as a method of uplifting the black race spiritually and materially. Because he was inspired originally by his distrust and contempt for the evil of the white—"of the *collective* white man's *historical* record" and "not . . . of any *individual*,"[221] he emphasized—his thrust at first was based on dialectical negation. He "equated 'black nationalism' and 'separation.' "[222] The white order had never accorded justice and equality to blacks and it never would: he himself did not "even consider myself an American," he confessed.[223] "I'm not an American. I'm one of the 22 million black people who are victims of democracy, nothing but disguised hypocrisy."[224] He was convinced that "the system in this country cannot produce freedom for an Afro-American."[225] Since victims were unable to continue to coexist with their victimizers, the two races could not live together in peace. Malcolm X sought independence.

But dialectically, he used the principle of nationalism positively to unite black people. Unlike many radical black associations, the Black Muslims considered all Negroes eligible for membership in their organization and made a bid for support among the Negro middle class, which, despite its professions of integrationism, was often more insidiously antiwhite than the black masses.[226] Malcolm X might have repeatedly denounced so-called house Negroes—the Uncle Toms of the modern order—and middle-class Negroes might have publicly rejected him. But he made constant efforts to bring the race together. He met with officials of conservative organizations—for instance, Percy Sutton of the NAACP—and fought against the intragroup jealousies that regularly undermined the black cause.

Malcolm X also used positively the idea of self-defense to lift black people in their struggle against white aggression. The Black Muslims, of course, had proclaimed the black man's right to defend himself. They preached not violence but self-protection. However, they seemed to founder in a kind of apolitical immobility that belied any implication of assertiveness. As Malcolm X admitted, "Privately I was convinced that our Nation of Islam could be an even greater force in the American black man's overall struggle—if we engaged in more *action*."[227] On the other hand he insinuated—if not threatened—that the black should militantly exert his rights as a citizen if he was attacked; that he was not bound by injunctions to love his enemy—injunctions that were in any case hypocritical. Malcolm X inhabited a nation of his own, albeit an ideological one, and he felt he had to safeguard its borders.

Again, he stressed the theme of a universal black nation. As the Black Muslims established links with Africa—Egypt and Ghana in particular[228]—so Malcolm X tried to instill in black people a sense of all-black identity. He did, like Marcus Garvey, revive their feeling of African roots. The white man has attempted to separate black Americans from Africans and Asians, he preached.[229] As the practical Black Muslim project involved separatism—or at least black community control, economic self-reliance and social self-discipline—his long-term solution to the black man's problems was based on his vision of an eventual return to Africa, where the black races of the earth could exist in justice and harmony. This mission was not founded just on religious eschatology: it also had a methodological function that served to intensify black consciousness. "A people without history or cultural roots . . . becomes a dead people," he said,[230] echoing historian Carter Woodson.[231] His mission also included a potential political program for a black party on which he later capitalized.[232]

Malcolm X was too much of a moralist and an activist to remain connected with the Nation of Islam. The Black Muslims were caught in a political dichotomy. They were inactive activists. In carrying their teachings to their logical extreme, Malcolm X exceeded the limits that Elijah Muhammad had imposed on his movement to ensure its and his own survival in an inimical order; in a way Muslim black nationalism was an end in itself. Also Malcolm X's ethical code denied him the luxury of disregarding the personal misconduct on the part of the man whom he looked upon as a divine prophet. Elijah Muhammad compromised with the world he lived in, both intellectually and morally, and Malcolm X would not. When Malcolm broke with the Black Muslims, he tried to adapt their theology to a secular plane. He still believed privately—perhaps even more fervently—in Allah. But whereas before he had assured his followers, "We don't mix our religion with our politics and our economics and our social and civil activities,"[233] he now proposed a Muslim Mosque which would be a "black nationalist organization with an international revolutionary orientation."[234] The black nationalism on which the mosque was founded involved the black man's political and economic control of his community[235] as well as his responsibility for its social uplift and fraternalism. "Our gospel is black nationalism," Malcolm X preached in 1964.[236]

Malcolm X had little time after he returned from Africa to fully develop his program: he was assassinated in February 1965. He further secularized it, however, in his newly formed Organization of Afro-American Unity by modifying his approach to the white enemy. Although the solution to the black's problems was "brotherhood"[237] and although black nationalism might have represented the potential negation of white power,[238] it did not necessarily entail antipathy to the white race as a whole.[239] In rejecting integration, "in separating ourselves, this doesn't mean that we are anti-white or anti-American, or anti-anything," said Malcolm X.[240] He would not be motivated by hate as an end in itself. It was not the white man per se; it was white racism that was the adversarial force. It was the morally bankrupt, self-seeking repressive society that exploited the black.

By abstracting the white man and identifying him with a criminal system, Malcolm X dialectically enlarged his thesis. Placing his cause within the framework of a "global rebellion of the oppressed against the oppressor, the exploited against the exploiter,"[241] he was explicitly attacking the industrial order that was "used to suppress the masses of dark-skinned people all over the world."[242] Capitalism was "vulturistic," he said. "You show me a capitalist, I'll show you a bloodsucker."[243] The system was in any case doomed, and Malcolm X consequently advocated a kind of socialism to lift the downtrodden Negro masses.[244]

He reached beyond the limits of the American nation both ideologically and economically. It was the white industrial world that had exploited, colonized and subjected the colored races of the earth. Malcolm X, in identifying with the latter, spoke for mankind in general. "One of the main objectives of the OAAU is to join the civil-rights struggle and lift it . . . to the level of human rights," he proposed.[245] Black nationalists, he insisted, "are more interested in human rights than they are in civil rights."[246]

His struggle had a transcendent moral objective for which he would militate politically. As he realized, his people "weren't conscious of the political maneuvering . . . which exploited [us] politically."[247] Blacks, who could vote in bloc, held a strategic position[248] in a society where all kinds of white groups were lobbying for particular interests. Indeed, blacks had to develop a power base of their own: "I believe in . . . any kind of political action," he affirmed.[249] "I believe in anything that is necessary to correct unjust conditions . . . as long as it's intelligently directed and designed to get results."[250]

The political alternative to independent black bloc voting was a military campaign of self-defense. In Malcolm X's words, "It's got to be the ballot or the bullet."[251] Since liberty, equality and justice had to be actively procured "by ballots or bullets,"[252] since "power . . . takes a back step—only in the face of more power,"[253] black people were necessarily bound to fight for their rights as citizens.[254] To know one's enemy was to confront him with his own weapons.[255] The white racist was not "passive, peaceful, and nonviolent";[256] rather, he was aggressive and dangerous, and the black man had to protect himself. For all its propaganda in favor of nonviolence, the white state was historically militaristic. "If it is wrong to be violent defending black women and black children and black babies and black men, then it is wrong for America to draft us and make us violent abroad in defense of her."[257] Malcolm X proposed the formation of retaliatory—guerrilla—units[258] in enemy territory where black people were being lawlessly persecuted. "We need a Mau Mau," he warned.[259] The OAAU could train southern Negroes and show "how to equip yourself and let you know how to deal with the man who deals with you."[260]

Insofar as his struggle in America for citizens' rights was on another level a worldwide revolution for human rights, Malcolm X was attempting to establish an international political foundation from which he could draw and to which he could lend support. It was this aspect of his mission that most threatened the equilibrium of the American industrial state. He realized that "if your power base is only here, you can forget it. You can't build a power base here"[261]—in the United States alone. The black man had to have "new allies,"[262] just as the black cause needed a broader interpretation. Since it was part of a universal movement, the "international situation"[263] could bring pressure on the government to cede to the Negro's demands. "The Negro problem has ceased to be a Negro problem . . . an American problem and has now become a world problem . . . for all humanity."[264]

Therefore, Malcolm X politically appealed for help—specifically at the Cairo Conference of the Organization of African Unity in 1964.[265] He was admitted as an observer and "a resolution came out . . . pointing out that . . . continued abuses of the human rights of the black people in America still existed."[266] He also looked to the United Nations as a potential political arbiter of black destiny. These tactics, of course, embarrassed American officialdom: his campaign for foreign allies worried the State Department and the CIA.[267] Particularly later—when Israel went to war against the Arabs—the strategy of the Muslim Malcolm X, which had attracted support among American blacks, took on the dimensions of an international power struggle. As Eugene Wolfenstein notes, "Malcolm was . . . becoming the middle term in a logic of international revolutionary action,"[268] which could affect the economic as well as political structures controlled by the United States. Obviously, Malcolm X knew he was in danger. Not only had he been threatened by orthodox Elijah Muhammad followers and by agencies of his government, but he was also being singled out by white European nations, allies of the United States. "The interests in this country are in cahoots with the interests in France and the interests in Britain," he explained. "And the governments in these different places were frightened" by the prospect of African Americans uniting with Africans.[269]

Malcolm X was assassinated by one of these terrorist factions. After his murder—and those of Martin Luther King, Jr., and of many lesser-known black martyrs—the black movement seemed to collapse. It died from integration, from the rise of a new Negro middle class and from the concerted power of the industrial system—from affluence, the opportunism of many black fellow-travelers and the instability of white allies. Indeed, white sympathizers, who lacked both endurance and historical roots, gave up when they realized they were part of a struggle to confront not just the present operation of the state, but also the cumulative whole of the American experience. As white SNCC workers created "more problems . . . than solutions,"[270] and undercut the revolutionary thrust of the operation, so leftist supporters of the Panthers sold out. The peace and women's liberation movements captured the attention of the media and distracted public interest from blacks. Beats and hippies faded out; white students graduated and went into business and yuppies emerged.

The black revolution was absorbed into the American system—as Cruse had feared[271]—and the power base on which it had built black solidarity, black pride, black self-defense and black self-determination was negated. The black revolution had to face the reinforced opposition of middle- and lower-class whites whose former, relatively silent, racism was exacerbated by political manipulation. In effect, whites of all strata accepted black civil rights only until they "infringed directly upon their own interests."[272] So black agitation gave way to what

NAACP president Vernon Jordan called "the despair of the seventies"[273] and to the indifference of the eighties. As Amiri Baraka lamented, "Robt Williams is quiet now / & Bobby Seale has disappeared / Huey skipped to Cuba / . . . Rap just got out of a behavior modification center / whispering of the sunni. . . ."[274]

The black movement accomplished little on a concrete political and economic level. The cynicism of regular Democrats,[275] which led to the failure of the Mississippi Freedom Democratic party—representing southern blacks' political bid for recognition in 1968—did much to destroy the idealism of black field workers. The equally cynical methods of Republicans in mobilizing the so-called silent majority along racial lines blocked the progress of civil rights. Whites did not believe in the "Negro Revolution . . . because we could not afford to lose votes," said writer Norman Mailer.[276] Liberals and conservatives united against it. The threat of black power aroused "a political white neo-ethnicity" representing middle-class pluralistic America.[277]

As writer Lewis Killian remarks, the white backlash was significant because it openly expressed "a reluctance to accept the *intermediate* steps that are necessary to make equality a reality for the many Negroes who are in no way prepared to live according to white middle-class standards."[278] Former allies of the Negro—like the Jews, for instance—gave up their role as Negro defenders and turned into neoethnic activists under the aegis of the same group solidarity which they denied the blacks—to the point, as Rabbi Jay Kaufman notes, that they denounced efforts for black self-determination as manifestations of anti-Semitism or "neo-fascism."[279] Since all ethnic collectivities—which are, with the exception of those of color, more or less advantaged—promote their particular interests within the context of the middle-class ethic, pluralism can function only within the same materialistic framework. Poverty is out. America, says Lester, "acts on the basis of power."[280]

The black movement actually lacked a clear economic direction. Harry Ashmore, a white critic, says that it was "never to attain philosophic coherence nor effective organization."[281] It was torn between integrationism and nationalism. Nevertheless, although it was beset with problems of method and of economic program, the black movement's essential philosophic base was solid: it sought human rights. Methodologically, it seemed progressively to arrive at a consensus. Almost everyone, from Martin Luther King, Jr., to Malcolm X to the Black Panthers, spoke for some kind of socialism. Some militants, like Angela Davis, George Jackson, James Boggs and, later, Amiri Baraka, were Marxists who blamed monopoly capitalism[282] and advocated its overthrow. Eldridge Cleaver would launch a revolution "by smashing and disrupting the machinery of oppressors."[283] George Jackson was for "socialism-communalism"[284] or "intercommunalism"[285] on the model of African social organization. Other activists identified class with race, as if race had swallowed class in a neocolonial world structure. Actually, the black internationalism of Malcolm X, Huey Newton and others was effective, although during the 1980s this strategy would be undermined by the deterioration of African economies and the spectacular successes of several Asian industrialized orders.

Also black leaders who were of exceptional quality did not have time to develop a coherent program: they died or were murdered or silenced young. They were not just the objects of solid white oppositional oppression, which had generalized cultural as well as economic roots and which erupted chiefly in violence. They were also hampered by their own psyches: most of them were victims of paranoiac instincts. They were fatalists. Although they had dreams of "universal identity"[286]—as did Martin Luther King, Jr., and Huey Newton—of creating a bright new world, these black leaders were obsessed by a premonition of tragedy that resembled a death wish and that seemed to drive them ineluctably to disaster despite themselves. As James Forman wrote, "There was a fatalistic streak in me—as in other young blacks— about our lives."[287] Newton, who at first believed himself "immune to death,"[288] soon began to think of himself as a marked man. King, said Bayard Rustin, became "a little too concerned about the possibility of death."[289] And Malcolm X "expected"—apparently all his life—"to die at any time."[290] He was—rightly—haunted by the idea that "any moment . . . could bring me death . . . that I would die a violent death."[291] And he did. But the spectacular rise and fall of the leaders of the black revolution worked to divorce them from the reality of the quotidian. Their fatalism, which reflected dramatically that of the long-suffering Negro masses, carried with it the implication of hopelessness. They were romantic heroes; when they were killed off or silenced, the people were left with no base on which they could build.

Certain blacks, including James Boggs and Manning Marable, blame the decline of the movement on its middle-class orientation. "Race consciousness which does not develop into a real and realistic attack of the causes of black oppression can only become false consciousness . . . a breeding ground for cultism, adventurism . . . opportunism," says Boggs.[292] "White folks realize now that they can concede

Blackness and still exercise control," wrote Rap Brown.[293] Potential race leaders turned into successful entrepreneurs by trading on their race and were, inevitably, separated from the new poor black masses. The gallantry of blacks and whites, according to Ashmore, "had . . . only opened the way for the advancement of middle-class blacks"—about a third of the black population—"who shared the material values of their white counterparts."[294] As Henry Martin, a black expatriate, commented on African Americans in service to General Motors, "I think I see a war going on between the action and the words."[295]

The emergence of a new black middle class has made possible the modern economic rationalization of racism. According to this theory, it is not color or historically rooted cultural attitudes but poverty and its ancillaries—crime, violence, drug dealing—that are responsible for the rejection and ghettoization of black people. Lack of education, the indispensable condition of job opportunity in the corporate age, is also an asocial effect of being poor and a further reason for consigning the black underclass to outcast status. Even black revisionists condemn the black community precisely because it has not become part of the white industrial middle class—as if this had been the implicit goal of the black movement for human rights. Perhaps, as Cruse suggests, the black middle class became "the tactical prisoner of its inherent pragmatism";[296] its ideology was lost in its practical opportunism, which benefited the few at the expense of the many. Indeed, strategic white groups—academics and intellectuals as well as businessmen and politicians—have tried to break down black nationalistic solidarity and disperse the black majority as a whole by dividing blacks into moral categories. The lawful, presentable moderate—who is integrated—is pitted against the lawless, brute extremist—who is not. It was this division that made for the differentiation between the house and the field Negro in slavery times.

The intellectual elite has, in fact, been particularly influential in discrediting the idea of black nationalism and has united in opposition to it. As social commentator Charles Kadushin points out, in the early sixties only the less prestigious of the intellectual elite members showed any interest in the black struggle for equality.[297] Leaders were often expressly against the movement. Poet Allen Tate, for instance, treated black militance as a resurgence of civil war. "The white race seems determined to rule the Negro race . . ." he admitted. "I belong to the white race; therefore I intend to support white rule."[298] By 1970, those who "were still concerned with civil rights were on the fringes rather than at the center of American intellectual life."[299]

Even institutional authorities discouraged independent studies of the black movement. Academia had "no sources of support for research on the impact of the Negro protest movement."[300] Many writers satirized the new vogue of Negrophilia. Saul Bellow's Mr. Sammler, in *Mr. Sammler's Planet,* ironized on the "idea of the corrupting disease of being white and the healing power of black."[301] Susan Sontag made fun of what she called James Baldwin's concept of white inferiority in *Blues for Mr. Charlie.*[302] But she missed the point. Baldwin was defending the tolerant, rational white liberal. Mailer seemed to resent the communality of the black experience through which the Negro "believed his people were possessed of a potential genius which was greater than Whites,"[303] just as he seemed to want to engage Baldwin in a literary—if not physical—combat for supremacy.[304] C. Vann Woodward mocked what he considered the second Reconstruction: the emergence of sets of "white romantics" and Negro "Noble Savage[s]" with the "simplicity, naturalness, spontaneity and uninhibited sexuality" to save a "bankrupt white civilization."[305]

In his book *The Confessions of Nat Turner,* William Styron exploited public interest in black subjects and, in the process, distorted black history. Disillusioned by black criticism and perhaps by his personal experience with a black convict whom he patronized and who deceived him,[306] Styron became disgusted with black agitation.[307] Speaking for the Negro race, he concluded that Frederick Douglass would be "horrified" by the foolishness of Negro militants with respect to their past.[308] Historian Daniel Boorstin denounced the rise of "New Barbarism," which he seemed to associate with blacks and their young white supporters. Modern radicalism was not a search for meaning in the pluralistic *"affirmation of community,"* he maintained, but an uncivilized form of sensationalism, an ego trip without ideology or content. Boorstin, who believes in the justice of American democracy and attributes its success to its lack of historical consciousness, has blamed blacks and their allies—student "apathetes"—for denying the existence of time.[309] Indeed, it appears as if the intellectual, following the political and social establishment, fears black idealism and black self-affirmation—maybe, as Sherwood Anderson's stable boy in "The Man Who Became a Woman" sentimentalized, because the "something we whites have got and think such a lot of, and are so proud about, isn't much of any good after all."[310]

The black is the only American who cannot get away from his history; he carries America's past in himself. Black consciousness is historical consciousness. Despite its apparent collapse, the blacks' movement had a significant impact on industrial culture—as was evident in whites' reaction to it. No matter how many incidences of tactical divergence and even inadequacy occurred, every branch of the black revolution of the sixties—from the SCLC to CORE to SNCC to OAAU to the Black Panther Party to the urban uprisings—posed a threat to the governing powers and called into question the premises on which industrial culture was founded.

There have inevitably been several concrete political gains. In the South, white leaders, in collaboration with industry, have been able to modify the caste system, if not to effect a change of racial attitudes. The black political challenge disrupted the solidarity of the white Democratic organization and led to divisions in white society between the lower and middle or upper middle class. Blacks not only hold a "veto power over White candidates in the old racist mold,"[311] but with the political thrust of Jesse Jackson, they have also been able to influence elections. Still they remain swallowed in the Democratic organization. As Cruse suggests, Jackson's movement, now disempowered within the Democratic party, "would . . . have been the core of a prepared black political base" if it had been focused on an independent black drive. *"A truly viable Third Party Movement in the United States has to be structured around the black political base."*[312] The fact is, as was pointed out in 1984, "with the exception of a relatively small proportion of progressives, whites of every social class have rejected the Jackson candidacy."[313] In 1988, after Jackson attracted a certain white constituency, he was buried in the white party structure. In 1992 he had little, if any, influence.

Nevertheless, Jackson's Rainbow Coalition, which was aimed deliberately both at colored ethnics and at the poor, did appeal to lower-middle-class white workers in economically depressed areas. The poor southern white—who had traditionally been subject to racial and religious demagoguery—has been confronted by regional industrialization. He has been uprooted; he could go either for or against the rising new southern rich. Under the impulse of Alabama's Governor George Wallace and his now-disinherited followers who were preaching the lost cause at any price, the cracker was a force of reaction. Unless he can be remodeled into the mass middle-class type, which is the staple of the consumer economy, he represents a potential source of discontent.[314]

Economically—if not culturally—speaking, the South and Southwest have conformed to the demands of the industrial state: they are the centers of new agribusiness and new corporate enterprise, including agribusiness in the Southwest, NASA, computer firms and television companies. Blacks have opportunities in these regions and they are quicker to take advantage of them than many whites. Jesse Jackson's purposeful depreciation of the significance of race was strategically effective in his appeal to lower-middle-class whites. A party realignment built on a black political base that minimized the importance of black and white might attract a white neo-Populist following[315]—although such a tactic would be a concession to economic rationalization and could suffer from a lack of cultural depth. The South's increased black voter registration[316] has brought a countermovement of previously apathetic whites, and more and more who are now voting do so along racial lines.

According to historian Andrew Hacker, the "greatest victory" of black power was "the demoralization of white society."[317] Actually, the black uprising led to the democratization of white society: the black was "a nationalizing force in American politics"[318] probably because he served to consolidate a white middle-class pluralistic majority. Implicitly, this majority stood in opposition not just to black power, but to the possible social and economic uplift of the black poor. This majority has also been responsible for the decades of Reagan-Bush Republicanism. In an election, for instance, in which only about 53 percent of the electorate voted, 73 percent of all white Protestants and 64 percent of all white women went for Reagan.[319] White Protestants, of course, constitute the largest ethnic minority.

In effect, Jackson's Rainbow Coalition represented a coalition of "outs" against the rule of the middle class. He lost the support of the Jews, who are conscientious voters, because he stood for what might have been interpreted as a challenge to the foundations of the industrial state and to its foreign policy. Although urban blacks are interested in concrete goals involving jobs, housing and education, they tend to be more ideologically motivated than whites.[320] They have a sense of black communality, which is associated with freedom and democracy and which could appeal to other disfavored citizens. But the industrial operation would have to slow down and produce more poor people for a black-led rainbow party really to take hold.

The emergence of a large, concentrated class of black and brown urban poor represents another threat to middle-class rule. "The building up of a mess of unemployed and frustrated Negro youth in congested areas of a city"[321] poses a problem to the smooth working of a state.

Not only would economic discontent hasten revolt, as Killian argues, but the menace of black rioting or uprising would also frighten the white community. Killian contends that black power concentrates on the "needs of the hard core of unassimilable Negroes."[322] In fact, the poor young black is inherently a potential black nationalist—if his sensibilities have not been deadened by incarceration or drugs.

Since blacks who are unassimilable are by definition thrust out of the system, they cannot hope for sufficient gains to reduce their dissatisfaction and their propensity to cause conflict. And since, historically and culturally, discontent is linked to race, blacks would be the ideological vanguard in any revolutionary challenge to white middle-class rule. Their tendency to violence could, of course, be harnessed to activist discipline, if they were given inspired leadership. On a political level, the outclass could be the incarnation of the internal logic—the principle of negation—of the dialectical process that to Herbert Marcuse represents historical truth.[323] By a social organization based on their substatus and by their growing numbers, black Americans who do not constitute a consistent political group still have a significant force: "They are the internal truth of the system, its principle of negation. . . ."[324] However, no one knows where blacks will go or whether they can obtain their ends by ballots or bullets, as Malcolm X put it. Nevertheless, the black revolution is not over, and the movement of the sixties was its precursor not just in terms of the sacrifice suffered and the heroes produced, but of its ideological accomplishments. A former black freedom rider remarked ironically, "There was some value in having achieved these rights and yet to understand that there was no basic gain."[325] As the lawyer for Marcus Garvey realized, although "the Black Star Line was a loss in money . . . it was a gain in soul."[326] It is perhaps this quality that must be exploited.

PART III

WHITE CULTURAL STEREOTYPES

CHAPTER 8

WHITE MONOCULTURISM

A merica's blacks and whites are intimately related—not just by circumstance and the common cultural environment in which they have cohabited, but also by blood. Indeed a new race, or what Melville Herskovits called a "homogeneous group,"[1] has emerged in the person of the American black. As Langston Hughes wrote, "You are white—yet a part of me as I am part of you."[2] In effect, the black's world is that of all America, while it is also different because race has separated white and black and has pitted one against the other. Therefore, each has developed his own viewpoint with respect to the same historical situation.

White American culture stems from the European tradition. In the seventeenth and eighteenth centuries, Americans who looked to the future and tried to break with their past wanted to create a society that would be the fulfillment of humanity. Their art was implicitly political. But with the establishment of the industrial state—which is an end in itself—Americans no longer devoted themselves to the historical project of redeeming mankind. Art became escapist and internalized; art for art's sake characterized the twentieth-century aesthetic from T. S. Eliot to John Barth and artists themselves, alienated subjects of a self-sufficient order, seemed content to use their vocation for their own interests.

Since European culture was grounded on the ideal that humanity had to fight against nature in order to survive, the industrial state represented the magnificent triumph of man by his mastery of natural adversaries—such as famine, flood, drought. The goal of material security and comfort seemed to have been attained in this industrial process. The philosophies of the modern era, which provided a framework for the cultural principles of industrialism, were those of Karl Marx and Sigmund Freud. Both philosophies are based on the original idea of

151

nature domination, both are deterministic and both use quantitative criteria or pragmatic results—through the concept of progress—to evaluate moral premises. In fact, both rationally justify industrial culture—Marx historically and Freud biologically. The materialistic theology of Marx parallels the psychological fatalism of Freud.

To Marx, capitalistic civilization (which is an advanced expression of nature domination) is a good in itself because it is a necessary step to human fulfillment. Man is governed by historical forces that will use him and sacrifice him and eventually redeem him on their way to their own inevitable self-realization. Marxism exists to perpetuate itself as form, regardless of content. To Freud, capitalistic civilization is built on sublimation, the perversion of Eros. The natural, instinctual love of life has, in western society, been repressed and converted to psychically destructive, but culturally constructive, power.[3] The monism of heterosexual monogamy, which has been transformed into the antithesis of love or the monism of death, has turned reality into an antagonistic condition to be conquered. Humans have borrowed the energy of the libido to wage war.[4] But every victory presented them with a more oppressive reality to overcome and the need for better and more technologically perfected tools in order to do so. They are caught in seemingly endless materialistic imperialism.

Industrial civilization has, therefore, evolved as a rationally organized process of domination, which operated on the basis of capitalistic exigencies of profit and gain. Indeed, capitalism made possible the development of industrial culture: to dominate the materials of nature necessarily entailed the domination of other peoples and things. Freud's theory of the superego provided him with an overall context within which the practical function of the system could be explained. It was not Eros, the expansive desire for life, that held civilization together. It was guilt, the need for self-confirmation that endlessly sought authority. As Eros lost in power, science and technology served methodologically not just to validate the system as a good in itself, but also to demystify the hopes and illusions that were inherent in human beings' quest for meaning. The creative urge was masked in artificial gratifications involving the consummation of things; it was swallowed in a narcissism that denied Eros.

If instinctual repression was, as Freud claimed, the condition of western civilization, then this civilization exists as a rejection of natural potential. Indeed, the denial of Eros was progressive and was correlative with the passage of time, with which money making—the principle of capitalistic accumulation and the driving force of the capitalistic proc-ess—has been associated. Money, "the universal condensed precipitate of property,"[5] represents time; it is time captured and capsuled as a symbolic defense against the lapse of time—or death. Money stands for the long and successful struggle of mastering nature through the control of products derived from natural materials. It implies, consequently, the separation of the human creature from his vulnerable human body, his mortality.[6]

Birth and death, the life cycle of the body, are the life-imposed limits of the mortal being and exist outside the will. Yet because western civilization was built on the assumed necessity of mastering nature—including human nature—it sublimated birth and death and tried to convert existence into a self-perpetuating process which feeds on itself, on the hypothesis that it is self-sufficient. Civilization attempted to turn itself into nature.[7] In the sense that life is said to resemble a death drive, related, like money, to the infantile anal complex,[8] life is based on the principle that outside nature is the other—the enemy. Man is doomed, therefore, to battle irreconcilably against himself, for it is his irrecon-cilable nature to die.

Freud was a pessimist who, unlike Marx, could not look for a so-lution to the sickness of civilization in a theory of history. His future was condemned by the past. Even if science and technology had enabled humans to transcend the struggle for survival, and nature domination no longer needed to be based on exploitation and alienated labor, which in the Marxist state are associated, people were still driven to repress their instincts. Or else—as in postindustrial society—they were encour-aged indiscriminately to give vent to all their impulses as long as their indulgences were controlled by consumer management. In any case, hu-man nature was on all levels pitted against itself. The minority of it that resided in white western civilizations wasted raw materials and ruled; the non-occidental majority suffered and served.

Since industrial culture represented the successful process of nature domination—at least materially—it was based on the Cartesian sepa-ration of subject and object, of the thinking or acting self and the thought or the thing. Western civilization had always been characterized ontologically by its division of reality into spirit and matter. Its oppo-sitional methodology stemmed from Christianity and was accentuated by the Protestant Reformation, which led to the capitalist revolution. White Americans and Europeans are driven not only to despoil nature, their adversary, but also to pervert history in order to prove their assumed power over both. Judeo-Christianity, for instance, has translated history into eschatology. It looks at the world manichaeistically: its approach is absolutist, not historically relativist. The industrial system functions as an entity in itself: it pits itself against the universe—the otherness. The industrial operation stands for mind, technique, performance—indeed, dematerialized mind—or subject—which absorbs all things in the process of working on them, and thus pragmatically prevails over them by the right of might or of the success of its workings.

Although the industrial system is presumably an end in itself, it had to depend on the outside—the object, the material other—in order to work. In fact, since white civilization has been built on repression and alienation, it can never escape its need of the natural forces which it negates but from which negation it derived its necessary energy. In Freudian theory and Marxist practice, the white has enclosed himself in an intricate labyrinth of his own construction in which, as long as he prevails, he has imprisoned other human beings.

Inevitably, industrial culture has rationalized its rule over and degradation of those people whom it ideologically and economically utilized in order to treat its hegemony as a good in itself. It pretends to racial or religious superiority. In the process of industrial development, non-Europeans (particularly blacks in America, who were brought here to facilitate the colonization and material exploitation of the continent) have been turned pragmatically from serviceable tools into an unemployed labor surplus. They have been thrust outside the civilizational order in which might is associated with right, or material advantage with spiritual primacy. The poor in America, for instance, who are disproportionately black and who constitute the contemporary antithesis to the privileged, disproportionately white middle class, according to the prevailing ethic, are undeserving and reprehensible.

Industrial culture is monoculture, as Ishmael Reed puts it.[9] Despite its much-publicized reputation, America is not a pluralistic society composed of an assortment of nationalities and collectivities. It is made up of a large middle-class majority and a small, but significant, minority. Indeed, middle-class hegemony, on which the health of the industrial state depends, has absorbed the aliens who, during earlier stages of capitalism, provided a necessary labor force. The Anglo-Saxon has lost his preeminence: immigrants, who contribute to the industrial operation as both producers and consumers, have turned into the backbone of the middle class. More than half the adult population no longer has "a meaningful . . . ethnic sentiment," writes a sociologist;[10] the national-

istic aspect of ethnicity "rarely survives the third generation," concur
Nathan Glazer and Daniel Patrick Moynihan.[11] Only the Jew remains
to claim special ethnic identity—which he associates both with his religion and with the cause of the State of Israel. Still, he, too, is more
American middle class than Jewish: if he was not relevant to American
culture in the days of "white, red and black," as critic Leslie Fiedler
observes,[12] he now stands high among the elite of the industrial order.

In joining the American middle class—necessarily by the renuncia-
tion of their own historical background—immigrants have embraced
and reinforced the standards of industrial culture. In the process of
modifying the values of Anglo-Saxon nativism (rejection of immigration), immigrants have adopted its chief biases: they have succeeded not
simply in rejecting but in reframing otherness in economic terms.
Whereas once "religion and race seem[ed] to define the major
groups,"[13] now—with the decline of religion and ethnicity—economic
status and race, which are historically and pragmatically related, are
the significant criteria for middle-class membership. "Isn't there a joke
about the immigrant who was in the country and after forty years could
only speak one word of English, 'nigger,' " asks Smart-Grosvznor.[14]
Racism, as Albert Einstein pointed out, is and always has been intentional, even ideological: it "is the result of the desire to maintain [the
Negro's] unworthy condition,"[15] and by contrast the worthiness of the
white. Contemporary social repression of the black poor is, in Freudian
terms, a projection of whites' own instinctual inhibition; blacks' material degradation is a substitute for and a projection against a Marxist
division of classes that would be a threat to middle-class solidarity. As
long as this social majority comprises a vast number of relatively advantaged Americans, the poor remain impotent. Economic rationality,
which is based on quantitative measures of productivity, abundance and
consumption, draws its confirmation from its stultification of cultural
pluralism, individualism and diversity.

Since culture is a statement of the situation of particular groups of
human beings in a specific period of history, it is by nature relativistic
and pluralistic. However, black and white cultures are syntheses of different attitudes, traditions and conventions within the same political
and social environment. Among the privileged strategic elites of the industrial order is the intellectual class whose members consist of white—
and some black—writers, scientists, critics and academics, and which
is traditionally supposed to set the cultural tone. Actually, modern art
as a whole, innovative as it sometimes pretends to be, reflects the po-

litical and philosophical sterility of industrial culture. Writers, for instance, are said to have shown a surprising "aridity"[16] since the Second World War. As Gore Vidal suggests, it is probably because of America's superpower status, its "world empire,"[17] that they are taken seriously—if, in fact, they are.

Traditionally, American writers have been accused of lacking originality and character. They have never really been able to emancipate themselves from the European tradition, no matter how much they tried to produce their own redemptive culture of universal man. Geographical rootlessness, status divisions, ethnic immigration and the anti-intellectualism that went with so-called democracy denied them a cultural center. They had neither a "long and solid cultural tradition" nor a "stable [and] homogeneous public."[18] And they all complained: American authors from T. S. Eliot to Thomas Pynchon have in common their distrust of—if not distaste for—their cultural environment.

Modern industrialized media culture has actually popularized art. Americans have no leisure class, which writers like Henry James and Henry Adams considered necessary for the development of a literary tradition. Professor and critic Richard Chase blamed intellectuals for not exploiting American materials, such as the heritage of both Puritanism and the frontier.[19] These subjects do involve the confrontation between self and otherness that has preoccupied the American mind. Puritanism posits a conflict between good and evil; the frontier, between man and nature. But as Roland Barthes has remarked of any self-styled universalist culture—in his case that of the petite bourgeoisie—"one of [its] constant features . . . is this impotence to imagine the Other."[20] The fact is that as American white culture evolved into an industrial world, it became more and more self-centered—megalomaniacal to Vidal[21]—if not evasionist. This tendency is particularly evident in its relation to black culture.

CHAPTER 9

THE STEREOTYPE OF THE BLACK BEAST

Although whites and blacks have inhabited the same territory for hundreds of years, although both groups have evolved their own styles of living—or culture—blacks are conspicuously absent or misrepresented in white literature, an oversight that could only be intentional. The black is ignored or distorted as a person. He is "more of a formula than a human being."[1] Critic Sterling Brown, for instance, counted seven Negro stereotypes that whites used in their writings. These were the contented slave, the wretched freedman, the comic darky, the brute black, the tragic mulatto, the local-color clown and the exotic primitive. It might be simpler to reduce these to three generic categories: the first would combine the brute and the exotic primitive in a classification that Brown called the "nigger,"[2] who, presumably, is the antithesis of the civilized white. The contented slave, the comic darky and the local-color Negro represent the second category, in which the black is also inferior to the white. The wretched freedman and the tragic mulatto come together in the third category, in Brown's "colored man,"[3] who is implicitly the white's antagonist. In all cases the black plays a role subordinate to the white.

The archetypical stereotype is the brute, through which the black is the manichaeistic antithesis of civilized whiteness. Indeed, he represents otherness in the process by which whites divided reality into good and evil, or spirit and matter, and sought to affirm themselves by mastering nature. The brute stood for unregenerate, non-Christian, non-European man. He incarnated the wilderness, the libidinous chaos of nature in its rawest and most hideous state. He came from the savage jungle and embodied not intelligent but malicious treachery, as had the decadent European whom the Protestant American associated with the hypocritical, Machiavellian Papist, but the evil of unredeemed darkness itself as Thomas Wolfe poeticized.[4,5] The black was barbarous, wild[6] and violent like a beast, and it was the white man's "duty" to "the white race"— or to higher civilization—to "take the gage of battle"[7] and to tame him.

Such a stereotype, which associates the black with animal nature, denies him human status. In using their civilization and their God as the criteria of human identity, whites hypothesized that there was a qualitative difference between white and black people. Marx might have argued that this assumption was a means of justifying whites' economic exploitation of nonwhites—as it certainly is. Freud might have considered whites' insistence on their civilization's supremacy as an attempt to sublimate the guilt of their imperfect suppression of libido. In any case, in negating the black, the white denied his own nature, which included dark and light gods, love and death,[8] Dionysius and Apollo, "unorganized, irrational forces of American life"[9] as well as reason. In effect, the white distorted reality because he distrusted it; he confused sin and joy, guilt and Eros.[10]

The stereotype of the black was, therefore, an antidote to the fears and fantasies of white people's cultural subconscious. "We . . . re-invest the black face with our guilt . . ." wrote James Baldwin.[11] "Responsibility rests upon recognition and recognition is a form of agreement," says Ralph Ellison.[12] One can face in others only what one can face in oneself and, therefore, in creating otherness out of what one rejects in oneself,[13] one is able to simulate self-purification. The symbolic mask of color by which the white has veiled the black's personality and reduced it to an abstract formula is a sublimation—perhaps like the edifice of American civilization—of what the white represses. As the white presumably subdues his own nature, however, he also subjects himself to it. He has turned it into Marxist alienated work or Freudian inhibition, both of which are products of the industrial age as well as sequels to the Christian doctrine of original sin. In this process of profiting from something, one proves oneself superior to it and rids oneself—superficially—of one's natural anxieties.

In construing the fable of the Negroes' difference, whites were expressing their subconscious fear that blacks were the same as they were. Whites were afraid that they were not special creatures among men. In hiding behind symbolic masks from what blacks represented to them, in inventing the stereotype of the black brute, whites were covering their dread of nonidentity, their self-doubt. As a character of Richard Wright's sentimentalizes, white hatred of blacks is the perverted expression of whites' need—even love—for them.[14]

From colonial days, religion prohibited and law banned intermarriage. This was the most important and most historic American civilizational taboo; it overshadowed those of witchcraft and incest—and entrenched the dogma that blacks were an inferior species. Whites decreed that only similar types could mate felicitously: a crossover might breed monsters. Abraham's posterity must keep to itself: it "may not marry nor give in marriage to the heathen,"[15] preached a churchman in 1609. "Religious racists . . . were monogenists."[16] The state of grace, of special election, was connected intimately with racism. And naturally the rationale that whites were different from blacks[17] was a means of justifying slavery. If the black was subhuman, then it was perfectly permissible to work him like an animal.[18] Race, religion and economic expedience were associated pragmatically in the development of American civilization.

Implicit in the concern over intermarriage is the link between race and sex. The emotional complex of fear, hate and doubt that underlies white attitudes toward blacks seems to vindicate Freud in the sense that racism would seem to have a sexual basis. As many blacks have pointed out, the ties are intimate. "The race situation will continue to be acute as long as the sex factor persists . . ." wrote James Weldon Johnson.[19] The stereotype of the black brute has engendered fantasies not only of the overendowed properties of the Negro male and female but also of their gross performances. It was—and still is—commonly believed that the black had "larger . . . sexual organs,"[20] as a psychologist recorded; the black was looked on as "an inexhaustible sex-machine with oversized genitals and a vast store of experience";[21] and the race problem was "inextricably connected with sex."[22] Moreover, the black was demeaned as an incompetent lover: blacks were portrayed "as hurried, inattentive . . . animalistic sexual brutes."[23] Their wild, unrestrained passion, their "always controlling force,"[24] was presumably for the white woman. As Ishmael Reed observes, "Everybody knew that all black men did was rape white women";[25] or, as Langston Hughes poeticized, ". . . a tall white woman / In an ermine cape / Looked at the black and / Thought of rape."[26] The black "lurks in the back of the popular mind always as the rapist."[27] His image is a projection of the white man's dark instincts that he can neither completely suppress nor rationalize.

In a Freudian sense sexual repression is necessary for the construction and perpetuation of civilization, which exploits the energy of Eros for its own ends. Since control of the id is related dialectically to the creation of the American system, sexual attitudes have a political and economic implication. They are linked to the profit motive and the power complex on which the industrial state is based. The stress on objects—on material gratification—is a compensation for the inhibition of instinct. Perhaps for this reason the recent sexual revolution—a reaction to repression—was taken over by the popular culture of the media and connected not just quantitatively with orgasmic performance, but also vicariously with the display of pornographic things[28]—as Marcuse points out—for the suppression of instinct is closely linked to economic operations. Sex projects its significance through objective criteria in the industrial state.

"The racism of sex . . . is but another aspect of the inequal political and economic relations" between black and white—as psychologist Calvin Hernton observes. If racism was to disappear, "the nature of the American politico-economic system [would] change."[29] The racism of sex reaches deep into the roots of industrial culture. White Americans' traditional anxieties and obsessions with respect to sex have been projected into their image of the black man. The idea that he stood for forbidden pleasures was a temptation as well as a prospective danger. On the one hand, whites could be titillated by the imagination of the black's overwhelming sexuality; on the other, they would place the black definitively out of bounds by magnifying the terrors that he represented. Whites are thus bound to him by "bonds of guilt older than [their] national identity itself."[30]

Erotic desire implies an irresistible yearning to succumb to natural impulses. If desire is inhibited, it turns in toward itself: it can express itself in a kind of apotheosized death wish, the narcissistic transformation of Eros into Nirvana. But desire can also be projected—often by necessity—onto the will to dominate nature. And since occidental civilization—the condition of whites' survival and the testimony to their accomplishment—subsists by stopping up and sublimating life's love impulse, it has evolved through a constant struggle between ego and id—between the drive for productivity and the desire for release. In effect, civilization is built upon the sexual distortions that came from this self-engendered but historically perpetuated battle. The Negro has been essential to the construction of whites' civilization. Whites' obsession with the black's sexuality[31] and their frenetic efforts to dam it— or in the case of many white females and sexual rebels, to let it flow— are means by which whites project their own internal conflict, which feeds on itself, onto the exploited black.[32] Using his stereotype, they have rewoven—even patterned—the intricate design of their subjective complexes from which stemmed their motivation to build their industrial structure—an assumed good in itself.

The white man has, therefore, perpetuated the myth of black brutishness in order to hide from his own morbid sexual urges.[33] He even used this myth to justify his own acts of rape. The white needed the Negro to hate, to love, to violate, to "keep from overtly hating, blaming and fearing himself."[34] Southerners—and often northerners—lynched blacks and castrated them almost always for presumed sexual crimes. Mob action is the expression of sexual fear[35] as violence is a form of sexual sadism.

The myth of the Negro is a necessary feature of American civilization; it is a "product of the American experience and of a crisis in the American mind."[36] Such a perversion seems to be inherent in a culture that derives its identity from its idealized will to prevail rather than from the relativistic interplay of historical experience, which invests all people with the quality of at least being human. Gunnar Myrdal wrote that a nation with a less emphatic democratic ethos would be able to uphold the caste system without an intense belief in sex and race dangers.[37] In effect, it is the oppression of a racial minority that permits the illusion of democracy to persist. The stereotype of the black brute symbolizes—in reverse—the historical process by which America climbed into ideological, as well as material, prominence. To the white, observes critic Leslie Fiedler, dark skins signify something ominous. The " 'Black Man' [is] a traditional name for the Devil himself."[38] The "savage colored man is postulated as the embodiment of villainy";[39] his natural barbarity had to be conquered for the good of mankind. By mastering him, whites convinced themselves that they were good. Even now a historian like Daniel Boorstin, the cultural homogenizer, justifies the white American's extermination of the red Indian. Boorstin dismisses "the idea of the Noble Savage" as a "bad joke"[40] for Americans who had been the target of his arrows and implies that he was an ignoble wildman who deserved to be massacred.

The domination of the black—or red—brute prefaces the triumph of the industrial state. Such a stereotype also reflects whites' fear of slave rebellion, a prospect that colored the attitudes of even humanitarian intellectuals. Herman Melville, for instance, who understood and condemned the corruption, even the sickness of western civilization, deplored the institution of slavery and was sympathetic to blacks. Nevertheless, he was too conditioned or too pessimistic to break out of his cultural bonds. Slave revolution would "jar our social systems," he warned.[41] Following the Puritan tradition, Melville concluded that the black, like all men in a state of nature—or savagery—was in servitude to sin and evil. In his ambiguous story "Benito Cereno," the misguided democrat Delano, who has faith in all men including Negroes, is undeceived by the European Cereno, and shocked by the brutality of the black slave Babo's revolt.

Perhaps Melville was, as Walt Whitman confessed himself to be, "tainted . . . just a little bit, with the New York feeling with regard to anti-slavery."[42] For Whitman, despite or because of his egalitarian pretensions, associated the Negro with the felon and other asocial types. The democratic principle of all America was tainted, as Mark Twain, who was himself ambivalent with respect to attitudes toward the black, observed. His Tom, the Negro son of Roxy in *The Tragedy of Pudd'nhead Wilson,* turned out to be the bad character, although he had been brought up as a white. And the stereotype of the inherently evil black brute was passed down in American literature to be fit into the fashions of the day. Every white would "project out . . . his own conception of the Negro."[43]

Southern writers, who knew the black best, reduced him to an abstraction. The myth of the bad black served to condone the racism on which society was based. Every Negro was an uncivilized threat to social order and harmony—when, in fact, social order and harmony depended on the Negro's presence. Although writer Ellen Glasgow was proud of her upper-class background—which presumably conditioned her to feel a sort of paternalistic sympathy toward Negroes—she still considered them "immature"[44] and hedonistic.[45] Her novels were concerned mainly with "the conflict between an individual's lower and higher nature"[46] and she strongly opposed the chaotic primitivism in which blacks rejoiced and which led to social disorder. Like the later agrarians (defenders of the southern way of life against northern industrialism), she sacrificed the freedom of the white and the autonomy of the black to her idea of civilization.

William Faulkner also portrayed the black as a potential brute and, therefore, as a threat to the white social order. Joe Christmas in *Light in August,* who—in principle—incarnated the good-bad Negro, was turned into a Christ figure only by his assassination, when he was no longer a danger to his white pursuers. Alive, however, he represented the black barbarian rapist—pure desire and fulfillment, swept out of the jungle, where death, like that of animals, occurs brutally and indifferently, into the midst of white society. Christmas reflected the utter indistinction of immanence: he was a nonexistent abstraction that Faulkner exploited to put across his theme. Critics, including Jean-Paul Sartre, have commented on Faulkner's taste for artistry, which disregards the reality of personality. He reversed the Sartrian conception of the for-self (*pour-soi*)[47] in order to "replace intuition of the future."[48] Likewise, Faulkner converted Nancy, his black dope fiend and prostitute—an unlikely nurse for Temple Drake's baby—into a sacrificial murderer and saint. In the process he deprived both Joe Christmas and Nancy of character and of humanity. They were there to serve Faulkner's purposes, which involved the salvation of whites. He did not truly believe that blacks were qualified to participate equally in white society. "Perhaps the Negro is not yet capable of more than second class citizenship," he admitted.[49]

The agrarians also were white supremacists and followed the southern tradition in reacting to Negroes either paternalistically or in fear of what historian Richard King calls the black beast.[50] For this reason, probably, they advocated a white hegemony. To agrarian Howard Odum, for instance, the black was different "not only in development but also in kind."[51] It was in the name of southern, presumably higher, civilization that the agrarians were apologists for the institution of slavery as well as for segregation and racism. These were the conditions of southern historical culture, which alone stood against the materialistic rootlessness of the North where "damned souls" ran "the way of sand / Into the destruction of the wind," as poet Allen Tate put it.[52] Since the agrarians tried to replay, not alter, the past, they refused to question the racial status quo, which alone assured the stability of the white order. Therefore, they were responsible, as Sterling Brown remarked, for "some of the most reactionary of modern comments on the Southern Negro."[53]

John Crowe Ransom, the aesthete, leader of the school of new criticism, defended slavery as practically humane.[54] Agrarians[55] Donald Davidson,[56] Stark Young[57] and Frank Owsley[58] were outright racists. Owsley claimed that Negroes had been kept in bondage because they were barbarians.[59] Robert Penn Warren treated his black characters as if they had no place in civilization. His black man Mose, for instance, was outside history. When Thomas Jefferson's nephew axed the slave John in *Brother to Dragons,* Warren was sacrificing him to his own view of reality. John, in effect, had no individuality and no personality:

he was an absence who represented the nephew's "darkest self." He was simply a slave on whom the white was able to vent his frustration; he was the "possibility of dark [that the assassin] feared."[60] And so Warren turned him into the white's "essential accomplice, provocateur." By the simple fact of his existence, John incited his master to hack him to pieces. As Warren concluded, it was the nephew who was "the real victim"; it was his "hand [that] was . . . elected to give the stroke."[61]

Allen Tate also refused to admit barbarian Negroes into the cathedral of historical southern civilization. The North, which he associated with black Republicans, had contempt for the past when it propagandized the notion of Negro rights. With northerners' "short memory" they turned honor into "a common entity."[62] Tate considered blacks qualitatively inferior to whites; they were lesser creatures. As lynching was the archetypal sacrifice to higher culture, so Tate's lynched Negro was not a person strung up by a mob: he was an abstraction. He was "owned by all the town" but "never claimed":[63] he was evidence of its transgression.

Tate, who confessed he once told "a stinking lie / that got a black boy whipped,"[64] did not take into account the pain of the unjustly beaten Negro. The Negro was a means: through him Tate atoned for his sin by repenting and in the process, presumably, by becoming more civilized. "Dignity's the stain / Of mortal sin that knows humility," he later philosophized.[65]

The black served to contribute to the moral development of the white. Agrarianism, for all its pretensions, lacked conviction as a cultural antidote to the excesses of industrialism precisely because its spokesmen capitalized on the image of the blacks as lesser human beings in order to bolster their own self-made myth. They were narcissists who enclosed themselves in a labyrinth in which dream was reality and reality dream—or, as Warren put it, *"the dream is a lie, but the dreaming is truth."*[66] By the 1950s, says a critic, "agrarianism and racism as concepts of Southern identity and vindicated reconciliation had failed . . . . Both . . . especially . . . race . . . paralyzed the South."[67]

Nevertheless, the stereotype of the black persists in southern literature in one form or another. Erskine Caldwell and Eudora Welty, both sympathetic to black people, thought of them as more or less primitive creatures.[68] Welty pictured blacks as having a "physical and spiritual intimacy with the land . . . and with the lower animals."[69] Flannery O'Connor pragmatically accepted segregation—the assignment of

blacks to lower status and whites to higher status in the social order—
because it existed in fact in the lack of communication between the
races. She was perfectly aware of the resentment, if not outright distaste,
that blacks felt for whites; she understood that whites resorted to stereotypes in their dealings with those whom they exploited: that even—
or particularly—liberals disregarded the humanity of Negroes whose
cause they pretended to defend.[70] Both races were at fault: neither
would meet the other. Whereas the white do-gooder was mired in sentimentalism, blacks either cooperated sullenly with the prescribed
rules[71] or took refuge, like James Baldwin, in clamorous, artificial rebellion against the tradition of the church and social order.[72] It was this
order that O'Connor, ardent Christian, upheld against all signs of anti-
Christianism. Whatever prevailed was right.

But it was William Styron who has most exploited the stereotype
of the black. As he admitted, "Most Southern white people *cannot*
know or touch black people . . . because of the deadly intimation of a
universal law."[73] Perhaps his insensitivity to them was the result of his
lack of contact with them. So he fell back on the myths which were
already encrusted in the southern tradition and which were linked to
the idea of black barbarism, black violence and black revolt. In the
background of *Lie Down in Darkness,* for instance, there hovers the
image of a drowned Negro "covered with scum and slobbering . . . at
the mouth . . . in search of beautiful white women to ravish and to drag
back to the unspeakable depths of his grave."[74] In contrast, Peyton, the
beautiful white heroine, flies like a heavenly spirit to her own death.

Worse, in his fictive biography of Nat Turner, Styron transformed
a historical figure, a militant black evangelist, into a sexual pervert.
Styron's Nat is driven by his obsessive attraction to whites—particularly
beautiful white girls "with golden curls"[75] who arouse his sudden barbarous "rage and confusion"[76] and, of course, lust. This Nat wants to
be white: "How white I was! What wicked joy!"[77] he exclaims as he
pisses like a male cat in a symbolic act of property and female appro-
priation.

There is no reason for Nat's wild rampage other than his imagined
fixation on whites. He is a slave, but his master is sympathetic and
tolerant. It is because of the slaver's "innocence and destiny"[78] that Nat
is inspired to revolt. Styron also discredits the real Nat's historically
recorded sense of religious mission, which is incomprehensible to the
rationalistic author. So he makes Nat set out on a gratuitous campaign,
which he baptizes with a homosexual orgasm,[79] to slaughter whites who

have been kind to him. Inevitably, Turner fails; white rule prevails. But
he blames his defeat on *"ass-sucking niggers"*[80] who are comfortable
only when they are under strict supervision and who are inclined to
turn against their own leaders. Imprisoned like a devil, Nat consecrates
his bloody assault by a narcissistic wet dream in which he pours out
his love to his fleshless ideal of white womanhood.[81] In Styron's hands,
a historical antislavery rebel is converted into the abstract incarnation
of evil—"part homosexual, part white man, hater of Blacks and admirer
of whites . . . a revolutionary without a cause." He is "the product of
a white man [afraid] to confront history."[82] Styron, says another critic,
looks at blacks "like animals."[83]

Such stereotypes are, as historian F. G. Davenport points out, unfortunately "within the tradition of historically oriented Southern literature."[84] In fact, they are an essential component of that tradition.
The white man could not pretend to be civilized if he did not entrench
the myth that blacks were savages. But these myths are common in the
writings of northern intellectuals, who draw on the southern example
for their own ends. The generation of the 1920s, apolitical, alienated
and self-centered, seemed to ignore the presence of the black in American society. Intellectuals tended to depersonalize the Negro whenever
they did include him in their cast of characters. They portrayed African
Americans as "robots who react only to immediate stimuli"—like Pav-
lov's dogs—or as outcast incompetents who "do not follow our mores
on one point and therefore cannot claim . . . benefits at any other."[85]
Langston Hughes's Simple complained that there was never any mention of blacks even in the newspapers except when they committed asocial acts like murder, robbery or rape.[86]

Sinclair Lewis took a positive stance against racism, but he was a
liberal paternalist who exploited the stereotype of Negroes as violent
and oversexed.[87] Actually, this myth provided writers with a rationalization for their own indifference to blacks. They could use it to justify their racial irresponsibility and to avoid the historical implications
of American culture. John Dos Passos was able to eliminate the Negro from his panoramic *U.S.A.*, just as John Steinbeck cut him out of
Depression-ridden America. Willa Cather wrote *Sapphira and the
Slave Girl*, a book against slavery, which seemed almost to be an
apology for it. Top, the bad Negro, finally had to be hanged by a
modern jury.[88]

Ernest Hemingway pushed the black underground in his artistic
consciousness to the point that he hardly even mentioned him. Never-

theless, Hemingway at least nurtured an image of black pugnacity: in one of his recurrent fits of bravado, he offered money to any Negro who could last three rounds in the boxing ring with him.[89] He pictured the black as a sniveling coward,[90] but Hemingway lacked moral imagination: his world, like his art, was artificially limited. F. Scott Fitzgerald, the striver, the prey of conventional opinions, was against African American rights, African American liberty and African Americans in general.[91] He, who was able to recognize both the promise and the corruption of capitalistic culture, dismissed the black entirely from its processes. Whereas his anti-Semitism allowed him to portray new rich opportunism and moral vulgarity, he ignored the role of the black in the rise of the industrial state. Of course, he tried to evade the issue: as a middle westerner, he protested, he was not a racist. And yet, oddly enough—perhaps intuitively—he seemed to have a premonition of what he appeared to have considered an eventual black upsurge. As *The Great Gatsby* was intrinsically a kind of "recognition of cultural defeat," so it contained a reference to a potential black takeover, which was introduced by Tom, the white supremacist.[92] Fitzgerald, who picked up and discarded ideas with unthinking facility, might have borrowed the notion from German philosopher Oswald Spengler or from various racist writers of the 1920s, including Joseph Hergesheimer and Lothrop Stoddard. But the mere suggestion of a black uprising adds a new dimension to Fitzgerald's work. He understood, even obliquely, that the black stereotype had a double meaning in the white sensibility. It was not just a means of black oppression; it was a projection of white fear. It was implicitly the admission that blacks were, in fact, human beings. It was the dialectical expression of the white's dread that he was not special.

The corollary to the stereotype of the bad black beast was that of the primitive exotic. This abstraction portrayed him as the good barbarian: he was Melville's Dagoo, close to nature but perhaps wiser than civilized man. Emancipated white liberals modernized the image of the Negro brute by transforming it into that of the noble savage. The concept was the white version of Alain Locke's "New Negro." Poet Vachel Lindsay, for instance, made the black the subject of a "cult of the primitive,"[93] which became a fashion during the 1920s and drew eager young white explorers to Harlem to stare at African Americans, as Langston Hughes said, "like amusing animals in a zoo."[94] At that time intellectuals—from surrealist poets to painters—were interested in Africa: Lindsay himself imagined blacks as "wild crap-shooters with a whoop and a call." They inspired his vision of *"THE CONGO CREEPING THROUGH THE BLACK,"*[95] the natural habitat of the hoodoo god, Mumbo-Jumbo.

Eugene O'Neill also took part in the cult of Negro primitivism.[96] The black, by his affinity to nature, did not inhibit his libido: he expressed himself by joyously singing, dancing and making love. To Ben Hecht, Negro music was Dionysian.[97] Gertrude Stein, although implicitly a racist,[98] was intrigued by the use of an all-black cast in the first production of the opera *Four Saints in Three Acts,* for which she had written the libretto and Virgil Thomson the music. However, Stein objected that their bodies created an effect that was "too much what modernistic writers refer to as 'futuristic.' "[99] The opera, she explained, was about saints who "did nothing and that was everything."[100] And yet, in a sense, the theme fit in with her idea of blacks who, except for their futuristic skins, might have been perfect for their roles because, she believed, in general their race suffered less from oppression than from nothingness. She was entirely occidental by disposition as well as by heritage and she considered African culture "very narrow," albeit "very ancient," even archaic. "Consequently nothing does or can happen."[101] Indeed, in Stein's linguistic experiment *Melanctha,* she used blacks as vehicles of immediate sensation and thus exploited their image as promiscuous and simplistic hedonists.

Of all white writers of the period, Stein's friend Carl Van Vechten was most known for his benevolence to and patronage of black art. He was sincere and loyal to his friends—including Langston Hughes, in particular. Like most of the uptown slummers of the day, however, he was caught up in what Ishmael Reed called a "monocultural attitude"[102] and was insensitive to the significance of the New Negro movement— as were many blacks themselves. Van Vechten was drawn to the exotic and the glamorous: he had a tendency to seek "chi chi publicity"[103] for blacks, as liberals of the 1960s promoted radical chic; he made a fetish out of the cult of blackness in his exploitation of the Negro Renaissance Man. Perhaps he was like poet Countee Cullen's white man who was asked by his hostess if his trips to Harlem had "an ulterior motive," if he came to look "upon us as some strange concoction which [he was] out to analyze and betray."[104] In *Mumbo Jumbo,* Reed satirizes him as Hinckle Von Vampton, the Atonist traitor of Jes Grew.[105]

Van Vechten was the leader of what Zora Neale Hurston called the "Negrotarians,"[106] the white patrons of black life and art. His novel to which he gave the controversial title *Nigger Heaven* has been criticized as the work of an unconscious white supremacist.[107] In fact, it is paternalistic as well as simplistic in its portrayal of sexually emotive naïve Negroes with "warm and passionately earnest" blood, a penchant for "exotic" low life and a tendency to spontaneous, childlike violence.[108] The book "gives the facts but . . . does not tell the truth," says writer Benjamin Brawley.[109] Van Vechten was attacked also by erstwhile friends whom, seemingly, he had betrayed. He was accused of "ruining, distorting, polluting, and corrupting"[110] Negro writers. And he did behave as if—in the spirit of the dilettante—he was taking up a fad that he would drop as soon as it went out of style. As he told H. L. Mencken, Negro jazz, blues and spirituals "stimulate me enormously for the moment. . . . Doubtless, I shall discard them too in time."[111]

Writer Alice Dunbar-Nelson made fun of middle-aged Jews who went slumming in Harlem, saying, "My what a wicked thrill I am getting. . . ."[112] Most of the New Negro exoticism seekers who visited Harlem were trying to gratify their own impulses for flapper unconventionality and vicarious sexual indulgence. They were looking for kicks and they were encouraged by blacks who needed patrons. When these whites went to nightclubs from which, more often than not, blacks were excluded, they felt culturally and materially superior—for the two went together—as if the so-called low life confirmed their image of what whites took for granted to be the high. Mabel Dodge, patroness of the arts, connoisseur of the avant-garde and friend of Van Vechten, could not seriously support a cultural movement led by Negro intellectuals:[113] her primitivism went no further than D. H. Lawrence and her husband, the Indian Tony Luhan. Virtuously she blamed the black race for being, in part, "rotted before it is ripe."[114] As whites pulled out of the Negro art movement, the New Negro himself became a stereotype.[115] He played at his role of "exotic primitive"[116] and "unfettered child."[117]

The cult of the primitive still enjoys a vogue: it is part of the liberal ethos. Of modern writers, Truman Capote's blacks are perhaps the most innocuous as they exist alongside whites in his world of innocent eccentricity. In fact, they hardly exist: they are art forms, like most of the creatures of Capote's imagination. They are simply fays in brown skins, a color that lends an extra air of exoticism. Capote's Zoo, the prancing Negroes who have been strumming on guitars since before birth in *Other Voices, Other Rooms*,[118] and Catherine Creek in *The Grass Harp*, part black and part Indian, "dark as the angels of Africa,"[119] are not real. They reflect what John Aldridge has called the "isolation of a mind which life has never really violated, in which the image of art has developed alone."[120] And the later Capote, disillusioned by his experiences with the social, literary and media-promoted stardom, identified with outcasts for whom Father Flanagan's Nigger Queen Kosher Café—in *Answered Prayers*—was to be the refuge.[121]

The American intellectual consciousness seems indelibly marked by the myth of the black if not as brute at least as exotic primitive. In both cases he is supposed to have pronounced sexual inclinations as well as capacities. To writer Norman Podhoretz, blacks, who appeared to be "free, independent, reckless, brave, masculine, erotic," were the neighborhood toughs, the "bad boys"[122] who beat on him. In *On the Road*, Jack Kerouac tried to imitate what he imagined to be their wild, animalistic life-style: blacks existed in the moment in a sensual heaven that he wanted to duplicate.[123] Jerzy Kosinski, who for a while played the role of a white chauffeur in black Harlem, inflated the stereotype of black sexuality and black hip in *Pinball* as if he were trying to hustle the image of a hustler. And radical chic took up the cause of the "primitive, exotic, and romantic" Black Panthers in order—says Tom Wolfe—to distinguish itself from the dull middle class.[124]

But it is perhaps Norman Mailer who most of all exploits the myth of the low-living, uncivilized black man. He bases his stereotype on his idea of what he calls existentialism—which differs from that of Sartre with respect to its omission of the concept of *pour-soi*. Since the black had been denied the social and material opportunities of western civilization, he was an outcast who had nothing to lose: he was absolutely free to seek sensation and rebellion as ends in themselves. He was an uninhibited psychopath who existed by gratifying the immediate needs and pleasures not of the mind but of the body as represented in orgasm. Consequently, the black could not be a serious revolutionary. He was a mentally undeveloped marginal "who kept for his survival the art of the primitive."[125] His state of consciousness was one that "elaborated a morality of the bottom"[126] because his self-esteem depended on his perversion of civilizational values.

Quite inevitably, Mailer had to face the elegant, perhaps overly sensitive, James Baldwin, who vigorously objected to such a characterization of black manhood. In any case, said Baldwin of "the New Lost Generation," "there are no formulas for the improvement of the private, or any other life—certainly not the formula of more or better orgasms."[127] Mailer, however, was not to be deterred and proceeded to expand his theme. He complained, somewhat incomprehensibly, that Baldwin was "too charming" to be a major writer: he was unable even to say "Fuck you" to his readers. Mailer's blacks did not suffer from this defect.[128]

Mailer's insistence that blacks are dominated by an overactive sensuality has led him into an ambiguous position. He attributes to them mysterious "psychic powers"[129] resembling those of the witch doctors, powers by which blacks are inherently opposed to the cold and uncaring industrial civilization of diabolical Anglo-Saxons.[130] Black power moves "obviously against technological society,"[131] which represents the "triumph of the white man," Mailer argues.[132] Since this society is triumphant—since Mailer is attracted by success—he assigns the black to lower human status in the cultural order. "There is no need to assume that the black man will prove morally superior to the white man," he has decided.[133] Perhaps he resents the fact that he had no role in the moral and much-publicized black movement of the 1960s. He admits he was "getting tired of Negroes and their rights."[134]

Consequently, perhaps, Mailer's black characters are variations of the stereotype of the black brute. Shago Martin in *An American Dream* is a grotesque image of sensuality and evil.[135] D.J. in *Why Are We in Vietnam?* imitates Mailer's idea of blacks. He speaks in the offbeat idiom of a jive-ass hipster, and he has, it is remarked, been graced with "a dick like a Nigger." Indeed, he has an alter-ego, a "shade,"[136] a black counterpart whose "genius"[137] might be as malicious as his own. D.J., the white disc jockey, is "conditioned by the electronic manipulation of [his] senses"[138] from which he cannot free himself. "Ass-head America contemplate your butt,"[139] he signs off as he goes to Vietnam. It seems as if Mailer is following a "program to make sacrosanct negative images of the black men": he uses them maybe unconsciously as a metaphor for "the substratum of human existence."[140] And this vision of the Negro, which, as Baldwin protested, is as "impenetrable" as it is "antique," appears to be common to the American literary establishment.[141]

The stereotype has been used as much by Jewish intellectuals, who are particularly prevalent in the literary elite, as by Anglo-Saxons. Since Jewish culture is traditionally dualistic in its division of reality into spirit and matter—or mind and body—Jews tend to denigrate the body. In depicting blacks as primitive and instinctive, they have adopted existing attitudes of white supremacy—or black inferiority. European culture, of which they are a part, is associated with the brain; African, with the id.[142] In this way, Jews, as Nat Hentoff remarks, have a "colonial" attitude toward the Negro[143] while at the same time, as victims of Christian persecution, they have pretended to be his ally. From James Baldwin, who condemned the Jew "for having become an American white man,"[144] to Harold Cruse,[145] blacks accused Jews of treachery. As Ellison reproached Irving Howe, Jews have deprived the black of individuality by stereotyping him because they looked at him from the viewpoint of their own collective bias. Blackness seemed to represent a "metaphysical condition" to which all blacks were subjected and, consequently, by which they were all humanly distorted.[146] In suggesting that blackness was a quality distinct from universal whiteness, Howe implied that there were different orders of men, which could be ranked. He, the northern liberal, adopted a modernized version of narcissistic southern racism, which was based on the assumptions of immanence.

Jews have accepted without question the idea that blacks were prodigious in their sexual capacities. Writer Seymour Krim went to Harlem—braving its garbage, dirt and crime—to seek kicks among hip local Negroes, the natural antidote to confining middle-class morality.[147] Philip Roth comments on Saul Bellow's opposition of " 'sexual niggerhood' " to " 'ethical Jewhood,' "[148] and himself associates the black with sexual power and social impotence. The black in Roth's *The Great American Novel* is the lowest race on the social scale, whom Communists would insert into the great American game of baseball in order to subvert it.

Saul Bellow in particular has seemed incapable of viewing blacks as people in their own right. They stand on the threshold of the civilized versus the primitive mind, as well as of social law and reason versus the contemporary chaos of voluntarism. The black lacks a sense of discipline and organization; and so his energies, if profuse, are misdirected. He is the welfare cheater, the criminal, "worse than the animals"—as an Italian ethnic calls him in one of Bellow's short stories.[149] The black pickpocket of *Mr. Sammler's Planet* has a huge purple penis, which he proudly exhibits.[150] The black in *Herzog* is, typically, paternalized. The blacks in *The Dean's December* are either hucksters or conventionalized social workers who imitate the manners of the bourgeoisie. Indeed, Bellow writes about blacks as if he had to work in abstractions. It is the white moderate's compulsive devotion to "order" that blocks his racial understanding, observed Martin Luther King, Jr.[151] As Augie March, Bellow's Jewish marginal, remarks, "Personality is unsafe. . . . It's the types that are safe."[152]

Bernard Malamud was perhaps even more extreme in his moral Manichaeism. He divided reality into ethical categories that seemed *a priori* to degrade the black. As Philip Roth suggests, the Jew—as exemplified by both Malamud and Bellow—opposes the virtuous Jewish Jew to the libidinous Gentile whose sexual and aggressive impulses are most pronounced in the Negro. The primitive "voice of the id" is that of the goy—and especially that of the black.[153]

Malamud also made fun of the Jew who tries to patronize the black by befriending him "if not because he's black, then because I'm white. It comes to the same thing."[154] The black lady who is the object of this kind of beneficence, of course, kicks in the teeth of the do-gooder, thereby demonstrating that "even the gestures of good carry their own peril in the real world."[155] In effect, Malamud suggested that the safest procedure for a Jew in a Gentile-preempted society was to remain within his own circle. In one of his stories, Levine—a disincarnated Harlem black—is the guardian angel of Manishevitz, who subsequently marvels, "A wonderful thing . . . There are Jews everywhere."[156]

But it was in *The Tenants* that Malamud most passionately illustrated his idea of the metaphysical antagonism of body and mind—or of black and Jew. Willie is the Negro writer whose animal-like immersion in immediate experience leads him to denigrate tradition and discipline for sensory gratification. His book is, therefore, fated to irrelevance: it can transcend neither the condition of "color or culture" nor the cause of "protest or ideology."[157] It is not universal: Willie cannot express himself, so he invents a fictional character "who will . . . love for him: and . . . love him."[158] He is determined by his voluntaristic blackness: "My form is *myself*,"[159] he proclaims. He is caught in the depths of his "unspent rage"[160] and limited by his self-centered arrogance to hostility as an end in itself. He is pure immanence.

So he goes wild—like an animal; he gives himself up to undirected violence. He advocates an anti-Semitic revolution that will begin with "the First Pogrom in the U.S. of A."[161] He will not accept the Jew Lesser's forgiveness because "no Jew can treat me like a man."[162] The story proceeds to a melodramatic finish—which is one of three that Malamud proposed. In the first, fire was to destroy everybody; in the second, Jew and black were to be reconciled in universal—and unlikely—harmony. In the last, in a symbolic reversal of roles, the black cuts off the Jew's testicles while, simultaneously, the Jew hacks out the black's brains.[163,164] *The Tenants* is significant not because of its abstract and gratuitously exaggerated characterization of Willie and Lesser and its portrayal of their cultural clash, but because its interest lies in the excessive intensity of Malamud's emotion, which is that, as a critic observed, of "pure rage."[165]

CHAPTER 10

THE STEREOTYPE OF
THE CONTENTED SLAVE

The second white stereotype of the black was that of the contented slave.[1] It included the images of the comic and the local-color Negro as well as that of the kindly, usually elderly, practically always sexless, humble servant[2] who, although not intellectually advanced, is the source of folk wisdom. In all cases, he loves and admires white people. In the hands of modern liberals, he is the would-be integrated Negro who looks up to whites and strives hopefully to be accepted into the prevailing social order. He is the white man with black skin who is delighted to hear that he is white at heart.

In branding the black as an inferior being who had to labor to become part of higher civilization, American whites were able to justify their exploitation of him. They pretended that he was happy to work for his superiors, whom he instinctively recognized as such. In fact, employment under the direction of his betters purged the black of his animal impulses; the white man's order and discipline schooled him for a state of grace of which he otherwise would have been eternally deprived. This stereotype of the African American served, as John Calhoun interpreted it, to resolve the possible problem of class war. As capital brought about the alienation of labor, so it was inevitably the cause of potential revolution by which the bourgeois state might be overturned. But if the Negro—an outside and originally lower human being—could be harnessed like a domesticated beast to perform the necessarily menial jobs of producing workers—as Calhoun put it—he would prevent interclass hostility between whites. Under control, the black was no longer Sterling Brown's "nigger"; he was the good, amusing, affectionate Negro, spelled with an " 'upper case N,' "[3] who asked for nothing but the approval of his superiors. Thus appreciated, he was considered, wrote Brown, "as contented slave, entertaining child and docile ward, until misled by 'radical' agitators, when he became a dangerous beast."[4]

Of course this stereotype of the black was entirely false. Even Booker T. Washington, who subscribed to the capitalist ethic and strove indefatigably to accommodate to white rule, had, he admitted, never been a contented slave. He had not known anyone "who did not want to be free, or . . . would return to slavery."[5] To survive, blacks had come to terms with whites and many did show affection for their masters and bosses. And to the white, who was protected by class as well as by caste barriers, paternalistic affiliation with Negroes was a confirmation of the white's assumption of superior worth. Because Ellen Glasgow, for instance, was proud of her status as a gentlewoman, she sought Negroes for her childhood playmates and "was ashamed of association with 'poor whites' " who might have threatened her sense of high standing.[6] Saul Bellow's Herzog was called a "mensch" because he stood up for the unfortunate black Tomkins.[7] Styron's innocence with regard to slavery was based on the presumably amicable relations his grandparents had enjoyed with the bondwoman who served them.[8] "Slavery was . . . a completely human situation. . . . In many cases there was a deep love and affection on the part of slaves for masters," he said.[9] "One of the chief characteristics of Protestants' treatment of the Negro . . . was a disconcerting tendency to ignore race problems altogether."[10] And immigrants—such as Mark Sullivan—refused to imagine that the blacks they knew were discontented or maltreated: "if they . . . were underprivileged they did not know it, and no one told them."[11]

In order that the black remain their admiring inferior and servant, whites blocked his opportunities for advancement. From the period of colonization they either forbade the education of Negroes or decreed that those who could read and write were still incapable of reasoning. The idea prevailed that "education discontented the Negro with his proper place in white society";[12] he was supposed to be "peculiarly adapted to servitude."[13] Literacy was at the time of the European Enlightenment a criterion of civilized behavior. As critic Henry Louis Gates, Jr., points out, the "sheer literacy of writing was the very commodity that separated animal from human being" and qualified a person for " 'the rights of man.' "[14] Blacks' analphabetism, therefore, confirmed the white humanist in his opinion that they were naturally inferior to him and good only for the meanest labor. So blacks were deliberately prevented from learning, and those who did teach themselves were dismissed as incapable of any profundity. Thomas Jefferson, for instance, who insisted that he had never found "a Black that had uttered a thought above the level of plain narration"[15] as both Gates and critic Houston Baker report, was prone to reject black intellectual achievement as inconsequential. He said of his African American contemporary Phyllis Wheatley, who was widely acclaimed in western intellectual circles, "The compositions published under her name are below the dignity of criticism."[16] Religion might have "produced a Phillis Whately [*sic*] but . . . not . . . a poet."[17]

Throughout American literature, white writers have drawn on the image of the unlettered, smiling, childish Negro. The Uncle Toms and the Aunt Jemimas of popular fiction are, in fact, white creations: whites themselves are contented slaves to such an idea of the black. Glasgow thought of Negroes as carefree children: she, who deplored the institution of slavery as a "symbol of human guilt,"[18] did not understand the implications of American racism. She blamed the South's defeat on its evasion of the problem—as if its very existence and economic viability had not depended upon its deliberate exploitation of black labor. Glasgow's acceptance of the notion that blacks could be happy in a state of enforced degradation was based implicitly on her assumption that they were qualitatively inferior to whites. They were endowed by race with what she termed "African fatalism . . . from out of the past"[19] and, therefore, were incapable of positive reasoning. In *Barren Ground,* Glasgow's white heroine, Dorinda, who understood blacks intuitively and was saved from economic disaster by them, considered them rationally incompetent, or, as she put it, "contentedly enough" to live "as inferiors . . . attached . . . to the superior powers."[20] Indeed, blacks' survival entailed their adaptation to the prevailing white world as if this were the will of nature and the law of right.

Katherine Anne Porter, whose grandmother was a member of a family of rich slave owners, took on the trappings of an upper-class gentlewoman with respect to her attitude toward blacks. She wrote of the complicity between post–Civil War blacks and whites, who gossiped together like old friends, happily remembering the good old slave past.[21] Yet Porter was a liberal activist who was horrified that Negroes had to riot "to gain something they should have had all along."[22]

It seemed that the more liberal a writer was, the more he was unconsciously subject to a cultural opinion that automatically assigned blacks to inferiority. Erskine Caldwell deplored southern racist practices and vigorously condemned the gratuitous violence that blacks suffered from the lower and middle white classes. In *A Place Called Estherville,* his George Swayne, the bank vice-president who rapes his black maid, Kathyanne, and the police captain who beats and jails her when she resists his advances are examples of this kind of terrorism.[23] Whereas Caldwell was able to give dignity and often individuality to his illiterate, unhealthy and hopeless poor whites, his Negroes had little personality. They were too nice and too compliant. Even when they resisted, they seemed to want to give in to the white system. Ganus Bazemore, Kathyanne's brother, is as subservient and willing and submissive as his sister. Handsome Brown, in *Georgia Boy,* repeatedly mistreated by his employer,[24] is "docile and dumb."[25] Moreover, in the tradition of the well-meaning white humanitarian, Caldwell tended to introduce into his stories a good white in whom blacks—even passive ones—can admiringly put their trust. "Dr. Plowden—God bless you!" cries Kathyanne to the benefactor who delivers her baby. And he, having vindicated the values of civilization, feels "satisfied with his life now." By her hero worship of him, "this mulatto girl . . . had rewarded him for a lifetime of labour."[26]

Erskine Caldwell, son of a minister, was beset by guilt from his experiences in the South. He had known and written about one black who was lynched for alleged sexual relations with a promiscuous white girl and another who was sent to a chain gang for supposedly stealing an iron pot that was too heavy to lift.[27] Caldwell was a liberal; Thomas Wolfe was not. He, the son of a lower-middle-class family of strivers, was inclined to dismiss blacks as inferior beings by nature who were, if not happy, at least well adapted to their lower stage of development. The Negro was an idiot, a clown,[28] a dog, an obedient child, who adored Wolfe for the attention he bestowed on him.[29] The black pimp who procured him women consoled him for these "bought unlovely loves [with] the warm shadow of his affection."[30] Wolfe's account of his visit to a Negro whorehouse is in any case unbelievable, but he derived satisfaction from the illusion of being liked. As Richard Wright's Tyree tells his son in *The Long Dream,* "Grin in their goddam faces . . . do what the hell you want behind their goddam backs!"[31]

William Faulkner, who seemed to draw on all the stereotypes of the African American, often resorted for relief to the myth of the black as the contented clown. He was a beast of burden who resembled the faithful and subservient ass. Indeed, Faulkner distorted black humanity in order to fit it into his preconceived idea of reality. Moreover, he was apparently unaware of the contradictions inherent in his characterization of black people. As a would-be gentleman who pretended to high-class status, he knew and liked blacks well, and was convinced that his affection for them was reciprocated. He had a mammy who was genuinely attached to his family. He was also conscientious and, within limits, liberal—as the southern gentry was supposed to be. He felt a deep obligation to expiate the sin of slavery:[32] southern whites "owe and must pay a responsibility to the Negro," he said.[33]

Faulkner went through a phase of integrationism. Like his Gavin Stephens, the staple of southern civilization, the good, just, intelligent white man whom blacks could trust in a cultural morass, Faulkner would not shirk his duty. He would stand up and do what he could for Negroes, if "not for the Negro," said Malcolm Cowley.[34] In a similar show of liberal moralism, he gave money to a Communist solicitor although he rejected the ideology. So he preached equity, racial consideration and peace. The opponents of civil rights were in any case not fair-thinking southern gentlemen: "It's the grown-ups and especially the women who keep the prejudice alive," he remarked.[35] Still he was careful not to overstate his position. Ultimately his integrationist stance was abandoned—much to the relief of his family and fellow townsmen.[36] But it had never interfered with his habitual treatment of Negroes: he had used them and mules—species which he associated—to plow his fields all through the period of black agitation. To defend the black was to be branded as a Negro lover and a Communist and anathema to higher civilization.

It was only within the context of the stereotype, which reflected the historical tradition of southern culture, that Faulkner could perceive the black. To turn him into an abstraction, to picture him as a simpleton contented in his place, was to uphold higher white values.[37] Such a myth favored attitudes of benevolence on the part of whites. The black was good when acting out the role of Mammy, like Faulkner's Dilsey who endures all things,[38] or of Pappy, like Simon, the stupid and God-fearing automaton in *Sartoris* who worships the Sartoris family and disdains liberty.[39] Dilsey, who actually managed the household of Quentin, is associated with Benjy, the idiot child. It is through Benjy that the narrator's point of view is expressed.

The black was adapted to civilization only when he played the part of the kindly, contented dumbbell who enjoyed plowing the fields of his superiors (although he often slept on the job); who looked up to whites admiringly; who was obedient, warm, and affectionate, like a child eager to please (although he might lapse into periodic drinking bouts and filching sprees); and who could be sheltered and protected from some evil called reality. Without "white guidance and sympathy," he would experience "moral, physical and economic deterioration."[40] The Negro might even be considered saintlike—like an idiot—as long as he remained passive and all-forgiving. He endured all and suffered all and instinctively, like an unthinking element of nature, understood all because he was endowed with animal-like fatalism. Faulkner's Nancy, for instance, "the murderer, the nigger, the dopefiend whore"— the beast to whose care Temple Drake consigns her baby in *Requiem for a Nun*—willingly sacrifices her "debased and worthless life" to her mistress[41] and to Faulkner's own contrived idea of good and evil. In *Light in August,* Joe Christmas, haunted like a savage, gives himself up to a certain lynching and unprotestingly serves as a scapegoat to purge superior whites of their neuroses. It would take immense creative will to imagine such compliance on the part of any human being.

Perhaps, as Baldwin suggested, Faulkner "needed to believe in black forgiveness."[42] It might have been his own neurotic guilt that caused him to attribute infinite innocence, endurance and tolerance to Negroes and to depict them as willing emotional and physical handservants of the white hegemony, which Faulkner considered higher civilization. Because they had been wronged, they seemed to confirm his conception of reality, which was based on victimization. Passively or actively, all men were, he thought, irremediably subject to fate. He constructed what Claude-Edmonde Magny has called a cathedral of evil, a "community of Sin,"[43] out of the pain and suffering that is common to human beings, including, in particular, right-thinking, just and sensitive white men. But in making blacks the tools of the white—or at least of his own aesthetic viewpoint—Faulkner deliberately robbed them of their humanity and their liberty. He denied their capacity for both. Why should blacks be free, asks Sam in *Sartoris:* "Ain't we got ez many white folks now ez we kin suppo't?"[44] Likewise in "Mountain Victory," when Jubal, the slave, is emancipated, he refuses to believe that his master no longer belongs to him.[45]

Faulkner had a tendency to be archly coy in his treatment of the Negro. But, more significant, he was justifying the subordinate position of blacks in his world. He was enforcing the doctrine of the good Negro as a composite of naïveté, passivity, infancy, senility, incompetence, stubbornness, irresponsibility, cowardice, silliness, affection and ignorance—sprinkled with a touch of harmless dishonesty.[46] This was the characterization of the Negro who was popular with whites, and who could not, therefore, be discontented. And naturally this picture of the old black mammy and the old black Sam and their jolly and brainless black relatives could not be tainted with any implications of sexuality.

Carson McCullers idealized Berenice, the kindly, all-understanding, blue-glass-eyed maid in *The Member of the Wedding*. William Styron followed the stereotype: he neither added anything to it nor questioned it. If, on the one hand, he pictured Nat Turner as the vicious black beast—the homosexual-onanist, the rapist and the assassin of friendly white folk—on the other he peopled his books with good, affectionate and contented Negroes, who were in general the servants of whites. In *Lie Down in Darkness,* his all-accepting, all-loving colored domestics—although emotionally and intellectually undeveloped—delight their white superiors with their low comedy and their religious fundamentalism.[47] In *The Long March,* it is the sentimentalized sympathy of a Negro maid that consoles the foot-sore Jewish hero. And in his play *In the Clap Shack,* Styron portrayed the Negro as a buffoon, albeit an amicable one, who hates Jews, likes white southern boys—including the protagonist—and has the power of a primitive witch doctor to predict the future. Perhaps, like many southerners, Styron is obsessed with a sense of culpability with respect to blacks: so he had to make them like him. The narrator of *Sophie's Choice* has "a compulsion to write about slavery" because he feels guilty about it.[48] Therefore, he sacrifices blacks simplistically to his neurosis and helps perpetuate the myths by which whites have rationalized their oppression of blacks. Once more a white, who appears to be unable to confront the black-white dualism that governs his cultural bias, has yielded "to the South in fantasy the victory it had been denied in fact."[49]

But the stereotype of the contented Negro was also particularly popular in the North. It comforted the white liberal's conscience while, at the same time, confirming him in the cultural pretensions of superiority. Social democrats like Hamlin Garland spoke of "negroes whose dusky countenances shone with . . . desire to make us happy."[50] William Dean Howells, who prided himself on his egalitarianism and devotion to human rights—especially with respect to blacks—paternalized Paul Laurence Dunbar. With the arrogance of the naïve, Howells expressed his satisfaction that a black man, son of slaves, could actually write poetry. He was amazed and delighted, he said, to discover "white thinking and white feeling in a black man."[51] Nevertheless, he encouraged Dunbar to stick to dialect. On the other hand, Howells disapproved of Charles Chesnutt's tempered account of black militancy in *The Marrow of Tra-*

dition. It was not a statement of Negro accommodation; it was "bitter, bitter," complained Howells.[52]

Howells reflected the liberal dogma that literacy was the criterion of being human and, therefore, that western civilization was the universal standard of mankind. Education meant learning to think and to reason, and thus to be white. Because whites considered it an amazing accomplishment for blacks, they assumed that there was an intrinsic intellectual difference between the races. Blacks who could properly read and write were treated like members of an intermediate species of animal that was making it up the human ladder. Even after the First World War, a socialist such as Max Eastman—a second-generation east European immigrant with relatively little historical and familial acquaintance with the English language—was astounded at the ability with which Claude McKay, a native of the British West Indies, handled his own tongue.[53]

Whites enjoyed playing benefactor to individual Negroes. They would often make exceptions in subscribing to conventional stereotypes as long as their chosen Negroes conformed to the image that was imposed upon them. The kind master of Willa Cather's slave girl Nancy in *Sapphira and the Slave Girl,* for instance, consoles her for the cruel treatment she has received at the hands of her mistress. Actually, he does little to help her. He defends the system as it stands and rests, he says, "on [his] confidence in [the Lord's] design."[54]

Sherwood Anderson wrote affectionately of lower-class blacks; he stressed the "happy-go-lucky sensuality of river-front Negroes."[55] But he was unsympathetic to the problems of black intellectuals—his potential equals. They do not "have much more to complain of than whites in this matter of their treatment in the arts," he claimed.[56] In *Buchanan Dying,* John Updike's fair-minded President Buchanan maintains that at the brink of the Civil War, slave holders wanted to free their slaves.[57] Updike was probably as uncomfortable with history as he admitted that he was with blacks. In *Rabbit Redux,* his Harry, the lower-middle-class "good-hearted, imperialist racist,"[58] believes that blacks are "certainly dumber"[59] than whites. But he, who is hardly an intellectual, has his doubts even in that respect because of the example of Bill Cosby, the television comic. In any case Negroes seem in general complaisant, particularly the old-time types—especially in the task of procuring women for white men, as if they are to serve perfectly any needs of their superiors. Harry, however, like Updike, feels "itchy"[60] in talking to blacks. Updike, himself a middle-class American, had not associated with them and had little desire to do so.[61]

In the North, the middle- or lower-middle-class white tended to accept the black only as an amusing and inherently stupid creature. The mass media "see to it that there is a comic Negro in every middle-class home," said Sterling Brown.[62] "White folks can't stand unhappy Negroes . . ." remarks Alice Childress's Wiletta in *Trouble in Mind*.[63] As James Farrell's ethnic racist, old man Lonigan, comments on Amos and Andy, "They're so much like darkies— Not the fresh northern nigger, but the genuine real southern darkies, the good niggers. . . ."[64]

A race-conscious liberal writer like Eugene O'Neill was inclined to turn the black man into a replica of the white, or at least the prevailing image of whiteness. Jim in *All God's Chillun Got Wings* is literally a "black slave" to the white woman, Ella, whom he "adores . . . as sacred,"[65] much to the disgust of his sister. Jim is popular with whites because he acts out the role that they have assigned him. Ella eventually turns on him and calls him "nigger."[66] Saintly, resigned and improbable as he is, he does not blame her. It is God who is at fault; Jim is the all-enduring victim of life. And O'Neill's Joe in *The Iceman Cometh* is happy to associate with his white cronies and to hear that he is the "whitest colored man" that one of them ever knew.[67]

Bellow's Negro sociologist in *The Dean's December* is a white do-gooder with a colored face. Malamud's Dubin, the liberal white intellectual in *Dubin's Lives,* accepts his half-black grandchild after first assuming that his daughter's interracial liaison will consign her to welfare motherhood.[68] The father of the child is, of course, an educated middle-class Negro, serious and responsible and in no way unworthy of or unlike an educated middle-class Jew. In both authors, however, the black is a type, not a person. The Negro "seldom appears to the white man as clearly individual."[69] As Roland Barthes defined the stereotype, it is "that emplacement of discourse *where the body is missing.*"[70] The black must conform to given white standards that entail the surrender of the very quality of being self and of being black—of the reality of skin color.

The liberal's ideology is integration, which presupposes the maintenance of the white cultural hegemony and reinforces the assumption that western civilization is the universal standard of mankind. Integration is the modern industrial means of upholding the existing order. It carries with it the implication that the white middle-class norm must prevail at the necessary expense of the outcast poor, who are identified with blacks—as Dubin suggests—and who present an inherent contradiction to the liberal ideal of assimilation as well as to the omnipotence of the consumer state. They are handicapped economically, and economic viability is the condition of membership in the middle class.

On a cultural level, integration implies that the African American past—the experience of being black—is a "stigma,"[71] as Podhoretz called it and as Howe supposed. The literacy that whites have posited as the condition of membership in their assumedly universal civilization is based on a particular tradition. As Houston Baker and Henry Louis Gates suggest, black linguistic expression,[72] which is incorporated in black culture, has been "locked in a relation of thesis to antithesis to a racial discourse embedded in Western philosophy." It has been associated with "strategies of negation":[73] to flow free, it has had to hide itself from whites. Black self-affirmation entails the denigration of the racist assumptions that not only are innate in it, but that constitute occidental thought. Color cannot be irrelevant as long as it remains "a fact of consciousness,"[74] which is essential to the formation of a white as well as a black point of view.

CHAPTER 11

THE STEREOTYPE OF THE MULATTO

The last of the three white stereotypes of the black is comprised in what Sterling Brown called the "colored person"[1] and Nancy Tischler "the arrogant malcontent."[2] The image of the mulatto— the wretched freedman—is "the basis for the black temptress, the black Christ and the new Negro."[3] In this image, the white mind reverted to its first premise regarding the natural incompatibility of black and white and of the qualitative superiority of the latter. Whereas the idea of the Negro brute represented pure and original evil in the midst of white grace, that of the colored person stands for the corruption of white blood. The mulatto is malicious; he is destructive; he is tragic; he is the product of miscegenation. He detests blacks and loathes whites, and he combines the rage of the beast with the cunning of the rational man. He has the black's emotions and the white's cleverness, and he would tear down the cultural order in which he has no place. It is he who is responsible for "racial hatreds."[4] He incites race riots and provokes lynchings. He has the vices of both sets of blood but all his accomplishments are attributed to his white heritage. "Yellow niggers," says George in Baldwin's *Blues for Mister Charlie*, ". . . ain't they the worst kind?"[5]

The stereotype of the colored person is also related to that of the contented Negro. Both assume that above all the black wants to be accepted in white society and that, therefore, he considers it the highest form of human achievement. Both take for granted the presupposition that the mulatto wants to be white—not because of what whites materially possess, but because of what they qualitatively are. While the nice, humble Negro knows his place and bows submissively to his betters, the nasty mulatto, miserably discontent and torn in himself, would take over the state and its women for himself, a feat he might be capable of because of his white blood.

Since racial attitudes are related intimately to sexual neuroses, it was the fear of amalgamation—which would bely the ideology of white supremacy—that led to whites' fabrication of the myth of the bad, and tragic, mulatto. It is interesting that the very term "mulatto" (which in Spanish means a young male mule, the sterile offspring of a horse and an ass) is habitually associated with the Negro.[6] The ideal of sacred white womanhood, which white men also concocted, was their means of keeping their mothers, wives and daughters from intermingling with black men. Whites would perpetuate the ideology of racial difference as a cultural norm—even though it was white men who were mainly responsible for the incidence of miscegenation. Wright's Tyree complains that whites "use this damned business about white women to make what they do sound right."[7] They set their females apart for the procreation only of whites; they invented and enforced the legend and ensuing reality of the asexuality of proper white ladies; they accused women who were attracted to blacks of degeneration or insanity, and the blacks who seduced or were seduced by them of rape. Whites would keep African Americans definitively outside the acceptable bounds of civilization. In fact, "it was probably . . . the idea of miscegenation and mulattoes rather than the quantity of interracial sex, marriage, and offspring that so outraged authorities" in early America.[8]

It was the white man, not the white woman, who propagated the specter of the black rape of white womanhood until all over America it became an integral part of the stereotype of the black. As one of Wright's characters says, it seemed as if a Negro had raped Uncle Sam's sister.[9] Despite the enforcement of segregation, the sexual separation of the races was not escapeproof, not even among properly raised women of the middle classes. One of the reasons for the rise of the original Ku Klux Klan was—according to Lerone Bennett, Jr.—the post–Civil War "miscegenation among average people."[10] Throughout history the white female has sneaked off into illicit relationships with blacks, aroused perhaps by the myth of black rape—and ferocious sexuality—that had been invented to keep her within bounds. "It is the racial meaning of Negro sexuality, in all of its pornography, that the white woman *expects and demands* when she becomes intimate with a Negro."[11]

The taboo was a challenge to many white women, who were sometimes not only sexually attracted to blacks to the point that they were the aggressors—as Calvin Hernton observes—but also subject to fantasies with respect to the black's alleged sexual powers.[12] They related to him chiefly on a physical level because they were under the control of prohibitive social customs: they were segregated from him. They hated and loved him alternately because he was culturally forbidden. But white women were always able to play a power role with him— which was denied them in their sexual commerce with white men. Because they belonged to the ruling order, they could condemn him with a single word. As Chester Himes put it, they were able to take advantage of the legend of Negro rape in order to lure him with their bodies and dare him with their color.[13] Amiri Baraka's Lula in *Dutchman* verbally seduces Clay before she murders him.[14] James Weldon Johnson warned blacks to beware of the white witch who robs her prey of his substance and castrates him cruelly.[15]

Since it is the white male, not the white female, who is chiefly responsible for the incidence of mixed blood, he has used the myth of black sexuality to rationalize his acts. He has hidden his "blood relations with Indians and blacks,"[16] one of whom stood for "alien perception" (cultural differences) and the other for "alien passion."[17] The white man has subjected the black woman to his sexual phobias and his sexual assaults. He has then stereotyped and dehumanized her for the gratification of impulses he could not control and, consequently, feared. The love-death narcissism seems to have obstructed the free play of sexual enjoyment. Since relations between master and slave and employer and worker are necessarily rarely reciprocal—since, as Toni Morrison puts it, "all unions between white men and black women be rape"[18]—it required an abnormal amount of sexual perversion, if not sadism, for white men to inflict themselves on their servants, who had to submit in order to survive. Black women should beware of white men, warned Pauline Hopkins at the turn of the century, for underneath burns "a living fire of hatred."[19]

The white male fabricated the legend of the promiscuous Negro wench to rationalize his sexual excesses and to justify his pretensions to civilizational integrity. He pretended "that no Negro woman can be raped because they are always willing."[20] The stereotype of the black temptress is the counterpart to that of the cunning and malicious colored person. White males, wrote Himes, turned "to Negro women because in them they saw only the black image of flesh . . . possessing no mind to condemn, no soul to be outraged . . . no power to judge or accuse."[21]

Writers of the post–World War I generation exploited the idea of the sexual dangers represented by the mulatto not only to maintain segregation, but also to avoid confronting the issue of racial discrimination. The sexual implications implicit in the stereotype of the colored person were an update of those comprehended in the stereotype of the Negro brute. "One was told," said Malcolm Cowley primly, that "the Negroes"—who by this time were in general of mixed blood—"had retained a direct virility that the whites had lost through being over-educated."[22] As Thomas Wolfe projected his own libidinal hang-ups onto the Negro, he contrasted his idea of the South (which incorporated the black presence and reeked with earthy female submissiveness) with the male Apollonian image, represented by the cold, orderly, correct and rational North.[23]

But it was Faulkner who was most preoccupied with the idea of miscegenation. He, who upheld the southern cultural ideal, used Freudian theory to rationalize southern racism. He would dissolve the guilt inherent in it—or, rather, he would disperse it by universalizing it. Civilization depended necessarily on repression, rapaciousness and acquisitiveness; it was the product of human sin; it was a curse.[24] In the South, man's inevitable transgression was symbolized by whites' oppression, rape and bondage of blacks. The moral infractions of gallant white men, whose splendor naturally entailed wrongdoing, had built the grandeur of the South.[25] Faulkner's thesis was an update of that of John C. Calhoun.

In effect, Faulkner vacillated within the limits of a traditional master-slave complex. He celebrated the magnificent sins of the arrogant conquerors of the wilderness while idealizing the fated endurance of the poor, victimized blacks, who were driven to work the land. His sympathies were "enlisted by the virtues of slave-morality and those of master-morality," says critic Philip Blair Rice.[26] Faulkner's characters were redeemed either by their submissiveness and victimization or by their assertiveness and self-sacrifice by which they presumably earned the reputation of heroes—at least in the imaginations of their fellow southerners.

Faulkner used his fatalism to justify his culture. It was the primal force of nature that had condemned blacks to subservient yet just labor and whites to noble but amoral deeds. Freud stressed the idea of the inevitability of biological nature to consign western man to instinctual repression and neurosis. Faulkner thought of nature as doom: blacks and whites had been assigned different roles in society because the dark and white races were not of the same kind. The two types of blood were incompatible, as was evident whenever they were incorporated in the same body. And this thesis was illustrated most clearly in the case of the tragic mulatto.

Mulattoes like Charles Bon or Joe Christmas were condemned by birth to inner conflict. Bon's son could come to terms with himself only by denying his white blood—"as the demon himself might have done."[27] Sam Feathers was "himself his own battleground."[28] Lucas Beauchamp alone, who was indifferent to his white heritage, was spared the internal strife of mixed blood, and he lived isolated, away from both black and white. Faulkner brought out the southerner's conventional and almost pathological fear of miscegenation—for which he was nevertheless the cause—and of the possibility that the black-white would rise against his progenitor in Oedipal fury. Since Faulkner was agonizingly aware of the white man's guilt in his violation of the black, he had to excuse it and he could do so only by attributing it to the natural order of things. As Magny observes, "In the absence of Salvation, Man is temporarily given over to Destiny. . . ."[29]

Ultimately, neither blacks nor whites were responsible for their destiny, as they were not to blame for their original difference and incompatibility. It was *"not through any fault or willing of our own who would not what we cannot."*[30] White men, wild, self-seeking and cruel, were cursed perhaps more than the black: they had misused freedom in magnificently erecting their civilization through their conquest of the wilderness. But they had been punished. Sutpen in Faulkner's *Absalom, Absalom!* lost the opportunity of founding his dynasty because, by the irony of fate, his only surviving son was black. All individuals, white or black, were irremediably subject to "the larger structure of the plot as a whole."[31] Nancy, the whore, is the agent of white redemption. Joe Christmas is not a person: he is the product and tool of everything that happens to him.

Because Faulkner's self-consciously universalist effort to rationalize black and white relations is contained within a white cultural framework, he subordinated the African American to the white man. The white, for all his sin and guilt, has dignity and individuality as well as an advantageous material position. Even if he is only what he can do, still his act of doing stands for positive cultural achievement. He is ennobled because he struggles splendidly although often futilely against his destiny. It is in his combat, in and to which he sacrifices himself, that he builds and preserves civilization. He is the warrior and the artist, the genius of the race. Indeed, Faulkner considered himself culturally doomed, as he put it tragically, "to keep on writing books."[32] He had been condemned in the face of failure to create truth out of "the agony and sweat of the human spirit."[33] Art, the antidote to "man's sense of failure, imperfection and impending death,"[34] was his predetermined role as a white man in the unending process of constructing civilization. He was elected as a doer.

But blacks were never so elected. They were neither heroes, nor artists, nor any kind of doer. Their experience of the agony and sweat of the human spirit lay in their working for whites. They endured passively their destiny: they were the silent bulwark on which the civilizational edifice rested for the glory of mankind in general—excluding colored people. The different roles of the white and the black complemented each other: as art "takes care of its own,"[35] so does poverty, but its anguish robs the sufferer of will. Negroes were supposed to resign themselves to their lowly status and inflicted pain in the knowledge that, like the artist, although on another plane, they would be redeemed in time.

The mulatto, the victim *par excellence,* the exemplary creation of white rapacious lust and black submissiveness, is the scapegoat who atones for the active and passive suffering of the races. He personifies the perverted sexuality—the curdling of mixed bloods—that presages his inevitably tragic end. Charles Bon is the image of the seducer; Joe Christmas brings his mistress, the white Yankee schoolmarm, to orgasmic heights, which she prolongs by calling him "Negro! Negro! Negro!"[36] The mulatto, however, is sexually adept only because he is fated to die—like the stinger bug. Absolutely free, rejected by blacks and whites alike, he incarnates the agony of the human experience.[37] He is a Christ figure, an abstract symbol,[38] not a person who crucifies himself. The battle between the two kinds of blood is resolved in his image: the white prevails and death, which is ordained, is martyrdom to the status quo.

As Faulkner came to feel more and more that the sordid and the commercial had replaced the glory of civilization and that true art was alienated from materialistic culture, his white men seemed to withdraw into themselves away from the world. Their main preoccupation involved an effort to preserve their innocence—their faith in their ability to possess a new Eden that had justified their original guilt—in the midst of a wilderness.[39] Ike McCaslin, for instance, who disapproves of slavery and has rejected all his property that issued from it, lives isolated in this reverence for the past as if it were "the *immobile* image of eternity"[40]—slavist as it had been. Perhaps it is the contradiction that is inherent in his regard for the past that imprisons him in impotence—in the sterility of Puritanism. He is stunted both sexually and morally. He will not face the present. In admiring the inevitable guilt of humanity and in protecting himself from it, McCaslin separates himself from living human beings—much as did Sutpen in his egocentric and violent obsession with his ideal. McCaslin is incapable of imagining the miscegenation in which his forefathers had freely and brutally indulged. The very thought of it shocks him now that blacks are asserting themselves, and sexuality is the reflection of their contempt for ancient codes of race incompatibility on which his concept of civilization has been built. In fact, his refusal to accept the reality of interracial sex is an expression of his attempt to safeguard his purity, which he associates with the lost Eden, America's primeval wilderness. "Old man," the Negro female partner of a mixed couple asks him, ". . . have you lived so long and forgotten so much that you don't remember anything you ever knew or felt or even heard about love?"[41]

McCaslin, probably like Faulkner, knows that civilization is based on slavery and on the destruction, rape and settlement of America's original natural environment, and that it had to continue on its course even if it led to the artificiality of industrial society. Blacks represented primitive nature over which whites had constructed their edifice. Perhaps that is why, as one of Faulkner's earlier characters observes, they make you feel so "immature."[42] Integrationists, both black and white, Faulkner concluded, were illusionists:[43] there would be no law of the land if it was not grounded on segregation,[44] the incompatibility of the two types of blood and the maintenance of the existing social order.[45] Faulkner would sacrifice life itself to his distaste for miscegenation and the intermingling of black and white cultural roles. He would prefer sin and violence—which were in any case inevitable—to what he imagined to be racial impurity. When Sutpen forbade his son, Charles Bon, to marry his half sister, the young man remarked that it was "not the incest" to which his father objected, but racial amalgamation.[46]

Most southern writers likewise sacrificed the black to a destiny, a natural order of things, which they universalized in the name of human civilization. Allen Tate feared miscegenation and damned the mulatto to a tragic end. "To educate a Negro beyond his station brings him unhappiness," he declared.[47] Emancipation had proven perilous for blacks, he and his fellow agrarians decided. The liberated Negro was obstreperous and unhappy: he was the wretched freedman. Indeed, as one critic points out, the picture of "the arrogant malcontent is . . . essential to post–World War I novels."[48]

Tate upheld the past, of which "no man can be free."[49] Even if it represented ancient and present failure—"the eldest in the latest crime"—it was the reflection of man's cultural achievement and the foundation of his future mission. Man's "fixed doom"[50] is death and the past is death remembered—and often mythicized. In a sense, therefore, it is the redemption of life's meaninglessness—as is civilization. It stands for the intellectual rendition, if not rationalization, of reality and, as such, it is a good in itself. It is "the intellectual sound / Of death's feet round in a reedy tomb," as Tate wrote in his elegy for Jefferson Davis.[51] The past is the idea to which black existence is subject as, presumably, blacks are incapable of such intellectualization.

Robert Penn Warren also resorted to the idea of inevitable destiny in order to rationalize the crimes of white civilization. History and its "savage comedy"[52] were to blame for the adventurism, despotism and exploitation that made up the American past. No one was free in reality, and it was this fact that pragmatically justified slavery, a social practice in which human beings of every race indulged. In the end, essentially nothing mattered because no one was responsible for what occurred: everybody was a tool of outside forces.[53] And Negroes seemed more qualified to deal with the inequities of existence than dynamic white men—the doers who controlled, if they had not created, the powers that stood for civilization.

In general, southern intellectuals (who were at least aware of the crimes of the white man) took refuge in a vague faith in their so-called civilization, which was based historically on the oppression of the black. The black symbolized the line of demarcation between the positive and the negative. The white's mind seized on the past tradition in an attempt to justify himself. "What was back there, hidden . . . ?" asked sociologist W. J. Cash of this mind. "The South was afraid. . . . Another great group of Southern fears and hates fixed itself on . . . the savage ideal— the patriotic will to hold rigidly to the ancient pattern. . . ."[54] And with time, as more and more African Americans were forced or disposed to amalgamate with Anglo-Americans to the point that they began to lose the color black, the mulatto came to represent the sexual neurosis of segregation. As miscegenation had once caused whites to enslave their children and grandchildren[55]—and themselves through their offspring— now it brought them to cultural confusion.

Northern intellectuals, past and present, might have deliberately tried to ignore the crimes of civilization, but they have used racism as a means of claiming a special—implicitly higher—distinction. It was important that they maintain a moral difference from blacks. Willa Cather, for instance, in the vein of Faulkner, pretended that her liberated slave, Top, couldn't "stand his freedom."[56] The white man's self-image was based on his self-engendered illusion of his superiority. Therefore, the mulatto posed a threat to his sense of identity. As Ralph Ellison's invisible man points out, his guilt and treason are equated with "any act that endangered the continuity of the dream."[57] After the First World War, writers like Lothrop Stoddard considered "the negro problem in this country [to be] essentially the problem of the mulatto."[58] He was the malcontent and his "protest was the desperate rebellion of 'a forceful Aryan in soul-entanglement with an utterly strange being.'"[59]

In the late 1960s, however, the intellectual class could no longer use the Negro for white cultural ends. It became ambivalent in its treatment of him. It disapproved of segregation and of racial stereotypes in principle, if not in fact. The intelligentsia was uncertain in its handling of sexual liberation, which had racial and political implications. It was faced with the inescapable fact that, as many whites were black—or at least octoroon—so most blacks possessed white blood. Both sex and race were ambiguous, but loaded, issues. The sexual revolution that followed the black movement for civil rights tended to undermine the patriarchal position of the white male at the same time, paradoxically, as it reinforced the authority of the industrial state. It brought women militantly into politics in support of middle-class norms at the expense of black freedom.

At first the sexual revolution confused the white male. He was uncertain of the role, particularly as the relaxation of sexual mores allowed the middle-class white female not just to run openly after blacks, but also to assume a contentious attitude toward him. Her new assertiveness seemed like an expression of natural erotic urges that the white male, apparently, had not been able to satisfy. In any case, her energies found a political outlet in women's liberation, the modern revival of a cause that had preoccupied females since abolition. But whereas before—in principle—women had assumed a cultural role as "moral custodians of society";[60] and whereas they had been interested in serving humanity for—as Rheta Childe Dorr, an early feminist, wrote—"purely a spiritual reward,"[61] now in postindustrial America their goals were chiefly material. Women competed in the market with white men: they looked for job status and reward. To the extent that their struggle has been successful, they have acted in conjunction with white middle-class males to reinforce the premises of the prevailing power and, therefore, to obstruct blacks' overall drive for economic and social equity.

Traditionally, women's movements follow those for black rights. Women were especially active after abolition, after southern populism and after the black revolution of the 1960s. History repeats itself, remarks Jeanne Noble: "Here they were, the women again, and . . . they were following immediately on the heels . . . of the black liberation movement. . . ."[62] Paula Giddings agrees. "The greatest gains made by women have come in the wake of . . . Black demands for . . . rights," she observes.[63]

Of course, women originally tried to associate their rights movements with those of the blacks. They claimed that their status as an undersex paralleled the outcast position of the black race. They, too, have been subject to the stereotypes of white male supremacists; they, too, have been used, exploited and misrepresented by the dominant white man. Their treatment in the North as sexual and in the South as asexual objects was, according to them, a side effect of white racism. Even in the post–Civil War era, women derived their rhetoric from the example of black oppression—from "images of slavery and prostitution."[64] Suffrage leaders in the North were, in principle, integrationists: they tried thereby to mobilize black women under their leadership.

Then, as now, despite their claims, women's struggles for rights, which seem to arrive propitiously in the midst of black agitation and have their "greatest currency in times of Black militancy,"[65] have served to dedramatize and depoliticize black movements. The two causes have worked at cross-purposes. While earlier feminists made much of their preoccupation with problems concerning the "*nature* of the sexes,"[66] they were actually striving for more social standing, which they related to humanitarian ideals. Women were envious of men's advantageous position in the existing order—which they upheld and which depended on the subordination of blacks. Many whites, including abolitionists, tended even to "discriminate against Black women,"[67] whom they viewed as a "different kind of humanity,"[68] inclined to impurity if not to immorality. Black women, says historian Page Smith, were not important to white women, who, in fact, hampered them.[69] Susan B. Anthony, who abandoned her black allies to attract the support of southerners,[70] considered women's suffrage and black rights separate issues.[71] When white women finally won the vote, they did nothing whatsoever "to change the status quo for blacks."[72] They had used black women for their own interests; so, once white women had achieved their specific goals they let their erstwhile sisters drop.

The two causes were qualitatively unlike. The experience of the middle-class white woman has always been different from that of the black slave, the black sharecropper's wife, the black slum dweller. The feminist appeal has been liberal and idealistic; the white female and the white male were and still are closely related on a cultural level, which includes the acceptance of white supremacy. Black women were fighting against economic and sexual exploitation by white males for the rights of their race as a whole—a struggle for which they sought the support and protection of black men. White women concentrated on political and material objectives—which concerned the middle class. Consequently, white feminism, which appealed only to bourgeois black women, tended to widen the gap between the black sexes as well as black classes, a phenomenon that has been characteristic of modern women's liberation. White women have constituted neither a social nor an ethnic nor an occupational nor an ideological group. They have never been oppressed. They have simply "invented a class [and tried] to make that class conscious," as Joan Didion puts it. A "litany of trivia was crucial to the movement in the beginning, a key technique in the politicizing of women."[73] Having no special angle on which to base their agitation, they have fallen back on the reformist tradition, which was a pragmatic endorsement of political capitalism in all its racist implications. As contemporary female militants in their individualistic quest for advancement have ignored the black poor and refused to recognize the potential of a black, possibly revolutionary, subculture, so they still exploit racism for their ends. Now as before, remarks Giddings, they "developed their feminism in a Black organization and then they turned the thrust of their activist energies elsewhere." Although they have branded themselves as "niggers"—perhaps to attract attention to themselves—they have failed to truly support the black cause.[74] "Does [Miss Ann—the symbol of the white woman] really want us to have the kind of power we want for ourselves?" asks Noble.[75] Giddings suggests that "the incipient women's movement was one means of maintaining the racial status quo."[76] The white female "is simply not as powerless as she claims," observes Noble.[77]

The women's movement has, in effect, served to divert the momentum of both the sexual and the black revolutions into conventionalized—even commercialized—channels. It has depoliticized the black's thrust and has turned him into a symbol of the traditional mulatto. Sexual liberation, the spontaneous but inchoate expression of discontented,[78] undirected,[79] white middle-class youth, at first helped break down the barriers of racial segregation and open the way for interracial sex. Feminism, however, which promoted female sexual power, brought women to the fore in the management of sexual relationships and, therefore, restored a new order in the potential chaos of Bohemian, beatnik, hippie and revolutionary free love. In conjunction with black nationalism, which would eliminate black-white couplings, feminism helped impose an updated version of traditional racial and sexual guidelines. The intellectual class, of which feminists were a vocal part, was shaken by the turmoil of the 1960s[80] and more ambivalent in its own distortion of the black image than were outright racists. If in principle it rejected popular black stereotypes, nevertheless it was uncertain in both its political and aesthetic reactions to sexual emancipation—with which it associated the black. It had to invent new rationalizations to rework the ancient myths. No longer could the intellectual class justify racism as the product of outside forces to which all humanity—white, black, red, yellow—was subject.

Since the 1960s there has been an intrawhite struggle over who the Negro should be—as Amiri Baraka observes. Quite naturally middle-class blacks have become the "semi-conscious pawns"[81] of this conflict, which was at heart political and sexual as well as aesthetic. It was based on the dichotomy between romantic experimentation and humanitarian essentialism, and in a distorted way, the conflict represented a modern version of medieval nominalism against medieval realism—the one which denies the other's affirmation of universal essences. Both artistic and philosophic positions were contained within the norms of middle-class democracy and both could be signified by the person of the mulatto—the white-black man.

Romantics have been disappointed by existing materialistic society. They have projected their disgust with postindustrial America into a new stereotype of the black, one that emphasized the antisocial, malicious and rebellious qualities of the colored person. He was the trickster, the hustler, the seducer. Love of and love with him were means by which bourgeois youth could revolt against prevailing conventions. The "image of the black man as superstud for white women . . . is . . . taken literally by both black and white," said Baraka.[82] Young white people used the sexual revolution as a counterpart to the black movement of the 1960s in order to relate to the Negro. He was typified as cool and hip and prodigiously oversexed. However, alienated youth was not durable in its antisocial impulses. Sexual liberation was simply a way of seeking kicks: like the slumming of the 1920s, like the contemporary drug culture, it was a form of escapism.

To Norman Mailer, a romantic, the black man is enviably sexual: only Mailer himself and his protagonists can outperform him. Indeed, Mailer replays the myth of the Negro beast on an updated level. Black sexuality—as incarnated in the mulatto—is more advanced than that of the black rapist brute because it combines the freedom of natural instinct with the refinement of social style. "Negroes are closer to sex than we are,"[83] says Mailer, a position that "makes the white man nervous and unhappy and miserable." Mailer is speaking not of himself, but of "the average white man all through the country."[84] For the Negro has the power to understand "the existential abyss of love."[85] All expressions of blackness are orgasmic,[86] including black music and art.

Despite his own sexual and aesthetic proficiency, Mailer seems unable to conceal his jealousy of blacks. Perhaps like Rusty, D.J.'s decadent father in Why Are We in Vietnam?, Mailer believes that blacks are making it with all kinds of white women. "The Niggers and the women are fucking each other" since the liberation of both, says Rusty. Women are free and "fuck too many," and "the Niggers are free" and have dues to be paid.[87] To Mailer, love is a competitive game to be won, a struggle rated by apocalyptic orgasms. The criterion that distinguishes fertile satisfaction from sterile degeneration is sexual athleticism. To be existential, hip and revolutionary, like a Negro, is to have and produce climaxes. Likewise on an artistic plane, a work of genius should necessarily arouse a furious reaction. As to John Barth, the pen has the power of the penis. Perhaps Mailer resents the fragile and sensitive James Baldwin, whose autobiographical and political essays whipped up a passionate white response that Mailer seems to lack.[88]

By Mailer's standards, the black is a cultural hero who possesses sexual powers and a political cause that the white can never claim. Yet in his literary characterization of the black, Mailer deprives him of his potency: he emasculates him. Alfred Kazin remarks that "blackness never interested Mailer . . . except as a syndrome for the 'hipster or psychopath.' It was orgasm. . . ."[89] As Carl Van Vechten followed the old myth and written of "impotence and sexuality" in Nigger Heaven,[90] thus castrating Byron, the hero, by turning him into the Nice

Negro and reducing Creeper to a personification of the phallus, so Mailer robs Shago in *The American Dream,* his black stud, of the capacity really to make it with his white woman. Mailer repeats the stereotype of the black man lusting after the white female: it is Shago who cannot help being "in love with . . . a nice White Southern Girl like [her]."[91] Because Shago cannot arouse her, his expression of love is the art of the devil—to whom, of course, the mulatto is traditionally related. " 'Shago, you're evil,' she declares."[92]

Obviously, Mailer is ambiguous in his treatment of black people—as Baldwin realized. He is confused. Blackness apparently does not fit into his manichaeistic view of the world. Sometimes he is paternalistic and praises the black for having survived in an inimical society. It is the black who undermined the rational pretentiousness of white computer logic. If there was "no magic to combat technology . . . there would not be a future for Black civilization, merely an adjunct to the white," Mailer observes.[93] Yet at other times he degrades black culture, which he associates with mysterious forces of nature. Whites' "moon shot had smashed more than one oncoming superiority of the Black," he claims triumphantly.[94] Mailer resents any manifestation of black nationalistic pride. He is "confounded," says his biographer, "as to the nature of the Black rebellion, which appears offensive in its exploring tyranny."[95] The assertive Negro, the unhappy freedman, the overeducated colored person, is a bad man, a threat to the established white hegemony. The "Negro does not want equality any longer, he wants superiority, and wants it because he feels he is in fact superior," Mailer complains.[96] The black's genius is antipathetic to industrial technology. Yet Mailer himself distrusts this regime. Which D.J., the black or the white one, he wonders, "could possibly be worse of a genius. . . . Harlem or Dallas is guiding the other, and who knows which?"[97] In the sense that he is inclined to stereotype, Mailer's imagination is "the same as that of the racists of old," as Addison Gayle observed. Even if he "raised anew the banner of white supremacy and black inferiority," he could not keep it up convincingly.[98]

Mailer's confusion, which reflects his attitude toward industrial civilization, seems to let him down. He admires the power of the presumably Anglo-Saxon scientific mind, while he detests the cold and bloodless plasticity of technologically oriented culture. He wants to regain a poetic—even magic—vision of the world. Narcissism, he suggests, has characterized the emotional climate of modern civilization:[99]

the self has absorbed all in erecting itself as a substitute for the primary, yet lost, object of love.[100] Mailer is, of course, himself an illustration of this phenomenon. And narcissists are inclined to stereotype: they "*love distorted images; they force others to reflect themselves.*"[101]

As Philip Roth observes, it is "vision of the self"—even the impotent, invisible or victimized self—"the only seemingly real thing in an unreal-seeming environment," that gives certain writers "joy, solace, and muscle."[102] It is difficult for such intellectuals, caught in their own image, to accept anything outside their orbit. They must rely on established myths in order to fit others into their own created context. A romantic poet like Robert Lowell, despite—or perhaps because of—his self-consciously benevolent feelings toward black people, nevertheless could not imagine them except with respect to whites. Lowell, for example, buried them in his reconstituted memory of a white heroism that no longer existed.[103] His approach to modern civilization was in any case nihilistic and resigned: "At . . . this point of the world, / the only satisfactory companion we / can imagine is death . . ." he wrote after the assassination of Martin Luther King, Jr.[104] John Berryman, a romantic as well as a "white, middle-class, liberal intellectual,"[105] who admired Negro art, was put off by the black movement of the 1960s. "Angered by the sexual implications behind the demand of black militants," he declared that "the two races cannot live together in peace."[106]

White intellectuals could not help but identify the black revolution with the sexual revolution: they were haunted by the sexual implications inherent in the black stereotype. Bernard Malamud, for instance, like Mailer, castrated his Negro. The white girl in *The Tenants,* who is excited and scared by Willie's "blackness,"[107] is not aroused by him as she is by Lesser, the Jew, who brings her to orgasmic heights. Indeed, Willie is completely done in: he loses his woman when Lesser abducts her, as he loses his brainchild, his book.

It is sex, which whites associate with blackness—as represented by the mulatto—that bothers the white-supremacist middle class. The very affirmation of black cultural autonomy, which whites have recognized and systematically demeaned, posed a threat to their own image of civilizational universality. Whites have been monoculturists and so they have paranoiacally suspected the black of wanting to undermine them. The mulatto—the mule—was identified with sterility. The colored race is a shadowy figure "with the attributes of death rather than those of fertility," writes Fiedler.[108] Voluntary interracial coupling between white women and black men—the metaphoric celebration of a union of body and spirit—would belie the dualism by which the white order operates. "*Difference* . . . prevails because it dispenses with or triumphs over conflict," said Roland Barthes,[109] anticipating Jacques Derrida. Such a union has troubled the American conscience that for so long was able to justify itself by the separation of impulse and ego, and the concealment of the one from the other.

It has always been the racial intimacy of male and female—not of male and male—that disturbed the white's image of himself. As Fiedler observes, American literature tended to substitute the Neoplatonic play of supposedly innocent young boys for explicit sexual expression.[110] The tradition of sexual innocence glossed over the white man's rape of the black woman. At the same time, it accepted the racial intermingling of blacks and whites of the same sex—relationships which seemingly had no sexual implications and so precluded any potential disruption of white cultural patterns—in the perverted sense, at least, that they were sterile. Fiedler even argues that James Baldwin, who succeeded in adjusting to a white world, used homosexuality to reconcile the races.[111] Fiedler's own Negro character Andrew Littlepage in *The Second Stone*, physically unattractive, obsequious and sardonic, represents a parody of the stereotype of black sexuality, black rebellion and black jive. He is the charlatan, the bourgeois Communist, who participates in a conference on love and accuses his critics of castrating him.[112] But Fiedler, like most white intellectuals, tries to fit the black into his scheme of things. "Both colored and white," he remarks, "are becoming . . . a *tertium quid,* more closely related to the myths of the black man than to the actualities of either."[113] They are, in effect, becoming mulattoes.

Fiedler is not a romantic; he is a liberal realist, an integrationist *par excellence* who accepts the modes of white culture and requires that blacks conform to them. Even more emphatically than he, Saul Bellow is the defender of the principles of western civilization that modern life has debased. And since his imagination cannot reach beyond the premises on which it is based—and which it transgresses—Bellow is able to see the black only in terms of this imagination—which amount to stereotypes. In any case, Bellow is not at home with the race. His discomfort does not seem to stem simply from a fear of black assertiveness, as does that of his character Herzog, who condemns Muslim nationalism because it is built on "*hate.*"[114] More significant, there lurks in the back of Bellow's mind the idea of both black sexuality and black disruptiveness—the two are associated as a threat to the existing order—which fascinates and repulses his intellectual protagonists. If, on the one hand,

Bellow's view of the black reflects the legend of the brute, on the other—in tune with contemporary trends—he relates this myth to that of the malicious colored man who is enough acculturated to be able—with cunning—to tear down the cultural edifice.

Bellow's Mr. Sammler, who with all his refinement is as prurient a voyeur as the traditional southern gentleman, is obsessed with his grotesque image of the Negro exhibitionist, the superman savage whose "large tan-and-purple" penis resembles a "tube, a snake . . . elephant's trunk."[115] But the black is not simply a brute. He is the kind of person who "goes about . . . robbing us, wrapped in ideologies designed by Nietzsche, Rousseau, Darwin and Freud."[116] And his sex is his "metaphysical warrant," the weapon he uses to destroy the order of the world. Western civilization is being undermined by "sexual niggerhood," a search for a "blameless state of madness" because it is related to biological nature, but which Sammler associates with the "envy and worship of [the] power to kill."[117]

Perhaps it is the idea of miscegenation that troubles Bellow's protagonist. The sex of the black is the affirmation of the id, on whose repression western civilization was constructed. Since sexual assertiveness appeals to and undermines the resistance of the white female—protector of the race—it endangers the whole process of cultural continuity. What a woman wants, says Bellow's Angela, is a "Jewish brain, a black cock, a Nordic beauty."[118] His Uncle Benn, the intellectual analyst of nature, is done in by sexual desire for a scheming and artificial woman. Above all, Bellow seems to be afraid of the infiltration of chaos or decadence in even an imperfect, unjust order. As a liberal universalist, he attacks the prevailing romantic literary mood of alienation which decries industrial society and yet which has become a convention. In opposing what he calls literature's acceptance of "romantic segregation or estrangement from the common world" because it "enfeebled literature," he implicitly defends the status quo, criticism of which must be contained within the limits of the dominant middle-class norm.[119]

The white male intellectual belittles the black's movement for liberation when he associates it with the white female's drive not for rights but for sexual emancipation. Like a medieval realist, he resorts to ancient stereotypes to restore the illusion of rational order to a society in flux. Women now expect nightly erotic "gratification . . . safety, money," writes Bellow.[120] One of John Updike's characters speaks of two modern revolutions: "One, women learned to say 'fuck.' Two, the oppressed learned to despise their sympathizers."[121] While blacks traditionally used to ache after white women—the blacks of Updike's fictional African state of Kush in *The Coup,* for instance, never "cease dreaming of intercourse between dark and fair skin"—now certain American females cannot "leave black men alone." Blacks have been consigned to ghettos not just because they are poor, thieving and disruptive, but, more significant, because whites have a "superstitious horror of their skins, their rolling eyes, their whiplike penises."[122] When blacks emerge from their enclaves, crudely and arrogantly, they claim their pound of white meat; and it is this kind of assertiveness that threatens the established structure.

Updike also updates the stereotype of the black brute rapist. His Skeeter in *Rabbit Redux* is a cool and hip colored revolutionist who fascinates Harry's son, takes away Harry's girl and then leaves her to die to save his own skin. And the girl is, of course, an enthusiastically consenting victim. She likes to be raped by him; she wholly supports the black cause, whose only positive effect seems to be sexual. Black and sexual liberation amount to the same thing. As another of Updike's white females remarks—perfectly vacuously—"once you're in a march you have no identity. It's elegant. It's beautiful."[123] Skeeter does not care about politics: to him sex is an expression of mastery as blackness inherently signifies the disruption of order. Black all by itself is, he says, "a political word" with an implication of blind rage.[124] "To be alive is to kill."[125]

By associating the black revolution with sex, Updike is demeaning the drive for black equality. The civil rights movement, says one of his characters, is a "god-awful phony imitation of a revival meeting."[126] Besides being a demagogue, the Negro is a state ward who gets everything on a silver platter, who "lives deprived and naked among us as the embodiment of truth."[127] His ideologizing is irrelevant, if not oppressive. The third world—chiefly the black part of it—is an enigma, a conscienceless noncivilization built on violence, or on the principle that "blood is spirit."[128] It is, thinks Bech, Updike's rational and cultured Jew in *Bech Is Back,* "a vacuum that might suck him in"[129] with his watch—the symbol *par excellence* of the white rational order. And yet, following the liberal tradition, Updike does try to maintain a tolerant stance. He defends his much-belabored Harry from any insinuation of racism on the grounds that Harry hates rich whites—his girl is one— "as much as the ghetto black."[130] Updike, having confessed that he has never felt at home with Negroes, worries about his discomfort with them. In *Buchanan Dying,* he even converts President Buchanan, actually a self-interested materialistic slave collaborator, into a moderate antislaver with a sympathy for blacks.[131]

By identifying the sex and race movements, white liberal intellectuals—perhaps unconsciously—were upholding the existing order in all its inequities. In reducing the black revolution to a sexual context—in effect, to forbidden desires for white females—they were attempting to control it; they were fitting it into the stereotype by which whites have traditionally subverted the black cause and perverted the historical reality of the black experience. "*Myth is depoliticized speech,*" said Barthes.[132] Some white intellectuals have accused blacks of vulgarizing their political struggle by limiting it to a sexual drive. Susan Sontag, for instance, criticizes black writers for portraying the "racial problem . . . in terms of sexual attitudes."[133] Baldwin, she says, equated white inferiority with "sexual inferiority"[134] and, conversely, black superiority with sexual proficiency, as if this show of force were the chief thrust of black power. Baraka's *Dutchman,* the story of a white girl's assassination of a bourgeois black man after he reclaimed positively his racial roots and turned on her, was presumably just an account of sexual and class anxiety. Sontag was unable to grasp its political implications.

Joyce Carol Oates, writing during the 1980s, was another liberal who resorted to the integrationist viewpoint in her characterization of blacks. Although they are "different" yet the "same,"[135] although it is in their neighborhoods that "forbidden thoughts are waiting,"[136] she turns them into whites with black skins whose only social distinction derives from their unjust treatment by whites. Perhaps for this reason they must be handled with extreme care. Oates's blacks have no culture of their own: in *Because It Is Bitter, and Because It Is My Heart,* her Negro protagonist Jinx, who dies in Vietnam and transcendentally unites with Iris, the white girl he rejected in life, has no historical ties to slavery or to his black tradition. His only racial specificity lies in the way Oates thinks he and his peers talk. They do not speak as do whites or, for that matter, as do blacks. They use a kind of offbeat jargon that rings embarrassingly false.

Such misrepresentations of the black have traditionally been employed as a means of repressing him. Stereotypes were cultural devices to subject him to the prevailing social norm. They have deprived him of cultural identity, as if he had to derive what self he had from the white, implicitly his better. When sociologists like Gunnar Myrdal claimed that Negro culture was a "*distorted development, or a pathological condition of the general American culture,*"[137] he wrote—as Ellison points out—as if black were the reverse side of white, which should be wiped away.[138]

Liberalism, its tolerance of black protest and its acceptance of black militants, including black intellectuals, into circles of relative power are reflections of the presumed primacy of white cultural norms to which blacks should submit. As Roland Barthes remarked, the bourgeois ideology has absorbed revolts and this ideology represents "the process through which the bourgeoisie transforms the reality of the world into an image of the world. History into Nature."[139] Tolerance, as Chester Himes observed, expresses neither recognition nor equality.[140] Robert Penn Warren tried to interpret the black "situation" in terms of the by now conventional intellectual pose of alienation. It is the archetypal "image of man's fate," he said. The black is the "prototype of the contemporary sense of existential dislocation."[141] To claim that the "melioration of the black man's agony in his transition to the larger white society"[142] is the liberal's responsibility is to pretend that the black can fulfill himself only as a member of the society, that he has no identity of his own. It is to try to turn him into another white man and to call such assimilation the realization of the American dream. It is also to avoid the significance of the past and the present in the name of a perverted idea of progress. "Our modern sentimentality," writes Arthur Schlesinger, Jr., "evades the essential moral problems in the name of superficial objectivity and asserts their unimportance in the name of an invincible progress."[143]

PART IV

BLACK CULTURAL AFFIRMATION

THE BLACK DIALECTIC WITH RESPECT TO THE STEREOTYPE OF THE BLACK BEAST

B lack literature has been marked—like all black culture—by its struggle not just for free expression but for survival in accordance with the exigencies of the prevailing white order. The black has had to battle for his identity and for his acceptance within the context of a stereotype that attempted to reduce him to a state of dependence. As W.E.B. DuBois pointed out, and as many contemporary African Americans emphasize, the black is subject to a double consciousness; he suffers from a split personality.[1] "The uniqueness of the Afro-American novel," writes critic Bernard Bell, ". . . derives from both the double-consciousness of its sociocultural and sociopsychological content and the double vision immanent in the pattern of oral and literary conventions of Afro-American and European-American sign systems that structure the content."[2] The black's revolution, which has not ended, has been a cultural as well as a political battle to clear the way for development of this original and independent voice.

Unlike the assimilated ethnics, the black has a definite and historical American culture of his own. Certain intellectuals, such as Baldwin,[3] Baraka[4] and Wright,[5] claim that it is based on his struggle against racism and oppression. To others, that culture is founded, even subconsciously, on a tradition that is distinct and separate from that of Europeans. However, it does exist and it is continuous. It has evolved through the centuries until it has a recognizable character of its own:

it "Jes Grew."[6] Black culture is unique and peculiarly American: the
stereotypes of the Negro themselves—with respect both to white attitudes and to blacks' reaction to them—are a product of the American
experience. In his response to the stereotypes, the black reenacts his role
as the oppressed, and still freedom-seeking, victim of white exploitation.
And he asserts his basic difference, his specificity.

The black experience in America, in which black culture is to a
great extent grounded, has been an agonizingly negative one. Not only
has the African American been denied a positive identity in the sense
that "there has always been a cultural and social boundary in America
beyond which [he] could not go,"[7] he has also literally been deprived
of a home on earth. He has been told that his native land is not his, as
Wright put it.[8] As a black, the writer William Kelley did not consider
himself a real American.[9] The African American, says Eric Lincoln, has
been made to feel that he is "not truly American," that America is the
"white man's country."[10] He is the outsider-insider: his very existence
is subject to stereotypical distortions that he must endure. Nevertheless,
as the outsider-insider, he has been able to achieve a vantage point: he
has absorbed the white man's culture as he has comprehended the white
man's character. He has played to the white's derogatory image of him
until he evolved not just a cultural personality of his own but, as sociologist Melville J. Herskovits notes, "a definite physical type."[11]

The stereotype of the Negro brute, for instance, "*the beast in our
newly found jungle*,"[12] was the means by which whites contrasted their
civilizational refinement to the savagery of the black, and rationalized
their exploitation of him. His presumed barbarism represented the primitive human past—which he carried on his back in the color of his skin
and which disqualified him for participation in white society. The
black's individuality was swallowed in the myth of darkness that he
could not escape. "Herself. Her race," thinks Nella Larsen's Irene in
Passing. "Race? The thing that bound and suffocated her. . . . A person
or the race."[13]

Because the black was treated as an irremedial cultural impotent,
he was not allowed to fall back on his heritage—as the original settlers
and later immigrants were able to do. His tentative overtures to his
African past were stymied—although many intellectuals from Phyllis
Wheatley to Martin Delany to Alexander Crummell made serious efforts to establish the link. His salvation, as Addison Gayle suggests, lies
outside the western orbit.[14] Leslie Fiedler, for instance, claims that the
black is not related to Europe despite the fact that he has been as much

formed by that civilization as any American.[15] Actually, as Baldwin points out, Americans of all kinds of ethnic and racial backgrounds have a common quality that seems to mark them no matter where they go.[16]

But the black was nevertheless singled out as the rejected American. As a reaction to the stigma of underman as reflected in the first stereotype of the Negro brute, black literature came to emphasize the theme of the outcast, a theme that in itself implies estrangement. "The descendants of Ham are permanently unpopular with white Americans," Gore Vidal archly comments.[17] To be black is to be at odds with white norms as well as with white authority. To Langston Hughes's Harriet in *Not Without Laughter,* Jesus, who is white, is "stiff and don't like niggers."[18] To Ishmael Reed in *Mumbo Jumbo,* Jesus "is a compromise" Atonist, one of those who sustain "the sacredness of Western civilization and its mission."[19] And Alice Walker's Ceilie in *The Color Purple* loses interest in God when she discovers that he is white and male.[20]

Only in the process of affirming his deliberate ostracism could the black develop his cultural independence. He derived existential and aesthetic integrity from his recognition of the fact that "to be a Negro is to be an outsider, not only in a sociological . . . but . . . in a moral sense," as Nathan Scott writes of Richard Wright's work.[21] Gayle comments with respect to writer John A. Williams that "the prototype of man is to be found in the literature of outsiders."[22] Zora Neale Hurston's *Their Eyes Were Watching God,* Gayle continues, suggests that "before men can move outside the tradition and mores which seek to enslave them anew they must become outsiders in the true sense of the term."[23] The black, however, was not the exemplar of estranged modern man in the same way as the intellectual white assumed this rather conventionalized role. In facing a world bound by an inimical white presence that threateningly hovered over him like fate, the black possessed a historical dimension which most whites have lost and which acknowledged the physical struggle of surviving not so much against brute nature as against the brute nature of men. Whites, whose concept of alienation was abstract, internalized and narcissistic, lacked the immediacy and the communality that went with racial confrontation. The black, however, whose culture of necessity had not been universalistic in its pretensions but had been imposed by a particular civilization, accepted conflict from his birth as a way of life.

Black literature, therefore, has been marked by a naturalistic strain that is deliberately contentious. Danger was inherent in existence; violence was an undercurrent in the black's relation to the white world.

As the expression of dialectical coherence with concrete historical content, black writing could establish the "link between the structure of thought and the structure of reality."[24] Black life was constantly menaced. From the time when the slave George Moses Horton bewailed the "slavish chain"[25] he was forced to wear and the free black Martin Delany denounced the greed of Europeans and the vacuity of their civilization,[26] to modern days when Baraka preached "hate whitey,"[27] black writing has been oriented to protest, if not to revolt. Since it "has been literature either of purpose or necessity," as Saunders Redding put it, the study of it "becomes . . . a practical, as opposed to purely speculative, exercise."[28] In effect, black literature has been political: "All art is propaganda," claimed DuBois. He objected to this quality in it only when it was "confined to one side while the other is stripped and silent."[29] Since "racial ideology . . . divided the peoples of the world into white and colored races,"[30] black culture is by nature revolutionary with respect to that of whites. Critic George Kent's black "*is-ness*" inherently resists Euro-American myths.[31]

Delany chose a Cuban rebel as a subject for one of his books. Sutton Grigg's *Imperium in Imperio* was an attack on the myth of white supremacy:[32] it introduced the theme of an all-black agency to protect Negro interests.[33] Arna Bontemps took up the theme of the slave Gabriel Prosser's insurrection[34] and poet Robert Hayden composed a poem celebrating the revolt of Cinque, the African slave, and a "ballad of Nat Turner."[35] John Brown would join Nat and Gabriel in an afterlife of martyrs. White critics, such as David Littlejohn, have accused black authors of "sadism or brutality."[36] "The *war* element . . . distinguishes the Negro literature of our day,"[37] he complains, forgetting that it has always been a part of the Negro tradition. Blacks do not write of Negro life "*except* as war against the envied and hated white majority."[38] But in the negation of white oppression, blacks dialectically derived a positive view of American culture, particularly in its moral implications. If whites, who championed freedom and equality, denied black rights, then to reject their standards was to posit the real truth of their original principles.

It was Richard Wright who most dramatically exemplified the naturalistic strain of black literature. It was the character of Bigger Thomas in Wright's *Native Son* that illustrated the desperation of the disadvantaged black man in confrontation with an all-pervading white world. In his original confusion, Bigger becomes the unwilling assassin, victimized by a seemingly conspiratorial white order to which he has no relation and by which he is *a priori* cursed, deprived and bereft even of a personality. "Wright . . . depicted the black American as the victim of modern America and the Bad Nigger incarnate."[39] But by his symbolic rebellion, by willfully becoming the "Bad Nigger," by the liberating act through which he turns deliberately into a brute killer, Bigger is reborn. He frees himself and assumes the role to which society has already consigned him. He is the Negro savage beast, as whites have stereotyped him. He is in fact the mythical rapist: as Benjamin Appel testifies, "In the original draft, Wright said, Bigger'd raped the girl before killing her," but an editor or publisher "convinced Dick to unrape . . . Bigger's victim."[40]

Bigger's emancipation, his very selfhood, comes from the fact that he intentionally creates himself as the mythic monster; therefore, he claims a part in the destiny that is thrust upon him. "He accepts the ascribed white definition of the Bad Nigger . . . as a rebel against social conventions and the status quo."[41] He has nothing to lose; having been oppressed by the system, he turns outrageously against it: according to the old Negro adage that Wright quotes, "If what is happening to me is right, then, damn it, anything is right."[42] Bigger's reaction was repugnant not so much to whites as to blacks. Indeed, whites bought the book with vicarious satisfaction: it was a best-seller. The black middle class, which, until Wright, had been working mainly on the strategy of cultural integration, was to a great extent shocked. As Ishmael Reed observes, "Richard Wright risked his neck."[43] Despite the final section of the book in which Max, the white leftish lawyer, tries to rationalize Bigger's actions in terms of environmental causes, *Native Son* was a prodigious accomplishment.[44]

In creating Bigger's savage revolt, Wright himself saw the absurdity of the individual rebel's action. The absolute freedom of the outsider was a source of conflict in his own aesthetic sensibility. Wright's man who lived underground (in the story of the same name) is innocent of the murder of which he was accused and from which he fled, and guilty—ridiculously—of the crimes that he confesses. Nothing that he does or does not commit has any relation to his subsequent execution. Just as Bigger is not seen by the blind Mrs. Dalton who employs him, so the underground, anonymous man is invisible to the people on whom he spies, from whom he steals and whom he possesses "now more completely than he had ever possessed them when he lived above ground."[45] But he loses his self, his name, his identity. He is a being-in-self totally divorced from the society in which he exists. The policemen who shoot him think he is crazy "maybe . . . because he lives in a white man's world."[46]

Likewise, Wright's protagonist Cross Damon in *The Outsider* is a man who exists completely cut off from the norms and standards of his society. He is a presence apart from the people with whom he comes into contact: he is an abstraction, an incarnation of a power drive, as the white hunchback—the monster—Houston explains it. Since he operates on the premise that he is absolutely an outsider, Cross thinks of himself as free to act as he will. Everything from deceit to murder is permitted him. He believes in nothing: he is living in a meaningless universe in a valueless era.[47] As a critic says, he is a man of "no myths, no traditions, no race."[48] Nevertheless, he is caught inextricably in himself; he is the victim of his self-destructive compulsions, if not of his self-hatred.[49] He is the slave of immanence.

Perhaps Wright punished Damon intentionally. Wright, almost despite himself, was primarily a moralist, a Puritan, as Margaret Walker calls him.[50] Critics have often reproached him for being under the influence of Jean-Paul Sartre's existentialism, but Wright's interpretation of Sartre was based on his particular experience. His faith, he said in *Black Boy,* was "welded to the common realities of life."[51] Therefore, when he deprived Cross Damon of Sartre's *pour-soi*—a projectural and thus an implicitly moral purpose that would limit the future—he was condemning him.

Wright was himself caught in a dichotomy. The protest novel, as Baldwin commented, is unable to free itself from the norms against which it reacts.[52] Wright personally could not reconcile his aspirations with imposed modes of existence. His life was "rootless without an absolute," as Himes remarked.[53] Wright himself admitted that he was "a rootless man"[54] and added that he did not care. He was torn in himself: perhaps as Baldwin said of protesters, he was trapped "in the sunlit prison of the American dream."[55] As in Jean Toomer's *Cane,* Lewis noted of Kabnis, he has two souls: "master; slave, soil and the overreaching heavens—Dusk; dawn. They fight and bastardize you."[56] "My position is a split one," confessed Wright. "I'm black. I'm a man of the West."[57] On the one hand, his entire aesthetic was based on his identification with the Negro race: his "feelings had . . . been formed by the South," he wrote, "for there had been slowly instilled into my personality and consciousness . . . the culture of the South."[58] Wright, therefore, had an instinctive sentiment for Black nationalism: he was aware of the "nationalistic aspects of Negro life" in "social institutions . . . as in folklore."[59] He disapproved of America's materialistic society: "will the Negro become just another American?" he asked. "If he does, he will have lost a great opportunity. . . ."[60] American white culture was built on "a lust for trash";[61] America's preoccupation with things made it impossible for people to relate to one another. They had no depth.

Wright's very concept of protest as an artistic theme was connected to his affirmation of a peculiarly black point of view. In *White Man, Listen!* he argued that black literature must defend the rights of black people who are in an oppressive environment. Like his protagonist Fish, who is ashamed of his dependence on whites and of his inclination to reflect their most brutal traits, Wright was seeking liberation as a black man. In this respect, he emphasized certain cultural phenomena that were peculiar to the black experience: he enjoyed "Dirty Dozens," for instance, the verbal games in which Rap Brown excelled and which, said Wright, "jeer at life . . . leer at what is decent, holy, just, wise, straight, right and uplifting."[62] He also, as critic Edward Watson points out, made Bessie, Bigger's girl, sing the blues.[63] He had a faultless ear for black speech. It is said that he "deconstructs Euro-myth and reconstructs it in an Afro-centric way."[64]

On the other hand, Wright was deeply, irrevocably influenced by the principles of western civilization. If he advised Negro writers to "accept the nationalistic implications of their lives," he did so in order that they "transcend them."[65] He was a universalist by inclination; indeed, he was too much of a rationalist to accept the racial destiny that he considered thrust upon him. "His inner world," writes Margaret Walker, "was neither mystical nor hedonist, but deeply contemplative and rational."[66] He repudiated his nationalism at the Présence Africaine conference of 1956;[67] he seemed to reject "the traditions of black culture, his Afro-American heritage as useless baggage from the rural Southern past."[68] Wright proclaimed defiantly, "I have no race except that which is forced upon me. I have no country. Except that to which I am obliged to belong. I have no traditions. I'm free. I have only the future."[69]

Wright felt outside the laws of black and white. Like Bigger, he was "estranged from both the religious and the folk culture of his race."[70] Margaret Walker observed that "black people were never his ideals."[71] He thought of them "as victims of society, demeaned and destroyed and corrupted to animal status." He seemed, in fact, to "hate . . . his own black self"; he had a "desire to be white."[72] According to James Baldwin, Wright's "real impulse toward American Negroes, individually, was to despise them."[73] As invisible subjects of an impersonalized structure, blacks were, concluded Wright, "lacking in genuine passion [and] void of great hope."[74] Therefore, he could not reconcile his aspirations with imposed modes of existence. The black was contemptible because he had been deprived of a being-for-himself.

Wright's universalism at times led him to deny that black culture had a character of its own. He tended to explain it behavioristically: to assume "that Negroes are Negroes because they are *treated* as Negroes,"[75] as he wrote in *Pagan Spain*; as if Protestants in a Catholic country or members of any minority would develop the same traits if they were oppressed. It seems as if Wright could not fully accept the particular implications of the Negro experience in its historical, social and aesthetic dimensions. Admittedly, he was a secularist who rejected Christianity and, in fact, any religion—as he realized when he went to Africa and confronted the world of African chiefs. Their "authority came from mumbo-jumbo and not from rational thought,"[76] he wrote; "this dense illiteracy and the astonishing oral tradition—transmitted from generation of generation . . . has . . . erected a psychological distance between the African and the Western world."[77] He was opposed to the concepts of "negritude, mysticism and tradition";[78] he "stoutly denied the mystic influence of 'race.' "[79] Léopold Senghor, the poet and ex-president of Ghana, complained that Wright looked at the African movement for liberation as an instance of "anti-racist racism."[80]

Wright's rationalist, secular and universalist orientation[81] had led him as a young man to join the Communist party. He said he had turned to the left because he sympathized with the poor and the oppressed, and because he did not want to be "alone in [his] loneliness"[82] and the party offered him the solidarity of group belonging. He found in the Communist and Bohemian circles in which he moved a way of life that excluded "distinctions or lines . . . between the Jim Crow black world and the artistic, intellectual white world."[83] Daniel Aaron, the historian of the left, however, claims that Wright only "paid lip service to Marxist universalism."[84] Negro members of the party were elitist; they were mostly "petit bourgeois opportunists or black decadents or cowards"[85] who made little effort to reach the black masses. And the organization itself was authoritarian; Wright soon "chafed under [its] dictates."[86] Like the white society it represented, the party disapproved of a writer who thought on his own.[87] Moreover, it "did not know the complex nature of Negro life."[88] Wright broke away, disgusted by what he called the "political dictatorship of the Communist Party of the United States."[89]

He could never free himself either from this country—which he did not reject no matter how much it persecuted him—or from the duality of his character. He loved and admired the white world for its power and its industrial technology, and he hated and disrespected it for its degradation of himself and his race. As Margaret Walker puts it, Wright had come out of hell in the South and had been wounded for life by its racism.[90] Perhaps, like his Fish, he "hated the enemy because he saw himself and his people as that enemy saw them": he had an "adoring hatred of [whites],"[91] by whom he was in general well received and appreciated. He was "wandering in a no-man's-land between the black world and the white," said Baldwin, who considered Wright victimized by "the war in the breast between blackness and whiteness."[92] Chester Himes made fun of his inability to rise above the weight of white stereotypes. In Himes's *A Case of Rape*, Roger Garrison, who is somewhat cruelly modeled on Wright, wants to prove that there is an "international conspiracy of racism which employed convictions of rape against Negro men to maintain the Negro race in subjugation and social inferiority."[93] He would thereby establish the fact that blacks were not intellectually unqualified. Perhaps because Wright was torn in himself, his characters are caught in inherent narcissism; they are beings lost in themselves. Again, because Wright was seeking some authoritative standard—which he tried to find in ideas—he grafted social and philosophic theories onto his protagonists until their personalities were overwhelmed. They were abstractions. Bigger is able to arrive at a kind of operational harmony through his act of violence and his subsequent acceptance of his execution. Still, he has to die uncomprehended; his message is misrepresented by the white lawyer, Max. Most of Wright's characters, however, cannot find themselves as either blacks or white-blacks. It sometimes seemed as if, in striving for universalism, Wright excluded pluralism. Yet throughout his life, he never ceased to strive.

Chester Himes was another black who, like Wright, stressed violence as the only recourse to the racism that turned "the whole structure of American thought against me,"[94] as his character Bob puts it in *If He Hollers Let Him Go*. Bob, who wants to be "accepted as a man,"[95] is unable to make out, no matter what he does, with "white folks sitting on my brain, controlling my every thought, action, and emotion."[96] "American tradition had convicted me one hundred years before."[97]

The black man who had to bear the burden of racism on his back was never free; the only issue was violence, as Himes concluded. "In 1969," he wrote, ". . . I had become firmly convinced that the only chance Black Americans had of attaining justice and equality in the United States of America was by violence."[98] In the heart of every American black person there "is the knowledge that the only way to fight racism is with a gun."[99] As for Himes personally, he set out to persuade blacks to combat their enemy by any means. He "was going to live as long as possible to aggravate the white race."[100] During the Second World War he urged Negroes to battle for freedom in their own land: he called for Negro martyrs to inspire the race.[101] He composed a short story about a black terrorist who systematically mows down seventy-three whites—forty-seven policeman and twenty-six civilians—wounds seventy-five more and experiences "spiritual ecstasy to see brains flying from those white men's heads. . . . Hate served his pleasure. . . ."[102]

Actually, Himes recognized the futility of violence as an end in itself. The black did not have the power to annihilate whites: he could not even wound them as they could him. When Himes was sent to jail for robbery, for instance, he realized that the judge who sentenced him— "this motherfucking bastard"—had, in effect, "hurt me as much as I could ever be hurt. . . . He had hurt me in a way I would never get over. . . ."[103] And, consequently, Himes understood the absurdity of his situation: it made no sense. He interiorized his aggression and attacked those to whom he was close. Chased away by racism, he became an expatriate and, like Wright, went to France. Although he pretended that his life "was free, unlike the lives of other brothers,"[104] he admitted that even in Europe, where he seemed to be accepted, he "never found a place where I even began to fit." Not only was his rootlessness cultural—for he neither spoke the language nor understood the mores of foreign lands—but he was also plagued by his "antagonism toward all white people who I thought treated me as an inferior."[105] He was caught in himself: he felt everywhere that he was being done in. He "went through life without liking anyone, black or white, living with a young woman whom I always suspected of infidelities and of whom I was always jealous."[106]

The naturalism by which Himes was at first influenced—after Wright's example—has been called "objective, pessimistic, and amoral."[107] Since naturalistic realists, including Ann Petrie and William Gardner Smith, viewed black existence as already determined by outside economic and social forces, they concluded that there was no issue for the black. Violence was his only means of quixotically upholding his dignity at the risk of his very survival: but violence could inevitably bury him in irrelevance. Social realism, according to Reed, is "field nigger romanticism."[108] Petrie turned violent against her heroine in *The Street*, who kills her black seducer, but she is driven by conditions beyond her control. Baldwin also intuitively acknowledged the futility of violence when he consigned his rebel in *Another Country,* Rufus, to the desperation of suicide. In his affirmation of the Negro killer, or would-be killer, the black writer brought out into the open his inherent hatred of the white man on which any cultural assertion of black nationalism would be based. "Nationalism is healthy! Go through it," urged Reed.[109] It has, in fact, become a norm for a "vast segment of the Black population."[110]

Even Baldwin, who accused Wright of disregarding the black cultural tradition and, therefore, of implicitly suggesting that there was no Negro writer articulate enough to interpret it,[111] that it could not even exist, shared Wright's murderous impulses with respect to the white man. But he too was torn—as much as if not more than Wright, whom in many ways he resembled. Baldwin participated comfortably in the prevailing white culture both as a member of the elitist intellectual class and, by inclination, as a cosmopolitan universalist.[112] His task for black writers was "to make the question of color obsolete."[113] As one of his protagonists says, eminent people "are trapped on their hill. They cannot come down," for "you can't afford to lose [your advantage]."[114] Since Baldwin was a success, removed from the struggles of ordinary black folk—except insofar as he later became involved with the civil rights movement—he was inclined to equate the black experience with that of any other American minority. "Gadge, baby, you're a nigger, too," he wrote to Elia Kazan,[115] whose novel *America, America* describes the trials of an immigrant on his way up the social and economic ladder. Baldwin also became a militant spokesman for his people during the black revolution—a role that was thrust upon him but in which he excelled to the point that it inspired some of his best nonfiction. He denounced whitey and called Americans "the emptiest and most unattractive people in the world."[116] In his novels and plays he resorted to protest realism, which he had criticized in others when he tried to transcend social issues. Yet often his creative art amounted to propaganda: although he located "the failure of the protest novel . . . in its rejection of life, the human being . . . in its insistence that it is his categorization alone which is real and cannot be transcended,"[117] he took refuge in stereotypes. Nevertheless, in his essays and in his speeches he was brilliantly moving.

Quite naturally Baldwin found it difficult to reconcile his militancy with his innocent desire to belong in and to please a world in which he seemed to be increasingly accepted. He had escaped racist America because, he told Nikki Giovanni, he could not find "a certain corroboration that I needed."[118] In Europe, he wandered, as he accused Wright of doing, in a racial no-man's-land. He knew, as had Wright, that "he does not belong to Africa."[119] Once "condemned" to move, he explained, "you, in a sense, become neither white nor black."[120] He informed Margaret Mead that his "whole frame of reference all the years I was growing up had been black and white . . . suddenly that frame of reference had gone . . . and . . . as far as I can tell . . . once that has happened to you, it never comes back."[121] He had been reared in Harlem, and was an unusually sensitive and intelligent boy who, in his search for security, had suffered rejection from the inimical white world and from his own hard and uncompromising father. He was both literally and symbolically the unwanted bastard child, tolerated superficially, repulsed in reality.[122] In trying to equate the frustration of a personal quest for affection and for a viable authority figure with the political implications of racism, he swung back and forth in a love-hate relation with American society, morally decadent and cowardly as he knew it to be.

Gayle accuses Baldwin of being "totally ignorant" of black history and "oblivious"[123] of black writers before Richard Wright, a failing which Cruse considers characteristic of the Negro intellectual. Baldwin lacks "an ethnic cultural philosophy," he says.[124] Indeed, black social realists have tended to disregard their cultural tradition in their focus on the present. Just as white sociologists—and novelists—are inclined to interpret the ghetto experience uniquely in behavioristic terms, just as certain slaves under the pressure of an inexorable system accepted the whites' pretensions of race superiority, so blacks, blinded by their disgust over the effects of the industrial machine, have sometimes ignored the affirmative, even creative, aspects of their culture. In his later novels, Baldwin was unable to externalize his hatred for white America—if not white Americans, whom he often quite sincerely liked. He allowed his protagonists to suffer like passive scapegoats for the sins of an order with which he was obsessed and by which he was besieged. He was, in fact, confused by the moral manichaeism which reduced reality to an elemental warfare of black against white, and which caught the militant in an impasse from which he had no exit. Baldwin acknowledged his quandary when—like Wright, who was profoundly influenced by western literature and art—he viewed his own life in terms of a choice either of "accepting without question the gift of the language of the culture . . . in which case you must betray your mother, your father, your brothers, or you can turn away from it, going back to your mother, father, and brothers and becoming absolutely useless."[125]

During the 1960s, social realism carried the theme of violence to its logical extreme in its absolute identification of art and revolution. To the black man, as critic L. D. Aldridge put it, "the struggle against injustice constitutes the basis of his morality."[126] According to the writer Hoyt Fuller, "New black literature is, where it is most dynamic, informed by a spirit of nationalism. . . ."[127] In effect, black intellectuals tried to eliminate the distinction between politics and aesthetics. But the movement that was the expression of what poet Don L. Lee called "a new consciousness . . . a *black consciousness*"[128] demeaned mere " 'protest' literature"[129] as an appeal to white morality and an imitation of white forms. Writers experimented with black speech and tried to poeticize the black idiom; they attempted "to embrace modern literary forms and to end the predominance of naturalism in Black literature."[130] They entered frankly and openly into the battle against whites. "We have recognized that we are at war. . . . We cannot have reconciliation until *all* the killing is done,"[131] wrote Nikki Giovanni early on. "We got to prove we can kill,"[132] for "this country must be / destroyed / if we are to live."[133]

Poet Judy Simmons also proposed "guns and deadly poems . . . / [as proper] For my race."[134] "We must Be . . . hate," wrote Ebon, "coiled around their hearts like a striking cobra."[135] Carolyn Rodgers was more pragmatic in her analysis of revolution. To her, living in Chicago "was guerilla warfare yeah. / letuh revolution come. / Couldn't be no action like what / I dun already seen."[136] Even an established, reputedly "integrationist" poet like Gwendolyn Brooks found out "suddenly there was New Black to meet."[137] She asked blacks in jail to cultivate "victory Over / . . . what wants to crumble you down."[138] And she called her people to arms: "First fight. Then fiddle . . . Carry hate / in front of you and harmony behind."[139]

The most virulent proponent of the dialectic of racial violence was Amiri Baraka, who, with Larry Neal, founded The Black Arts Repertory Theatre/School in Harlem. It was he who insisted that art was politics: "We want 'poems that kill,' " he wrote.[140] He agreed with Ron Karenga that black art must be "functional, collective, and committing."[141] In effect, he preferred drama and poetry to fiction because these forms could be played or read directly to the people. And he felt, as he had written in *Dutchman,* that violent action would take the part of creative

work: "just let me bleed you, you loud whore," says Clay to Lula, "and
one poem vanished. . . . If Bessie Smith had killed some white people
she wouldn't have needed that music."[142]

From the days when, as LeRoi Jones, Baraka wrote *The Slave*, he
had preached revolution. He viewed contemporary issues in terms of
an ineluctable struggle between elementary forces. There is, as his protagonist Walker says, an unbreakable wall between black and white,
between himself and the white wife he has—symbolically and actually—
loved, who "if any white person . . . could . . . would understand,"[143]
but who cannot. And his war was not just against the white "soulless
monster":[144] he despised the bourgeoisie of any color—except, of
course, when his nationalism forced him to make up to the black middle
class.[145]

In the tradition of the revolutionist, Baraka looked chiefly to the
future. He thought in terms of power, which, he said, "must include
the positive evolution of all the forces."[146] To him reality was an ideal:
he spoke, for instance, of "that . . . reality / that we must all work to
force reality into reality."[147] In truth the present did not exist; it was
corrupt. The past was finished: history was "an old deaf lady / burned
to death / in South Carolina."[148] He concluded, "BE, we say to the
epoch of / tomorrow. And tomorrow now. And Now is when we
mean."[149] He championed blackness in its adversary role and used art
to call all blacks to arms against their enemy. ". . . i am prophesying
the death of white people in this land / [and] the triumph of black life
in the land / and all over the world."[150]

Baraka was putting himself dialectically outside the norms and standards of the industrial middle-class hegemony. As the old Negro adage
cited by Richard Wright claimed absolute moral freedom to reverse the
white man's injustice, so Baraka reasoned that "since there is a 'good'
we know is bullshit . . . we will be, definitely, bad, bad, as a motherfucker."[151] Bobby Seale and other Black Panthers had deliberately assumed the role of "bad nigger."[152] Malcolm X was admired for his
badness. "Our beauty is BAD cause we bad," wrote Baraka. "Our terribleness is our survival as beautiful beings, anywhere."[153]

But it was difficult for him to maintain his nationalistic revolutionary fervor in a situation in which he, as an artist despite himself, had
to invent new political and new aesthetic modes. He might have protested that "form is emptiness"[154] with respect to his radical mission.
But still he was trying to evolve an "*advanced*" form in the style of a
musician like John Coltrane, which was drawn "so much on the people

that it comes together."[155] Moreover, he could not help but doubt the viability of the revolutionary system. "Can we make a world and do actual work in it? Can we find actual love in it?" he asked almost wistfully.[156] The problem, as Don L. Lee (who nonetheless advocated "art for people's sake,"[157] and considered himself first a black and then a poet) observed, was that "i ain't seen no stanzas break a honkie's head."[158] Hating whites as an end in itself was essentially not only to fortify "the white man's sense of power,"[159] as Cruse suggests, but it was also to observe both revolution and art in the vainglory of words. The manichaeism implicit in the act of screaming " 'whitey' " and " 'honkie,' " as critic Stephen Henderson puts it, amounts to "masturbatory art."[160] And Houston Baker explains that "much of the work produced under the aegis of black . . . nationalism is deemed the sound and fury of a troubled past."[161] Baraka, who was accused of exoticism, if not narcissism, was in many ways—like Wright and Baldwin—fighting himself. He was a bourgeois intellectual who renounced his background and was seeking wholeness in an environment which was torn apart and in which his own creativity often was reduced to self-celebration.

After the 1960s, Baraka seemed to realize that his cause had no real issue. He took up Marxism, Leninism and world communism in order, he said, to make revolution scientific and directed. He also returned to his original campaign against all the bourgeoisie, including that of the blacks. Again, he found in this ideology—especially in the period of the cold war—that "it was much easier for a work of mine screaming 'Hate Whitey' to get published than work which suggests unequivocally 'BUILD A REVOLUTIONARY MARXIST-LENINIST COMMUNIST PARTY in the U.S.A. . . . .' "[162] And yet he still apparently had difficulty, at least philosophically and aesthetically, in reconciling a universalist world view with a nationalism that identified "race, nation, and culture."[163] He was also, it appears, unaware of the historical failure of communism with respect to black people.

CHAPTER 13

BLACK ATTITUDES TOWARD INTEGRATION

H istorically, the feeling of black solidarity has been the basis of black cultural expression. Since African Americans were subjected to a white hegemony, they have had—in order to survive—to adapt to white-imposed norms that presumed the superiority of white civilization. Blacks were allowed no alternatives to the standards of an order that pretended to be the absolute criterion of human achievement on earth. The second stereotype which whites propagated to control the black was that of the contented slave, the happy servant who recognizes his inferiority and looks up to his master admiringly. This image, the sequel to that of the black brute, carried with it the implication that the white had tamed the inherently violent nature of the original savage and had redeemed him in the higher values of white society.

Just as whites were subject to their own fabricated stereotype of the contented slave—until they convinced themselves by it that they were, in fact, superior beings—so blacks played to the stereotype in their struggle to adapt to white standards. They tried to make it in the white man's world: an ambition that characterized the ethnic process of assimilation, but which implied that white society was all that it assumed to be; that it was, in effect, worth the effort of striving to belong. Whereas whites, who controlled the order, forced blacks to submit to their will, blacks, who were subservient, had—and still have—to deal with different white modes of treating them.

One of blacks' first efforts to gain some autonomy in their lives was centered on education. This struggle involved their acceptance of white cultural norms, since obviously in the white man's world only Euro-American standards were promulgated. Besides, as Henry Louis Gates,

Jr., has pointed out, whites would not allow their slaves to become literate because they wanted to keep them in a condition of civic, moral and political inferiority. Whites, who equated " 'the rights of man' and the ability to write,"[1] were able to justify their consignment of blacks to the status of brutes by the fact that blacks, who were forbidden to read and write, could not do so.

Education, therefore, became the criterion for the "social and ethical betterment of the black person."[2] It would elevate him from his primeval nature to a state in which he might participate in the universal good of white civilization. Faith in education, therefore, had two implications with respect both to whites and blacks. It confirmed the whites, who were often liberal humanitarians, in their conviction that they did possess a superior civilization to which blacks must be necessarily—and happily—subject. It forced blacks to create themselves in a white image in order to be accepted and acceptable. Education was, indeed, the ground on which integration was based. The French abbot Gregoire, for instance, and the French Society of Friends of the Negro paid homage to the talents of Phyllis Wheatley: they considered her poetic accomplishments proof that the black race could attain intellectual fulfillment.[3]

Frederick Douglass, the slave who made himself into a national leader, deliberately learned how to read and write in order to set himself free—both physically and psychologically. He would use the white man's tools against the white man's system. His text, says Gates, was "the . . . mediator between the world as the master would have it and the world as the slave knows it really is."[4] Yet Douglass was subject to the temptations of a culture that has produced enviable words, if not deeds. As Richard Wright's "reading . . . created a vast sense of distance"[5] between himself and the harshness he suffered, as James Baldwin discovered possibilities through books that contradicted the impossibilities of the environment in which he was caught,[6] so Douglass was influenced by the literate he devoured and the intellectual circles in which he was received. As Houston Baker suggests, Douglass adapted to the white liberal image that represented one sector of the accepted white authority of the day: he projected a common destiny for himself and put himself in "harmony with a white, Christian, abolitionist framework."[7]

William Wells Brown, also a former slave, adapted to the humanitarian image of white liberals. His book *Clotel* featured what critic Barbara Christian calls the mulatta,[8] the white-colored slave daughter of the master, who, cloistered by her sex and his position in the big house, poses—unlike the mulatto—no threat to white male hegemony and yet who, distinguished by her gentility and moral integrity—as well as education—is designed to arouse sympathy, particularly that of a white female audience. Harriet Wilson also tried to appeal to white women in her novel *Our Nig*. She traded on the current of sentimentality that prevailed at the time. Half white and half Negro, she suffered relentless hardship at the hands of a cruel mistress, for she "was black, no one would love her." But she was the daughter of a colored man with a white heart, she wrote.[9] Booker T. Washington, in *Up from Slavery*, "adopted a public mask that displayed a Black self in harmony with its era."[10] There has existed, and still does exist, in black culture a pronounced inclination to integration. As Baker puts it, there is a "strong drive . . . toward a larger white society."[11]

This inclination is balanced by a contrary impulse: to integrate is not only to negate the distinctive features of the black experience but also to expose oneself to white malevolence. Black writing in all its aspects is characterized by the dualism inherent in the black situation in America. As Baraka wrote at Howard University, "All we were being readied for was to *get in*, to be part of the big ugly which was that ugly because it would never admit us in the first motherfucking place! We were being taught integration and nothing of the kind existed."[12] Naturally, therefore, the black cannot help but be torn in himself: he is intrinsically as much a part of white society as he is outside it. On the one hand, he has been raised in white culture and he knows its attractions, while on the other, he is as aware of the deceptions of this culture as he is of his own history.

As DuBois said with respect to his two souls, "How can love for my oppressed race accord with love for the oppressing country?"[13] Even without this cultural fission, the literate black has been faced through the centuries with functional problems regarding his creative activities. He has been forced to address himself to a literate audience that—obviously—has been chiefly white. "The black writer must not merely live in two worlds; he inevitably writes for two worlds," remarks a critic.[14] Until recently the black public has been deliberately restricted: black literacy has been curtailed. At the turn of the century there were "relatively few black readers in comparison with the large and nationwide white readership."[15] All the publishing houses were in the hands of whites, who also catered to a mass readership. As writer Charles Chesnutt observed, "There is undoubtedly a large and growing reading class among the colored people, but as yet they are mostly poor and I do not know how large buyers of books they are. . . . "[16]

Consequently, black writing has traditionally been aimed at a white public and its themes have been universalistic and integrationist. Since social protest, even of a moderate kind such as Chesnutt's, tended to alienate whites,[17] it was suppressed—at least until Richard Wright. The black author played the role—or depicted the condition—of the contented Negro in accordance with the white stereotype. He could not remain silent about glaring brutalities such as lynchings or riots, but otherwise the black author tried to minimize the difficulties of his situation. He realized and could not help but admit—to himself at least—that his compliance was a façade. "We wear the mask that grins and lies, / . . . With torn and bleeding hearts we smile," wrote poet Paul Laurence Dunbar.[18] "My position is most unfortunate . . ." he confessed. "I am a black white man."[19] And, indeed, his position *was* unfortunate. He suffered from what he called a "double-consciousness":[20] while "living with and for a particular section of the populace with a unique origin and experience [he was] writing for . . . a . . . national audience."[21]

It is probable that Dunbar—even if financial necessity had not led him deliberately to try to please the white public—did to some extent endorse the thesis of the contented slave. He was fixed on the past, according to a critic, even if he wanted to people it "with heroes of his race, whether real or legendary."[22] But he played to the image of the black and portrayed Negro "types of subservience, idleness and vanity."[23] Sterling Brown said that Dunbar "idealized the Negro, *in his place*."[24] He composed happy pictures of the old plantation: "you kin jes' tell Mistah Lincum / fu'to tek his freedom back,"[25] he had one of his characters proclaim. He also confined his fiction and most of his so-called literary poetry to the bounds of the genteel tradition, which was then in style. Son of slaves, he had worked his way up to the point that he was accepted by the eastern intellectual establishment and was revered as the "Poet Laureate of the Negro Race."[26] Black people were proud of him; whites respected him. And he wrote in dialect, as he told James Weldon Johnson, because that was "the only way he could get [the latter] to listen to him."[27]

But he felt that he was being paternalized. Dunbar resented William Dean Howells for praising the verse which typified him as a Negro and which he considered less worthy than poems composed in literary English. He did not want to differentiate himself with respect to white culture: he did not accept the fact that the Negro dialect—which he represented with remarkable skill—was not a mutilation of the English language, but a new and melodious adaptation of it. In any case, he set a style which appealed to whites—perhaps because, caught in their own myth of superiority, they believed that dialect was inferior[28]—and which his black imitators exploited in their own bids for fame. As it fell into disfavor—as Gates points out—"black poetry . . . the oral component of black poetry . . . was sacrificed on the altar of the universal to the spirit of Western art."[29] James Weldon Johnson himself realized that blacks needed "form that will express the racial spirit by symbols from within rather than by symbols from without."[30]

Dunbar could not have suffered from a double-consciousness had he not felt a profound spiritual affinity with his people. He could not have written his folk poetry without a deep feeling of racial identification. He had, says a critic, "a sense of the validity of an Afro-American view of life."[31] He celebrated black music and the black oratorical tradition—such as church sermons. The voice of his Malindy, before which "robins, la'ks, an' all dem things, / Heish dey moufs an' hides dey face,"[32] was that of his own mother. At a time when blacks were being violently consigned to underclass status, he wanted to militate for them. "Unless we live the lives of protest . . . we are as guilty as the lynchers of the South . . ."[33] he wrote to a white friend. And yet his hands were tied. He lost faith: he "suffered loss and grievous pain, . . . / And wounds so deep that love . . . / Had not the pow'r to ease them or to cure."[34] He concluded that "a colored man has no business with ideals—not in *this* century."[35]

Actually, Dunbar was writing at a time when the black community was sharply divided into classes, and the middle class had a long tradition not just of literacy but also of cultural refinement. Before the Civil War, the black community had seemed to be more united. Slaves were all subservient despite their differences as house or field hands: they were of the same caste. In the North, free and educated blacks—joined by escaped slaves of exceptional force and purpose—were caught up in a mission to liberate their brothers, with whom they felt a deep sense of solidarity. But with Reconstruction, the literate, mostly mulatto Negro rose to political and social prominence. In fact, in accordance with DuBois's concept of the talented tenth, the bourgeoisie stressed the theme of uplift. Black leaders wanted to raise black people to a level where they would be acceptable to whites; black writers tended to turn their heroes and heroines into paragons of virtue in order to convince the white audience, to which they were necessarily appealing, that blacks were worthy of integrating into the larger society. "A demonstration of intellectual parity by the Negro through the production of literature and art" would eliminate racism, said James Weldon Johnson.[36] "Far, far the way we have trod, / From heathen kraal and jungle den, / To freedmen, freemen, sons of God, / Americans and Citizens," he poeticized.[37] The purpose of Angelina Grimké, of the renowned—almost white—abolitionist family, was, as she put it, to "counter the stereotype of the 'darkey' by presenting 'the best type of colored people'. . . educated, cultivated and cultured . . . in many instances, more moral than the whites . . . [who] do not talk . . . in the Negro dialect."[38]

Most writers, therefore, chose very genteel, very worthy and very white protagonists. Passing was a favorite theme. At that point, many colored people of light skin had been easily able to pass into the white world. Authors used the subject both to make fun of white people in their exclusivist pretentiousness and to prove that there was, in fact, no cultural difference between the two races. Chesnutt, an almost white mulatto, showed how passing divided siblings and brought on unnecessary social tensions. Novelist Frances Harper wrote of an octoroon who refused to pass[39] and Pauline Hopkins of mulattoes who did so in order to emancipate slaves. Both idealized their characters to the point that they lacked life in their exemplary roles.[40] And both denied any qualitative, civilizational distinction between whites and blacks, thus bowing implicitly to the assumption that the white world, which prevailed, was the universal criterion of mankind.

Passing was the theme, also, of James Weldon Johnson's *The Autobiography of an Ex-Coloured Man*. With the Negro migrations that came with the First World War, black culture was losing its rural folk roots and becoming subject to urban influences. Since the metropolitan middle class had trouble identifying with the deracinated, directionless crowds that were invading and creating the ghettos of northern cities, color was more and more emphasized as the measure of class. Freed field hands were likely to be pure black; free Negroes—either manumitted or established citizens—were obviously kin to whites. Implicit in Johnson's novel is the association of higher class standing with light skin: a Negro who is able to pass must necessarily be practically white in color, and Johnson's protagonist is not only indistinguishably white, he is also the heir of "the best blood of the South."[41] His father is a recognized aristocrat. Although he lives with his dark mother and is put with the colored kids, he is remarkably different from those in the Connecticut town in which he lives. He is perfectly aware of his status: he finds that the shiny black boy in school "was in some way looked down upon";[42] he later calls him "nigger."[43] As the Negro doctor who befriends him in his adulthood scorns "loafing darkies," so he himself is repulsed by the vulgarity of lower-class blacks.[44]

As color tone stood for class distinction within the black community, it served positively to deny cultural difference between black and white. Johnson's ex-colored man is—as his white patron tells him—"by blood, by appearance, by education, and by tastes a white man,"[45] indeed, a white man of exceptional refinement. The light Negro was particularly torn in himself, not just because—by his education—he identified with the white civilization that rejected him, but because this very education separated him from his black world. As the millionaire who adopts Johnson's protagonist remarks, "I can imagine no more dissatisfied human being than an educated, cultured, and refined coloured man in the United States."[46] Certain black intellectuals (such as Dunbar, who was racially able to feel an instinctive and inherited solidarity with the agrarian tradition of slave parents—and with the South) blamed the city for destroying the integrity of formerly simple black folk. In his novel *The Sport of the Gods,* Dunbar portrayed a country family that, in escaping southern racist injustice, was unprepared morally for urban life and succumbed to a malignant environment of hustling, prostitution, crime—and even jazz. Following his experience with Philadelphia Negroes, DuBois thought that the inherent goodness and innocence of his people was perverted by the atmosphere of the city.

The post–World War I Harlem Renaissance reflected class differences between blacks. Perhaps its thrust was blunted because of the distinction that separated the educated intellectual from the uncultured black masses and intensified the black intellectual's sense of double allegiance with respect to his position in America. As historian David Lewis points out, the Renaissance was a time when, although sincerely preoccupied with their project to affirm black culture from its African origins through the slave experience to its present state, most writers implicitly accepted DuBois's idea that "there was nothing wrong with American society that interracial elitism could not cure."[47] Alain Locke, a proponent of the New Negro, was extremely educated, refined and Eurocentric. The Chicago sociologist Charles Johnson, who came east and chose the field of the arts as the one area from which Negroes were not excluded and who thus helped spark the Harlem aesthetic movement with his magazine *Opportunity,* was perhaps the most significant of the "handful of Harlem notables"[48] who deliberately managed "downtown contacts, prizes and publicity."[49] He sought white support. The prevailing spirit was integrationist and high-toned. "Locke and Johnson," says Lewis, wanted art "untainted by racial stereotypes or embarrassing vulgarity."[50] DuBois objected to the funkier aspect of the Renaissance: he did not appreciate the shenanigans of what he thought of as the "debauched tenth."[51] And Pace Phonograph's Black Swan Records rejected Bessie Smith, Lewis notes, because "of her unmistakable nitty-grittiness."[52]

In his poetic romance, *Cane,* Jean Toomer illustrated that the black soul was divided in itself psychologically as well as culturally. Toomer was the son of a distinguished colored family, particularly on his mother's side. His grandfather, Pinckney B. S. Pinchback, himself the son of the white Major William Pinchback and a mulatto slave, was a former lieutenant governor and governor of Louisiana and had been elected senator from the state. As a boy Toomer lived as both a white and a black and had no strong racial identity. Eventually, he denied his Negro blood: "I am of no particular race. I am of the human race," he insisted.[53] He could not maintain race consciousness in the white world in which he moved: "in my body were many bloods," he wrote.[54] "I am an essentialist . . . a spiritualizer, a poetic realist."[55]

As a young man on a visit to the South, he was, however, struck by the spirit of African American culture as reflected in its music, its sensuality and its rural folk tradition. When he heard black spirituals, Toomer felt his African American roots so intensely "that I lost my own identity," he said.[56] The South seemed to be the last point of resistance to the mechanical, industrial civilization of the North that was swallowing beauty and grace, and Toomer looked nostalgically back to it. Because he was an irrepressible womanizer, a man who celebrated the free expression of instinct, Toomer was quick to sense the relationship between sexual and racial repression. He found purity of love in the black community. "Particularly black folks were made to mate," he wrote.[57] Whereas he decided that "black life seems more soluble in lump," it was white life, "pitiably agitated to superiority," that was "more palatable."[58]

Toomer was an aesthete, torn between his inner and outer selves; he considered his inner self the more real. He wanted to free not just black and white, but spirit and body in a mystic union. Encouraged by white friends, including intellectuals Waldo Frank and Sherwood Anderson—who were both attracted to Negro exoticism—he tended to romanticize the primitive over the civilized, the rural over the urban,[59] almost as if he were looking longingly to the days of slavery. His poetic masterpiece, *Cane,* is a symbolic interpretation of the southern drama of color. Its first part celebrates uncorrupted instinct in the soul of the farm Negro on the ancestral soil—where "most anything can come to one."[60] The second part represents the emotional tensions the colored man and woman suffer in the suffocating atmosphere of the city. The third part presages the inevitable defeat of both as guardians of their specificity in their color.

But if in *Cane* Toomer was seeking not just a new form, but also a real identifiable self, he had to renounce both. He might have felt and seen the integrity of the Negro experience—which had contributed so strongly to black culture—but he was unable to render it in its entirety. The spirituals that had so moved him, he realized "with deep regret," would, "meeting ridicule, . . . be certain to disaster." *Cane* itself was "a swan-song . . . a song of an end."[61] Toomer was representing in his romance an antithesis of black and white, which a critic has compared to an implicit opposition of the spiritual versus the material.[62] For this reason, he did not seem to believe that the black could survive as such in a modern industrialized civilization.

In the first part of *Cane* blacks sing and dance and make love with elemental dignity; they are sadly acting out a transient moment in a way of life that is passing. "The sun is setting on / A song-lit race of slaves," he wrote. "O soil, it is not too late yet / to catch my plaintive soul, leaving, soon gone."[63] Toomer was describing love-lost women in illicit, even interracial passion. Karintha is beautiful, but promiscuous; the infidelity of Carma, who dances with an African spirit, drives her husband to murder. Fern is used by men; Esther dreams of the vagrant trickster, the lover of women *par excellence* and the craftsman of words who leaves his mark indelibly on her. And Becky, the white, dies when her two mulatto sons leave town. Perhaps she represents a haunt: as critic Gérard Cordesse remarks, "The imposed infusion of white blood parallels the infusion of white culture through exile and servitude. . . ."[64] The white is the curse in the South; in fact, the whole drama is played under a blood-burning moon that symbolizes the violence that the South inflicts on its colored folk.

In *Cane*'s second part, the black's natural creative spirit is stultified by the city. Avey, the new urban bourgeoise, is promiscuous, "no better than a whore."[65] But she is rootless, an "orphan-woman"[66] whose outlet lies not in song but in indolent romantic dreaming. John, the high-class Negro (Toomer was sensitive to status discrimination within the metropolitan Negro community), is attracted to Dorrie but she cannot inspire him, even by her dancing. He has renounced his original spirit: his face is "a dead thing."[67] Paul, the black who loves Bona, knows that "people saw not attractiveness in his dark skin, but difference."[68] He is separated from his girl by the kind of barriers that Toomer detested in materialistic society. It was this kind of artificial order that was killing off "the Negro of the folk song" and "the Negro of the emotional church."[69] Toomer felt that the loss was irreparable, and he had no faith that blacks possessed a culture resilient enough "to resist."[70]

Toomer could not resolve the cultural dichotomies that he found in the black soul. In the third section of *Cane,* he left the problem of split consciousness unsolved. Since he associated "spiritual fusion" with creativity, he looked to the intellect—as to the Logos, the word—to reconcile the warring elements of the Negro consciousness.[71] Kabnis, his artist, who is "a dream," returns from the urban North to the South where he confronts Lewis—perhaps his alter ego whom, since "life . . . has given him in excess of what he can receive . . . , he vomited,"[72] as Lewis puts it. It would be through the reclamation of this same Lewis that Kabnis might discover a new and transcendent voice. If Carrie, the innocent young girl, is the symbol of love and of the integral future and also of redemptive art, then the old man whom she tends and who cannot speak is the past with its sin and violence and antithesis of black and white. But Kabnis cannot find his voice: he condemns the old man as the "father of hell"[73] and will not recognize the girl. He can neither purge himself of sin nor conciliate his warring souls: "the form that is burnt into my soul is some twisted awful thing that crept in from a dream," he says.[74] And Lewis, finally exasperated, goes away. "Their pain is too intense" for him to stay.[75]

Eventually, Toomer, who sought the forces that would create "a new people in the world, a people to whom all Americans . . . belong,"[76] turned his quest to psychic explorations. He renounced the real world. As he wrote in *Blue Meridian,* one must "fix . . . / [on] the symbol of Universal Man— / . . . outgrow clan and class, color, / Nationalism, creed all."[77] Because he refused to be either black or white, Toomer suffered from a duality of personality—from his experience of "separated selves."[78] He was divorced from his people, whose soul had so moved him, and he felt "curiously broken":[79] he could not "will [himself] into new life"[80] and he could not revert to his old sensation of spiritual belonging. He could not integrate his revolt against the social and sexual conventionality of bourgeois standards—black as well as white—"of an environment which [obtrudes] itself between the spontaneous union of souls,"[81] as one of his characters puts it, with his implicit affirmation of the essence of being black. He confessed he had no center: he was a complex of extremes, "a devil and a saint,"[82] never satisfied, always questing for some kind of transcendent fulfillment. "We are split men," he wrote, "disconnected from our resources, / almost severed from our *selves,* and therefore out of touch with reality."[83] He died, withdrawn into himself, unreconciled and unrecognized, "a weakly inferior colored boy . . . who never grew up," as he put it.[84]

Gates thinks that it was by denying racial difference that "passion and lyricism inform[ed Toomer's] use of language."[85] Certainly, like his character Nathan Merilh, Toomer cared only about "two things . . . creation, and the power to achieve it."[86] Unfortunately for him, he was caught in a subjectivity that could not accept otherness; passing never enabled him to recover his poetic inspiration. Perhaps he missed his racial identity. His sensibility and inwardness, said Redding, "were narcissistic": he would swallow himself in the "universal oneness. Nirvana. Oblivion."[87]

Toomer was perhaps the lyrical genius of the Harlem Renaissance whose books caught the poetry and the agony of the black experience. It is certain that the Negro movement of the 1920s was not a coherent unified literary manifestation. It included various types and trends of black writing, but it lacked "an intrinsic and vital literary tradition of its own."[88] Nevertheless, it was, in principle, brought together by a common purpose. It represented an attempt "to assert . . . a dissociation of sensibility from that enforced by American culture and its institutions," as George Kent put it.[89] Since the Negro literary tradition was theoretically interpreted—if not led—by cultivated members of the Negro bourgeoisie who had little to do intellectually and socially with the experience of the ordinary ghetto black, it was cut off from the indigenous Negro tradition. It operated within a white framework, either liberal or left wing, and it was always oriented to uplift or to integration or to "interracialism," a philosophy subject to the "cultural paternalism" that "makes the Negro intellectual 'outer directed.' "[90] Black writing depended to a great extent on the patronage of whites to whom black artists played for approval. As a character of Wallace Thurman's observes, "Being a Negro in these days is a racket and I'm going to make the most of it while it lasts."[91]

A writer like Jessie Fauset, for instance (Phi Beta Kappa at Cornell, spinster schoolteacher, competent literary editor of *The Crisis* under DuBois, and member of the upper Negro bourgeoisie), was hardly the type to launch a radical movement of black art. Although she spoke of the duality of the Negro spirit, she was too preoccupied with maintaining her respectability and with upholding white civilizational standards[92] to comprehend the aspirations and impulses of black people as a whole. She inserted middle-class goals into her race consciousness[93] and insisted that the Negro "is not so vastly different from any other American, just distinctive."[94]

George Schuyler, a brilliant black social critic who was white in color, refused to acknowledge any qualitative difference between white and black[95] and, therefore, the possibility of the development of an integral black culture. If the Negro "is merely a lampblacked Anglo-Saxon," as Schuyler maintained, then a special kind of Negro art was impossible to cultivate. "It is sheer nonsense to talk about 'racial differences' as between the American black man and the American white man," he wrote.[96] Actually, he suffered because he was an outspoken individualist who wanted to transcend the onus of racial identification; he refused to be categorized as anything but himself. Schuyler rationalized the color caste system on pragmatic grounds: it was a policy "to spare the nation the enervating presence of a destructive social caste system,"[97] he argued in the spirit of John C. Calhoun. He would not consider Jim Crow, personally or collectively, as a reason for racial distinction on the part either of blacks or of whites.

Melvin Tolson, an aesthete to whom "the artistic subsumes the political,"[98] used poetry to establish the universality of human civilization. He was not really a part of the Harlem Renaissance: he came to it late and he was not involved in its original thrust. He was an academic intimately involved in the study of western civilizational trends, so he viewed the world in western terms—usually those of economic progress. "With the Peoples of the World . . . / We advance!" out of illiteracy, poverty, superstition, disease and Jim Crow, he wrote. "The New Negro . . . / Strides . . . Along the Highway of Today / Toward the Promised Land of Tomorrow!"[99] In his *Libretto for the Republic of Liberia,* which was praised by Allen Tate, Tolson envisioned a cultural progression in which America would emerge from the "charnel-house" of Europe and "Black Lazarus" would "rise . . . from the white man's grave."[100] The curator of his Harlem gallery is a "voluntary" Negro—a man of all races of Afroirishjewish ancestry"[101] who chooses to be a black. But Tolson was a loner as well as a latecomer to the New Negro movement and he took refuge in esotericism.[102] In many ways, he was, like Toomer, a mystic. He looked forward to the apocalypses, the revelation of spiritual realities; he was, indeed, divorced from the ordinary Harlem scene.

Nella Larsen was a scientifically trained middle-class woman married to a physicist. In her novel *Passing,* she made clear the problems of double-consciousness that plagued the Negro not just of whitish skin, but of white cultural orientation and of high Negro social standing, for the three seemed to go together. Larsen appeared to be torn between the black and the white worlds. If she made an effort, like her heroine Irene Redfield, to defend the race to which she belonged; if she recognized the loveliness of black features and the warmth, gaiety and spontaneity of the black personality in contrast to the coldness of the repressed white; nevertheless, she was confused and hesitant with respect to passing. "We disapprove of it and at the same time condone it," says Irene.[103] Perhaps she "found the vagaries of a white identity preferable to the pain of Africa," as Lewis remarks.[104] Perhaps, as her books suggest, she just wanted to be left alone—even in a segregated situation—away from the humiliations and intrusions and patronization of whites. Perhaps, like Irene, Larsen was caught between two allegiances.

It was this same double allegiance that seemed to smother the very extensive talent of Countee Cullen. He had started out in a favored situation: adopted son of a leading Harlem minister, gifted student, personable young man, he was a poet of whom black intellectual circles expected much. Nevertheless, he, too, was torn.[105] He was a universalist who wanted to be accepted in the larger culture not as a Negro but as a poet in his own right. As Rampersad says, he "wished to be seen not as a Negro poet, but as a poet who happened to be Negro."[106] In this sense he dealt adversely with race consciousness: as he admitted, "Although I struggle against it, it colors my writing. . . ."[107] Yet he resolved to be his black self: "Lord, I will live persuaded by mine own," he wrote.[108] This same inner battle obtained on a religious as well as a cultural level. He was both Christian and pagan: he was two men, one who believed and one who doubted.[109] He was the "black sheep" who questioned the validity of a faith in which he had been raised and by which he was excluded.[110]

Cullen tried desperately to reconcile his two sides. He wanted to balance the tight and logical discipline of the English language with melodic "heights and depths of emotion."[111] He idealized Africa as the symbol of black freedom and autonomy, while at the same time he modeled his poetry on occidental forms. "What is Africa to me?" he asked. Reason told him that it was a foreign and alien culture; his sensibility drew him to it, to the voluptuousness of music and love and dance. Confused, he wondered, "Do I play a double part," and then justified himself. "Lord, I fashion dark gods, too / Daring even to give you / Dark despairing features," he confessed.[112] He was profoundly estranged in a white-preempted world where, he realized, he could at any minute be reduced to the category of "nigger," as he was once called.[113] "We were not made eternally to weep,"[114] he asserted and then ruefully complained, "Yet do I marvel at this curious thing: / To make a poet black and bid him sing."[115] He had been given the language, the tool, that—culturally—worked against him.

Isolated with respect to his situation in a white-dominated civilization in which he had been schooled and by which he was rejected, and to that of the Negro bourgeoisie from which he hailed and which was exploiting the vogue of blackness during the so-called jazz age, Cullen's confusion was reflected in his aesthetic attitudes. Privately, he was beset by religious and cultural doubt; publicly, he was condemned by those of his peers who practiced the cult of the New Negro. Cullen reacted: "Aloof and lonely must he ever walk,"[116] he wrote as he defied his black critics. He abandoned his identification with his people and sought a refuge in his own novel brand of Christianity: he came to believe that Christ symbolized and incarnated the contradiction between black and white, between spirit and body, between death and life. In *The Black Christ* his lynched hero, Jim, is resuscitated as a sacrificed figure,[117] and the poet finds solace as well as faith in the submissive image of the scapegoat.

Because black writers were in general under the influence of an integrationist philosophy, they tended to underplay race and emphasize the fact that whites and blacks were the same. Therefore, they took up the theme of passing. Georgia Douglas Johnson, hostess of a literary salon and friend to most of the intellectuals of the time, admitted that she did not enjoy "writing racially."[118] Yet she wrote plays on racial themes: lynching, exploitation, the mulatto offspring of white potentates.[119] Alice Dunbar Nelson, wife of Paul Laurence Dunbar, was governed also by what critic Gloria Hull calls "intergrationist ethics."[120] With the exception of lynching, black writers shied away from controversial subjects. Since they depended on whites—to the extent that they were addressing a white public and receiving aid from a white literary establishment—they had to temper their approach. Even incipient nationalists were torn by a love-hate relationship with the white world that they admired and despised.

Rudolph Fisher, promising, attractive and energetic, died young. He burned out. Wallace Thurman, who was not of the proper middle class, who was decidedly black and, therefore, self-conscious about his skin color, believed that the Negro movement should identify positively, culturally, with race. He never doubted, says Lewis, that "artists could recognize the need 'for a truly Negroid note' and would go to the proletariat rather than to the bourgeoisie for characters and material."[121] His magazines, which unfortunately went under, were dedicated to this principle—and were criticized by more genteel aesthetes as vulgar. Nevertheless, he did not seem to be able to impose his point of view, perhaps because he himself was torn. "He craved the company of whites and mixed bloods," says Rampersad.[122] Thurman's books were not affirmative statements of black cultural identity but, rather, attacks on his peers. *The Blacker the Berry* denounced color prejudice within the black community. *Infants of the Spring* satirized the reigning Negro intelligentsia that he and Zora Neale Hurston labeled the "Niggerati."[123] Talented and ambitious as he was, he was unpopular. It is said that Thurman was a "victim of his own self-hatred arising from his racial identity."[124] Like Fisher, Thurman died young, disillusioned "with the outcome of the Renaissance, as well as his own personal failure as an artist."[125]

Zora Neale Hurston, student of Franz Boas, protégée of Annie Nathan Meyer and secretary to Fannie Hurst, took her hometown in Florida as a model for her fictional and anthropological studies of black culture. "When I pitched headforemost into the world I landed in the crib of Negroism," she wrote proudly.[126] But her collections of African American folklore—as well as her highly original novels—were rejected by the black middle class. It was ashamed of the hoodoo, conjuring and signifying on which she reported, which were part of the African American tradition but were not taken seriously by rational western culture. The better types of blacks are against "the spirituals, the Blues, *any* definitely Negroid thing," she remarked.[127] They snubbed the folkways of their people. "They lacked the happy carelessness of a class beneath them and the understanding of a top-flight Negro above them," Hurston observed.[128]

She became disillusioned. She was too much of an individualist to

be a black nationalist. She turned her back on the past and denied
that there was such a thing as race pride. She refused to endorse the
ideology of "Race Pride and Race Consciousness," she said.[129] Hurston distrusted "Race Solidarity," which did not exist in America
"with any group."[130] The black race was anything but solid: Negroes
were individuals; "why should [they] be united? Nobody else in
America is."[131] There was a class difference in the community, which
had divided it into upper and lower strata, and the first disesteemed
the second.

As an individualist, Hurston looked at all people—blacks and
whites equally—as sufficient unto themselves. There was no advantage
in being of one race or another. Perhaps it was her early success and
her subsequent—obstinate—refusal to recognize the weight of factors
such as poverty, racial oppression and prejudice on a group's potential
mobility that led to her ultimate defeat. Although she rose from disadvantaged economic and social conditions to the privileged intellectual
class, her community, deprived as it was, was all black and relatively
free of the intrusion of whites. Yet her education had separated her
from it. She had "to have the spy-glass of anthropology to look through
at" her roots, she said.[132] Perhaps because she was a liberated spirit,
she was all her life, she said, shadowed by "a cosmic loneliness." She
was isolated in herself: "Nothing and nobody around me really touched
me."[133] Eventually, Hurston was abandoned by her benefactors; she
made a living as a maid in a white household and died in a poorhouse
alone. "There is something about poverty that smells like death. Dead
dreams dropping off the heart like leaves in a dry season and rotting
around the feet."[134]

The youthful militancy of Angelina Grimké may have been silenced
by the disapproval of her would-be publishers. An editor refused one
of her race poems because "it is the implied threat of a bloody rising
on the part of the negro."[135] It was, of course, nothing of the sort, but
Grimké was deeply affected by the brutality of whites against blacks:
she wrote plays and short stories particularly about lynching. She tried
to appeal to the maternal instincts of white women: in "The Closing
Door" a black mother smothers her young son so that he will not have
to face the possibility of mob assault.[136] As writer Fenton Johnson said,
it was "better to die than to grow up and find that you are colored."[137]
Grimké was too genteel, however, to maintain the pace of protest. She
gave up writing, retired to New York and resigned herself to the apparent futility of her career. "The days fall upon me; / One by one, they

fall, / Like Leaves ... Who will never find me / Under the days?" she concluded.[138]

Even Claude McKay, a dedicated and self-conscious militant from the West Indies who stressed race and attacked the integrationist intellectual advocates of uplift as propagandists, suffered from a cultural dualism. He, who chafed under the realm of white supremacy to the point that his soul, he said, was full of "searing hate,"[139] nevertheless felt a prolonged allegiance to the white man's civilization.

McKay celebrated blackness. The Negro loved and accepted life— as did he in principle and as did his character Jake in *Home to Harlem,* who "thrilled to Harlem,"[140] the "Afro-American cultural capital," mythic landscape to writers of the 1920s, as historian James De Jongh points out.[141] In *Banana Bottom,* McKay praised the marginals who lived from day to day, taking whatever came with equanimity, and the peasants who were free from repression and inflicted guilt to be themselves. His Bita, for instance, preferred her people to those she had known during her education in England and to her cold, restrictively moral benefactors. Locke, who disapproved of McKay's approach, accused him and those like him of "spiritual truancy and social irresponsibility."[142] For McKay deeply resented the oppressiveness of white culture: "The white man is a tiger at my throat ..." he wrote.[143] "I was born / far from my native clime, under the white man's menace out of time."[144]

But McKay, contentious, discontent, resentful, was also perhaps, like his Ray, "a misfit ... with my little education and constant dreaming,"[145] a slave "of the civilized tradition."[146] Neither Ray nor his author could be happy in the carefree instinctual existence that he imagined blacks enjoyed. He was a universalist who took up socialist ideology before he became disillusioned with it, its spokesmen and the proletarian literature that it championed.[147] Above all, he sought racial harmony: he was even interested in the theme of passing. Indeed, McKay was more of an introspective neurotic than a gay celebrant of the joys of life.[148] He was cut off from people who "don't have any idea of words like freedom and restraint":[149] he could not indulge himself— morally or intellectually—in "irresponsible happiness."[150]

The black, Chester Himes said, was "in conflict with himself, with his environment, with his public."[151] DuBois wrote with respect to being black, "[I am] sensitive, I am artificial, I cringe or am bumptious or immobile, I am intellectually dishonest, art-blind, and I lack humor." Whites would not let him stop being so, he added.[152] The integrationist, presumably contented Negro was forced to play a role, for which he hated himself. Countee Cullen "was very taken with the art of lying."[153] As Langston Hughes put it, "It is we who use words / As screens for thoughts / And weave dark garments / To cover the naked body / Of the too white truth / It is we with the civilized souls. / We are liars."[154]

But Hughes found elemental strength in racial identity. He needed his people and so, like McKay, he turned to the folk and lower-class features of Negro culture. On the surface he was an avowed integrationist. Although he often found himself at odds with the reigning white—and black—intelligentsia, he refused to impose himself on others. He was a pragmatist who rode with events: he was pleasant, even conciliatory and certainly careful not to reveal his own opinions. He made his way as he went along; he followed most of the aesthetic and political trends of the day—from primitivism to socialism—to please his white patrons and black associates, from DuBois to Countee Cullen to Jessie Fauset to Wallace Thurman to his "godmother" Mason to Carl Van Vechten.

Hughes was part of the younger group of Renaissance writers who wanted to cultivate the black tradition in what the literary elite considered its rawest aspects. He used dialect in his first book of poetry, *The Weary Blues;* he established a close relation between the cultures of Africa and African America; he protested forcefully against the injustices of racism. *Not Without Laughter,* his novel, was the story of a boy growing up in a Negro family that urban migration had begun to uproot. He represented in it all kinds of black experience and black types—all affirmatively—in the persons of his aunts (one a blues-singing streetwalker, the other a prim materialist); of his father, a traveling gay blade; of his old-fashioned, all-understanding grandmother. As his Mamie says in "Simply Heavenly," "I loves my people."[155] Those Negroes who have passed, "who've crossed the line / To live downtown / Miss . . . Harlem of the bitter dream, / Since their dream had come true."[156]

Yet Hughes, too, was torn, because as he realized he was a part of the American civilization that rejected him and his people. "I'm not a white man . . ." he protested to a group of Africans, only to be told, "You no black man neither."[157] He had to make his way as a writer in a society that seemed to have no place for him, and he had to play for the patronage of rich white sponsors in order to do so. Indeed, Hughes was forced to be an integrationist—although he was oriented in that direction. Despite himself he attested that skin did not matter, that he found "his birthright as a man no less than . . . as a black man."[158]

The "Negro sensibility is socially and historically conditioned: that Western culture must be won," said Ralph Ellison.[159] Robert Hayden's thoughts were "caught in that filmy / trap";[160] he had a "divided self."[161] The black cannot assert his liberty within a context in which he is indoctrinated and also by which he is controlled. The white world belongs as much to him as to the white. Ellison, for instance, insisted on the "duality of the cultural experience"[162] of being both Negro and American.[163] Consequently, he tried to separate art from ideology as if literary creation had an autonomous existence that did not depend on cultural influences. Inevitably, like Baldwin, who also tried to disregard social issues,[164] Ellison could not do so. His novel, *Invisible Man,* was involved implicitly in the racial politics of his day.

Many whites preempted the book as a part of their tradition, as if Ellison had passed on a cultural level. "Until fairly recently," wrote critic James McPherson in 1970, "not many blacks—perhaps even college-educated blacks—knew that [Ellison] existed."[165] Whites praised his book: they seemed to imply that he had taken up Euro-American aesthetic themes—such as those of New England transcendentalism and alienation. Richard Kostelanetz, a literary analyst, called Ellison a "brown skinned aristocrat."[166] His novel was Kafkaesque, argued writer Jonathan Baumbach; it was not really a Negro novel; it had more "in common . . . with Joyce, Melville . . . than . . . with Baldwin and Wright."[167] It was "not a Negro novel," agreed Littlejohn, who denied that there is a distinctive " 'Negro experience' in America."[168] Actually, to a qualified degree, Ellison was in accord with him. As he did not "recognize any white culture" of which blacks were not a part, so he did not "recognize any black culture the way many people use the expression."[169] Indeed, many blacks actually disowned his book, perhaps because they felt it was lionized by whites or because Ellison, personally, refused to adopt a militant stance in the black struggle for rights. They accused him of aestheticism, of noncommitment and of excessive individualism—even tokenism and Uncle Tomism.[170] Ellison's protagonist, said Gayle, "chooses death over life, opts for non-creativity in favor of creativity, chooses the path of individualism instead of racial unity."[171]

Invisible Man is, nevertheless, a black novel; no white could have written it. In many ways it is a commentary on—and extension of—the themes of *Native Son.* In the sense that Ellison's protagonist has suffered conspicuously from the dualism that is inherent in the black American experience—as his author, like Wright and Baldwin, absorbed the black and white cultures to which he was exposed—the book reflects the black American tradition. Ellison's aesthetic method involved the ironic use of negation to establish an affirmative place for his invisible man, the victim of the pretension that white civilization is the absolute measure of human worth. Black boys "were men outside historical time,"[172] as if history—the record of mankind's achievement on earth—were indeed white, and blackness, as a critic remarks, were "equivalent to the reverse of things."[173] As the invisible man puts it, "By all historical logic [blacks] should have disappeared around the first part of the nineteenth century, rationalized out of existence. . . . They were outside the groove of history, and it was my job to get them in, all of them."[174] In order to do so, he must create himself as an individual, discover his identity as a black and inevitably force the outside world to recognize him as such.

Ellison was recording an actual historical aspect of the black American experience, which he transferred to the level of myth. His romance, which reflects the American picaresque tradition, moves not progressively, but cyclically, as does Toomer's *Cane*. It goes back to where it started: its end is in its beginning. He was depicting a quest outside of time, which, in universal terms, could be associated with the quest of every man. The Negro symbolized not just the person "lowest down," as Ellison put it, but "the mysterious, underground aspect of human personality. . . . [He] was the gauge of the human condition as it waxed and waned in our society."[175] Ellison represented the black and the undiscovered, if not rejected, dimensions of the white. The narrator therefore does not go forward; he simply opens himself to possibility or to deeper levels of experience. He is passive: he endures the relentless assault of forces outside himself, like Ellison's protagonist the "King of the Bingo Game" in the short story of the same name, who felt "that his whole life was determined by the bingo wheel."[176] By negation, by refusing one by one the roles which are thrust on the invisible man and by which he is rendered unseeable, he slips from unconscious to conscious invisibility, from the pseudo-light of the street to the glaring opacity of the cellar—lit with city electricity—whence, like Job, he can move nowhere but up.

Richard Wright's Bigger Thomas had to kill in order to be seen by his blind employer. And he found himself at the point that he could brave his own execution. Ellison's invisible man deliberately buries himself below ground. In reacting against the ruling norms—against "all the representations of social power [who] seek to control reality,"[177] he digs his way to the bottom of himself as well as of his world. Because he makes a willful, personal choice—like Bigger—he is trying to "reconcile the individual to the chaotic reality of contemporary life without ... despair and without false optimism."[178] Ellison's purpose is to transcend the desire for freedom by accepting the paradoxical fact that it is realized only in limits—that it is "rooted in its opposite."[179] The protagonist renounces nothing; he does not retire into subjectivity; he does not grow—either in years or accomplishment or accumulation, as in white fiction. He develops in the depths of consciousness: the implication is that he will resurge. "The American novel is ... a conquest of the frontier," according to Ellison; "as it describes our experience, it creates it."[180]

Wright left Bigger on the brink of execution, misunderstood and misrepresented, credible only to himself—and to his reader. Ellison granted his narrator certain options. The circle was not closed. As an implicit commentary on *Native Son, Invisible Man* rejected the determinism that characterized Wright's aesthetic approach. Ellison is a craftsman who associates technique not simply with self-discipline and will, but with ideology in the sense that freedom is transcendence through the recognition of limits. As writing is inherently the delineation of cultural relationships, so the "greatest freedom" of the writer is his "possession of technique."[181] It is by his art that he defines—indeed, creates—himself, within the civilizational framework in which he has been placed. The unrelenting environmental pressure that weighed on Wright's protagonist was signified in the solemnity of his style. Form was secondary to content. To Ellison, however, "protest" as "an element of all art"[182] was intrinsic in the act of writing; but since he believed that "style is more important than political ideologies,"[183] he incorporated ideology in his very focus on style. Since true freedom was rooted in its opposite, blacks had art—as exemplified in black music—"in place of freedom."[184]

It is what Ishmael Reed calls the monocultural pretension of white civilization that has stultified black literary expressiveness in America. Quite naturally blacks, who have absorbed the techniques of this civilization, have, like whites, used them as bases for communication. They provide the necessary framework within which writers are able to place their creative efforts; they supply the rules of the game. When black writers militantly defined art as politics, they were, in effect, attacking artistic as well as political forms and, therefore, destroying the linguistic context in which literature and ideology were placed. It was this attack that Ellison apparently resisted because he was a cultural universalist.

James Baldwin, another universalist, confronted this same dilemma of cultural revolution, seemingly without knowing what the implications were. Like Ellison, he was a gifted stylist, profoundly attached to the occidental influences—from Dickens to Henry James—that had formed him. It was perhaps to Baldwin that Reed referred when he spoke of "the white literary—and factions of the black literary—establishment's fascination with the epicene, small-boned, slight and delicate black writer."[185] But Baldwin was torn—at least intellectually—in himself: he swung from side to side in the battle of the races. As one critic points out, he was "crying to white hearts and brains."[186] He was "a very ambitious man," says Reed. He was "a hustler who tried to come on like Job."[187] He ached for success in the white-run world; he left the church and Harlem, he said, because he "was icily determined never to make peace with the ghetto."[188] And he set forth into the white intellectual world in which he progressively made good. He attempted, he explained, "to make myself fit in . . . to wash myself clean for the American literary academy."[189] Baldwin became a representative of the modern talented tenth who spoke more to the white than to the Negro. He was the integrationist whose life ethic was "love, acceptance"[190] and who had "faith in [human beings] and love for them."[191] Indeed, love was his principle theme: "The key is love," he told Nikki Giovanni. "Your suffering is your bridge."[192] He spoke as "a convinced universalist," remarks Quincy Troupe, "who, while he . . . contested the diminution of his humanity in American racism did not . . . see culture as an instrument of combat."[193] Therefore, Baldwin sought what he called a "color-blind" society.[194] He would ignore the question of race.[195] "The Negro simply wants to be dealt with as another human being. No more. And no less," he concluded.[196]

Yet Baldwin, as fervent spokesman—or "witness,"[197] as he put it—for his people, denounced all whites in general and his liberal followers in particular, who, nevertheless, masochistically seemed to revel in his attacks on them. "Color . . . is a political reality,"[198] he claimed, and he used it aggressively. "All attempts at dialogue between subdued and subduer, between those placed within history and those dispersed outside, break down."[199] He was proud of his part in the black movement: he compared his commitment to it to that of his early ministry when he had been "saved."[200] But his militancy was often reduced to "comments on 'radical chic' issues," observes Reed.[201] He was marked with the guilt of needing to bind himself to blacks in the sense that they and he shared a "precarious . . . inutterably painful relation"[202] to whites, from which they had to remake a world in their image. Baldwin's success, however, separated him from his people even more radically than his ambition as a young man to rise above ghetto victimization, as Margaret Mead was quick to observe.[203] In many ways he was closer to her than to them.

He consequently agonized not just over the irreconcilable struggle into which he had been called and with which he was intimately involved, but over his own position in it. He felt "lonely," "trapped" in his legend, "divorced" from what he thought he was and what he was truly. He was trying to avoid an estrangement "between myself and my generation," he told Quincy Troupe.[204] But the way the world treated him was unbearable. As one of his white friends remarked, "The conflict in him . . . was ever present."[205] His life "was a never-ending struggle between Good and Evil," said another.[206]

Baldwin was by nature a prophet and a preacher—"an artist priest."[207] He was profoundly marked by the Calvinist tradition: his first and probably most moving novel, *Go Tell It on the Mountain,* was an account of his personal quest for identity—which involved his being saved. Whereas Ellison's protagonist found himself through his reaction to the outside forces that worked on him to mold him to their ways, Baldwin's selfhood depended on his struggle against an interiorized adversary: he was fighting the father image that rejected him. Ellison sought guilt by intelligible choice; Baldwin was persecuted by it. In effect, he would sacrifice consciousness to gain freedom. In *Go Tell It on the Mountain,* Baldwin's experience was tied to the black world of family and church. It was from both that he derived his pervading sense of alienation and sin, which cut off his access to the acceptance and love that he craved. And since the church and its minister, his stepfather, equated evil with sex, Baldwin celebrated art, sex and love in an almost mystic equivalence—to which he added black power after he joined the black revolution.

Art and sex served double—even conflicting—functions. On the one hand, he used them as means of escaping his personal and racial frustrations. As such they were not signs of rebellion; they were ways of assimilating into the white world. And on the other hand, they were weapons through which he sought transcendent gratification. Art was more than a cause: it was a kind of apocalypse. Through sex—particularly homosexual and interracial sex[208]—Baldwin could defy a restrictive and oppressive authority; he could rise against his father. While his artistic dedication enabled him to become a member of the intellectual set and lose the racist framework under which he had suffered, his sexual mission drove him to negate the norms of the white superstructure in which intellectuals functioned and to assert the virtues of both black innocence and black power. Consequently, he was caught in a cultural confusion.

Critic Robert Bone accuses Baldwin of being "sealed in a narcissism so engrossing that he fails to make emotional contact with his characters."[209] He looked uniquely to the "holy . . . orgasm"[210] for self-liberation. Actually, Baldwin's protagonists lack authenticity. His whites—usually liberals—have no life, from David to Eric to Victor to Parnell; the blacks of his later, more political novels are also abstractions. Nevertheless, the sexual content of his books was not simplistic, as Bone would have it. Baldwin was acutely aware of the sexual implications of racism and he made them explicit—even though he tended, perhaps sentimentally, to envision interracial harmony in terms of male homosexuality. He knew, as he put it, that "there are no formulas for the improvement of the private, or any other life—certainly not the formula of more and better orgasms."[211]

Before the jazz age, black writers—probably in reaction to the white stereotype of the oversexed Negro brute—tended to minimize sexuality. In accordance not only with the image of the nice colored person, but also with the prevailing literary genteel fashion, they made the Negro practically asexual. The proper mulatta was as cold as her white counterpart; in *Our Nig*, Harriet Wilson passed over even her married life; Jean Toomer alluded to the respectable bourgeoise as "a powdered and scented proper bundle of donts and prohibitions."[212] But the 1920s gave rise to a new affirmation of sexuality—particularly that which was associated with the black. Whites flocked to Harlem seeking the instinctual pleasures that they imagined abounded there, and blacks were more than willing to indulge them—at least artistically. Writers who rejected the middle-class theme of uplift and wanted to assert positive features of black culture through the common folk tended to contrast the repressive civilization of the whites to the emotional and physical expressiveness of blacks.

Black intellectuals often romanticized the idea of black instinctual release and sold it to whites, who were demanding that blacks behave primitively and wickedly. Of course, whites compared pejoratively the black's "emotional urgings, indolence and potential savagery"[213] to their own intellectual and physical self-control. As George Schuyler put it, they assumed that even when the black appears civilized, "it is only necessary to beat on a tom tom and he is ready to . . . ride off wild-eyed on the back of a crocodile."[214] Blacks, on the other hand, wanted no part of a white society that stultified the free play of instinct and sensation. It was rotten; it was degenerate; it was cold and overbearing and artificial; it was a veneer to cover over the disorder of reality. It made Fenton Johnson "tired";[215] it bored Nella Larsen's Clare, who snuck up to Harlem "to see Negroes, to be with them . . . to hear them laugh."[216] Rudolph Fisher celebrated what was called the "saturnalian quality of Harlem life."[217] Countee Cullen's middle-class hostess refused to pass because whites "don't know what [enjoyment] is";[218] he himself praised the pleasure of the body. Black folks were natural dreamers, singers, dancers and lovers.

In the sense that blacks have shared the cultural framework of whites, they were and are ambivalent in their attitudes toward sex. As Eldridge Cleaver pointed out, modern society is sexually disconnected. He, a socialist revolutionary, put this Freudian concept in a Marxist context. "The source of the fragmentation of the Self," he wrote, " . . . lies in the alienation between the function of a man's Mind and the function of his Body."[219] The division presumably was based on the class war between profiteering capitalists and exploited workers, among whom were numbered the mass of blacks. His universalism, however, did not hold when it came to sex, which he used as a weapon in his personal rebellion against the white power structure.

Historically and traditionally, the black was subject to white men's sexual exploitation of the black woman. The black man was reduced to impotence: he had no arms to protect her. He "was forbidden by definition, since he's black, to assume the roles, burdens, duties and joys of being a man."[220] He was also exposed to a white value system and bombarded by the idea that *"ideal* woman"[221] meant white; he was the victim of "the myth of white womanhood."[222] Hernton observes that he has a sociosexually induced predisposition for white females, who symbolize his "freedom and bondage,"[223] who have been placed "beyond the pitch of reality," as Richard Wright put it.[224] Quite naturally he has been ambivalent in his relations with them.

Wright, according to Michel Fabre, his French biographer, associated the white woman with the mind and preferred her for her "intellectual capacity"[225] to the more sensuous black—whom, according to Margaret Walker, he disesteemed.[226] Wright thought that the whites he knew strove "instinctively to avoid all passion."[227] Insofar as he was an integrationist, he seemed to view interracial sex as the definitive evidence of cultural assimilation. As one of his characters observes, "The sex of a white woman is practically a religion"; to take one is to prove "to yourself and to the white man that you're really *mentally* white."[228]

Chester Himes also illustrated the contradictions in the black's attitude toward the white woman. To make love to her was to avenge oneself on the white man. This necessarily involved her humiliation. Within the black's "homicidal mania" was an urge "to possess a delicate, fragile, sensitive, highly cultured blond white woman bred to centuries of aristocracy."[229] Inevitably, this kind of desire led to perverted relationships. Himes's Jesse Robinson in *The Primitive,* for instance, always thought of sex as "a little soiled . . . tainted by his Protestant upbringing and his grotesque imagination, his strange indignation."[230] Himes's Scott Hamilton in *A Case of Rape* also did not know the white woman "he had dreamed into existence,"[231] and she could never give herself to him. At heart she was always a white supremacist: "She believed in her race as she believed in her God."[232]

The desire to possess the white woman was based neither on affection nor sexual instinct; indeed, Himes's white females are frigid while his black women, like Baby Sister and Iris and even Mabel, are irrepressibly hot. Affairs with whites were rather tainted with pathological racial implications: "The very essence of any relation between a black man and a white woman in the United States is . . . generally sex of a nature which lends itself to pornography. . . ."[233] Himes's Bob in *If He Hollers Let Him Go,* for instance, wanted "to make [the white girl] as low as a white whore in a Negro slum—a scrummy two dollar whore."[234] Black-white sexual relations led inevitably to violence, "the final answer of any black to a white woman with whom he lives in a white society."[235] Jesse Robinson murders his white mistress after a sordid affair in which he does everything but make love. Himes himself almost killed one of his girls,[236] and he beat up others with whom he was living; his love intrigues were embittered by his uncontrollable jealousies.[237]

Like Gore Vidal's Indian who wanted "a *white* woman . . . to humiliate,"[238] the black was often sadistic toward his conquest. Baldwin's Rufus, the black jazzman, took pleasure in savaging his white southern girl. Malcolm X admitted when he was trying to be white that "to have a white woman who wasn't a known common whore was—for the average black man, at least—a status symbol of the first order."[239] Nevertheless, he periodically roughed up his middle-class white mistress— to her presumed sexual satisfaction. Amiri Baraka always regretted the

false Bohemianism of his Greenwich Village days when he married a
white and when, he confessed, he had "straight-out white supremacy
bourgeois opinions mixed with . . . revolutionary ones."[240] Even after
his divorce he was beset by "guilt" about his life at that time.[241] And
Eldridge Cleaver went into a rage against white women and himself
because, as he realized, at one point he really preferred "white girls over
black."[242] In fact, he associated interracial sex, with its implications of
violence, not with integration but with revolution: when he put his arms
around a white, he was hugging a chance at freedom; when he attacked
her, he was rebelling or aggressing against society as well as the girl.
"Rape was an insurrectionary act," he wrote. Like Bigger Thomas's
murder—and originally intended rape—it was the only resolution to
the conflict he felt with respect to whites. "Loving you and thus / And
hating you so," he addressed a white girl, "My heart is torn in two /
Crucified." He hated the girl more than he loved her. Blacks' attraction
to whites was, he pointed out, "often of such a bloody, hateful, bitter
and malignant nature" that it was anything but flattering.[243] As Malcolm X agreed, blacks had little respect for their white mistresses.[244]

It was natural that black militants should relate sex to revolution
on both cultural and political planes. As Baraka broke out of interracial
circles, he called for violence. "Rape the white girls," he wrote. "Rape
their fathers. Cut the mothers' throats."[245] George Cain, caught in the
throes of narcotics addiction, hated Nicole, the white whom he had
married and deserted. "Loathe her, her whiteness, her love. . . . Her love
is . . . a tenacious clinging thing, choking me to death," he cried. He
could have "killed her easily with pleasure."[246] It was not only the
black's "obsessive image of the white woman, projection of terror and
racial resentment"[247] that threatened the harmony of a mutual relationship: it was also her equally obsessive image of him. In effect, as Himes
seemed to understand, it was the element of thrill that appeared to
attract white women to blacks. They were either like Malcolm X's girl,
"in love with lust—particularly 'taboo' lust,"[248] or, like Alice Walker's
Lynn in *Meridian,* and Cain's Nicole, they were "nigger struck." This
attitude was particularly prevalent at the time of the interracial movement for civil rights. These women were arrogant and stupid in their
naïveté: they embraced integrationism, "knowing only the myth"[249] of
the character of their partners, believing ahistorically in human universalism and relying blindly on sex to resolve their guilt. The interracial
marriage in *Meridian,* fruit of two inherently shallow pseudo-
revolutionaries' sexual experimentation in formerly forbidden fields,

was from the beginning condemned to sterility, as the death of their child suggests. It ended in the abortion of love and in the subsequent rape of Lynn, the white wife, by one of her black husband's friends.

White women—perhaps unconsciously and thus stupidly—used black men as much as they were being used. Their higher caste status always gave them political, social—and sexual—advantages over their Negro lovers. Malcolm X's girl was able to marry a white man while she carried on her affair with Malcolm. As Himes put it, since "the female of the oppressors" possessed "the hammer of persecution over the male of the oppressed,"[250] there seemed to be "some capacity for self-destruction in the traditional status of Negro men which only white women could release."[251] The black, concluded Himes, is not primitive in his sexual emotions: he is "neurotic, complicated, schizophrenic."[252]

And yet Himes—and his protagonists—played the role of seducer—cool, cynical and irresistible to women. The main preoccupation of the politically nonmilitant black seemed often to involve his racking up of white conquests. As writer Cecil Brown's Doc says in *The Lives and Loves of Mr. Jiveass Nigger,* "A black man is a gigolo as a poor man; if he's successful . . . he becomes a Don Juan."[253] Never would he fit into the old stereotype of the rapist; as the modern integrationist, he is the swinger. Brown's George is a "hustler . . . jiveass . . . jazz player"[254] who turns against his father—"a nigger [who] cursed all the time"[255]— and seeks his identity in sexual intercourse with all kinds of uncontrollably willing white females. As he remarks, "The black lover was a true warrior . . . who is doomed . . . to fighting a perpetual battle with an elusive enemy, and with the foreknowledge that he can never be the victor. . . ."[256] He involves himself wholly in the situation at hand and tries to find his meaning immediately in it; he wins only by the perfection of the techniques by which he plays a fruitless game. His never-ending sexual accomplishments are a compensation for the nonbeing he fears—precisely because he realizes that they are meaningless. He is the modern Sisyphus—until, like George, he gives up the vanity of his effort.

The relations between black men and black women had also to be ambivalent. The sexual pathology that accompanied race oppression affected intragroup behavior. Both black men and black women suffered: men from the white man's policy of the threat of castration, and women by his rape. It was inevitable that the black would turn on his woman, as James Baldwin[257] and Alice Walker[258] pointed out, and make her the victim of his frustration. It was inevitable also that she, often wearily, would resent him. As Nikki Giovanni wrote, "i make up with you / because you aren't strong / enough to reach out / to say / come home i need you."[259]

Historically, the black woman has had to deal with one of the white's favorite and most entrenched stereotypes: the mammy, the Aunt Jemima, an image that encompasses the myth of the contented Negro. Even as the victim of the white man's rape and dominance, as the white family's nurse, as the mother of the mulatto and of her own black offspring, the black slave woman nevertheless managed to build a sense of community solidarity. "The Black mother," it is said, ". . . hands on the spark, the legacy of Black strength."[260] Poet Carole Gregory praises the woman, "African in ancestry, / woman of intelligence / to raise generations / victoriously through Jim and Jane Crow."[261] She was the purveyor of the black tradition. In spite or perhaps because of the pressures and the legends that were fabricated on and around her, the black mammy was anything but the prototype of the contented Negro.

According to critic Erlene Stetson, there were three concepts implicit in the black mother's creative strategies, which involved her very survival: the quest for identity, "a subversive perception of reality and subterfuge and ambivalence."[262] She was an actor: she played a game. Barbara Christian speaks of "the innate contrariness of black women," beneath which lies "a grudging respect for . . . even a gleeful identification with, a resistance to authority."[263] The female might have been "de mule uh de world,"[264] as Hurston's Nanny describes her in *Their Eyes Were Watching God,* but she was an especially determined and stubborn one. She was a fighter underneath her sometimes cheerful, often obstreperous, façade: the "minstrel-smile" hid "the surging / Of my sad people's soul," as Gwendolyn Bennett put it.[265]

The black woman's traditional fidelity to the black tradition was expressed through her undercover militancy: she was the mammy not of the white man's family but of her race. "The cultural continuity of people of African descent, from South to North America"—of which Christian speaks with reference to Paule Marshall—constituted "a stance from which to delineate the values of the Northern world."[266] As Sojourner Truth, herself a myth and a symbol in Alice Walker's *Meridian,* said of her own maternal heritage, "If the first woman God ever made / was strong enough to turn the world / upside down, all alone / together women ought to be able to turn it rightside up again."[267]

Blacks have always mythicized the black mother, or often grandmother. Since the black cultural experience—in slavery—involved the truncation of all natural human ties, from marriage to family institutions, she was the signification of blackness. Although she had to submit in order to endure, she preserved her militant contrariness through the archetypal sacrifice and resilience of selfhood: she submitted to the white rule she abhorred in order to survive. Therefore, Toni Morrison's black maid in *Jazz* steals a ring from Tiffany to assert her spiritual independence from her mistress. The black mother handed down throughout generations a sense of precious value of the black heritage. Black writers have consequently idolized the woman. "Three hundred years in the deepest South, / But God put a song and a prayer in my mouth / God put a dream like steel in my soul," wrote Langston Hughes about her.[268] She had suffered and has continued to suffer. Gwendolyn Brooks's black mother of Emmett Till "kisses her killed boy / And she is sorry / Chaos in windy grays / Through a red prairie."[269]

Alice Walker's Meridian may have lost her relation to her real mother, but she reclaims her tradition just as her author—in search of her mother's gardens—finds the wholeness of the black community in its maternally transmitted heritage, from Africa through slavery to the present. In *The Autobiography of Miss Jane Pittman,* Ernest Gaines's Miss Jane Pittman, whose life is recorded by a young black historian, brings the defiant spirit with which she escaped from slavery down to the battle for civil rights: her neighbors, scared as they are, follow her as well as the young martyr Jimmy. Toni Morrison's Sethe in *Beloved* defies the entire white world by murdering her beloved baby to keep her from being enslaved. In Gloria Naylor's *Mama Day,* the character Mama Day is responsible for the historic continuity and autonomy of her island off South Carolina. As Baldwin remarked, "It evolves upon the mother to invest . . . her manchild with some kind of interior dignity which will protect him";[270] his own "long-suffering females" had a "dignity and largeness of movement which outsize life," says Gloria Hull.[271] Ralph Ellison also idealized his mother; William Gardner Smith spoke of the "old African tribal feeling" of his.[272] "My mother," as Carolyn Rodgers puts it, "religious—negro proud of / having waded through a storm, is very obviously, / a sturdy Black bridge that I / crossed over, on."[273]

It was just this strength and sturdiness that gave rise to a counter-myth within the black community. The black mother was the matriarch who kept her family intact, often at the expense of the socially, economically and politically impotent male; she was assigned the qualities of the castrator. With the upsurge of the Negro bourgeoisie, the black mother sacrificed the spirituality of her black heritage for the materialism of society at large: her middle-class orientation tended to stifle the creative instincts of her children.

She therefore exists sometimes in black literature as a veritable harpy. E. Franklin Frazier stressed her sterile vulgarity and Daniel Patrick Moynihan transferred her to the ghetto where he made her reign supreme in an amputated family.[274] In Chester Himes's *The Third Generation,* she is light in tone, frigid and destructive;[275] in Ntozake Shange's *Betsey Brown,* she is antimilitant, even antiblack: she reproves her daughter for picking "the most niggerish people in the world to make her friends."[276] The mother of Walker's Meridian emotionally smothers her child.

The cultural dichotomies implicit in these myths affected the relationships between black men and black women. Often the latter resented the man's seeming preference for the forbidden white. Jessie Fauset questioned the motives of her lover when he praised her black hair. Did the girl "of your young manhood's dream" have "blue eyes? Did her hair goldly gleam?" she wondered.[277] Particularly after the civil rights and sexual revolutions, the black woman was disgusted by the brazenness of apparently sex-starved white females who wantonly pursued her men. For centuries she, who had been the object not only of the white man's sexual fantasies but also of his outright rape—his "racial barbarity"—who bore not only the black but most of the mixed colored population, now found herself in a sexual free-for-all with white girls. Moreover, white females used the myth of their own "social position and reputed virtues"[278] to win their prey. As Walker's Meridian (whose enemies were the black bourgeoisie and the white racist power structure) remarks, white women are "sexless, contemptible and ridiculous." She is ashamed if not demoralized when her man takes up with them: "obviously their color made them interesting . . . as if she were less."[279] According to Carole Gregory, "a white wife / tames the Black man's struggle for freedom."[280] Blacks, says Toni Morrison, "look at white women, and see the enemy."[281] This "hatred of the white woman"[282] has a social dimension that has affected the relationship between the black sexes.

The women's movement for equal rights brought about an alliance between many black females and their self-professed white sisters. The black woman was advancing in both intellectual and commercial areas to the point that she often overshadowed the black male—a development that reinforced the tension between them. Since traditionally he had used her as a scapegoat for his frustrations and disappointments, her revolt involved her turning against him. Morrison's Chilly in *The Bluest Eye,* for instance, had hated his woman, whom he had not been able to protect from the intrusion of armed whites when they were making love.[283] Nikki Giovanni protested that she could not deal with men, not just because they physically abused women but because they "build their standards on false rationales."[284] It is they, remarks Walker's Fanny in *The Temple of My Familiar,* who "help create [the system]. At least the part of it that oppresses women." In fact, all governments are nothing but "male-supremist private clubs."[285]

Moreover, social solutions—like that of Moynihan to black economic problems—have traded on stereotypical antagonisms between black males and females. Maya Angelou speaks of "the built-in suspicion between the sexes."[286] After the Negro woman challenged the male, it was she—the upwardly mobile black—who was to be deprived of her opportunity in favor of unemployed black men—as Paula Giddings points out.[287] Likewise it was the African American man who was doubly demeaned when his woman rose on the economic scale and became a part of female activism. Ishmael Reed suggests that the alliance between white and black women was engineered by white men to undermine black men. As his Jake Brashford says in *Reckless Eyeballing,* "It's these white women who are carrying on the attack against black men today, because they struck a deal with the white men who run the country. . . ."[288] Reed's Tremonisha Smarts, the black, is subverted by Becky French, the influential white, and writes a propagandist play in which the black protagonist, Mose, is depicted as a sexual demon—an incestuous, woman-bashing rapist. She therefore confirms what "everybody knew" in any case: black men did nothing but rape white women.[289]

The fact that the black woman chose the decade of the 1970s "to stand outside [her community] to define herself as in revolt against it"[290] caused the breach among the blacks. The end of the civil rights movement, the death and imprisonment of all its young heroes, brought the desiccation of the idealism that had inspired black solidarity. The sexual revolution itself seemed to react adversely to the morale of the black female. As two social analysts report, there has been an increased incidence of frigidity among women because, as they put it, the male "overdoes the sex mores."[291] Nikki Giovanni, who always prided herself "on being a child of the sixties," speaks of herself as "the unrealized dream of an idea unborn," and simply stays alive "among the tired and lonely."[292] Carolyn Rodgers concludes, "We are talented, dedicated, / well read / BLACK COMMITTED, / we are lonely."[293] Jeanne Noble sums it up: black writers began to express "an unusual loneliness which is the result of too few positive relationships between black men and women."[294]

CHAPTER 14

BLACK RACIAL MEMORY

T he third stereotype whites imposed on blacks in order to control them was that of the tragic mulatto. According to the white version, the colored man is doomed by nature because he is at war with himself: he is a living battlefield of "intellectual strivings and self-control [against] emotional urgings, indolence and potent savagery."[1] This mulatto image is related to whites' sexual pathology: their concept of a mulatto—of black and white in one body—is a projection of a neurotic taboo that whites have violated and forbidden desires that they cannot suppress. It is the white rape—far more than white seduction—that is responsible for the incidence of miscegenation in America. Most blacks do have a white ancestor of some kind; the races have indeed been indelibly intermingled. By 1910, three quarters of the Negroes in America were of mixed blood, according to Joel Williamson.[2] By the mid-twentieth century, as James Baldwin pointed out, there were "few but very few"[3] blacks who were not to some degree white.

Therefore, to the black person, mixed blood is a common fact: it is an intrinsic aspect of the black experience. It does not necessarily connote taboo violation, tragedy or neurotic repression because it is almost universally present in the black's very being. Jean Toomer was perhaps prescient—although maybe perversely so—when he saw "*a new world, / A new America*"[4] in terms of its "new people, . . . / Growing towards the universal Human Being."[5] The American Negro, as Herskovits determined as early as 1928, has created a new homogeneous type of person, "a veritable New Negro,"[6] a "mixture of all races"[7] with less variability than other existing types. "Mulattos in America," agrees Williamson, "are a new people. . . . New in the vital way of constituting a new culture that is both African and European. . . ."[8] If passing had reputably brought Negroes unhappiness, then this is not the effect of any stereotypical war between disparate personality strains involving reason against emotion. Rather, according to the black point of view, the assimilated Negro who hides his blood is discontent because he has had to forsake his cultural tradition. As Larsen's Clare explains, family and background, so precious to the African American, do not matter in the rootless and heterogeneous society of American whites. "It's easier with white people to drop down . . . from nowhere."[9]

After what have been called the protest and integrationist phases of the black experience—both of which threatened to divide the Negro community—blacks have been exploring the sources of a tradition that is peculiar to their American history. They have rejected middle-class norms—both black and white—as they have in the past.[10] They are trying culturally to identify the black in terms of his heritage and his present situation. In effect, the black has often turned away from both conformism and militancy. He does not want to be "just a black copy of the white mind";[11] he does not want to depend on white criteria—even antithetically—in order to define himself. As Walker's Grange Copeland sums up his own cultural development in *The Third Life of Grange Copeland:* "The white folks hated me and I hated myself until I started hating them in return and loving myself."[12] Then when Copeland loved his own kind in the person of his granddaughter, Ruth, he was free of them; he could ignore them.

Aesthetically, the black has had to break out of the intellectual narcissism in which white thinking is ensconced. The curse of Western European culture, says Gates, is "the presence of an enshrined collective cultural memory . . . that can confine and delimit."[13] Black literature—which until recently was peripheral to the main currents of the American tradition—has been able to recognize realities that go beyond the values and limits of industrial occidental civilization. If ideally—although perhaps not in fact—the black writer is not interested "solely in 'getting ahead,' "[14] his message could be irrelevant to success standards that imply the acceptance of set norms. The black cultural perspective has often excluded the escapist idea of progress by which writers have rationalized and justified their discrepancies between principle and act, as well as their scientific and technological accomplishments. As writer and activist Julian Mayfield remarks, "Writers of the mainstream, reflecting the attitude of the American people generally, seem determined not to become involved in any of the genuine fury, turmoil and passion of life; and it is only such involvement that makes life worth living.[15]

Black culture has been built on foundations different from those of whites. Even now, to reach the source of the logocentric ontology of the white so-called book, or canon—the point at which writing invaded the perception of truth, inscribed in the soul, and invented the Other (either manichaeistically or dialectically) in order to create identity through difference—white thinking has had to rely on all the supplements of this "book" until it became entwined in itself. Europeans came to assume that their civilization was universal, that its values—from an elemental battle against nature to mastery of the earth's environment— were those of all mankind. This monoculturism, as Reed refers to it, evolved not simply from the missionary eschatology that was the basis of the Judeo-Christian ideology, but also from historical circumstances. In their development, European literature and art and music had a pluralistic quality. They were characterized by a folk tribalism that gave them life and trenchancy and that derived from the use of the vernacular and the rise and rivalry of nation-states. The Germans, French, English, Spanish and Italians possessed special, identifiable traditions as their countries swung up and down, in and out of power. But they all functioned within the set context that had been established religiously by their Christian heritage, culturally by the Greek Logos and empirically by Roman imperial politics. The trend to monoculturism reached full expression after Europe broke out of its circumscribed limits, which had been imposed by Islam, conquered its territory and began to view the world as its domain. White American culture was an offshoot of this latter phase; it has always operated self-consciously in terms of occidental patterns of thought: it has tried to preserve its Judeo-Christian roots in its cultural development.

Black culture, on the other hand, has had to define itself within boundaries that have been imposed on it. Where white civilization worked from inside out, black culture has been a process of discovery that went from the outside in. The Other is not intrinsic to the Logos; it represents the adversary world. The black has been subject to the standards of his rulers and his oppressors; to the extent that he has turned back to his original experience, he is defining himself. His spiritual survival depended on his "awareness of the power system enforcing . . . myths . . . the ability to use this awareness to resist (and when possible subvert) that system"[16] and his awareness of the limitations of his countermyths. The black's attachment to his folklore—as Ellison remarked—showed his "willingness to trust his own sensibilities as to the definition of reality, rather than to allow his masters to define these crucial matters for him."[17] Not only was his self-education an act of resistance to prevailing norms, but it was also self-invention: he had to create the book in order to explore his sources. Contemporary black critics have analyzed the black American tradition and have concluded, as Houston Baker puts it, that "African life, black American culture and black men and women in society contain values that must be preserved, fostered, and communicated."[18] Black literature, which is much less rigidly formalized than that of whites, centers on human possibilities,[19] on new ground to be cleared and not old to be replanted. Situated in a world context, black literature is modern in its acceptance of social and political fluctuation—despite or perhaps because of its devotion to roots.

Black writers look to the past as the source of qualities that might define the state of being black. The black aesthetic point of view is based affirmatively on a racial memory that involved what some call the dream and others call the historical reality of blackness. In a holistic sense, the two are the same because the black man's image of Africa has been idealized if not mythicized throughout the generations he has lived in Africa. Therefore, from Phyllis Wheatley, who boasted of her African roots, to Nikki Giovanni, blacks have celebrated their African heritage.

Of course, the black American has links to Africa as the white has ties to Europe. But where the white willfully separated from his mother country and then tried to preserve his connection to it, the black's relationship with his native land was deliberately truncated so that his memory of it existed as a dream. It had assiduously to be re- and deconstructed. So although the black's cultural filiation with his original continent might have disappointed Richard Wright,[20] confused Langston Hughes and, for a while, Amiri Baraka[21] and amused Chester Himes,[22] it was as real as the color consciousness that was at the root of black identity. It provided the black American not just with a native subconscious and not just with a tradition that is outside that of Europe, but with a concrete existential bond with the nonwhite majority—particularly the black third world, which had the potential numerical force to undermine postindustrial power by the sheer weight of its mass and the debilitating pressure of its destitution.

Indeed, Africa represents to the black the antithesis of the materialism that has inspired industrial progress. Africa is the expression of spriri*tuality*; the idea that "spirit inhabits all life"[23]—as one of Alice Walker's characters puts it—is the legacy of African civilization. "What is the absolute truth about the man of color on this earth?" the father of her Olivia in *The Temple of My Familiar* would ask, and then answer himself, "He admits spirit. . . ."[24] And spirit implies sentiment. It was an African who claimed that "emotion is African, as Reason is Hellenic."[25] Locke spoke of the Negro's "emotional inheritance a deep-seated aesthetic endowment" as an offshoot of the African soul. His "primitive tropical heritage," characteristic of "group experience,"[26] was African. The New Negro's ancestral pride—which in modern times has evoked the conviction that "black culture is superior to white culture,"[27] derives from the faith that black people are able to relate to natural forces. "Blackness / Is a going to essences and to unifyings," writes Gwendolyn Brooks;[28] "the rays / of God roared through us all," says Baraka;[29] a patient who saw Reed's Jes Grew—the force of life— "felt like the gut heart and lungs of Africa's interior."[30] The very capacity to feel profoundly is, to the black, something that whites, who have been emotionally repressed in the plasticity of a rationalistic and technological order, increasingly lack. As DuBois predicted, the black race has a message to give the world.[31]

The positive assertion of an indefinable quality called blackness could sometimes be reduced to bluster, the baseless exercise of pretense. Black aesthetics, as Baker observes, often represent the effort "*to will into being a new art and criticism*" by means of purely "*conative utterances,*"[32] which either intrigued or irritated whites to the extent that they were militant. Nevertheless, the cultural reality stands: blacks were insisting on their difference. The feeling of being black does evoke a response from all kinds of nationalities and types of blacks and even, in many case, from whites. When Gwendolyn Brooks visited Kenya, she told herself excitedly, "This is BLACKland—and I am *black*."[33] She realized "that I am essentially an essential African, in occupancy here because of an indeed 'peculiar' institution [and] that in the black fellow-feeling must be the black man's encyclopedic Primer."[34] Zora Neale Hurston was attached to her "crib" of Negroism,[35] and Jean Toomer, whose Kabnis "discovers, mystically, the strength of his people,"[36] referred, equally mystically, to "the soil of my ancestors."[37] And whites— from Joseph Conrad's Kurtz to Harlem's thrill seekers to Mailer's white Negro—seem to perceive a distinction, an intimation of some unexplored dimension of reality in the black spirit that, of course, they deform when they intellectualize it as sexuality, primitivism, the unconscious, black existentialism or even as primordial metaphysical truth.

Religion in any form—from theology to fundamentalism to expressionism to art—has been central to black life in both Africa and America. History itself—which to blacks is not progressive and makes no pretenses to objectivity—is an ideal. It is a dream; it is fact and fiction combined in the consciousness of a people. "History and myth intertwine," says a critic.[38] Given its religious foundations, history is myth, as myth is reality in its most profound significance. Since history does not advance, it is as it always is: it is "usually cyclical."[39] To historian and writer Arna Bontemps, history is a pendulum;[40] to Ellison it repeats itself.[41] The black experience is viewed as a whole: to be black, writes Stephen Henderson, is to feel "a sense of fidelity to the observed and intuited truth of the Black experience" as a "totality."[42] If black myth is not a signification of some universal human predisposition—as anthropologist Claude Lévi-Strauss would define myth—but, as critic Jane Campbell has it, a "dramatic embodiment of cultural values, of ideal states of being found in Afro-American history and experience,"[43] it incarnates all facets of specifically black life. The myth included the African American's emotional response not only to his mortal condition but also to his situation in the world. Unlike the white, the black was able to bow to the irremediability of death—which, remarks Walker, can be beautiful if it is not inflicted and not sullied by the effects of technological civilization.[44] Yet blacks who have been socially and politically maligned have had to accept the existence of evil. They have been subject to an imperialistic and racist ideology that "divided the peoples of the world into white and colored races"[45] and that represented a force as inexorable as that of nature. They have suffered oppression through colonialism, slavery and segregation. As Toni Morrison observes, "Black people in general don't annihilate evil.... We are not surprised by its existence or horrified or outraged."[46] In effect, they have been enriched by the experience of it.

One of the most revealing links between the African spirit and the African American spirit involves the religious ontology common to both. The African relates to nature by his worship of the gods who mediate between himself, his people and the mystery of existence. His civilization, which reaches beyond the constricts and constructs of language, reason and structured literature, is based on the ambiguity of man's position in an unintelligible universe and on his consequent attempt to come to terms—at least approximately—with his inner and outer nature. As social thinker Sunday O. Anozie writes, in primitive society "myths are shown to operate from an awareness of oppositions to their satisfactory mediation."[47] In the sense that they are formalized, that they stand for "systems of the abstract relations,"[48] they are pro-pitiatory. They represent a way of compromise with the potentially menacing unknown and, thereby, they offer a person an area in which he can function with relative freedom and even power. For if, as Senghor suggests, the nature of things—or "super-reality,"[49] the essential life force—is perceived only through emotion and intuition, then these modes fill the role that westerners have in general assigned to reason. Emotion is supposed to signify "intuitive reason":[50] the god-spirits are mythicized in feeling.

These African spirits, or loas, are mythical creatures that somehow followed black prisoners on their route to enslavement. They showed up in Haitian vodoun and crossed the Caribbean to New Orleans voo-doo which, as Ishmael Reed writes, was "based upon the belief that [they] are present in the Americas and often use men and women as their mediums."[51] Lafcadio Hearn—a pronounced racist when he lived in the South[52,53]—was the lover of Marie Laveau, queen of voodoo.[54] Zora Neale Hurston actually experienced the rites of voodoo in New Orleans and felt, she reported, its unearthly terror.[55]

Voodoo, the use and refuge of the spirit world, was present every-where blacks went—from South America to North America. Black Christians turned the saints into loas in Brazil and Mexico and other Latin American countries; black festivals, particularly those on Shrove Tuesday, represented incantations to hidden powers. Avey Johnson, Paule Marshall's North American black bourgeoise in *Praisesong for the Widow,* discovered in the revelries of Grenada her true black iden-tity. Chesnutt's conjure woman, Aunt Peggy, in *Conjure Tales* was a voodooist who resorted to rites and charms and goophers to settle ac-counts among her people and to ward off the malice of the master.[56] Ntozake Shange's Indigo in *Sassafras, Cypress and Indigo* is a kind of modern sorceress who believes that black people need "Access to the moon. The power to heal. / Daily visits with the spirits."[57] Gloria Nay-lor's Mama Day in the work of that name had not just premonitions, but powers to cure, both psychically and physically.

In all these spiritual ways the African American nurtured a deep and vital attachment to his African past, which, as a racial memory, affected and still affects his view of the present. Within this context, his historical experience is a whole. As Phyllis Wheatley, the converted neoclassical Puritan, was proud of her "peculiarly African gift,"[58] so modern poet Jayne Cortez sings to Orisha, gods of the Yoruban.[59] Blacks' sentiment of racial identity has two dimensions. In the first place it is the subconscious imagination of Africa as an "ideal civilization":[60] it is a dream of glory. "I remember Kings. / A blossoming palace. Silver. Ivory. / The conventional wealth of stalking Africa . . . My right to raid the sun, consult the moon,"[61] writes Brooks. Locke, too, spoke of "a sense of 'remembered beauty.' "[62] Countee Cullen's brown girl has "beauty like a queen,"[63] and poet Kettie Combo pictures her black sister as a "beautiful, ancient / African queen."[64] Moreover, this memory has implicitly subversive implications: it represents the black's reaction to his present American condition. Paule Marshall's West Indian peasants idolize and ritualistically honor the black rebel, Cuffee Ned, while blacks from the beginning of slavery have celebrated the exploits of black revolutionaries—from Denmark Vesey to Toussaint L'Ouverture to Malcolm X, the modern "prince of the earth," as Baraka calls him.[65]

Not only does the black have a mythically indelible attachment to his African past. His second racial memory involves his fall from glory into physical and mental subjection, or into what George Kent describes as "the chaos swirling at the root of transplanted black life."[66] Brooks, for instance, thinks back on the "blazing dementiae . . . the mate and captain . . . Their retching rampage among their luminous / Black pudding among the guttural chained slime."[67] But also the idea of slavery as a descent into forced inexpressivity, the negation of affirmation, involves a feeling of historical communality through the very struggle for survival—or survival through the feeling of group solidarity.

Since the black's "intensely political perspective"[68] is implicit in his race consciousness, his culture is ethical in spirit: it is founded on moral premises and it affirms certain values that relate to the black's collective experience. Ralph Ellison has criticized nationalists like Amiri Baraka for imposing ideological content on the blues,[69] but this music does make a positive statement regarding black norms, as writers from Douglass[70] to Baraka[71] have pointed out. If aesthetics is not politics, as some artists have pretended, nevertheless it is ethics, as Henderson, for instance, notes.[72] The view that "true art is moral as well as social"[73] has inevitably led to a confusion between theories of art as propaganda and of art as itself. Since the black, unlike the white, did not presume that his culture—even in its musical form—was an end in itself and since he had to accept the boundaries in which it was enclosed and which were essential to its development, he was able to distinguish more clearly and self-evidently than whites between ethical absolutes. Where white people were led to believe that white was right and that all thought was logocentric, the black, who suffered moral violation in the name of right, was able to recognize with conviction that certain principles transcended the pretentions of white civilization. The black, therefore, had access, as Richard Wright put it, to a "truer and deeper life"[74] than did whites; "black is a tremendous spiritual condition," said Baldwin.[75] "The core of the black world's vision remains intact," wrote Cleaver.[76]

For instance, the black has been able to assume possession of certain of his oppressor's favorite tenets. Gwendolyn Brooks claims that "democracy and Christianity / Recommence with me."[77] Melvin Tolson likewise used figures and tropes from occidental as well as from African culture to illuminate his dream of apocalyptic pluralism—of cosmic manhood, through which Africa would save the white and the whole world.[78] Tolson blamed the whites for "counterfeit[ing] our Christianity / And bring[ing] contempt upon Democracy."[79] Ellison, who considered the principle but not the fact of western democracy the "framework that promises a harmonious future coexistence between blacks and whites,"[80] remarked, "Today the most dramatic fight of American . . . ideals is being sparked by black Americans."[81] And poet Robert Hayden observed that where "no other beings / . . . make more extravagant claims / for their importance and identity"[82] than white Americans, it is they who "fear, mistrust, betray . . . the freedom / They boast of in their ignorant pride."[83]

As the black dialectically adopted certain principles of white civilization, so he affirmed values that persisted from his African heritage. The social structure of African tribalism was based upon communality. In America, where racism was a source of black solidarity, it reduced all blacks to an equal status and imposed on them all a common destiny—in theory, if not in fact. And it was this affirmation of communality that resulted in black cultural expression. Just as, in slavery, black folk tales and black songs were positive assertions of the black spirit in implicit reaction against white constraints, so in the 1960s, black art was "the aesthetic and spiritual sister of the Black Power concept," said Larry Neal.[84] According to Houston Baker, the black aesthetic "has given rise to a newly realized black collectivity and its artists a sense of holism, a sense of essential reciprocity between black art and black culture."[85] The black slaves and black sharecroppers of the South used communality as a means of surviving in an inimical world; the Black Panthers utilized it politically in order to enlist mass black participation in their projects. The ghetto itself took on a positive significance through this type of group affiliation. Baker refers to the "laudatory delineation of black urban culture,"[86] and writers from George Cain to Kenneth Clark have spoken of the fellowship that facilitates and distinguishes slum survival. It was communalism, not communism, that was characteristic of the black tradition. W.E.B. DuBois considered the practice—as in "the Afro-communal group"[87]—a criterion of being black.

The theme of communality has always been featured in black writing. Critic Michael Cooke speaks of "*kinship*"[88] as one of the successive conditions into which black literature developed. What Henderson calls "SATURATION," the "communication of Blackness in a given situation,"[89] and Gates considers the collective character of black art[90] are aspects of the feeling of communality. Since literature is essentially an attempt at human communication rather than a form of transcendence by the elevation of mankind over animality and one type of cultural expression over all others, it has served as a means of solidifying group relations. Hurston's Negro storytellers brought the people together in a sense of their own past with their tales of old Massa and slave John.[91] Alice Walker, depressed by her political weakness—her incapacity to use violence—was restored by writing: it brought her close to her community.[92,93]

Insofar as black culture does not pretend to transcendence, it is deliberately not a literary culture in the white sense of the word. The black is cursed by "the *absence* of a printed, catalogued, collective memory," says Gates.[94] This does not mean that it opposes or even devalues writing: Jes Grew, the self-presence with "no end and no beginning," had been "*seeking its words. Its text. For what good is a liturgy without a text.*"[95] Nevertheless, black culture has resisted western theories that equate literary with moral—in fact, human—good. These theories tend to enclose thought within a vicious circle: to be readable, literature must utilize concepts that are articulated in the particular linguistic framework of a particular stylized way of thinking—or a canon. In Africa, civilization would reach beyond the constrictions of writing; it would enlarge the latter and base its art on "*la parole*,"[96] a form of communication that included speaking, rhythm, empathy, intuition, call and response as well as formal language. In America, where slaves were not permitted to read and write, culture was founded on the oral tradition[97]—which was in itself an assertion of black communality. The African American novel is, therefore, not just a branch of Euro-American literature. The fact that it stems from oral art expression differentiates it from white disciplines.

Oratory was a type of expression peculiar to Americans as distinct from Europeans. "Oratory . . . moving by the Revolution from the pulpit to the political forum was . . . the one branch of literature in which America . . . had a formal tradition," said critic F. O. Matthiessen.[98] Black oral culture, uninhibited by the restrictions of formalized schooling and the pressure of more and more extensive and pervasive journalism, was able to develop not just through the pulpit but through folk songs and narratives. It particularly stressed the device of call and response.[99]

Black literature is not simply a " 'literature of necessity,' a literature concerned with the urgent realities of the racial situation,"[100] as Saunders Redding had it—although it is political in the sense that it is by nature black, as the negation of a white canon which "has always been political from the beginning."[101] It is, however, more than just protest, more than what Henderson calls "masturbatory art [that] screams, 'whitey' and 'honkey.' "[102] It is the expression of black identity. The black creative movement of the 1960s was to be "an art of liberating vision," as Larry Neal put it, "an art that validates the positive aspects of our life style."[103] Of course this life-style calls into question the criteria of the white ethic. Insofar as the white tradition is monocultural in essence and logocentric in method, insofar as it uses the intertextuality of the canon to claim its literary preeminence, it would either not understand or not tolerate cultural difference.

Therefore, resistance to white standards is necessarily a part of the black cultural tradition—as it is of the black life-style. As Baker writes, " 'An index of repudiation' characterizes [it]. The ideology of white America is rejected and replaced by a black American cultural experience."[104] According to writer June Jordan, "The functions of protest and affirmation are not ultimately distinct. . . . The affirmation of Black values and lifestyle within the American context is . . . an act of protest."[105] Gayle thinks of "race and super-structure"[106] as the pillars of this culture according to Gates, who locates the distinguishing features of black literature in its oral, collective and repudiative traditions.[107] To critic Robert Stepto, the black's use of authentication represents his efforts to affirm himself against a white-controlled world. It is by seeking "their own literary forms"[108] that writers create a coherent continuity and new types of literary discipline. As Ellison suggests, blacks would "create the race by creating ourselves and then . . . we will have created something far more important . . . a culture."[109]

Certain critics have used a model to characterize the black literary viewpoint. This trope had in general been inherent in black culture from its African to its American phases, from the past to the present. Gates and Baker, for instance, have taken the image of the so-called signifying monkey to represent the historical black tradition in all of its expressive aspects. "Signifyin(g)," says Gates, is a black "rhetorical concept . . . by which a second statement or figure repeats or tropes or reverses the first."[110] On the one hand, repetition is an aesthetic device that parallels the technique of call and response and controverts the idea of progress: repetition serves the same function as the classical chorus and allows not only for a textual relationship between the author—or the narrator—and his audience, but also detachment from the written text and parody. On the other hand, reversal questions the text in hand. Troping includes parody: it is an ironic comment that affirms and denies—by mocking—the original statement; it swings back and forth like a monkey in a tree. The parody recapitulates and repudiates; it imitates and debunks; it simultaneously preserves and disrupts.[111] Reversal is repudiation: the signifying monkey rejects even as he submits to the forces that overwhelm him, and in his act of signifying, he exercises his right of freedom. His reversal is not dialectically all-absorbing: it is a game that he plays as he hops from one side to the other.

The signifier is the trickster, the duper, the con artist. He is Brer Rabbit, John de Conquer DuPester; he is Hurston's Slave John; he is Ellison's Rinehart; he is Reed's Pompey, the ventriloquist, or the cowboy in the boat of the good sun-god, Ra, the victor over Set, the evil one, the protector of the vessel. "Look out Set," sings the cowboy, "here i come Set / to get Set to sunset / Set / to unseat Set to Set down Set."[112] He is Baldwin's devil, "subtle, charming, cunning, and warm."[113] The art of the trickster is reflected in dozens, the verbal game in which black kids excel by insulting one another and which, writes Eric Lincoln, is "implicit in the very structure of black-white relations": blacks deprecate one another before whites can.[114] The trickster was Rap Brown, "Rap the dicker the asskicker / the cherry picker the city slicker the titty licker."[115] Langston Hughes's *Ask Your Mama,* a parody of intellectual modernism, was constructed on the word play of dozens as reflected thematically in black music. "The tell me of the mama / is the answer to the child,"[116] said Hughes, who himself played the role of poet as "mother . . . to the race."[117] The signifier is the personification of the mulatto as seen from the perspective of the black: he is the sin of the father turned back on the father. And he has existed throughout history—both black and white. He is Esu and Hermes; the European figure of Harlequin[118] was originally the African man. He is Legba, "the spirit of the 'crossroads' and the medium between two worlds"—a young loa in Africa, an old one in the Americas.[119] He is the flying Ibo of Paule Marshall's *Praisesong for the Widow*.[120]

Signifying, indeed, has been more than aesthetics: it is art as a way of both physical and spiritual survival. Black culture is the creation of black identity in a world that has been socially, politically and economically preempted. The black "protagonist begins to understand the limitations imposed on him by the white world, and he plays the role of trickster and bagman in order to avoid capture."[121] Since the black has been forced to adapt to norms inflicted on him, he has had to invent himself out of nothing. All he has had was his existence. His mythicizing, fabricated or rediscovered, is his act of self-creation. The slave, Baker points out, had to construct his humanity under conditions in which he was defined as less than human: his being "had to erupt from nothingness."[122] His movement was a necessarily oppositional one—as is that of all black art. But it was not dialectically progressive; it did not intend to envelop the being of things. The black aesthetic movement, like the signifying monkey, would "alter existing structures to accord with the wishes of black America."[123] It would clear room for itself. Where aesthetes like James Joyce tried to expand western culture from within by playing on the intertextual signification of its multilingual and allusive structured words, which caught themselves in the limitations of his traditional culture, blacks would challenge the structure: they would open it up.

Black artists have been dedicated to the task of creating themselves free. Frederick Douglass, the slave, adopted the English language as "his instrument for extracting meaning from nothingness, being from existence."[124] Jean Toomer, who had faith in the coming of a transcendent—colorless—American man, felt that through his gift of naming things with words "I had in my hands the tools for my own creation."[125] Ralph Ellison's narrator, who has sunk to the depths of the world, acknowledges his American identity by realizing, while he is eating red-sauced white cream, that he is black and blue all over. He suggests that he has changed from Jack the running rabbit into Jack the hibernating bear, perhaps to arise phoenixlike anew. The African American female, "as poor, woman, and black," was also forced "to generate her own definition in order to survive."[126] The life of Toni Morrison's

Sula, in the novel of that name, is "experimental," but in abandoning her community she loses herself.[127] But in *Song of Solomon,* Morrison's Pilate invents herself all by herself through her devotion to her heritage. Born unconnected—without a navel—she is "self-created and self-contained"[128]—a myth in herself who perpetuates her own tradition by reconstructing it. She is heiress to the flying African. Alice Walker's Meridian writes of "we, cast out alone / to heal / and recreate ourselves."[129] In *The Color Purple* Celie, who is convinced she is ugly, defies God because she knows that he doesn't like ugly. She projects her truth in her own terms and makes herself herself. "Whether God will read [her] letters or no" she "will go on writing them; which is guidance enough" for her sister Nettie.[130]

It is through the project of re-creation that blacks have taken American English—their native tongue—and molded it to fit black cultural norms, which often seem to resemble those of Africa. The language of the African American, as Gates points out, is mythopoeic; that of the westerner is rational and technocratic.[131] Language in itself serves contradictory roles both in its ontology and in its method. On the one hand it is more than a perception of reality, the translation of things as they are into concepts. It is the stuff of existential reality in the sense that it alone represents the process of existing relations and thus the power of human communicability. On the other, however, by its very exercise language exposes its inherent limitations: by itself it cannot transcend the particular historical, geographical and cultural situation in which it functions. Because it is by nature relativistic, it is a barrier to human communication. It is not only incapable of reproducing and representing reality, but it actually misrepresents things as they are, as well as its own workings. There is a necessary gap between the signifier and the signified: the linguistic word or phrase is only functional; it is caught in a system on which it depends ideologically, socially and historically. It is *"a form and not a substance"*;[132] its value and character are conditioned by difference and not similitude.

As the black has had to operate in a preempted world, so has he had to express himself through a language that was culturally not his. As James Weldon Johnson's ex-colored man remarks, "The colored man looked at everything through the prism of his relationship to society as a *colored* man. . . ."[133] He had been named; he had not named himself. "The black poet's mythopoeic function has never been to look plainly at the world through its veils; it has been to recreate in metaphor an outer world and in metonym an inner world in the image of a people, in terms where any opposition between the two is resolved . . ." says Gates.[134] Necessarily, as Baker points out, the black's conceptual field "must have differed in its systematic organization from that of his white American master."[135] Therefore, his rendering of reality through the tools of his master would involve his deliberate mythicization or distortion or revision of his master's usage of them. He would remold them to fit his vision; his response was parodic. He would unname in order to rename: he would find his own voice in the specificity of himself— as have black nationalists from Malcolm X to Amiri Baraka. Robert Hayden, whose true name was a mystery "like my life my mother fled / Like the life I might have known,"[136] interpreted the character of Malcolm X, El-Haji Malik El-Shabazz, as a metamorphosis of Ahab the native son. At last, "rejecting Ahab," though "of Ahab's tribe," he struck "through the mask" and "rose renamed, became / Much more than there was time for him to be."[137] As it was said, "for the Afro-American . . . self-creation and reformation of a fragmented familial past are endlessly interwoven."[138] Naming is genealogical revisionism. The aesthetic interest of the black would not involve the mystification of reality in the style of the white postmodern writer. The black would not refabricate it in the process of writing a story about writing a story or of investigating a hieroglyph that might lead to nothing. Rather, he would try to represent his self, as he perceives it, at the core of the fictitious facts that surround his way to it—which are in truth nonexistent. Whereas, for instance, the conspiracy by which Thomas Pynchon's characters are persecuted is either real and rational or paranoiac and imaginary, that of Ishmael Reed in *Mumbo Jumbo*, regardless of reliable but irrelevant testimony, stands for the actual attempt of white civilization to destroy mankind's creative spirit in the incarnation of Jes Grew.[139]

CHAPTER 15

BLACK
CULTURAL COMMITMENT

Black art has issued from the inexpressible depths of the historical experience which represents black reality, which is necessarily and admittedly limited to the African American context and which is outside language in that it is felt and not recorded. But to the extent that blacks affirm their reality, they more than whites would express themselves directly in concrete terms: they would speak out loud to be heard. The African American literary tradition exists because authors and texts "seek their own literary forms," says Stepto.[1] In order to transcend existing political, social and economic structures, blacks have addressed themselves to actual conditions. They have not been "inclined to neglect moral and social issues in their narratives,"[2] writes critic Bernard Bell: they have not been art-for-art. Whether they have been labeled postmodern or neorealist or even esoteric like Tolson, they have assumed that "man is a social being who ought not to separate from the historical context . . . in which he finds his significance and develops his potential as an individual."[3] If blackness has no essence but exists as "signified . . . by a signifier," as Gates suggests[4]—and history itself is the signifying monkey (the trickster, the fast-change artist, the mulatto)—the truth of being black has to be created out of the varying black texts that punctuate successive stages of American history. There may not be or ever have been a black essence, but there can be its is-ness to be written. Blackness cannot be thought of as a transcendent quality that stands protectively and morally behind black people because—as one of Gloria Naylor's characters points out—it just is: it is not beautiful, it is not ugly.[5] It exists, "but only as a function of its signifiers," Gates observes.[6] Reed also questions the ideal of a black subject. It must be construed in relation to signs displayed by all kinds

270

of performing artists, past and present, and to the occidental structure within which it has taken meaning. "Each writer writes the missing parts to the other writer's story. And the whole story is what I'm after," comments Alice Walker.[7]

In Reed's poetic parody of Ralph Ellison, "the figure of history . . . is the signifying monkey," the dualistic invisible man is both "outside of / history . . . inside of / history."[8] Like the mulatto, the signifying monkey "seems to dwell in [a] space between two linguistic domains,"[9] which he plays against each other. He breaks cultural rules at the same time that he opens the way to the re-creation of new cultural forms. He does represent "a new race of man; the only new race of man to come into being in modern times."[10] Since blacks are "uh mingled people,"[11] as Hurston's Janie puts it in *Their Eyes Were Watching God*, they are culturally mingled. Since they can "ask the rhetorical question, what man is white,"[12] like Tolson's curator, they are outside and free of, inside, and subject to western cultural standards. The American black now personifies "liminality";[13] he stands in the space between one cultural place and another; he is not irreparably caught in a labyrinth with no exit. He is potentially incarnate, and he *is* also potentially as the being of nothingness.

The mulatto theme had been exploited as much by blacks as by whites, but in a different way. For whites, the colored man is tragic because he is between two worlds and at home in neither. He is beset by an internal struggle between his two incompatible kinds of blood, one savage, one civilized: one brute and dumb, the other rational and intelligent, although perhaps conniving. It is this inner battle that makes for his confused and often desperate personality. Faulkner drew on this stereotype to dramatize Joe Christmas out of existence, just as he used the image of the black brute sexpot to fabricate his impossible character of Nancy. But mixed Negroes were not only tragic because they were "discontented, aspiring."[14] The white man looked at them, the fruit of his seed, as downright evil. They were tricksters, con men, rogues, signifiers who posed a threat to the intrinsic harmony of the white cultural order. As in pre–Civil War days the feeling prevailed that "only the mulatto influence . . . made slaves unmanageable,"[15] so in modern times "too often 'bad' Negroes . . . were the educated, or the propertied, or the militant."[16] Baldwin's white man in *Blues for Mister Charlie* thought that yellow Negroes were the worst kind.[17]

To the black, however, the mulatto's tragedy stemmed from the fact that it has historically separated him from his people. Light skin made it possible for the mulatto to make it either in the white or the middle-class Negro world. Johnson's ex-colored man became "an ordinarily successful white man who has made a little money"[18] and who, almost despite himself, abandoned his black heritage simply by acceding to the success ethic by which white culture functioned. Color in this way was a commodity in both the white and black materialistic societies.

Yet to the black, color was a symbol with an ideological connotation: it was a tragic reminder of the historical subjection of a people. Both Alice Walker and Malcolm X recognized with a more or less pronounced feeling of shame and aversion that their lightness was the result of the white man's rape and that, consequently, they possessed the spirit of both the oppressor and the victim. Walker's great-great-grandfather had raped a child of eleven years: she was "the thing itself."[19] To revise the theme of DuBois, the Negro's vision is contorted because of his veil of white, not black, blood that clouds his perception of reality. Whereas before the twentieth century—in general—color-class differentiation divided the black community and light skin signified distinction, recently dark skin tone has come to stand for black cultural integrity. Since most blacks are to some degree mulattoes, the pure black is the exception. Charles Chesnutt's protagonist in "The Wife of His Youth" reclaims his black wife, who is socially unpresentable, in a turnabout of social roles. His accused half-white murderer attacks the sheriff, his father, who ultimately saves him.[20] Langston Hughes's mulatto, in the play of the same name, is not so lucky. Renounced by his white father, he kills the old man. "*I am your son, white man!* / A little yellow / Bastard boy,"[21] wrote Hughes in his poem in which he defended, as Johnson had before him, the dark woman who is rejected with her offspring.[22]

If there is no direct or rational link between the powerful gods of creation and the more or less pitiable creatures they have set on earth, then signifying would be the only way of relating to the caprices of these mysterious universal forces. And if the shape of the world has been preempted in a white image which the black must break apart in order to get back to where he started, then he must seek himself by means of a dualism that is inherent in his mixed skin color. The black, like all Americans, divides reality in two. Bigger Thomas looked at the world in terms of the black ghetto versus white overrule, and Ellison's invisible man viewed reality in terms of the unseen inner I and outside pressures. Since this oppositionism precludes dialectical imperialism—involving the progressive mastery of otherness—it is unlike that of whites. It represents a process of epuration, a falling back, a return to sources, a divestment of burdensome obstacles. Black idealism challenges the moral infallibility of American society, but it does so not just because this society is—as Wright[23] and Ellison[24] put it—"too shallow," too superficial and too immoral, but because it is stultifying. White intellectuals also have denounced the vulgar materialism of a civilization that, as poet Henry Miller pointed out, has the worst-paid poets in the world.[25] Rather, blacks tend to turn their backs on America because it impinges on them: it leaves no room for them to develop their cultural potential.

Rationalistic, logocentric westerners defined blackness as their otherness. It was the negative quality through which Europeans established not just their pretensions of universality, but also the inner dynamics by which they were able to sustain their civilizational mission to prevail ethically. Occidental thought, which is metaphysical in inclination, derives its assumption of moral right from its creation of otherness. It is this that nourishes its tendency to absorb, swallow or consume difference. And it is this that characterizes the white dialectic.

Therefore, in a reversal of orientation, the black must play the role of the signifying monkey not merely to affirm his blackness, not merely to bear witness to the inscrutability of his natural context, but to lay bare the undeniability of his and others' existence. As noted in so-called primitive societies, myths operate from "an awareness of opposition to their satisfactory mediation."[26] They stand not only as tropes to prevent a culture's absorption and loss of identity but also as traces of some inexpressible and unreachable truth. To create is, therefore, a revolutionary act, but not in the totalitarian dialectical sense of occidental revolution, whose synthesis depends on the progressive negation of negation and so on the creation of adversary otherness. Gates, for instance, debunks the idea of blackness as negative essence because this would imply the reality of an absolute dualism or ineluctable manichaeism in the white cultural sense: he would not "substitute . . . one sort of essentialism [that of blackness] for another."[27]

The mulatto, consequently, could be the exemplar of the signifying monkey. He tricks; he mediates; he does not categorically oppose. He is not all black; he possesses some white. His image serves as a criterion of difference to a white world that, as poet Gerald Barrax writes, wants to integrate "me into your anonymity / because it is my right / you think / to be like you."[28] The mulatto signifies ambiguously on the black man's relation to and place in white society. As black folk art rarely judged, but simply presented itself as a form in itself, it proposed an

alternative to the rigid disciplines of white aesthetics. The mulatto is a
con man in that as his whiteness is the signification of his historical
kinship and long-suffering experience with the white, so is his blackness
a witness to his distinction, by which he can attune to a reality outside
white cultural restrictions. It is his ideal freedom.

The signifying monkey is, of course, a trope that is common to
many cultures. He is Melville's hustler in *The Confidence-Man,* whose
role is played by many characters, from the preacher to the artist to the
Negro cripple, "an embodiment of the Confidence Man."[29] He is Mark
Twain's Duke in *The Adventures of Huckleberry Finn.* He is the African
Esu, the Greek Hermes, god of the language, distinguished by his ability
not just to trick, to steal, to charm, but also to make love. He is Brer
Rabbit, equally a womanizer. "By and large," writes Norman O.
Brown, "the primitive mind makes no distinction between trickery and
magic."[30] The con artist is a craftsman: he possesses skills that raise
him to the level of culture hero and creator. Phyllis Wheatley, the so-
called capitulator to white norms, has been characterized as a "trickster
... who disguises her real message behind innocuous 'appearance' " in
order to win concessions "for Africans like herself."[31] The sexual powers of the con man are connected to his magical gifts, which approach
those of the conjuror. He is always endowed with an oversized phallus.
He is also proficient in trade and commerce, a talent that relates him
to the sources of civilization—the exchange-communication between
various societies. Hermes was not only the god of education and culture;
he was also the symbol of democracy. He represented the religious aspirations of the Greek *demos,* the lower classes. He was a group figure:
he could stand for the totem, which, in Senghor's poem, is *"the real
self of the poet."*[32] The image of the mulatto encompasses all these
attributes: he is smart, he is uppity, he is slippery, he is seductive, he is
tricky. He makes fun of authority; he is manipulative; he is a hustler in
the marketplace; he is a lover of women; and, like Hermes the thief,
he is loyal to a communal code. He incarnates the soul of an outcast
people.

In his aesthetic function, the signifying monkey plays a part different from that of the traditional western hero. As European art was
oriented toward the monopolistic control of human ethics—through the
Manichaeism of otherness—so the art of the signifier is neither moral
nor immoral.[33] Insofar as it is the affirmation of selfhood within a special group context and, reciprocally, of group identity through the self,
the art of the signifier is relativistic. As much as it champions certain

ideal principles and precepts, it rejects, mocks or reverses others. Black art is based on both continuity and revisionism.

As critic Jay Edwards points out in the context of Lévi-Strauss, there are two types of character roles in the traditional plot. The first, which is univocal, is based on lack. It involves the hero, who has a task to accomplish; he plans his operation and he succeeds or fails. His outlook is pragmatic. The second, which is bivocal, is that of the trickster. He has no clear project: the plot is inclined to be picaresque; it is ambiguous with respect to the controlling theme. The con man may lack something that he strives to possess, or he may be threatened in his experience. But he is apt to violate the contract that is implied in the superstructure of the narrative. He may, for instance, state a moral principle at variance with that contained in the original plan, or he may go off on a new, seemingly irrelevant mission. His art is indeterminate; it has no end. People do not live happily ever after, nor do they fall from grace. They do not feel agonizingly obliged to set right times that are out of joint.[34]

If, as Stepto quotes a critic, "structure, or all that which holds people apart, defines their differences, and constrains their actions, is one pole in a charged field, for which the opposite pole is communitas, or anti-structure, the egalitarian 'sentiment for humanity,' "[35] then there is an inherent tension between plot and setting, between the literal and the figurative, that characterizes the writing of African Americans. The writing is relatively free of the moral manichaeism implied in the premise of the western plot, a concept which applies even today: that the protagonist has something to achieve. Indeed, the signifier often questions whatever he signifies. As the author, he might stress setting over plot in one case, and in another the reverse. In a third, he might confound the two.

It is perhaps the sense of circularity, the free flow from a source or a theme, the play of double narratives and of double beginnings and endings that seem to characterize much modern black writing and to liberate it from western literary modes. Stepto maintains that the black "myth of the quest for freedom and literacy has occasioned two basic types of narrative expressions, the narratives of ascent and immersion,"[36] but the two resemble each other. Stories of ascent, which are based on lack, in many cases seem to parody the conventional white plot. Frederick Douglass's autobiography, for instance, illustrated "the positing of fictive selves in language,"[37] as Gates defines this tradition. Douglass made himself up: he "subverted the terms of the code he was meant to mediate" in that his text was to serve as "the . . . mediator between the world as the master would have it and the world as the slave knows it really is."[38] Douglass, therefore, was "a trickster" because his mediation turned to irony in the context of double meanings.

Richard Wright's *Native Son,* on the surface another novel of ascent, also excluded the possibility of mediation in a world where meanings are deliberately obscured. The doctrinaire rationalizations of the socialist lawyer Max serve on one level to parody the true significance of Bigger's action—which is absolutely absurd when seen from the point of view of the white world against which it is aimed.

Ralph Ellison's narrator is at heart a trickster. Ultimately, he achieves a condition of brilliant luminosity at the end of his story of ascent-descent. At the same time that he is most profoundly entrapped in his own invisibility, he is the signifier of himself.

Jean Toomer's *Cane* is a narrative of lack or of what Stepto calls soullessness. Kabnis, the poet who would find fulfillment in art, starts off from awareness that he is divided in himself. He is on the quest for wholeness because he suffers from the double-consciousness that characterizes the black psyche forced to cope in an inimical society. "The whole world is a conspiracy. . . . I'm what sin is," says Kabnis paranoiacally. He is "the victim of their sin."[39] Although he seeks redemption through folk-culture immersion in the sense that he returns to the South to find his roots, he still cannot pull himself together. In the South, "identity was regional, connected with the earth,"[40] but Kabnis, like his author, is a mystical creature of the air looking for transcendence. He cannot discover a voice to reach his folk and, therefore, to accomplish his would-be ascent to poetic expression. Lewis, the tall copper-colored mulatto alter ego of Kabnis, is in a way the true artist because he signifies on Kabnis: Lewis puts him down and then leaves. Kabnis had vomited Lewis.[41]

On the other side of the narrative of ascent—or of lack—there is that of immersion. Both are characterized by the irony and the ambivalence of the signifying monkey. Since the black quest, unlike that of the white, is a kind of symbolic epuration, it does not run along closely plotted lines. "The white mind leans . . . to the idea of planned search in its conception of progress," says a critic. "But the black mind, left with a memorial history, rather than a formal chronicle of guilt to work with, leans . . . to the area of broad and undirected search."[42] Because, as Gayle writes, the black is struggling "to maintain a sense of historic and cultural peculiarity . . . against the forces that [would] assimilate

him on American terms or construct definitions to limit his human potential,"[43] he must explore uncharted depths of experience. He must go
back into what Redding calls the "jungle"[44] and others call "chaos,"[45]
which is "swirling at the root of transplanted black life."[46] Since his
past, unlike that of the white who equates the process of history with
evolution, growth and the pursuit of happiness, is static and unre-
corded, there is no progression. The black discovers himself in archaic
dimensions of time. Langston Hughes knew "rivers ancient as the world
and older than the flow of human blood in human veins."[47] Morrison's
Sethe, who separates from every human community because her "love
is too thick," has at least her timeless "rememory" in which she can
take refuge.[48] Baldwin's Louisa in "This Morning, This Evening, So
Soon" also thinks that "our culture is as thick as clabber milk."[49] As
one of Toomer's characters remarks, "There is no such thing as happiness. Life bends joy and pain, beauty and ugliness, in such a way that
no one may isolate them. No one should want to. . . ."[50] The episodes
of *Cane* itself, as Toomer conceived it, reflect the movement of a circle.[51]
Where the white American tends to look at the world as his oyster and
arrives at maturity triumphantly to claim that he is free, white and
twenty-one, the black ironically accepts a set destiny. "All I got to do
is stay black and die," said Billie Holiday.[52]

Going back to the symbolic American jungle might represent a return in the present to the slave region—as Toomer and his Kabnis went
back to the South, the symbol of geographical "*comunitas* and *genus
loci*,"[53] of moments in and out of time. In an Ellison story, Todd, the
imperfectly assimilated modern black, is saved morally and physically
by the old southern Negro from whose spirit he has struggled to dis-
associate himself.[54] In one of Alice Walker's stories, the emancipated
daughter comes home to patronize her peasant sister and mother, to
the sister's disgust.[55] And Shange's Betsey Brown, in the work of that
name, learns to identify with her people against the wishes of her bourgeois mother;[56] Shange's Indigo, a southerner endowed with spiritual
powers, actually "was the folks."[57]

The search for roots is an especially ambiguous experience for the
black striver, and it is one that lends itself to signifying. There are two
popular traditions on which black culture is drawn: that of the deprived
rural folk and that of the dispossessed ghetto masses. Both not only lie
outside prevailing white norms but they also serve to comment on the
validity of these norms. Houston Baker, for instance, has used the
Trueblood episode in Ellison's *Invisible Man* to point out the irony that

underlies the relationship between a poor, uneducated—sinful—black sharecropper and a respected white philanthropist. It is not merely that Trueblood shares his incestuous urges with his social class better—who has repressed them but who is still human enough to entertain them. More significant, it is by admitting and expressing them that Trueblood plays to—and profits from—white stereotypes that condemn him to amoral self-indulgence and thus rationalize his poverty and illiteracy.[58] A variation on the theme of playing white myths involves the so-called integrated black, like Himes's Scott in *A Case of Rape,* who regales liberals with "such anecdotes of racial abuse, both real and imagined, which white Americans find so fascinating."[59]

Toni Morrison's middle-class blacks also turn their backs on the incestuous family in their midst.[60] But it is Ellison's narrator—the striver—who is most appalled by Trueblood's self-exposure. Trueblood is a con man; he assumes voluntarily and openly the character of the amoral brute and capitalizes on the image: he impregnates his daughter. He therefore frees himself from social constraints and from the white harassment that usually dogs the black man's existence. Trueblood's sexual comportment is both outrageous and public, but since such excess is expected of and permitted to the poor black, he gets along perfectly with whites, who vicariously feed on his scandalous tales and even pay him for them. He verifies their idea of him and is, consequently, able to use his incestuous libido as a commodity. Black incest, as William Faulkner made clear, is more acceptable to white norms than interracial sex.[61] It is the mulatto who signifies the danger. Trueblood is safe because he is beyond the pale: he represents the inherent nature of blackness, which whites repress; he is the scapegoat for their forbidden desires. Nevertheless, his signification has prostituted the souls both of womanhood, in the persons of his wife and daughter, and of his own cultural integrity, as poet Irma McClarin writes in the voice of a mother whose two daughters have been impregnated by their father: "Look at the skeleton children . . . no heart remains . . . to bring them back as women / into their bodies at dawn."[62]

It was white society that brought on Trueblood's self-prostitution. As he explains, it was the dream of interracial sex that inspired his incestuous relationship. Haunted by the imagination of impossible love, he turned to his daughter, thereby staying within the bounds imposed by whites. Since he commercially exploited his intrafamilial adventures, he is in his way signifying upon his condition in white society. It is in his role as a trickster that Trueblood publicly exposes what whites hypocritically degrade as his blackness. Because he accepts his asociability and uses it to titillate his adversaries, he and his wife and daughter survive in a white-preempted world. But he still sings the blues.[63]

Ellison is trading on Trueblood's misdeeds in order to point up the anomalies of a culture in which blackness is invisibility. On one level, the narrator is seeking acceptance of self even in his experience with Trueblood. Other writers have used the theme of sexual abnormality to comment ironically on the distorted norms of a white sexist world. Alice Walker's Celie, the object of sexual violence that she thinks is incestuous, has to find herself sexually in an affair with her friend Shug before she can be herself. Toni Morrison's proper colored in *The Bluest Eye* discovered and created their own feeling of black beauty when they "stood astride [the] ugliness"[64] of their black playmate, Pecola. In fact, they derive a sense of human dignity from her, the small, uncomplaining victim of incestuous rape who craves love and loveliness in the form of baby-dollblue eyes. It is white norms that have instilled in her, poor rejected creature, such a perverted image of beauty and lovability. "The horror at the heart of her yearning is exceeded only by the evil of fulfillment,"[65] writes Morrison, who muses on the fact that "innocence and faith were no more productive than . . . lust and despair."[66] When the soil is bad for certain types of flowers, "when the land kills of its own volition, we acquiesce and say the victim has no right to live."[67]

Suffering serves not just as a base from which a writer may point up the perversions of an inimical order, but also as an opening through which he may discover his cultural particularity. Blacks are traditionally inspired by the dispossessed folk of rural America—especially of the South—the "black and poor and small and different," as Margaret Walker puts it, about whom "nobody cared and nobody wondered and nobody / understood."[68] Many artists also seek their black reality in the slums among "the lower mass of disinherited ghetto Negroes, for whom the American middle-class liberal establishment offers no way out."[69] Actually, this part of the population is the only expanding community in America today. The lower class is the desperate class, wrote Johnson many years ago, which conforms "to the requirements of civilization much as a trained lion with low muttered growls goes through his stunts under the crack of the trainer's whip."[70]

It is in these rejected slums that many blacks find the positive characteristics of racial belonging. "The outcasts of the earth," wrote Claude McKay, "A race oppressed and scorned by ruling man; / How can they thus consent to joy and mirth."[71] To Gwendolyn Brooks, it is in the back "where it's rough and untended and hungry weed grows"[72] that are found "dusky folk, so clamorous! / So colorfully incorrect, / So amorous, / So flatly brave!"[73] The slum, no matter how unsavory, possesses a spirit that cannot be stifled: Jayne Cortez, for instance, praises Harlem, "hidden by ravines of sweet oil / by temples of switch blades / beautiful in your sound of fertility . . . in your camouflage of grief."[74] George Cain felt something inside him "kindle and reawaken" when he came up to Harlem, "land of black people, dead people, my people."[75] He did not want to leave the "warmth and protection of the community."[76] Langston Hughes loved Harlem as much as he did his character Simple. "There is so much richness in Negro humor, so much beauty in black dreams, so much dignity in our struggles, and so much universality in our problems . . . that I do not understand the tendency . . . that some American Negro artists have of seeking to run away from themselves, of running away from *us*," he concluded.[77] "Oh child," says Ossie Davis's Missy in *Purlie Victorious*, "being colored can be a lotta fun when ain't nobody looking."[78] And Nikki Giovanni hoped that no white person would have "cause to write about me / because they never understand Black love is Black wealth and they'll / probably talk about my hard childhood and never understand that / all the while I was quite happy."[79]

It was at the root of oneself, of one's communal links, of one's history, of one's fate—in effect, of the human condition—that one could experience the feeling of true liberation. At the bottom of this white man's cave, the invisible man was illuminated by electric light bulbs furnished free by industrial society. "I Yam what I am," he affirms.[80] When Gloria Naylor's Willa in *Linden Hills* "had actually seen and accepted reality"—down in her black husband's cellar—"reality brought . . . a healing calm. For whatever it was worth she could rebuild."[81] This quality of acceptance in the face of disaster—indeed, of inevitability—adds a deeply human dimension to black writing that goes beyond narcissism. To find the self, one must delve into the remotest, the most unattractive recesses of mortal existence. Gwendolyn Brooks's Lincoln West, ugly, savage, black and odd, is comforted when he can reassure himself, "After all, I'm / The real thing!"[82] Brooks militantly, or, as she puts it, "firmly"[83] believes that blackness is her people's ultimate reality. As a critic points out, the vision and endurance of people like Brooks's Big Bessie in the last part of *In the Mecca*, who, poor, black and unlovely, stands with sore feet in the "wild weed"[84] of the slums, will redeem the city where little girls are callously slain. Alice

Walker's Celie creates herself out of her realization that "I'm pore, I'm black, I may be ugly and can't cook. . . . But I'm here."[85] And Langston Hughes, discouraged by the vagaries of his career and his reputation as well as by the rise of white-promoted black stars like Ellison and Baldwin, who disdained him intellectually, wrote a poem in which he compared himself to a mule, the symbol of the toiling Negro. Whites could lynch Jim Crow, beat him, he admitted. Nevertheless, he was "here to stay. It'll never be *that* easy, white folks; / To get rid of me. . . ."[86]

On its deepest level, the feeling of black communality stems from the discovery that human beings are able to accept and to survive and consequently, often gracefully, meaningfully, even politically, to surmount the store of life's outrage and pain. As this capacity is the source of dignity—as Job found—so it is the fountainhead of human expression or of art. And the black artist creates his literature, his music, himself and a sense of blackness—whatever that might be—out of it. Since it was from the lowdown, outcast minority of Negroes that black music, America's original contribution to world civilization, developed, black art was based not just on people's suffering but on their spiritual transcendence of it—whether in rural outposts or slum tenements. The poor who lived around Brewster Place in Naylor's novel of that name went to Canaan Baptist Church to worship God "loudly" because "they took no chances that He did not hear them." They sang the same words as their forebears in the cotton fields but "with the frantic determination of a people who realized that the world was swiftly changing but for some mystic complex reason their burden had not."[87] Margaret Walker speaks of her "lost disinherited dispossessed and happy people,"[88] of "the boys and girls who grew . . . to laugh and dance and sing and . . . marry . . . bear children and then die / of consumption and anemia and lynching."[89]

Black American culture is original in its sources. European civilization was built as a self-conscious synthesis of already-established modes of thought and evolved within a set context. Europeans adapted and reworked intricate themes, a pastime that preoccupied the upper literate classes. In modern so-called democratic times, they have stretched their cultural path from the top down, from the clergy and the nobility to the middle classes to the rising audience of the mass media. The individual artist, confused by the disappearance of class guidelines, disillusioned by the irrelevance of his resistance first to industrial and then to political materialism, has sought refuge in an intellectual circle which matches that of other strategic elites in the social order. Or he has been lost in a kind of cultural labyrinth whose terminal point is the naked self stripped of both meaning and connection. Or like many postmoderns he has tried to refashion his significance in an aesthetic cobweb of intertextuality.

The black American slave, from whom black art derived, operated in a state of practical nothingness. He had to struggle to create himself from the bottom up and—through himself—to invent his humanity. He might have existed in a kind of chaos, but his self-awareness was all he had and he sought to find in it a wholeness in which he could cohere both spiritually and physically. He could do no more than ground his expressiveness, his only outlet, in the elemental fact of his given existence in a world to which he had no relation. Perhaps because he worked from the bottom up—from brute physical labor to intellection, from pure sensation to spiritual articulation, from total dispossession to communality—he, alone of all Americans, has produced the only indigenous American culture.

Both blacks and whites have acknowledged his accomplishment. Calverton, the socialist critic, wrote that "the contributions of the Negro to American culture . . . are more striking and singular in substance and structure than any contributions that have been made by the white man."[90] Whites—looking back to their European heritage—imitated their sources or tried self-consciously to surpass them by using their same form. The Negro, said Johnson, is the "creator of the only things artistic that . . . have sprung from American soil and been acknowledged as distinctive American products."[91] His culture is "central to American culture,"[92] as writer Bruce Franklin has been cited. It is "superior to white culture," states Julius Lester flatly.[93] "The cultural and artistic originality of the American nation is founded, historically, on the ingredients of a black aesthetic and artistic base," agrees Cruse.[94]

It is his music that has earned the black the reputation of a cultural originator. Black music has influenced not just Africa and America, but also people of oriental and European civilizations—which habitually have never recognized trends that they could neither assimilate nor control. This music, including gospel, spirituals, blues, jazz, and rhythm-and-blues, is a whole: it manifests the characteristics of an identifiable tradition. It has social and political as well as artistic content and it represents a reaction to middle-class industrial values. In its "most profound manifestations [it] is completely antithetical to [these] standards."[95]

This music is distinctly black: it is "Afro-American in its totality,"[96] says Baraka; it reflects "an attitude"[97] that is specifically and historically black. William Handy, the father of the blues, "aimed to use all that is characteristic of the Negro from Africa to Alabama."[98] He tried "to combine ragtime syncopation with a real melody in the spiritual tradition,"[99] and he succeeded. The blues are "so basic because it is black speech at its earliest articulation as a New World speech," explains Baraka.[100] In this way, black music is an aesthetic guideline for other forms of black art. As the call-and-response pattern that it utilizes is the affirmation of the collective voice,[101] so it proclaims the feeling of communality that was its inspiration. Together, "Southern Negroes sang about everything,"[102] wrote Handy—from sledgehammers to mean whites to death to mules. Yet within this framework, black music is the expression of individual yearning: it brings together "the personal and collective experience of the black masses."[103] According to Ellison, jazz is the "art of individual assertion within and against the group."[104] Baraka more violently contends that "New Black music is this: Find the Self, then Kill it."[105]

Essentially, black music is immediate, emotive, expansive and impulsive. Because it rejoices in the spiritual indivisibility of soul and body, it is not closed in: it is "the interpenetration of the One and the All," which Michael Cooke terms intimacy.[106] It actually celebrates indeterminacy and, therefore, it transcends the negativity of alienation as an end to itself. On the one hand, black music is based on the pain, sorrow and suffering of an oppressed and uprooted people. "Suffering and hard luck . . . birthed these songs"; "the blues were conceived in aching hearts," wrote Handy. "All of our music is derived from suffering. . . ."[107] Langston Hughes remarked that bebop is "not to be dug unless you have seen dark days too."[108] Yet if the spirit of the music is founded in suffering, then it is its form that makes for its feeling of release—if not of joy. "Rhythm was [the] basic element," Handy explained.[109] "Negroes react rhythmically to everything. That's how the blues came to be."[110] Through this rhythm—perhaps a reflection of the bonds of communality resting on call-and-response—black music was able to deprecate the very trouble of which it was the living witness. It is the outpouring of grief and gaiety, of love and stultification, of hate and forbearance—all at the same time. As it deceives, mocks and secretly humiliates the prevailing white world, it simultaneously raises its haunting hymns to hope and faith, and then comes back to earth. There is in this art, as Baraka points out, the "commitment and will to *be* the *truth* as well as to express it."[111] According to Ellison, the blues "are the only consistent art in the United States which constantly reminds us of our limitations while encouraging us to see how far we can actually go."[112] They "at once express both the agony of life and the possibility of conquering it through sheer toughness of spirit."[113] Black music is ambiguous: it signifies on the very process of living. Toni Morrison's latest novel, the story of a black couple who reach a state of relative peace through violence and suffering, is called *Jazz*.

Black music has been unrestrained in its mode of expression. The church sister, the jazzman, the rhythm-and-blues singer were free to pour out their souls in their own way; music was their personal release. Baldwin's Sonny in "Sonny's Blues" resurrected himself from the "terrible things"[114] he had done to himself by playing his music. William Kelley's Uncle Wallace Bedlow in "Cry For Me" sang out not for "money or for people even but because you wanted to."[115] Then having sung, he died because "he'd done everything that he ever wanted to do."[116] Unlike whites, blacks were unafraid to emote: they had historically been repressed by outside forces and not by internal inhibitions. As Hurston remarked with respect to subdued Anglo-Episcopalian hymns, "If white people liked trashy singing like that, there must be something funny about them that I had not noticed before."[117] Blacks were not subject to bourgeois judgment and guilt in their practice of non-European forms that had roots in an African past. The black musician, says Ellison, was "less torn and damaged by the moral compromises and insincerities which have so sickened the life of our country."[118] He could project the yearnings of a captive people as well as the mysteries of a tradition that was related to paganism and that found an outlet in the occultism and evangelism of southern folk faith. "The Frenzy or 'Shouting,' when the Spirit of the Lord passed by, and, seizing the devotee, made him mad with supernatural joy, was the last essential of Negro religion. . . ."[119]

It was also in the subversive implications of this art, in the game contained in rhythmic repetition, that the black musician created his freedom. Because he could make fun of the governing white community without fear of recrimination (since it did not understand what he was doing) he cleared a space in which he could play, in the most profound sense of the term. True art, as Friedrich Schiller defined it, is play against limits. The black musician used atonal techniques to express the double-edgedness that is characteristic of the black approach to the white world—or of the signifying monkey. The monkey, says Cooke, "announced with ironic humor what the blues announce with sorrowful yearning, the pretense of powers and qualities as undeniable as recognized."[120] The black musician did not have to lie: with ambivalence he could sound out all he had known and felt. He could improvise; he could parody; he could deliberately misconstrue; he could soar and then collapse; he could weep in one breath and laugh in another. Toni Morrison's "effort is to be like something that has only been fully expressed in [black] music"; she wants to catch the "quality of hunger and disturbance . . . that never ends."[121] Maya Angelou uses music as a metonym for her roots: she would sneak out to church services—although she was not religious—to hear the spirituals in order to escape her white husband, who would never have understood what she was doing.[122] She loved the music. Paule Marshall's Avey Johnson found herself through her participation in black dancing.[123]

Indeed, black musicians tend to treat their art ironically. They have turned hymns to God into calls for liberty, popular dance tunes into offbeat social commentaries and platitudinous love ditties into takeoffs on middle-class sentimentality. In black hands, irony is a means of asserting one's right to freedom within bounds, just as misrepresentation is a way to truth. Through both, the artist makes room for himself against the limits in which he is enclosed. Parallelly, dissimulation is characteristic of the unconscious in its signification of a deeper truth than what appears. Philosopher-psychologist Jacques Lacan explained, "The Other which my lie invokes [is] a gage of the truth in which it thrives[, thus] the dimension of truth emerges only with the appearance of language."[124]

If the white artist often uses irony to establish a kind of complicity with the enemy and so to assert the sanctity of the victimized self through its inverse relation to an alien world, then the black does so in order to reverse the assumptions of an order in which he has been assigned to inferior status. His irony is "bound up with American color caste" or with a social taboo that exposes the falsehood of democracy.[125] The Negro experience has produced values through a "tragicomic confrontation of life,"[126] and irony includes not just resistance but acceptance of the conditions of living through which the artist alone exercises the freedom of selfhood. In this sense, irony is in kinship with the inherent nature of things, good or evil as they may be. Langston Hughes saw the beauty of "black dancers because of their poverty; singers because they suffered,"[127] and concluded that "no matter how hard life might be, it was not without laughter."[128] The blues are "ironic laughter mixed with tears."[129]

Irony includes sympathy. "We're sorry for everybody but our-selves," complained Chester Himes.[130] Through this sympathy, black music expresses the striving of all people: it is a synthesis of human feeling; it is a universal language which is perceived if not understood and which addresses itself to the emotions over reason. "What ya think music is, watcher think t blues be, & them get happy church music is about," asks Ntozake Shange's Uncle John in *Sassafras, Cypress and Indigo,* and answers, it's "talkin' wit t unreal what's mo' real than most folks ever gonna know."[131] Perhaps because black music is the product of a particular folk tradition and because it has a definite political and social significance, it profoundly reflects the human condition. Black musicians have developed an art that reaches back through history: they are the "symbol of the spontaneous creative impulse of the race . . . often crude, sexy, uninhibited, uneducated, yet wise with . . . folk wisdom."[132] Jazz, said Rudolph Fisher, "was not mere sound, it was a vibrant throb that took hold of the crowd and rocked it [as crowds] had rocked . . . a thousand years ago in a city whose walls were jungle."[133]

As a developed and still developing art, black music has had to struggle to defend its integral character against the incursions of con-sumer society. Its every form, from spirituals to blues to jazz to rhythm-and-blues, has been at first deprecated by official culture and then exploited. Systematically, white enterprises have looted, prostituted and commercialized black music as white industry has sought to control it financially. During the Harlem Renaissance, as writers and painters lost their drive before the paternalism and indifference of their white spon-sors, black music alone held its own: it kept its intimate relation with the black masses. In the years between the 1920s and the 1960s, re-marked Cruse, "in *quality* the Negro has retrogressed in every creative field except jazz."[134]

Yet in a society that functions according to a consumer ethic, as Baraka observes, as soon as a new jazz form reaches a certain stage of development, it is "duplicated by corporations, diluted commercially, bowdlerized for the sake of mass profit."[135] "Traditional jazz had its *Dixieland;* Big-band jazz its *Swing;* BeBop its *Cool;* RB its *Rock;* and Contemporary black music its *Fusion,* all of which . . . were corporate creations aimed at a white middle-class audience with mainly white performers."[136] Industrial culture moves inexorably to swallow every kind of original expression in its operational momentum. "The race exploiter," says Cruse, "has, by its own inner dynamic, swept everything before it by its power of rapid development and ability to absorb and institutionalize *even anti-capitalistic features*."[137] Nevertheless, black music has not only maintained its tradition but it has also continued to renew itself. It has again brought black intellectuals into immediate relation with their aesthetic heritage.

Since the Harlem Renaissance, black poets especially have tried to model their verse on black musical forms. Langston Hughes, for instance, was one of the first to adapt the techniques of jazz to poetry. He would, he hoped, be able to capture the quality of the black and of the human spirit. Black music had a strength like the "beat of the human heart," it had "humor, and [was] rooted power,"[138] he wrote. Since "poetry is rhythm—and, through rhythm, has its roots deep in the nature of the universe,"[139] he tried to construct his on a jazz beat. *Ask Your Mama,* for instance, was the verbal rendition of "twelve moods for jazz" including the blues, Dixieland and bebop; it was an ironic comment on the Negro condition.[140]

Larry Neal, Amiri Baraka and many other writers of the black aesthetic movement of the 1960s also tried to integrate literary and musical modes of artistic expression: they wanted to make words take the place of notes. "The soul of Black poetry is *sound,* not print or image," says Ihab Hassan.[141] Baraka even collaborated in the composition of poetic-musical drama. To create verse in the same style as music would be to utter a cultural statement: it was a political act, as the Beats realized in the 1950s when they imitated black forms. The categories of poetry, as Carolyn Rodgers put it, are "signifying, teachin / rappin, covers off, spaced, bein, love, shoutin, jazz, du-wah, and pyramid."[142] Nikki Giovanni is a stylist who deliberately seeks the rhythm of jazz, blues and African drumming.[143] Yet musical forms, even when they are sung, resist the restrictions of words. As James Emanuel, biographer of Langston Hughes, remarks, "Jazz poems can reveal jazz even less than blues poems can reveal the blues. . . ."[144]

CHAPTER 16

BLACK
AESTHETIC FORMS

In their poetic adaptation of black musical forms, black writers have been trying simultaneously both to inform and devise a literary context in which they can function free of the constraints of the institutionalized European discipline, and to clear a place for themselves through their identification with their peculiarly black tradition. Ishmael Reed, according to Henry Louis Gates, Jr., is concerned not just with "the process of willing-into-being a rhetorical structure, a literary language, replete with its own figures and tropes," but also with "the relation his own art bears to his black literary precursors."[1] In both cases Reed would be following the aesthetic methods of first ascent and then immersion—involving implicitly a rejection of conventional western norms. Reed's language, Gates goes on to explain, allows him "to posit a structure of feeling that simultaneously critiques both the metaphysical presuppositions inherent in Western ideas and forms of writing and the metaphorical system in which the 'black-ness' of the writer and his experience have been valorized as a 'natural' absence."[2] Methodologically, Reed's project parallels that of many white postmodernists; substantially, it is his invention of being black. In the first case, the narrative of ascent is often caught in itself—or in the inevitable constraints of a preempted language that not only misrepresents reality *per se,* but, historically, distorts any affirmation of the black cultural presence. In the second, that of immersion or descent resembles the attempt of the mulatto—the new American race—to discover his spiritual affinity with his black heritage as well as to signify on its relation to the world in which it was enclosed and against which it raised its voice. In this way, literature's preoccupation with black music—regardless of the formalistic difficulties of rendering sound and soul in words—serves a significant purpose in the development of a black aesthetic culture.

Many writers who adopted, even hesitantly, the way of immersion were inspired by their feeling for music, the original black art. DuBois's *Souls of Black Folk,* whose "soulfulness" Stepto contrasted, perhaps summarily, with the "soullessness"[3] of *Cane,* was in one sense a narrative of descent. DuBois was seeking to express the spiritual essence of a race. "There is no true American music but the wild sweet melodies of the Negro slave . . . ," he wrote.[4] "That plaintive rhythmic melody . . . still remains the most original and beautiful expression of human life and longing yet born of American soil."[5] Through his art, DuBois was describing the American black as the spokesman for the human condition. "The 'I' of the Sorrow Songs" is not just the "quintessential atemporal Afro-American 'we,' " as Stepto remarks; it is the "we" of all mankind.[6] It is the statement of a communalism embedded in a historical context that belies change and answers only to the absolute and eternal triangular cycle of life on earth—birth, existence and death.

But DuBois's alter ego, his scientific, white-trained self by which Stepto claims that he authenticates his voice and his plotless tale,[7] serves almost to parody his lyricism: it signifies on it, and is signified by it. It is DuBois, the white, who is "measuring his soul by the tape of [an outside] world";[8] it is the disciplined sociologist who referred to "bastards and . . . prostitutes"[9] in the Negro community and then—in a reversal of tone—counterposed his political and educational treatises on Negro uplift with race-proud and race-moving tales of mythical folk heroes—like John Jones and Josie—and of "life and love and strife and failure" in a small settlement.[10] Progress is ugly in comparison with these kinds of basic truths, DuBois commented, denying his scientific strain. Were stories like these, he asked, introducing a question that Ellison's invisible man would later pick up, "the twilight of nightfall or the flush of some faint-dawning day?"[11] Ellison's narrator would wonder in his struggle to see himself, "Will it be death or spring?"[12] The circle completes itself.

James Weldon Johnson's *The Autobiography of an Ex-Coloured Man* uses the methodology of ascent to point up its message—which is that of immersion. On the surface, *Autobiography* is the tale of a mulatto, son of a southern blueblood and worthy Negro woman, who passes willy-nilly into white society. Unlike conventional stories of the alienated and passive protagonists who are tools of circumstance—like Saul Bellow's Augie March or Kurt Vonnegut's Rudy in *Deadeye Dick*—Johnson's ex-colored man lives in a world of upside-down values. If sense is nonsense, then nonsense is sense: life has a point that Augie and Rudy can never discover. Johnson's viewpoint is not that of "a human being, but . . . of a *coloured* man."[13] Indeed, the entire narrative movement depends on his inversion of prevailing norms and standards: as he succeeds, he fails; as he becomes white he loses his soul and turns into another member of an amorphous middle class. The author is the signifier, commenting on the black situation.

The ex-colored man has no control over his life because—progressively—he rejects the heritage with which he is saddled: because he is as much a part of one race as of the other. He is forced by social norms to make his transition into the black world.[14] And through his musical talent he enters "really . . . into the race."[15] He is captivated not only by the "weirdly sweet . . . wonderfully strong"[16] melodies of blacks but also by the ragtime he discovered in New York clubs. Following the inclination of his dual personality he wants to transform the music into classical forms; through his playing ability, he attracts the attention of a rich patron and reaches the stage where he can pass. As much as he is morally appalled by the hypocrisies of so-called civilized whites, he is disgusted by the vulgarity and the abjection of lower-class blacks. He is rejected by both his mother's and his father's folk. As his color and his ethics keep him away from the latter—including his own sister—who permit, even promote, the burning of human beings, so his refinement separates him from low-class Negroes whose "shambling, slouching gait and loud talk and laughter" repel him.[17] He even associates ragtime and the cakewalk, which he admires, with Mammon's lair.[18]

Ideally, of course, he would renounce both his blackness and his whiteness. He would be the ahistoric new man of the new world—the type about whom Henry James had written and to whom Jean Toomer would mystically refer. Johnson's story reflects the spirit of the burgeoning industrial age. The American new man, from whom capitalism derived its impetus, was supposedly nature's nobleman—free of European social structures. He was the frontiersman hacking his way to a continental empire; he was the financier, the manufacturer, the speculator, who unified the country in economic networks of control. He was the latest and the best development of the evolutionary process, to whom all mankind would look. And the ex-colored man was "a perfect little aristocrat"[19] who with alacrity—as he passed—contracted "the money fever."[20] Implicit in Johnson's account, however, was the contradiction between what was and what appeared to be: this kind of successful new man was an artifice.

The hedonism for which Johnson's ex-colored man has been criticized is a characteristic of his white acculturation. It is inherent in the materialistic society which he joins, which loses itself to the pursuit of money and on which—finally—the mulatto signifies. He is lucid despite his success. He comments dispassionately on the treasures by which he is surrounded, including his later lovely white wife, his children, his comforts, even the code of honor that he has observed. Still he realizes that he has sacrificed his soul. He is "possessed by a strange longing for my mother's people" toward whom he feels like a "coward, a deserter."[21] He has missed his calling; he has sold "my birthright for a mess of pottage."[22] In effect, he affirms the fact that he had a birthright by negation.

During the Harlem Renaissance, Zora Neale Hurston, an enigmatic character herself, played the role of the signifying monkey. Hurston's double vision did not explicitly involve the dissonance between the call of black self-expression and the negative response of a white racist world—although, as a critic remarks, the title of *Their Eyes Were Watching God* might be taken as "an encoded critique of the color line . . . and especially of white power."[23] But she was able to make her way coldly in a competitive white-controlled intellectual field: she was in a sense an opportunist who had perhaps less use for the black than for the white bourgeoisie. In fact, she suffered from a contradiction between her inner and outer selves. Her writing represented the former, and she gave herself to it and disregarded political and social realities. She tried to "turn [her] back on the past" as if it were not included in the present. She would seek her happiness on her own. "But the way!" she admitted. "Its agony was . . . certain. . . ." Nevertheless, she "must go the way."[24]

If Hurston's life was a story of ascent—and fall—her writing involved her immersion in the spirit of the people, with whom she, child of an all-black community, intimately identified. It was a projection of her inner, nonintegrated self. Like her character Janie—who believes not simply that she is free to be as she is by nature, but that this attitude, this "dream," is "the truth" above reality—Hurston seemed to have taken it for granted that she, an intelligent and ambitious black woman, could indeed make her way. Janie gives up financial and social security to realize her dream. Because she glosses over the harsher facts of her life, especially with her man Tea Cake—facts that ironically bear witness to the truth of her deep feeling for him as well as of the inevitable transitoriness of love—she does fulfill her dream.[25]

Like her author, Janie is subject to constraints that she refused to accept. In rebelling, she learns—perhaps more than Hurston—that her inside and her outside could not mix.[26] Tea Cake does not have "doodly squat";[27] Tea Cake is too black; Tea Cake is a rouster and a gambler and a migrant field hand, often out of work; Tea Cake "slapped her around a bit to show that he was boss."[28] Tea Cake dies irrelevantly and uselessly, the victim of a dog bite during the flood, but Tea Cake is able to make happiness: he is "a glance from God."[29] After his death, Janie has forever her true life with him: she can bring her inner self in harmony with her outer. She finds her voice and learns to express herself and so to "utilize [herself] all over"[30] almost as a work of art, or, as Tea Cake had put it, as "something tuh make uh man forgit tuh git old and forgit tuh die."[31] Janie's life is truth: it is "a great tree in leaf with the things suffered, things enjoyed, things done and undone. Dawn and doom was in the branches."[32] And, in inventing her, Hurston's art also is truth. "In the mingling of their complementary voices [Janie's auto-biography, Hurston's metaphor] reading themselves into the canon, Hurston gains immortality in the literary tradition, whereas Janie inserts her voice into the Afro-American oral traditions."[33]

In creating Janie's narrative and using it to testify to the improbable joy of existence amid the pressures of an exacting world, Hurston created her own self and her own higher truth. According to Hurston's old man Mentu in *Moses, Man of the Mountain,* who personifies the signifying monkey, stories are "unexpected visitors" who stand "outside his door until they were asked to come in."[34] It does not matter if they are factual or not as long as they can make something really be. Moses, for example, who feels like "two beings,"[35] who is either an Egyptian ruler or a Hebrew slave, becomes one in himself by inventing a role as leader of the Jews. He deliberately "crossed over":[36] he passes from the higher caste to the lower because he follows his inner truth. As he makes himself up, he calls into being a new God whom no one—neither the Egyptians nor the Hebrews—had ever heard of before.[37]

Moses, of course, was the archetypal trickster—as he was known in Negro folklore. In Hurston's tale, he learns the secrets of nature, which he uses to authorize his role. He takes over the art of language. He borrows the magic of his tutor and then father-in-law, Jethro. And he finally signifies on his God by mysteriously naming him I AM WHAT I AM in order to establish his omnipotence.[38] Actually, it is the smoke of incense that is deified as His Presence: "It was not understood so it became divine," wrote Hurston.[39] Then Moses manipulates Pharaoh and by the force of speech rallies a reticent, grumbling, sullen Hebrew tribe. He gives them manna, which he passes as a miracle: "Manna was a word that didn't mean anything in particular anyhow, so they called the grains of bread by that name."[40] The Ten Commandments are also verbal artifacts: they are created out of "ten words of power."[41] Finally, in accordance with the realities of existence, Moses' end, once he has accomplished his mission, is anything but heroic. It is, on the contrary, banal. He simply comes down from the top of Mount Nebo and heads "back over the years."[42] But he, too, having construed his truth out of art, has really experienced it.

Langston Hughes, who in real life had to tolerate the erratic behavior of Hurston, was neither as flamboyant nor as individualistic as his erstwhile friend. (They had a falling out over a play on which they collaborated.) He, too, tried to make it in the white man's world: he was the attentive courtier of his rich patroness—his "godmother," Mrs. Charlotte Mason—whom he sincerely liked. He was the faithful friend of Carl Van Vechten and his second patron, Noel Sullivan; he was for a while an ardent fellow-traveler of the left—although, as Rampersad suggests, perhaps Hughes was merely stringing along in his difficult struggle to survive.[43] "Writing for a *living* . . . makes nothing but a literary sharecropper out of a man," he confessed.[44] Hughes was commercially oriented,[45] and in that sense in harmony with white standards. He was never able to make it financially, but if he acceded to the values of an inimical white order to get by, at heart he resented the compromises that were exacted of him as much as he basically deplored the arrogance of power of white people. "So far in this world . . . only my writing has been my own, to do when I wanted to do it . . ."[46] he complained at a time when, with anguish, he wrenched away from the despotic benevolence of his godmother.

Hughes used his writing ironically to comment on prevailing norms. Conciliatory in behavior, integrationist by public pronouncement, ever smiling, ever affable, ever pleasant, he often seethed with rage underneath. At bottom he did not like whites in general; he was a militant: "Good morning, Revolution," he wrote.[47] But he played a required role. The way to kill racists, he advised actress Vinette Carroll, was "with kindness."[48] He identified profoundly with downtrodden black folk, although perhaps by nature as well as by circumstance he was unable to attack their oppressors militantly. Still, he did keep to his principles. He broke with his godmother when she tried to control his art; he retreated from his stance of radical socialism to the point of repudiating the theme of an earlier poem, not simply because he could not earn enough to make a living, but because his affiliation "tended to estrange him from black masses."[49] He had never joined the Communist party, he said, because of its attitudes toward discipline and jazz.[50] And he left the luxurious protection of his friend Noel Sullivan to live in Harlem, which he loved.

Perhaps Hughes was simplistic in his analysis of the racial situation. Implicitly, he did accept the values and even the basic professions of the Anglo-Saxon world, not only in its materialistic ethic but in its factitious idealism. He believed in Negro uplift,[51] looked for Negro heroes and criticized the school of black protest not because it was enclosed in an impasse of negativism, but because it depicted blacks as race-crazy murderers, rapists and hustlers.[52] He also opposed aesthetic esoterica: to him, "art never transcends life."[53] Nevertheless, throughout his life, he signified on the ways of white folks. And he adopted the voice of the common American Negro as, said William Gardner Smith, "few have heard him speak."[54] If he could not be overly militant, he could at least express himself with irony, humor and an undercurrent of irremediable sadness. His character Jesse Semple, or Simple—like Hughes—was the personification of the signifier: he was, remarked Arna Bontemps, "the very hipped, race-conscious, fighting-back, city-bred greatgrandson of Uncle Remus."[55] As Hughes wrote in his poem "Motto," "I play it cool / And dig all jive / That's the reason / I stay alive."[56] The folk tradition with which he identified has, as George Kent says, "is-ness. Things are. It is not rational."[57]

The oppositionism of black versus white was, if not an end in itself, an inherent feature in the process by which writers were creating an autonomous culture. Chester Himes, for instance—obsessed by the race war to the point that, ideologically, he foresaw violence as its only issue[58] and, emotionally, considered pornographic sex the only basis of a relationship between blacks and whites—led a tormented existence. But his idea of the "absurd nigger"[59] allowed him to go beyond his almost pathological suspicion of whites—both abroad and in America. In fact, he began to signify on himself. In his detective stories and in his play, *Baby Sister,* he spoofed the whole gamut of the Harlem scene from the pimp—"narcissistic about his smooth black self"[60]—to the hustler-preacher, to the black siren, as well as the commercial literary market that published and paid him well. His hard-shooting, hard-loving, hard-playing con men—including his black detectives—were models for suspense movies and novels to come: they were takeoffs on popular and profitable art. And, almost despite himself, he projected a picture of Harlem that affirmed its special black character. He made it come alive, "labyrinthic, equivocal and wickedly comic,"[61] wrote a critic in praise of him.

It was in concentrating on black themes and in reviewing those of past black literature that writers developed, revised and perpetuated a culture that was intrinsically American and that was their own. Regardless of Ellison's statement that he recognized neither "any white culture" nor "any black culture the way many people use the expression,"[62] his roots were, as Larry Neal pointed out, "deep in the Black American folk tradition."[63] With respect to his form, as Ellison admitted, he drew it from black music and used it to define his "identity: as an individual, as a member of the collectivity, and as a link in the chain of tradition."[64] According to Ellison, "The perfection, the artistic dedication which helped me as a writer, was not so much in the classical emphasis as within jazz itself."[65] Neal said that his novel was "one long blues solo" whose structure was derived from Louis Armstrong's "music . . . forms."[66]

With respect to his characters, Ellison filled his book with tragicomic Negro folk types, from Trueblood, who signifies on the hypocrisy of white social norms, to Tarp, who, having been jailed for saying no, symbolically gives the links of his prison chain to the invisible man, the renunciant of imposed roles, the preserver of his culture. From Mother Gresham to Ras the nationalist to Rinehart the con man to Tod (Death) Clifton—whose attack on the white policeman is a reenactment of the murderous despair of a Bigger Thomas—all Ellison's people are overrun by constrictive decrees. If, as Ellison claims, American literature *"is built off our folklore to a large extent,"*[67] then it is black folk culture that informs his art and allows his protagonist eventually to establish by negation his independence through his group identity. Ellison is a humorist; his is a fiction of manners which represents the American scene much as the *commedia dell'arte* represented that of the southern European Renaissance.

With respect to his literary predecessors, Ellison's book constitutes on one level an ironic commentary on Richard Wright's *Native Son* and *Black Boy*. As such, it is an extension of the black cultural experience in its attempt to harmonize black and white culture in a pluralistic framework, and to relate art to politics within the context of the black's quest for freedom. In this sense, *Invisible Man* provided a corollary to protest fiction. Although consciously, the narrator does not take his grandfather's advice "to overcome 'em with yeses, undermine 'em with grins, agree 'em to death and destruction," he does in another way "let them swoller" him to the point that they might "vomit or bust wide open."[68]

To Ellison, freedom was the right and the power to express oneself. The old slave woman who appears to the narrator defines it as "nothing but knowing how to say what I got up in my head."[69] Liberation lay in language, the being of culture and of communal existence. Whites, having been indoctrinated in their rational canon, might—like Wittgenstein—recognize its barriers. But the invisible, nameless man was seeking a voice through which he could not only speak, but also be heard and identified. Nevertheless, his objective goal was not consonant with his subjective, almost pathetic, naïveté. He suffers from his goodwilled innocence; he chases illusions; he allows himself to be duped; he loses himself in his good intentions. So he cannot find his tongue. Because he would not take his grandfather's and his headmaster's advice, he digs his own hole—from which, however, this might be an exit. He is making freedom for himself. He is expressing his real self through his narrative. In finding himself, he turns himself into the trickster—"whose name is 'freedom,' whose name is 'human,' " writes Baker.[70] The invisible man was "Buckeye the Rabbit," the precursor of Brer; now he is the hibernating bear. As he adopts his many roles as masks and then discards them, he is progressively defining himself in the sense, as Ellison says, that "masking . . . is a play upon possibility." Through his struggle to rise to self-consciousness and become "the poet . . . the . . . Language-Maker"[71] who makes his name his own, the narrator falls to group consciousness and liberates himself within the limits of this possibility. As a critic explains, self-conscious literature "isolates the experiences of individuals; is addressed to individuals . . . and is experienced by this individual as an individual." Folk literature "isolates the experience of a socially defined group; is addressed to all of the group; and is experienced by a group . . . as a group."[72]

The leading trope in *Invisible Man,* which represents man generically and not just Ellison's protagonist, is that of the trickster. Trueblood and Rinehart, for instance, are both duplicitous and, in accord with the attitudes of the narrator's grandfather and headmaster, tell the white man what he wants to hear. But both are inhibited by the cultural restrictions that define their roles: they are not themselves. Trueblood plays automatically to a given stereotype from which he can never be free. And Rinehart, "the elusive rogue [who] becomes 'one' only with the metamorphic flow which he, like Ellison's Poet, sees as the essence of experience"[73]—as critic Kimberly Benston puts it—is caught narcissistically in his own self-image. He has no real self. The narrator alone has the possibility of liberating himself. When he comes to realize that his experiences "were me . . . defined me"[74] even as he repudiates their sway over him—he recognizes the fact that he is actually he. And like Walker's Celie, he knows that he is there—wherever he is. He has been led by his experiences to the point where he understands that he is free. The liberating grace of the trickster, as Benston observes, lies in his exposure of "the world's duplicity, its lack of correspondence to a simple referent, its ability to name two things at once which amounts to an inability to name any one thing conclusively."[75] In effect, the trickster plays the part of language itself.

It is through the metaphoric trope of trickster that Ellison not only brings his complex American panorama together, but also comments ironically on the black cultural tradition. He signifies on social realism, on traditional black race solutions, including Washington's work ethic and DuBois's concept of uplift through the talented tenth, and on white power structures. Perhaps in this sense Ellison claims that the work of art is "a social action in itself":[76] he thinks of art as a mission; it is inherently moral. He criticizes the lost generation for its "disengagement from public morality."[77] Michael Cooke says that signifying concerns two sets of relationships: the first "between two equals where the position of one party relative to the rest of the world has taken on distortions of definition or value"; the second "between two people where a long-standing and yet not intrinsically legitimate authority is given to the one over the other."[78] The invisible man's journey to potential liberation leads him through black cultural alleys against a relentlessly overbearing white order—all of which he satirizes.

Ellison's novel—which has carried on and developed the black tradition—is in turn open to further revisionism and cultural enlargement on the part of black writers who followed him. Toni Morrison, for instance, signifies on him and, therefore, enriches her black literary heritage. Trueblood, the incestuous sharecropper—ironically the progenitor of racial purity—transforms his shame and that of his wife and daughter into a commodity that he sells to sexually prurient whites for a little material comfort. Morrison's Breedlove in *The Bluest Eye*, in many ways a takeoff on Trueblood, infects a whole community by his rape of his daughter, Pecora. He "dropped his seeds in his own plot of black dirt."[79] By shocking the respectable black population—much as Trueblood had shocked the invisible man—Breedlove exposes it to its own perfidy. By its comportment, it indicates that it has adopted prevailing middle-class norms: the community will not have colored people behave like "niggers,"[80] so it repudiates the poor, black, unattractive and pregnant Pecora. "We cleaned ourselves on her," says her friend, Claudia. "We were so beautiful when we stood astride her ugliness. ... Her poverty kept us generous."[81] Pecora is the scapegoat of the bourgeois community, as the black Truebloods are the scapegoats of white society, as the Greek *polis* (city-state) seemed "able to sustain its identity only by allowing a certain admixture of the alien, the 'debased' or 'useless.' "[82] Claudia, who at first had rejected white standards, learns herself, albeit sadly, to adjust and to play the game. She, who had hated white baby dolls and then little white girls, goes from "pristine sadism to fabricated hatred to fraudulent love"[83] of white norms. In the process, inevitably, she defiles her own nature.

As the scapegoat, Pecora acts out the schizophrenia that characterizes the spirit of the community and that it covers up. She "stepped over into madness."[84] Obsessed with her desire for blue eyes—and therefore, symbolically, for purity, beauty, acceptance, whiteness—she defies God, as does Walker's Celie in another sense. Pecora seeks help through an old trickster-preacher,[85] who is interested in the material aspect of religion. She accepts his fake miracle and believes that she has been discolored—that she has become white. But, in fact, neither the father who profaned her nor the rogue-magician who deceived her is evil. If the first raped her, still his hatred for himself as much as for her is "mixed with tenderness."[86] If the second knows that she is desperate in seeking to appropriate the most trafficked, the most insidious and the most artificial of the dominant white world's attitudes, still he feels profound sympathy for her. Both the father and the con man are free in a white hegemony—by circumstance and by profession—and, as Morrison perhaps ambivalently signifies on Ellison's Trueblood, "the love of a free man is never safe."[87]

Morrison is concerned with the dualism within the black group, hemmed in as it had been by a world governed by white materialistic standards. She is seeking an integral black community, and she is not afraid to examine the forces that disseminate it. In Morrison's *Sula,* despite the fact that "all freedom and triumph was forbidden" to her Sula and Nel, since they are "neither white nor male,"[88] Sula—unlike her more respectable friend—takes it on herself to defy social convention. She has a daring and a sense of independence that are lacking in the spirit of the proper bourgeoisie by which she is surrounded. She lives "an experimental life"[89] to the extent that she is rumored to sleep even with white men[90]—as she does, with little compunction, with Nel's husband. The love of a free woman might be as unsafe as that of a free man. Sula is outlandish; she observes no rules; she transcends polarities of good/evil, virgin/whore, self/other, says a critic.[91] But she stands up for herself, whereas the correct folks, whom she shocks and who, like Nel's mother, appear to be tall and proud and elegant, might on the inside be "really custard."[92] It is they who surrender their birthright. But Sula, who is separated from them, "had no center, no speck around which to grow."[93] She is alone and rootless. As she comments of Nel, "She will walk down that road . . . thinking how much I have cost her and never remember the days when we were two throats and one eye and we had no price."[94]

In seeking the integrity of the black community, Morrison is the novelist of immersion. The black must journey back into Redding's jungle where he can find himself.[95] And Morrison does—both geographically and historically. Her strength lies in her ability to glimpse a beauty implicit in this jungle through the often sordid reality that enshrouds it. In *Song of Solomon,* Milkman, whose father has embraced the crass materialism of America, goes back in time and place to look for his heritage, which he thinks is buried family gold but which turns out to be the spiritual roots of his racial and his essential being. He discovers his integral community, which his weird old aunt, Pilate, incarnates. She, uprooted in modern industrial times, has been forced to reinvent herself in a distorted world. And she prevails.

She has to die in the process as Milkman will, in all probability in his act of finding her and his meaning. Ironically, he is traduced by the greed of his friend Guitar, the nationalist trickster, who believes that he is being traduced by Milkman. They are both after the gold. But in the end, Milkman is transported: his death will be his apotheosis. There is hope in Pilate's dying words: "I wish I'd a knowed more people. . . . If I'd a knowed more, I would a loved more," she says. It is she who inspires Milkman; she who can fly "without ever leaving the ground."[96] The class, the color cleft in the black group may be irreparable, but since it involves sacrificial redemption, it bears the promise of a healing future.

Morrison posits the cultural integrity of the agricultural South— which is fast disappearing—as the antidote to the corrupted consumer society that engulfs the urban black. Son, the adventurer of *Tar Baby*, comes from an all-black Florida town—much like the community of Zora Neale Hurston—which, despite its simplicity and deep, enduring loyalties, seems like a desert to the metropolitan sophisticate Jadine. Son is a purist: he believes that whites and blacks "should not eat together or live together or sleep together."[97] Jadine lives perfectly well— at least on the surface—with both whites and blacks and especially with the upper classes of any color. Son is the scamp, the trickster, the apparently absolutely free, unattached, uncompromised incarnation of the Brer Rabbit who breaks into the "fenced-in garden world of Farmer Brown, the self-appointed keeper of the bounty of the world,"[98] embodied in the person of the refined, rich and degenerate white man Valerian Street.

Jadine, Street's beautiful protégée, rootless and successful, is as naïve and as uncaring as her patron. Only once in her life has she been forced to face herself, and that was in a Paris supermarket when for no apparent reason she was affronted by a coal-black African in a brilliant yellow dress. Valerian, the benefactor of his entourage, which includes his neglected wife and his sullen Negro help—the aunt and uncle of Jadine—is guilty of willful innocence. "An innocent man is a sin before God. Inhuman and therefore unworthy."[99] Valerian—with whom Son might have discovered a lost home on a black island—has constructed his own interior castle apart from the everyday preoccupations of ordinary folk. He is like the characters of Thomas Pynchon who live in entropic rooms, withdrawn from the world.

Jadine plays the role of the tar baby by which the farmer would ensnare Brer Rabbit, the intruder, and tame him to his will. Actually, however, she is the catalyst through whom the trickster escapes to his own briar patch and, therefore, makes his choice of race and his sacrifice to his heritage. Jadine's uncle, the butler, knows "white folks play with Negroes,"[100] and Son realizes that "people don't mix races; they abandon them or pick them."[101] Jadine is the white man's trap who has opted for his materialistic ways. But Son is also the tar baby, who cannot adapt to the realities of the uncaring world.

Morrison seeks the meaning of the black experience through its geographical and historical sources. As critic Susan Willis says, "everything is historical" in her.[102] And in this respect she also finds that the prevailing white culture is responsible for the disjunction which characterizes the black psyche, both individually and collectively. "There's no bad luck in the world but white folks," says Baby Suggs,[103] the mother-in-law of Sethe in *Beloved.* Because they arrogantly assume that "under every dark skin was a jungle,"[104] they plant the jungle in the souls of black people. Indeed, blacks would go to any extreme to escape the pressure of whites. Sethe cuts the throat of her beloved baby daughter to keep her from the horror of slavery. The theme of child murder is common in black literature: Angelina Grimké's fictional black mother smothers her little boy;[105] Georgia Douglas Johnson's black woman refuses to bring children into the world of "cruelty and sin."[106] Robert Hayden wrote of an abandoned black woman who dresses up her children before she shoots them to spare them the suffering of their poverty. "They were so happy they forgot / They were hungry, daddyless. / Garland got away. Cleola, Willie Mae / Won't be hungry anymore, / Oh they'll never cry and hunger anymore," she moans.[107]

In Toni Morrison's *Beloved,* there is nothing that Sethe ever does in all her life that can attenuate the pain that her act causes her. "Sadness was at her center, the desolated center where the self that was no self made its home."[108] She fastens eventually on a substitute daughter who flies in with the wind—perhaps in the world of dreams and essences the resurrection of her own—but her obsession only exacerbates the disorder of her psyche. Sethe confines her universe to the room in which her beloved is enclosed. She is the victim of the fact that "anybody white could take your whole self for anything that came to mind. Not just work, kill, or maim you, but dirty you."[109] And yet, ambivalently, Morrison implies that it is this same overbearing pressure of the white presence that has in part brought about blacks' feeling of communal solidarity, which overrides the ordinary tensions of human relations. Perhaps because the last of the "Sweet Home" men, Paul D., had suffered as a fellow slave, he understands Sethe and loves her and for a time dehaunts her. He sticks, at least in spirit, with her: "She's fixed me and I can't break it," he says.[110] And to her death, Baby Suggs supports Sethe, as does her living daughter, Denver.

In *Jazz,* Morrison goes back to Harlem in the 1920s and rural black America before that time to point up her concept of black communality. It is the blacks who seem on the surface most to suffer the "evil [that] ran the streets":[111] it is they who undergo the broken relationships of rootlessness and ill chance, and yet it is they who somehow—through mutual pain—reach a kind of self-knowledge. Violet Trace killed the self in her who wanted to be what she was not and then "killed the me that killed her." Her real me is left.[112]

Writer David Bradley used the theme of immersion to discover the integrity that distinguishes the black group and to establish a counterpoint to the epistemology of rationalized historical research. *The Chaneysville Incident* is another voyage into the regional past. Professor of history John Washington, happily integrated in his profession and in his marriage, returns to his father's rural community. John finds little factual evidence of the blackness that he hoped had characterized his family. Yet his father, Moses, had played the role of the trickster by duping a lynch mob and had sought his grandfather C.K., an ex-slave, who really exists only in John's imagination, not in historical proof. It is John who must invent the lives of his fathers: he must reveal them and their blackness at an intensity beyond that of evidence.[113] By hypothesizing their backgrounds, John creates the reality of their lives as well as of blackness in general. Even then he cannot transmit the truth in any objective form for the world at large to comprehend, so he leaves it for others after him to figure out and for his white wife to accept on faith or love.[114]

The past, as John sees it, is not fixed: it involves discovery, if not re-creation. As a detective painstakingly proceeds from clue to clue, so John interpolates history, introducing intuition, natural conditions, even coincidence, to unravel the puzzle of his particular—seemingly irrelevant—heritage. But history is as fictive as fact. So John finds at the end the core of a drama, which includes his great-great-grandfather's militant resistance to slavery and the reality of group solidarity. The blacks—women, men and children—who escaped the South killed themselves not only to avoid recapture, because they preferred to be buried in their graves before they'd again be enslaved, but also because they knew that the blessing of nature was on them and that death—as the old slave Azacca advised, repeating the words of Legba—"was not an ending of things but a passing on of spirit." A spirit, like Morrison's Pilate, "could fly wherever he willed."[115] Of course, this message was distorted by whites, who pretended that it applied to them in heaven, but not to blacks. The spiritual gift was the blacks' in the solidarity of group belonging. And it was also John Washington's, who could have confidence through it that history, although it moves aimlessly, awkwardly and cold-bloodedly, "does move . . . always forward."[116] The black conserves his hope.

Writer Ernest Gaines's group in *A Gathering of Old Men* is moved to collective resistance because its members are militating against white autocracy and because they have been robbed of their spiritual heritage and integrity. They organize, they arm themselves, old and impotent as they are, in defense of Mather, "the only one we knowed had ever stood up,"[117] who is accused of killing a white. They do this for reasons that involve their inner sense of dignity. Mat says that such action gives "an old nigger like me one more chance to do something with his life."[118] Johnny Paul protests the fact that the white man's tractor "was go'n come in there [to the black cemetery] and plow up them graves, getting rid of all proof that we ever was,"[119] reducing the significance of being black to irrelevance. And Tucker goes along to atone for the fact that he gave in—through his fear of whites—to the beating of his brother. Finally, the real murderer comes forth and confesses, thereby asserting his manhood.

Alice Walker, who also defends the idea of black spiritual integrity, would free the black even from his dialectically negative relation to whites. Although her Grange Copeland has gone through the traditional steps to self-emancipation—from hatred of whites to violence against them—and he, like his son, has been reduced by whites to a life of stultifying bondage, he is finally able to affirm himself despite them. Through his positive love for his granddaughter and his ensuing sacrifice, Copeland realizes that his identity is his own, that it is by his individual will that he must determine his destiny. In effect, he kills himself for her. It is his inner self that the white world cannot touch. "When they got you thinking that they're to blame for *every*thing they have you thinking they's some kind of gods!" he reasons.[120] "We are not different from them; . . . We are the same. / And we do not worship them," writes Walker in one of her poems.[121] ". . . i must train myself / to want / not one bit more / than what i need to keep me alive," she tells herself while "talking to my grandmother who died poor" and while "recognizing beauty / in your / so nearly / undefeated face."[122]

It was from the concept of self-reliance that Walker arrived at her idea of black cultural integrity. From her first stance as a rebel against both white social oppression and male dominance—which could be related—she decided that self-affirmation involved group affirmation through the continuity of an inherently distinct black tradition, despite—or perhaps because of—the fact that it was perpetually under siege by that of the ruling whites. But Walker associated this tradition with spirit. "I am preoccupied with the spiritual survival, the survival *whole* of my people," she wrote.[123] For we "know that no matter what *they* do / all of us must live / or none."[124]

It was in the South, her birthplace, that Walker felt most the "sense of *community*."[125] She also found this solidarity together with race pride in the civil rights movement, in which she participated. It "gave us each other forever," she said.[126] Martin Luther King, Jr., "exposed the hidden beauty of black people in the South, and caused us to look again at the land our fathers and mothers knew."[127] Walker, by nature nonviolent, discovered in art the means of avoiding "the sin and *inconvenience*"[128] of the killing that went with revolution, although she was realistic enough to admit that "my art . . . would probably change nothing."[129] Nevertheless, through her writing she was able to follow and perpetuate the black cultural tradition.

She adopted Zora Neale Hurston in particular as her literary model because she admired her precursor's expression of "racial health; a sense of black people as complete, complex, *undiminished* human beings."[130] They were whole in themselves, regardless of the pressures of the white world by which they were surrounded. And through Hurston, Walker learned to affirm the maternal tradition against which she had earlier rebelled and which had been so necessary to the continuity of the black cultural heritage. In the first part of the twentieth century, the emancipated striver broke away from her background of subservience and endurance, lost her roots and was spiritually destroyed, but the modern female intellectual now seeks herself in the cultural entirety of the black experience. "Our mothers and grandmothers, some of them: moving to a music not yet written. And they waited,"[131] explained Walker. Therefore, she would explore "the history and psychological threads of the life some of my ancestors lived." It was in writing that "I felt the joy and strength and my own continuity,"[132] and the black cultural history was like a patchwork quilt that could be artistically assembled.

In effect, Walker learned—as Morrison's Ondine tells her niece, Jadine—"to be a daughter first . . . a woman that cares about where she come from and takes care of them that took care of her."[133] Walker turned to the black female tradition to synthesize the contradictions in the black communal experience. If her Meridian has been deceived by the intrigues of the black movement and harrowed by her incapacity to kill for it, her final recourse is her symbolic assumption of the role she has resisted: that of "Black Motherhood personified." Meridian has herself given one child away like "some kind of monster,"[134] as her own middle-class mother puts it, and she has aborted another. Now she is mother to her people.

Walker was influenced by the mythical black heroines who dominated her early fancies. The black women whom Meridian remembers from childhood stories are "always imitating Harriet Tubman—escaping to become something unheard of."[135] The magnificent Sojourner Tree, symbol of the maternal tradition, which was planted on her college campus and which authorities had threatened to cut down, had been nurtured by the slave fabulist Louvinie—whose tongue was dissected and yet whose stories perpetuated the tradition—and was reputed to shield the lovemaking (and, consequently, the unsanctioned conceptions) of young black students. The casket of Wile Chile, the pregnant ghetto urchin whom the chapel refused to reverence, was wreathed by its leaves: it was witness to the child murder of Fast Mary, and, at one point, shade to her body. Meridian had her own abortion in its protective vicinity.

The tree symbolized the mutual self-defense of the black community: it was a mother image. And it is in assuming her own personal responsibility to the black community that Meridian resolves the disjunctions that seemingly individually ripped her apart. She takes refuge in all kinds of traditional expressions of black solidarity, and finds a following among the illiterate and the impoverished. She is inspired by the "communal spirit, togetherness, righteous convergence"[136] of the black church and to her final resolve by the death of a young black man. She will be true to her own experience; she will stand by her people at any price. "The respect she owed her life was to continue, against whatever obstacles, to live it, and not to give up any particle of it without a fight to the death, preferably *not* her own. . . . Under a large tree . . . she made a promise . . . that . . . she *would* kill, before she allowed anyone to murder [her neighbor's] son again."[137]

In *The Color Purple*, Celie also finds herself and her voice in the community solidarity, which in her case consists of the fellowship of women—Shug, Squeak or Mary Agnes, and ultimately her sister, Nettie. Celie lives in an all-black environment, enclosed in its poverty by the white order that presses in on it, but nevertheless responsible to its own self-devised standards. In discovering the autonomy of her own voice, Celie carries on a tradition that has preceded her: she affirms the validity of the world. If, as Gates suggests, Shug is a figure for Hurston,[138] Walker's literary idol, then Walker's narrative is a commentary on Hurston's *Their Eyes Are Watching God*. Walker is signifying on Hurston not just in the sense that as Janie speaks herself into being, so does Celie write herself; but that as Janie discovers what Tea Cake calls "uh love game"[139] by availing herself of all God's natural gifts—involving, ultimately and ironically, Tea Cake's death—so Celie creates herself in her wholeness by addressing and then renouncing God. If Janie's Tea Cake "seems the idea bee-man"[140] as Michael Awkward says, if he is the essence of natural being, then Celie's I is the resurrected female offspring of the divinity.

In telling her tale, Janie projects her inner self outward and asks for an objective response—and thus a confirmation of herself—from her listener, Phoeby. By writing down her inner feelings, Celie objectifies herself and discovers that she is she. Janie, however, speaks within a context: it is Hurston, her author, who is the mediator between herself and her audience, representing the black community from which she wants acceptance. In this sense, Janie's narrative is one of "division," as Hurston called it.[141] Like those of ascent, it recounts a struggle to relate one's innermost being to a world of implied primal otherness. The call demands a response without which it would fall into meaninglessness. Janie has not been integrated into her society: she is a fabulist, a fabricator of illusion who invents in order to survive. She was always creating through the power of words. "Maybe [Stark] ain't nothin'. . . but he something in my mouth," she says. "He's got to be else Ah ain't got nothin tuh live for. Ah'll lie and say he is."[142] Again, she talks Tea Cake and their often stormy affair into the idyll it finally turns out to be in truth. Hurston herself was known, as Langston Hughes put it, as a "book of entertainment in herself."[143] She was a book seeking readership, in some respects like a Narcissa searching for her reflection in the God she watches.

Celie, somewhat similarly, creates her audience as she relates to her community, which has a spirit of solidarity against the outside "other" world of whites. The written word is her communal voice, and in this she differs from Janie. The God of the Bible that, as Toomer's old man says, "the white folks made . . . lie,"[144] is the big, graybearded white man whom Shug describes and whom Celie renounces. Shug's God, like Janie's, is associated with nature: with trees, air, birds and "being part of everything, not separate at all."[145] It is at this point that Celie begins to believe that a real God exists to please his creation: she notices the things he made to make her happy, like corn, the color purple and wildflowers, and she starts to write to Nettie. She does not chase imposed ideas: she finds her inherent freedom.

As *The Color Purple* signifies on the work of Hurston, so, in a sense, does Walker's *The Temple of My Familiar*. In this novel she uses intertextual techniques to inform the narrative. She goes back in time to recapture the methods of the black oral tradition and to relate the living past to the present through mnemonic undercurrents that resemble the subconscious truth of history. Walker takes up figures from black literature, including her own books, to integrate the apparently disparate elements of black culture. *The Temple of My Familiar* unites the African and South American traditions with those of the American South and of contemporary culture.

If, as Gates insists, "the very act of writing has been a 'political' act"[146] in the sense that it is an affirmation of the black's presence to negate what the West has treated as his absence, then black literature is implicitly a denunciation of western standards. As the African thinker Wole Soyinka puns, language signifies *l'engage*—a verbal distortion of the French langage.[147] Language is not, as it has been to many westerners, a constraint inaccessible to reason; it is an arm to the black by the very fact that it "disguises thought," as Wittgenstein noted.[148] Walker goes beyond linguistic boundaries to evoke an international black community that is both practically free of whites and spiritually opposed to them. In *The Temple of My Familiar*, Fanny, for instance, does not like them, does not understand them and does not want to. Miss Lissie, Mr. Hal and Mr. Rafe, to whom Suwelo returns to discover himself, live unto themselves away from the white slayer, segregator, rapist and lyncher.[149] In a more extreme sense, John Edgar Wideman, in *The Lyncher*, a fanciful account of a black plot to lynch a white policeman, calls for freedom in the form of "metaphysical revolt."[150]

Walker is not a black militant. She is acutely conscious of the role of the white and through him of the mulatto, who has been eminently present in the black cultural tradition since the beginning of the period of white imperialism. Blacks and whites together are writing "one immense story," she observes.[151] Blacks, she admits, "are black, yes, but we are 'white,' too, and we are red."[152] Walker's Fanny refuses to be a racist because she has too much pride to "do to [whites] what they've done to black people."[153] Besides, she is afraid she might kill. Decent, even heroic white women are scattered, although sparsely, throughout Walker's narrative. The role of the artist, as personified by Arveyda, is that of Hermes, the communicating trickster-seducer-thief. He is the messenger on whom "fell the responsibility for uniting the world."[154]

Mainly *The Temple of My Familiar* is an attempt to harmonize certain black cultural themes. It is a literary quilt constructed from swatches of black colonized existence all over the world. It is, therefore, dialectical in Gates's sense of the world: in negating the negation of the white idea of blackness, Walker makes signifying a direct political act.

Zede—the South American mother of her namesake Zede, the accused
Communist; the grandmother of Carlotta, the intellectual—is a seam-
stress, a sewing magician. Her daughter Zede and Carlotta escape to
California with the aid of the white woman Mary Jane, who later saves
the African Dahvid by marrying him. Carlotta becomes the wife of
Arveyda, who falls in love with Zede as well as Carlotta. He is the
artist, the phallic genius, who brings people together in spirit by teaching them how to love. Blacks must affirm the fact that they are at "the
banquet of life."[155] Fanny, granddaughter of Walker's Celie, daughter
of Dahvid, the African liberation leader, leaves her man, Suwelo, because he is like the males of the generation of the 1960s who "had
failed women—and themselves."[156] Finally, Suwelo redeems himself in
a community of spirit which excludes jealousy, rationalism, possessive-
ness and materialism, and which is peopled by Miss Lissie and Mr. Hal,
the lover and friend of Suwelo's dead uncle Rafe.

It is the spiritual quality of the black psyche that Walker wants to
explore. Her swatches of black existence are drawn from a submerged
but enduring past as well as from a flowing, sensate present. Miss Lissie,
who remembers being sold into slavery, thinks of "the memory, like the
mind [as] the capacity to dream." She explains, "Just as the memory
exists at a deeper level of consciousness than thinking, so the dream
world of the memory is at a deeper level still."[157] Reason, in other
words, distorts truth. Hurston also claimed that—unlike the white—
the "Negro thinks in hieroglyphics"[158]—in action words, not in written
forms. And Wittgenstein opined that "in order to understand the essential nature of a proposition, we should consider hieroglyphic script,
which depicts the facts that it describes."[159] Therefore, Miss Mary, who
lives with Gaines's Miss Jane Pittman, criticizes the young black historian for trying to organize chronologically Miss Jane's narrative.
"Well, you don't tie up all the loose ends all the time," she says.[160] In
The Temple of My Familiar, Walker's Olivia who was raised in Africa
relates how

> the Olinka use humming instead of words and . . . that accounts
> for the musicality of their speech. The hum has meaning, but it
> expresses something that is fundamentally inexpressible in words.
> Then the listener gets to interpret the hum out of his own experi-
> ence, and to know that there is a communality of understanding
> possible but that true comprehension will always be a matter of
> degree.[161]

Certain black writers have bypassed the political implications of the black experience and tried to picture the integral black community—relatively free of white influences. William Kelley, for instance, suggested this theme in his book *A Different Drummer,* in which the farmer Tucker Caliban—the great-great-great-grandson of the African slave who liberated his people and was ambushed and killed—salts his land, shoots his cattle, chops up his clock, burns his house and leads away all the Negroes from the southern town of Sutton. He is liberating himself completely from white norms: he is the kind of man who—to spite liberal programs—proclaims, "Ain't nobody working for my rights; I wouldn't let them."[162] He fights "all my battles myself." His wife, Bethra, an educated Negro, explains that maybe those who have gone to school, inevitably on white terms, "lost a faith in ourselves." Tucker is responsible to himself and his principles: he "just knows what he has to do."[163] Of course, the whites are appalled at the exodus—with the exceptions of the Willsons, the family which at first had enslaved the Calibans and then employed them. David Willson, a gentleman who renounced his youthful ideals, feels that Tucker, in emancipating himself, "has freed me too."[164] Dewey, Willson's son and Tucker's boyhood companion and betrayer, wants to find his old friend. But ordinary white folk, who blame Tucker's African blood for his apostasy, as usual go on the rampage and attack and lynch the visiting northern black minister, an old associate of David Willson in his days as a leftist crusader.

Necessarily, Tucker's movement has the quality of a dream. There is no place to which his blacks can really go. Like Octavia Butler, who constructs new life forms out of all kinds of species, including humans, and a combination of sexes—including neuter *its*—in her book *Imago,* Kelley goes beyond political circumstances. In *The Women of Brewster Place,* Gloria Naylor situates her all-black community more credibly within the context of an environment in which they are irremediably placed. She describes the trials and satisfactions of the people who reside in a housing project on the edge of the ghetto. She pictures the various, often conflicting, preoccupations of individuals who are pulled irresistibly together by a feeling of black solidarity, while at the same time their self-interest tears them apart both personally and collectively. As Michael Awkward summarizes the book, it "has to do with how . . . to depict the disunity of Afro-Americans while . . . acknowledging and . . . representing Black cultural impulses that insist on unity."[165]

What Naylor is describing is the lives of—as the bourgeois Mrs.

Browne tells her militant Kiswana—"proud people who . . . lived asking only one thing of this world—to be allowed to be." Mrs. Browne
realizes "that black isn't beautiful and it isn't ugly—black is!"[166] And
this fact—which is, in effect, the basis of true black liberty—is the thesis
of Gloria Naylor's writing: she discovers—or creates—the black specificity that lies at the core of the black cultural experience. It does not
matter how the black character came into existence; it just simply is
and will be. Of course, the feeling of black solidarity stems in part from
the pressures of the white order: Brewster Place is isolated in a slum
neighborhood because of an inimical white society. But its communality
cannot be explained away because it derives from environmental disadvantages. Its unity is founded on inflicted but "common *disunity* . . .
a shared failure to achieve wholeness,"[167] which is peculiar to it.

In its own characteristic way the congregation of the neighborhood's Canaan Baptist Church stamps and shouts, by which people are
released and opened to new experience and new togetherness—as was
Etta Mae. The white influences that malevolently enter into the formation of an antiwhite or nonwhite or eventually all-black spirit are
subsumed in the process of living and in the consequent feeling of black
solidarity that has nothing to do with whites. The thrust of Naylor's
narrative lies in the fact that the separated women of Brewster Place,
each involved in her own problems, do come together in a block party
in which they all attempt to tear down the walls of their ghetto and
expose themselves as a whole to the world at large.

In *Linden Hills,* the story of a black suburb, Naylor describes the
class distinctions that separate the black community. The materialist
Luther Nedeed is rich and influential because he has successfully speculated on his conviction that the future of America "was going to be
white": that blacks were going to give in to white standards. He believes
in the omnipotence of the industrial ethic to which blacks, like whites,
are subject, and which is based on "white money backing wars for white
power."[168] Unfortunately, however, he finds his own bid for black
power frustrated in the universal prevalence of the American dream,
"the *will* to possess."[169]

Linden Hills gave up its character of blackness. "People have . . .
lost all touch with what it is to be *them*,"[170] says young Lester. They
live in a faceless, disjointed community. And Luther Nedeed is traduced
by his white child, whom he rejects, and by his nameless wife, whom
he imprisons in the cellar of his house. In a sense, Naylor is ironically
signifying on Ralph Ellison's *Invisible Man*. But her woman rises like

an avenging fury of the past: she claims her roots in her dead son and in her rediscovered name, and comes to Luther in an act of retribution that ends in the destruction by fire of all he has and is.

In *Mama Day,* Naylor situates her black community in a mythical autonomous southern island that belongs to no state, although it lies within the territorial borders of the United States. The black character of the island might have stemmed from the fact that the people on it were "brought here as slaves [and] had no choice but to look at everything upside-down."[171] But this character exists and has created a tradition in itself, which has nothing to do with whites—or even with a slave mentality—but which seems to reestablish the right-side-up nature of things.

The leading Day family is mulatto by heritage. Bascombe Wade, a Norwegian immigrant, loved the slave woman Sapphira to such an extent that he freed her, his issue and all the other island blacks. He deeded them his land and pined away in lovesickness at her disappearance—probably back to her home. It was she, pure African conjure woman, "the great, great, grand, Mother . . . goddess," "the Mother who began the Days,"[172] who taught her children the art of divining nature's secrets, an art that has come down through generations. So it is not its white blood that the family prizes. Cocoa, for instance, the great-great-great-granddaughter, who is culturally assimilated in the larger society, is—says her husband, George—"as black as they come"[173] in spirit, if not in skin tone. She is proud of having descended "from that slave woman who talked a man out of a whole island":[174] indeed, Cocoa hates to admit the fact that she is carrying a little bit of Bascombe Wade.

The confrontation in the narrative is based on the theme of technological man—represented by George—against natural woman, and of man in general against the forces of nature. George, the bastard orphan who has nothing but himself and who has used this gift to make good in the rationalistic white world, comes up against Mama Day, Cocoa's great-aunt, who is rooted in the mysterious processes of nature—its cycles, its past, its human and her ancestral blood ties. To George, the island "smelled like forever."[175] He is not prepared, however, to accept the existence of the unknown powers that lie beneath the surface of the apparently clear façade of the Days. He has never had a family heritage—a feeling of the bond of blood and nature. It is only his capacity for love that transforms him from a normal, conventional, successful American into a spirit with an eternal home; it is his common mortality that redeems him even as he loses his life. He, the scientific engineer who refuses to believe in either the unconquerable fury of nature's hurricane or in what he calls Mama Day's "mumbo-jumbo,"[176] nevertheless breaks "his heart 'cause he couldn't let [Cocoa] go."[177]

Actually, George learns another language. Just as Walker's humming is black speech in its original a-rational context, so Mama Day's collaboration with and preventive measures against the vicissitudes of nature—in effect, her mumbo-jumbo—are a form of primeval affinity with it. She, who redefines time and right and wrong[178] by acceding to natural cycles as if they were part of her being, is able to protect and to perpetuate the values of her community. Mama Day's message is inexpressible and incomprehensible; but by its effect on George, it manifests the validity of a particular cultural approach. As Hurston wrote:

> The Negro is a very original being. While he lives and moves in the midst of a white civilization, everything that he touches is reinterpreted for his own use. He has modified the language, mode of food preparation, practice of medicine, and . . . the religion of his new country. . . . [179]

Indeed with respect to religion, Naylor's later work *Bailey's Cafe* is a practical allegory set in a place on "the edge of the world."[180] The book ends with the birth of a new mulatto Christ in the home of homeless people. Modern black writers have modified existing linguistic structures to suit black needs. In assuming the role of a black militant essayist, James Baldwin, for instance, was impressive for his stylistic innovation. It was not what he said; his politics were implicit in his act of writing. It was rather the way he said what he did. His emotive capacity made the black cause for which he was pleading an affirmation of black cultural integrity. He was obviously influenced by the techniques of black preaching: he applied oratorical forms—including those of call-and-response—to his prose. Writer Jamaica Kincaid has complained that she has had to speak of the crime of her oppressors in "the language of the criminal who committed the crime."[181] But to do so adroitly is to turn the very arms of her enemy against himself. As Toni Morrison addressed the late Baldwin, "You went into that forbidden territory [of American English] and decolonized it, robbed it of the jewel of its naïveté and un-gated it for black people so that in your wake we could enter it, occupy it, restructure it in order to accommodate our complicated passion . . . all the while refusing 'to be defined by a language that has never been able to recognize [us].' "[182]

Blacks—particularly poets—often tend nowadays to prosaism in order to render their experience emotionally. This is sometimes so intense that the artist can sustain its dramatic effect only by making it banal. As Ntozake Shange put it, "i couldn't stand bein sorry + colored at the same time / its so redundant in the modern world."[183] But it is by reducing the written word to the level of ordinary speech that the black not merely carries on the oral tradition, including the technique of call-and-response, but also assumes a political stance in rejecting the diction of whites.

Implicit in the distortion of white linguistic structures is the black's rejection of white norms. When Maya Angelou comments on her disadvantaged position as a struggling unmarried mother, she takes comfort in the fact that "the sad light" in which she is seen "had been shared and was to be shared by black girls in every state in the country."[184] She feels a special sense of black solidarity: "I was young . . . unmarried . . . but I was a mother, and that placed me nearer the people."[185] Whites were different. "Black was Black and White was White and although the two might share sex, they must never exchange love."[186] There was no material achievement that could close the gap. Whites were by nature an incompatible species: they were less interesting, less "respectful . . . merciful . . . spiritual."[187] Although Angelou refuses to be militantly antiwhite, although she takes pride in her capacity to survive—and even at times succeed—in an alien world, although she has recited a poem for the inauguration of President Clinton, she preferred to ignore whites who controlled her destiny and that of her son. It was, in fact, her love for him that brought coherence to her picaresque career.

Love is evidently the dominant theme of most modern black writers. And, unlike that of whites, black love is deliberately and paradoxically de-Platonized and often desexualized. What has been called the "built-in suspicion"[188] between the black sexes has often resulted in the dissociation of love and sex. Sex is a satisfaction that is healthy and fulfilling, but inclined to be perfunctory and transitory; love is an emotion that binds individuals of any age and gender and situation in a collective whole.

CHAPTER 17

BLACK POSTMODERN FORMS

Perhaps the most radical of the manipulators not just of the American English language but of its literary tradition is Ishmael Reed. In transforming existing white structures into black tropes and in creating a black cultural perspective from the inside of an all-white framework, he has redefined the significance of white culture itself. He is playing the part of the mulatto trickster. In many ways, he is like the white postmodernists who exploit the intrinsic reality of language as a means of communication—and thus call into question the reality it is supposed to depict. But where whites confine the act of writing to the limits of their canon and often assume the role of a solipsistic god, the creating genius, Reed's approach is pluralistic. White intertextuality depends on texts which have been sanctified by western civilizational accumulation and which they rebut, or parody, or try to improve or even misread, in the spirit of critic Harold Bloom. Blacks must make themselves up. Reed is writing for the enlargement of literature in all kinds of cultural contexts. Because he is a moralist, he has a transcendent frame of reference that prevents his art from turning into the intricate reworking of themes as a good in itself. Since the concept of intertextuality—"the profaned or 'fallen' history of [existing] relations"[1]—is founded on the principle of relativity both in fiction and in fact, and since fact and fiction are both transmitted only by language—necessarily the misrepresentation of the thing and the idea—fact is fiction as much as fiction is fact. History is a vast narrative and truth exists merely in the process of using words for any purpose whatsoever. Consequently, when an author summons all kinds of texts to parody, signify or lean on them, he is implicitly calling for authentication. He is working for some kind of end. He is admitting his need for, and by negation the reality of, some point of reference outside himself. If intertextuality is defined as "the profaned or 'fallen' history of [existing] relations" as depicted in a text, then it points antithetically to historical relations that were assumed in the past to be genuine and unprofaned—although they cannot be definitely expressed. Intertextuality makes a comment on a significance that is presumably no longer—in many ways the intertextual narrative is like a detective story that goes from clue to clue to some absent kind of resolution. Again if language—both voice and "the concept of voice,"[2] as philologist Mikhail Bakhtin had it—is a structure requiring dialogue, if in other words it is a call demanding response, and if "parody is the exemplary case of Bakhtinian dialogue,"[3] then intertextuality involves the parodic utilization of history. History—meaningful or not, true or false or both—is there like the past, and its thereness—however impenetrable—is the only possible basis on which a voice can initiate a dialogue with some reality outside itself.

Nevertheless, to parody the fictive records of an impenetrable thereness—comprehending integral relations that no longer exist—is to reduce the reality of these relations to the self. The parodist, having assumed that relations once were, sets about to create their past being. Parody, says a critic, can be regressive or progressive, in the sense that it looks either backward to a significant lost authority or forward to some unrealized moral ideology.[4] In both cases parody posits an evaluative criterion that is independent of textual commentary, and so leads the writer to associate not just value, but the very act of artistic creation with his own process of writing.

Barthes, in defining intertextuality as "the impossibility of living outside the infinite text,"[5] made, as critic Linda Hutcheon points out, "intertextuality the very condition of textuality."[6] In this sense Barthes encloses the writer in an assumed quantum. The use of texts amounts to an exercise in the fabrication of what has been called chimeras. The artist builds himself a labyrinth, infinite in operation, finite in idea, in which he imprisons himself. The reason for writing is lost in its operation: the "need for the author's parodic intention to become obvious in the text . . . seems to defy the concept of intertextuality."[7]

It might be because many white postmodernists have lacked an evaluative criterion—both moral and aesthetic—that they have fabricated a refuge for themselves in an art that answers to nothing more than their need or their lack. Their writing is its own justification as an exercise of itself. Writers and their characters seem to abandon the very field on which they perform. Postmodernist William Gass's *Omensetter,* the inexpressible nature of truth, leaves the town in which he is not and cannot be received. After the capitulation of his generation, Thomas Pynchon's Zoyd cops out, as do most of the personae of *Vineland*. Prairie, the hope of the future, finds her home only through the affection of her dog, which, like Gertrude Stein's dog, at least knows who she is—or that she is she. John Barth's Fenn and Susan, Peter and Katherine, and Frank and Lee turn away from the political murders and insoluble messes of their times, exile themselves on their boats and amuse themselves by making love, stories and babies, and by investigating thrown-out manuscripts and resurrected literary exemplars. In the meantime, Clarence Major's black Mason, in his book *My Amputations*, which signifies on *Invisible Man*, goes on a quest to make himself a writer after his manuscript is stolen. In so doing, he becomes an impostor, a signifying monkey. Yet he recognizes that "the world history" might be changed. "People made it all up: it could be remade. But," he adds realistically, "how, when and where."[8]

Dialogue, relations, history itself depended upon the summoning, repositioning, rephrasing and reworking of texts that are tangibly there. These, which to be sure might exist in a seemingly endless quantity, are in fact limited to the finite reach of the individual explorer: they are infinite only in potential. In signifying on them, in parodying them, the writer just adds himself and his particular cultural breadth to them—whether they are real or fictive or misrepresentative. In this sense, the apparent political and moral indifference of the white postmodernists is based implicitly on self-doubt, timidity or lack of value. With the exception perhaps of Pynchon, who suggests cultural alternatives, white postmodernists are, despite themselves, apologists for a civilization that they assume to be absolute and which, therefore, in deceiving disempowers them. They are logocentrists bereft of a center. According to critic John Matthews, Barth "domesticates the women's liberation movement," which he considered the significant revolution of the 1960s, "by absorbing its subversiveness into metaphor, psychology, theme and metanarrative."[9] Likewise, he glosses over the more insidious activities of America's cold-war agents. Margaret Mead softened James Baldwin's revolutionary thrust by universalizing racism. She placed it within the context of minority oppression, a common phenomenon in the presumably universal history of the West. Baldwin replied, "I know it's universal, Margaret, but the fact it is universal doesn't mean that I'll accept it."[10] Ishmael Reed's Quicksill tells the ambitious integrationist, the Indian princess Quaw Quaw, "Drat your universality."[11]

Reed is a so-called postmodernist who is expressly political. His parody or his signifying amounts to a denunciation of the values—or lack of values—of the civilization whose linguistic tools he employs. Therefore, he has a reference outside himself on which he can base his art. His satire is relevant to his times—even or perhaps because of its slapstick comedy and jargonized punning. In many cases his writing could be considered exaggerated, tasteless, misdirected; but Reed is an artist who is not afraid, either aesthetically or politically, to confront the society in which he functions without having to resort to propaganda or to aestheticism.

In *The Free-Lance Pallbearers,* for instance, Reed is making a judgment on the corrupted values not just of America's ruling powers, but also of its black population. *Free-Lance* relates the American success ethic to power, to the anal complex, to materialism, to death. HARRY SAM, the so-called "master of HIMSELF"[12] who learned from his mother "always be at the top of the heap,"[13] is, in effect, the pint-sized top dog, the "great dictator, former Polish used-car salesman and barn burner"[14] who has lived in the water closet for thirty years. However, he rules the social order with an iron hand, inspiring strivers such as Bukka Make-um Shit Doopey Dunk, the upwardly mobile black who inhabits the HARRY SAM housing projects, to make good. Reed is signifying on Charlie Chaplin, perhaps on Thomas Pynchon, and through Bukka on Booker T. Washington and Ralph Ellison. When Philip Roth composed his one-dimensional satire on Tricky Dick Nixon, who was as hairy as Sam, he was following Reed's technique.

Bukka suffers a series of picaresque misadventures in which he is put upon as much as was Ellison's invisible man. His ambitions come to nothing through the agency of Entropy Productions, which is headed by a character named Cypher X—or Zero, "the white BECOMINGS king."[15] As a robot throws baseballs in his face while a tape praises blacks and threatens whites, the audience applauds "its own doom."[16] The truth, as Bukka at last understands, is that the world is a chaotic free-for-all, a production of nothingness or of waste. As SAM, finally exposed, explains the principle of success, "If you don't stop others where they are, before ya know it, they'll be surrounding NOTHIN' which is ME like a bunch of Free-Lance Pallbearers."[17]

Mumbo Jumbo is perhaps Reed's best-known work. It is the story of the mysterious appearance of Jes Grew, hungering for a text, in the American society of the Atonists, the entropists, the purveyors of words without the accent or character. Jes Grew, which just is,[18] is present in black songs, which "belonged to nobody,"[19] as James Weldon Johnson put it, and therefore to all. It is a part of black music, and indeed of black itself: *"Jes Grew absorbs Black as Black does Jes Grew."*[20] It is historical: it was in the nature religion of Osiris, the Egyptian dancer and lover and signifier, who was done in by Set because he had no text. As the Atonists know, Jes Grew "needs its words and steps, or else it becomes merely a flair-up."[21]

The plot of *Mumbo Jumbo* involves the Atonist antinatural effort to stifle Jes Grew by depriving him of a text. Papa LaBas, the detective-conjuror, struggles to keep the powerful enemy from procuring the words of the book. It has been in the hands of Abdul, the nationalist and the practitioner of a "chimerical art."[22] Papa LaBas's quest is fruitless: Abdul burns the book without really knowing what is in it and "Jes Grew sensed the ashes of its writings, its litany and just withered up and died."[23] Nevertheless, the issues have been clarified. If, as Derrida says, original illegibility—which might be the Being of the world—is "the possibility of the book,"[24] then Jes Grew will continue to seek its words as it already found its notes. Jes Grew is everywhere in black music. As Herman explains, blacks were "dumped here on our own without the Book to tell us who the loas are. . . . We made up our own. . . . The Blues, Ragtime, the Work that we do is just as good."[25] So even if the book, the text, the canon, has yet to be written; even if, when it is composed, it will fall inevitably into the opposition that is inherent within it "of 'rationalism' and 'irrationalism,' "[26] which has marked the logocentrism of western thought, it will be able to discover its own potential. Jes Grew has already proved that it deserves its writing. It has, in fact, been everywhere: the blues, for instance, inspired even Jean-Paul Sartre's intellectual Roquentin in *Nausea* to a soulful realization that would justify himself to himself.[27] Jes Grew is indestructible spirit to be taken up by whoever and whatever recognizes it. It has its roots in art of all kinds and its source in history, the impenetrable presence of being there. It is "life"; it "will come back and when it returns we will see that it never left," remarks Papa LaBas.[28]

In *Yellow Back Radio Broke-Down*, Reed takes off on the materialistic ethic of American culture. Through the figure of Loop Garoo, a black kid cowboy who represents not just the western frontiersman but also the folk incarnation of a Haitian rebel initiated in the art of voodoo, the town of Yellow Back Radio has been liberated by children. They have revolted because their reigning elders "made us learn facts by rote. Lies really bent upon making us behave."[29] Immediately, Drag

Gibson, powermonger and speculator, defends the exiled adults in order to take over the town for his own interests—in implicit collaboration with the government and the Roman Catholic Church. By attacking this venerable, symbolic and allegedly Atonistic institution, Reed is upholding African civilization with its mysteries, its nature worship, its emotiveness. In the suppressed African American culture, he says, the objective correlatives "are invisible and abstract."[30]

Loop, the hero, is forced to serve the cause of moral right against the corrupted orthodoxy of law and order. Moreover, he is not just signifying on American myths (the materialistically motivated concept of the West, for instance) but he is also reinterpreting literary as well as religious and cultural conventions. He is, he confesses, "the cosmic jester"[31] who introduces untraditional forms into society. Where Bo Schmo, the neorealist,[32] argues that "all art should be for the end of liberating the masses," Loop resists such monoaestheticism. To him the novel does not have to follow a formula: "It can be anything it wants to be, a vaudeville show, the six o'clock news, the mumblings of wild men saddled by demons."[33] As Skinny, one of Drag's men, points out, "We cowpokes make up a language as we go along."[34] The principle of African art is based more on improvisation than on form.

In effect, voodoo—or insight into nature—is art. Loop himself fictionalizes spiritual arms to combat his materialistic, power-hungry adversaries. He uses charms; he enlists the aid of animals like pythons and pigs to suffocate and chew up his enemies; he practices "Hoodoo, an American version of the Ju-Ju religion that originated in Africa."[35] And he does all this ironically: he parodies the passion of Christ in his confrontation with the devil-making pope who is out to steal his magic lucky piece, his mad dog necklace. It is not Loop, however, with his supernatural forces who wins over Drag. With the conquest of the frontier comes industrial civilization with government agents and Chicken Delight and urban crowds. Drag, though arrested and disempowered, is like the old inner-directed capitalist absorbed in the ubiquity of consumerism. Loop climbs down from his cross and follows the pope.

Most of Reed's novels include a con man, a prototype of the signifying monkey. Pompey, the ventriloquist in Reed's historical fiction *Flight to Canada*, is the precursor of Black Peter, the impostor in his contemporary and political narratives *The Terrible Twos* and *The Terrible Threes*. But if, as has been suggested, history is "a kind of parodic ventriloquism that speaks through . . . the intrinsic intertextuality of the subject,"[36] then it does represent a thereness that like art signifies on

something. No matter whether it is factual or fictional, history compre-
hends a certain cultural environment that its narrator cannot help but
reflect. "The historical career of legends" may be "unimportant," as
Black Peter observes, but the legend itself is the witness to its particular
time.[37]

Reed combines fact and fiction to mock America's historical legends of slavery, of abolitionism and of emancipation. "Who is to say
what is fact and what is fiction?" he asks.[38] "Where does fact begin
and fiction leave off?"[39] The Uncle Tom legend, for instance, has been
represented and misrepresented by Harriet Beecher Stowe, who stole
the idea, the etheric double, from an ex-slave; by William Wells
Brown, the escaped so-called slave satirist; and by Reed's own Uncle
Robin, domestic of the feudal slave ruler Arthur Swills. Stowe profited literarily and financially from the characterization; Brown gained
recognition through the narrative of his escape; and Reed's Uncle
Robin is a trickster who turns on his master and takes over his empire. As Reed comments with respect to *Uncle Tom's Cabin,* originally the black was "the Man Who Was a Thing"; then, as in the
works of Mary Ovington, he was "Half a Man"; and finally in writer
J. A. Williams, he became "the Man Who Cried I Am."[40] The black
went from being a slave to being a cultural integrationist to being a
self-created individual. If, as Benston puts it—after Ellison's *Invisible
Man*—"I yam what I am [is] the topos of un[naming] in Afro-
American literature,"[41] it is also the signification of Hurston's Yah-
weh—the natural God of miracles and powers who appeared to
Moses. It is in this guise that the black, the trickster, wins. Robin, for
instance, remarks—after he is enriched by the wealth of his late
duped master—who is the fool, Uncle Tom, me or Nat Turner?
"Who pushed Swill into the fire? Some Etheric Double, the inexorable
forces of history? A ghost? Thought? Or all of these? . . . Who?"[42]

Raven Quickskill is the artist of the book—another con man in his
own right. The raven is the figurehead of an Eskimo organization that
predated the coming of Columbus: it is the symbol of a culture that has
lost its sense of beauty and hope with the deterioration of its liberty.
The raven is also the spirit that haunts the mad poet of Edgar Allan
Poe. Raven Quickskill, who has escaped slavery, comes back to the
scene of his bondage to record the narrative of Robin who also symbolizes the first sign of spring, and thus in a way to signify on the future.
"Time past is time present," as Reed says,[43] so writing is the unconscious determination of what is to come. Raven's writing, like that of

William Wells Brown, is his "freedom": it is his magic, his "Hoodoo."[44] His poems "were 'reading' for him from his inner self, which knew more about his future than he did."[45] In effect, if the artist is conditioned by history, if he reflects it in his work like the ventriloquist's dummy, so he determines it in his turn. The artist is the agent, the messenger, the signifier who is responsible for the transmission of legendary fact and, therefore, for cultural continuity that makes for historical interpretation and reinterpretation.

For instance, it was Raven Quickskill's book, *Flight to Canada,* that "was responsible for getting him to Canada."[46] It would be his revision of the Uncle Tom legend—as it applied to Robin—that would carry on the black tradition in its racial particularity. As history is implicit in legend, so is fact in fiction. "Words built the world and words can destroy the world," says Quickskill.[47] "*The limits of my language* mean the limits of my world," wrote Wittgenstein in another sense.[48] The raven is a predacious bird: Quickskill uses his literacy "like that of old Voodoo."[49]

History is also real: Quickskill's reach, like his new freedom, is limited: he cannot really create and destroy a world. He must carry on a given tradition. Liberation, the overthrow of the oppressor, does not necessarily usher in an ethical order. Quickskill realizes that slaves were not only "enslaved by others, but they often, in subtle ways, enslaved each other." He wonders whether "overseers [were] to be replaced by new overseers."[50] As Papa LaBas remarks in *The Last Days of Louisiana Red,* "The philosophy of slavery has been handed down through the ages and has appeared under different names. Moochism for example." Moochers, who subvert the operations of conscientious individuals, "cooperate in their 'oppression.' "[51] Major's Mason learns at the end of his quest that "one can carry the disease one covers oneself against on the fingers one uses to secure the cover."[52] Perhaps, ultimately, the difference "between a savage and a civilized man is determined by who has the power," as the pragmatic materialist Yankee Jack puts it in Reed's book.[53] Still, the very fact that Quickskill is dealing with a concrete historical experience, and that his writing would bear witness to "all the changes that would happen to make a 'thing' into an 'I Am,' "[54] gives his narrative an authenticity that is lacking in intertextual surrealism and solipsism. The raven's statement "Nevermore" is not wholly an enigma: it is not the inner voice of a mad man; nor is it just "the . . . stock and store, caught from some unhappy master whom unmerciful Disaster / Followed fast and followed faster."[55] It represents the political struggle of people who stood up for themselves against their depersonalization.

Even if literature is a magic art in the sense that it is the expression of the inexpressible, it nevertheless testifies to some kind of cultural particularity. In this way, as Quickskill says, "writing always catches up on me."[56] The raven also caught up on the soul of Edgar Allan Poe's narrator, which lay in its shadow. The black experience, which derives from both the African and the American traditions, is not only a quest for liberation against social and political oppression; it is also the affirmation of concealed layers of consciousness which can never be rationally exposed but which white civilization has suppressed—as it has suppressed its own inexplicable impulses. The western rationalist approach to reality can function on a comprehensible or logical dimension only by means of invented antitheses: it is caught in its own line of sight. Perhaps it is in this sense that Wittgenstein wrote, "Solipsism . . . coincides with pure realism. . . . [Its] self . . . shrinks to a point without extension, and there remains the reality co-ordinated with it."[57] James Joyce's Bloom and H. C. Earwicker took seemingly infinite journeys around the circle of western languages through puns and references only to arrive back at the natural cycle from which they had started. Derrida's insistence that there is nothing outside the text and that everything in it is relative to it has led him to separate the writer's intention from his meaning, and, therefore, necessarily to fall back on the sources from which his language has been historically derived and toward which it is ineluctably oriented. Since "whatever we see could be other than it is,"[58] everything can be and nothing is. The African world view, which posits the material and spiritual unity of things, sees the universe as a hieroglyphy that balances—not opposes—antithetical powers. " 'Opposites' constitute interdependent interacting forces which are necessary for producing a given reality."[59] Hermes, the thief; Esu, the signifying monkey; Legba, the spirit of the "Crossroads"; the modern mulatto; and the "new man" are workers of mystery: they practice subterfuge, they are endowed with the key to natural contradictions. Signifying is metacommunication that functions on different levels of being, and not simply those of interpretation and application. Black literature, as Cooke points out, makes metamorphosis a datum.[60]

Since language is misrepresentation in its limited capacity to render reality in any form, it can only provide clues to what exists. And this existing thereness in all its facets is an ever-living, nonprogressive *is*— at least in the imagination of the signifier. That it is logically a tautology is irrelevant. Unlike blacks, says Reed, Europeans "are after themselves. They call it destiny. Progress. We call it Haints."[61] As the black idea of history is cyclical, black literary techniques included repetition, suggestion, mystery. In Reed's *Reckless Eyeballing,* the mother of the writer Ian Ball has the Indian gift of clairvoyance and Ball himself "knew about Afro-American signifying."[62] It is his brother who—at least in his dream—stands guard over nefarious feminist influences that involve white Becky Smith and black Tremonisha Smarts. Becky, in collusion with white males who control the cultural order, has propagated the stereotype of the black male brute-rapist; Tremonisha, her protégée and collaborator, has capitulated to the materialistic myths by which industrial culture functions. Women like Minnie the Moocher in *The Last Days of Louisiana Red* are vampires who drive men off; they are black widow spiders. They "deprive . . . the victim of the ability to express itself";[63] they stifle him, as Ball is himself artistically castrated in his own creative thrust. He gives in to the demands of his white producers and softens the message of his play in which a black is sentenced for allegedly eyeballing a white girl. This female aggression is the inevitable result of the pragmatic, materialistic and rationalistic impetus of women's liberation.

Reckless Eyeballing is also making an ironic commentary on Baldwin's *Blues for Mister Charlie,* in which the author seemingly capitulated to liberal opinion and morally refused to condemn the southern cracker who murders the black protagonist. "He's not a wicked man," explains the good white Parnell; he just "suffers—from being in the dark."[64] No one is bad from within one's own perspective: everything makes sense. Reed's book likewise signifies on the American success ethic—which deceives as much as it entices. It satirizes the state of black art in general, which, forced to affirm itself in an inimical cultural environment, has no apparent alternative but to accede to the demands of the white mainstream. In the recent political era of Reagan and Bush, blacks were no longer interesting: radicals had opted for security if not power control by any means, and confrontation was outmoded.

Nevertheless, as Reed makes clear, aesthetics is economics and politics. In *The Terrible Twos* and *The Terrible Threes,* the black street performer with red hair and a dummy, the descendant of Pompey, the master ventriloquist of slave days and a takeoff on Ellison's Tod, is the impostor, the magician who usurps the place of Black Peter, accomplice of Saint Nicholas. Actually, *The Terrible Twos* is a parody of Dickens's *A Christmas Carol* and a satire of the political practices of industrial

America: Scrooge is the "guiding spirit of . . . America" in 1980;[65] the president, a good-looking model is, like HARRY SAM, "NOTHIN'." He is the real dummy, put in by the ruling powers, and, like Santa Claus, the manufactured clone of Saint Nicholas and symbol of industrial profiteering, the president is the product of publicity and promotion. In fact, "the highest order of [the] species of Moocher is the President," as Reed writes in *Louisiana Red*.[66]

The ventriloquist con man impersonates Black Peter, the Ethiopian Saint Nicholas's attendant, makes a Santa Claus out of a murdered snowman and speaks through him for the masses. He exposes the plan of plotting officials of the power structure to monopolize Christmas and to rid the world of the surplus poor. The president is touched by the ploy of the false Santa Claus; he changes heart and shares his Christmas dinner with John, the black butler at the White House, and John's family, including, of course, a sweet-natured crippled boy, a black replica of Tiny Tim. The president, comments Reed, "really, if he wanted to, could change the course of—there I go again. My idealism."[67]

The book is a political attack on "European-centered ideologies of domination," as Linda Hutcheon puts it.[68] "You know how two-year-olds are," remarks one of Reed's characters. "Their plates will be full but they'll have their eyes on everybody else's plates. . . ."[69] It is not enough to say no, no. They take what they want anyway, rapaciously, with no thought for anybody else. In Reed's novel, monoculturalism wins again. The false Santa Claus is exposed; the true commercial one— the moral fraud—comes back; Nance, the black detective, is frustrated in his efforts to locate Snowman, who has served as the dummy; the president is arrested; the old order is reinforced. The rich hire "surplus people"—whom they groom to be vital—"to keep their own kind off the premises of these high buildings where the vital people dwelled." They drive their high-powered machines "through the dirty hands reaching . . . from the gutter."[70]

By the time of *The Terrible Threes*, the false Black Peter—whose image has been commercialized and incorporated into the operation of consumer society—has fallen to the status of a surplus person. Reverend Jones, a mad preacher; Bob Krantz, an extraterritorial spy; and the president, another Moocher type, have launched a worldwide plot involving Africa and nuclear weapons: they, the terrible three, are aiming for a third world war. The real Black Peter comes to reclaim his rightful role from his impostor; the pope, who resents Black Peter's voodoo techniques, sends Saint Nicholas to contest him.[71] Saint Nicholas, indoctrinated in the methods of western civilization, outdoes his former accomplice with a series of spectacular miracles, while Black Peter, who "just can't resist helping those in distress,"[72] wastes his time by acting on a small and modest scale and by concentrating on individual and irrelevant cases.

Inevitably, Saint Nicholas falls into the commercial trap. The terrible plot continues; Black Peter returns to save his mulattoized brother, Saint Nicholas. Black Peter is like Jes Grew: he keeps coming back, and "Americans would . . . find out. . . . It's hard to prevent Black Peter from going where he wants to go."[73] Nance, the detective, is vindicated and hired by the Satan-obsessed Catholic Church. And since, as Satan himself admits, blacks are not related to him: they are "none of my kin,"[74] hope remains in the political universe of Ishmael Reed—as it does in the world view of many black writers.

Blacks, Satan concludes, have "their *language*"[75]—which is by implication different from that of whites. Black art, which reflects the black point of view, is—as Reed points out in *Mumbo Jumbo*—an entity, albeit indecipherable in itself. It does not have to depend entirely on words or on discourse. The figure of Jes Grew, which never speaks, which is an *it*, represents "disembodied rhythm," as a critic puts it, "the essence of anti-growth" before which people "turn once more to mystery, to wonderment."[76] Jes Grew is a thereness in which they would be expressed.

The text and the essence of Jes Grew are, of course, a contradiction in terms. But as tautology could be irrelevant to world reality, so might opposition be. Because a written record is open to continuous perusal throughout generations of time, it attests to absolute changelessness in the presence of change. It can never be read in the same way, and so it signifies historical recurrence or historical growth or ahistorical lack of order, depending on the conditions and manner in which it is seen. The indeterminate thereness of Jes Grew, for instance, is defined by its absence, says Gates.[77] Papa LaBas's effort to track down the text is in a way a parody of the act of writing: for Reed comments on the techniques by which artists express themselves in language and thereby try to relate human understanding to the truth. After all, the distinction of human beings lies in their ability to use and to create language. The battle between the Atonists who seek absolute unity—or logocentrism—and the Jes Grew carriers is an elemental one: it resembles the effort of western monoculturists to possess the language of the people and, therefore, to prevail over pluraculturists.

Actually, the text of Jes Grew could be the "vast and terrible text of Blackness itself"[78]—as it has been called. Papa LaBas's quest for it stands for black people's struggle simply to be in whatever integrity they might possess. The text has been suppressed by whites, misrepresented by blacks, distorted by time. But it is, nevertheless, there in its inexpressible presence. The search for it might expose the foundations on which a new and undissimulated American culture could be built. The question concerns the process by which whites and blacks with different experiences and orientations could eventually produce a fruitful civilization. " 'How,' " Reed's turtle asked the lobster, " 'can [white] Nick and [black] Peter, who are opposites, be the same? . . .' But the lobster wasn't saying."[79] Perhaps the answer lies in the mulatto, represented by the Ethiopian Nicholas.

To create a black voice might, in a sense, preserve white cultural themes in a context that would strip away the traditional will to dominate. In introducing values that do not depend uniquely on the materialistic criteria of achievement, American blacks might free the social order of the polarization which divides it into the relatively advantaged majority and the deprived minority, which consigns the minority to poverty, crime and ill health.

The identification of poor with black represents a tendency to subsume black consciousness in class rationalizations that would deny the historical significance of the black experience. To associate poverty with all its asocial implications is pragmatically to degrade the positive qualities of being black. At the same time as the black mass is devalued, the possibility of full, pluralistic integration is blocked, and black culture is reduced to material criteria for the better function of the postindustrial state.

The development of African American cultural forms could even open the world to the diversity that is implicit in human nature and that has yet to be revealed. However, if the black, who has been excluded from and who has held out for so long against the all-consuming state, should be absorbed in it, there would be no point for the coming-into-being of the American experience. It would be a grotesque historical mistake.

NOTES

Chapter 1: Cultural and Economic Segregation

1. Herbert Marcuse: *L'Homme Unidimensionnel*, p. 86.
2. John Dollard: *Caste and Class in a Southern Town*, p. 433.
3. Waldemar Kaempffert: "Democracy and the Machine," *This America*, p. 174.
4. Marcuse: *La Fin de l'Utopie*, p. 43 (author's translation).
5. Milton Gordon, cited by Harold Cruse: *The Crisis of the Negro Intellectual*, p. 9.
6. Amiri Baraka (LeRoi Jones): *Daggers and Javelins*, p. 140 (italics in original).
7. Victor Ferkiss: *Technological Man*, p. 50.
8. Stuart Sherman: "The Point of View in American Criticism," Charles L. Glicksberg: *American Literary Criticism*, p. 167.
9. Benjamin Brawley: *A Social History of the American Negro*, p. 57.
10. George M. Frederickson: *White Supremacy*, p. 70.
11. Louis M. Hacker: *The Triumph of American Capitalism*, p. 5 (italics in original).
12. William E. B. DuBois: "Reconstruction and Its Benefits," *Black History*, p. 280.
13. John C. Calhoun II: "Life and Labor in the New South," *The Transformation of American Society*, p. 30.
14. Stokely Carmichael: "Toward Black Liberation," *Black Fire*, pp. 120–121.
15. Quoted in Whitney M. Young: *Negro Protest Thought in the Twentieth Century*, p. 292.
16. C. Eric Lincoln: *Sounds of the Struggle*, p. 202.
17. Kerner Commission, quoted in *American Vistas*, p. 255.
18. DuBois: "Prologue," *Black History, op. cit.*, p. 9.
19. Cruse, *op. cit.*, p. 282.
20. Louis Lomax: *The Negro Revolt*, p. 21.
21. Frederick D. Patterson: "The Negro Wants Full Participation in American Democracy," *What the Negro Wants*, p. 280.
22. Langston Hughes: "My America," *The Langston Hughes Reader*, p. 501.
23. Ralph Ellison: *Shadow and Act*, pp. 25 and 19.
24. Lloyd Warner, quoted in Lincoln: "The Black Muslims in America," *American Race Relations Today*, p. 181.

25. E. Franklin Frazier: *On Race Relations,* p. 257.
26. Lincoln: "The Black Muslims in America," *op. cit.,* p. 181.
27. DuBois, quoted by Charles E. Silberman: *Crisis in Black and White,* p. 109.
28. James Baldwin: "Many Thousands Gone," *The Partisan Review Anthology,* p. 108.
29. Robin M. Williams, Jr.: *American Society,* p. 467.
30. Gunnar Myrdal: *An American Dilemma,* p. 89 (italics in original).
31. DuBois, quoted in Francis L. Broderick: "W.E.B. DuBois: Entente with White Liberals, 1910–1920," *Black History, op. cit.,* p. 364.
32. Hannah Arendt: *Crisis of the Republic,* p. 90.
33. James M. McPherson: "The Negro: Innately Inferior or Equal?," *Black History, op. cit.,* p. 238.
34. Malcolm X, *Negro Protest Thought, op. cit.,* p. 383.
35. Thomas D. Clark and Albert D. Kirwan: *The South Since Appomattox,* p. 306.
36. Dollard, *op. cit.,* p. 98.
37. See Kenneth M. Stamp: "The Tragic Legend of Reconstruction," *Myth and the American Experience,* p. 64.
38. Robert Wiebe: *The Search for Order,* p. 58.
39. C. Vann Woodward: *The Strange Career of Jim Crow,* p. 82.
40. Baraka, *op. cit.,* p. 284.
41. Michael Harrington: *The Other America,* p. 156.
42. See Earl Raab and Seymour Lipset: "The Prejudiced Society," *American Race Relations Today, op. cit.,* p. 51.
43. Myrdal, *op. cit.,* p. 381 (italics in original).
44. Francis O. Simkins: *The South Old and New,* p. 180.
45. See "*Plessey* v. *Ferguson*," *Great Issues in American History,* pp. 55–57.
46. "Declaration of Ninety-six Southern Congressmen on Integration," March 11, 1956, *ibid.,* p. 65.
47. Duane Lockard: *The Perverted Priorities of American Politics,* p. 88.
48. Quoted in Lerone Bennett, Jr.: *Before the Mayflower,* p. 219.
49. Herbert G. Gutman: *Work, Culture and Society in Industrial America,* p. 81.
50. "*Plessy* v. *Ferguson*," *op. cit.,* pp. 56–57.
51. Quoted by Louis R. Harlan: *Booker T. Washington, the Wizard of Tuskegee,* p. 430.
52. See Woodward: *The Burden of Southern History,* p. 78, and Bennett, *op. cit.,* p. 198.
53. James Comer: *Beyond Black and White,* p. 117.
54. Russell Nye: *This Almost Chosen People,* pp. 331 and 351.
55. Oscar Handlin: *Race and Nationality in American Life,* p. 84.
56. *Ibid.,* p. 81.
57. Gordon B. Hancock: "Race Relations in the United States: A Summary," *What the Negro Wants, op. cit.,* p. 226.

58. Theodore Parker, quoted by Joel Kovel: *White Racism*, p. 28.
59. Thomas F. Gossett: *Race: The History of an Idea in America*, p. 167.
60. See Eric Goldman: *Rendezvous with Destiny*, p. 147.
61. Wiebe, *op. cit.*, p. 58.
62. William Howard Taft: "Inaugural Address, 1909," *In Their Place*, p. 92.
63. Woodrow Wilson: "Letter to Oswald Garrison Villard, 1913," *ibid.*, p. 93.
64. Wilson, quoted by F. Garven Davenport, Jr.: *The Myth of Southern History*, p. 13.
65. Warren Harding, quoted in *The New York Times*, October 27, 1921, *In Their Place, op. cit.*, p. 95.
66. See Harvey Wish: *The American Historian*, pp. 99, 210, 214, 221; see Gossett, *op. cit.*, pp. 284–285.
67. Rhodes: "History of the United States," quoted in *In Their Place, op. cit.*, p. 110; see Stanley B. Hirshson: *Farewell to the Bloody Shirt.*
68. Bowers: "The Tragic Era," quoted in *In Their Place, op. cit.*, p. 113.
69. Commager and Morison: "The Growth of the American Republic," quoted in *ibid.*, p. 107.
70. Merle Curti: *The Growth of American Thought*, p. 606.
71. DuBois, quoted by Hollis R. Lynch: *The Black Urban Condition*, p. 103.
72. DuBois: *Autobiography*, p. 256; see John C. Teaford: *The Unheralded Triumph*, p. 47.
73. Gossett, *op. cit.*, p. 262.
74. Ralph Bunche: *Negro Protest Thought, op. cit.*, p. 113.
75. Wiebe, *op. cit.*, pp. 107–108.
76. See Page Smith: *The Rise of Industrial America*, vol. 6, p. 654.
77. Harlan, *op. cit.*, p. 239.
78. Woodward: *The Strange Career of Jim Crow, op. cit.*, p. 82.
79. Woodward: *Reunion and Reaction* (italics in original), p. 53.
80. *Ibid.*, p. 246.
81. William Riker, quoted in Lockard, *op. cit.*, p. 82.
82. Dollard, *op. cit.*, p. 58.
83. Kovel, *op. cit.*, p. 198.
84. Kenneth Clark: *Dark Ghetto*, p. 21.
85. See Juan Gonzales: *Two Blocks Away*, p. 91.
86. J. C. Furnas: *The Americans*, vol. 2, p. 847.
87. Myrdal, quoted in Woodward: *The Strange Career of Jim Crow, op. cit.*, p. 105.
88. Maury Maverick: *This America, op. cit.*, p. 400.
89. Myrdal, *op. cit.*, p. 677.
90. Sherwood Anderson: "The Man Who Became a Woman," *Portable Sherwood Anderson*, p. 487.
91. Thomas Wolfe: *Look Homeward, Angel*, p. 95.
92. Kovel, *op. cit.*, pp. 32 and 184 (italics in original).

93. See Jane Jacobs: "The Death and Life of Great American Cities," p. 324.
94. Hollis R. Lynch: *The Black Urban Condition*, p. 74.
95. August Meier and Elliott Rudwick: *From Plantation to Ghetto*, p. 215.
96. Martin Grodzins: "The Metropolitan Area as a Racial Problem," *American Race Relations Today, op. cit.*, p. 93.
97. Ernest Van Den Haag: "How Not to Prevent Civil Disorders," *Basic Issues of American Democracy*, pp. 253–257.
98. Quoted in Clark, *op. cit.*, p. 2.
99. Reinhold Niebuhr: *Leaves from the Notebook of a Tamed Cynic*, p. 169.
100. Grodzins, *op. cit., American Race Relations Today*, p. 98.
101. Carmichael: "Toward Black Liberation," *op. cit.*, p. 123.
102. Myrdal, *op. cit.*, p. 591 (italics in original); see *ibid.*, p. 585.
103. Harlan, *op. cit.*, pp. 190 and 192.
104. Theodore Rosengarten: *All God's Dangers: The Life of Nate Shaw*, p. 217.
105. George E. Peterson: "Finances," *The Urban Predicament*, pp. 98–99.
106. Robert Hutchins: "Permanence and Change," *The Establishment and All That* (collection of major articles selected from *Center Magazine*), p. 124.
107. James S. Coleman: "Equal Schools or Equal Students?," *Anatomies of America*, p. 354.
108. V. D. Key, Jr.: *Public Opinion and American Democracy*, pp. 211, 217, 228.
109. "Declaration of Ninety-six Southern Congressmen," *op. cit.*, pp. 64–65.
110. James S. Coleman and Sara D. Kelly: "Education," *The Urban Predicament, op. cit.*, p. 248.
111. Nathan Glazer and Daniel Patrick Moynihan: *Beyond the Melting Pot*, p. 46.
112. Clark, *op. cit.*, p. 132.
113. William Julius Wilson: *The Truly Disadvantaged*, p. 102.
114. See Judge William C. Booth: "Racism and Human Rights," *Black Anti-Semitism and Jewish Racism*.
115. See Meier and Rudwick: "Early Boycotts of Segregated Schools: The Case of Springfield, Ohio, 1922–23," *Along the Color Line*, pp. 290–301.
116. Frazier: *The Negro in the United States*, p. 396.
117. *Ibid.* p. 409.
118. Stephan Thernstrom: *The Other Bostonians*, pp. 202, 208, 214.
119. DuBois: *Against Racism*, p. 145.
120. Talcott Parsons: "Some Theoretical Considerations on the Nature and Trends of Change of Ethnicity," *Ethnicity Theory and Experience*, p. 77 (italics in original).
121. Peter Heinz: "The Problem of 'Pariahs,' " *Max Weber and Sociology Today*, p. 248.
122. Frederickson, *op. cit.*, p. 205.

123. A. Philip Randolph: "Lynching: Capitalism Its Cause; Socialism Its Cause," *The Messenger,* March, 1919, *Negro Protest Thought, op. cit.,* p. 74.
124. Clark, *op. cit.,* p. 41.
125. Parsons, *op. cit., Ethnicity,* p. 77.
126. Frederickson, *op. cit.,* pp. 209–210.
127. DuBois, quoted in Brawley, *op. cit.,* p. 320.
128. Frederickson, *op. cit.,* pp. 220 and 215.
129. Quoted in Rosengarten, *op. cit.,* p. 488.
130. Gutman, *op. cit.,* pp. 14–15 and 24.
131. DuBois: *Autobiography, op. cit.,* p. 234.
132. DuBois: *Against Racism, op. cit.,* p. 126.
133. Quoted in Gutman, *op. cit.,* p. 152.
134. Quoted in *ibid.,* p. 206.
135. Meier and Rudwick: *From Plantation to Ghetto, op. cit.,* p. 191.
136. See Clark, *op. cit.,* p. 43.
137. Patrick Renshaw: *The Wobblies,* p. 166.
138. See Richard Edwards: *Contested Terrain,* especially pp. 195–196.
139. St. Clair Drake and Horace R. Cayton: *Black Metropolis,* vol. 1, p. 224.
140. Clark, *op. cit.,* p. 106.
141. Drake and Cayton, *op. cit.,* p. xxviii.
142. Edwards, *op. cit.,* pp. 195–196.
143. Gutman, *op. cit.,* p. 31.
144. Richard Wright: *American Hunger,* p. 80.
145. Richard Drennan: "Introduction," Lillian Symes and Travers Clement: *Rebel America,* p. xxiv.
146. Drake and Cayton, *op. cit.,* vol. 2, p. 735.
147. Cruse: "My Jewish Problem and Theirs," *Black American Anti-Semitism and Jewish Racism, op. cit.,* pp. 181 and 185.
148. Hugh Armstrong, quoted in Vivian Gornick: *The Romance of American Communism,* p. 163.
149. See Gornick, *ibid.,* p. 51.
150. Ellison: *Invisible Man,* p. 432.
151. See Cruse: *Crisis, op. cit.,* p. 49.
152. Wright, *op. cit.,* p. 123.
153. John Gates: *The Story of an American Communist,* pp. 166–167.
154. *Ibid.,* p. 108.
155. Drake and Cayton, *op. cit.,* vol. 2, p. 736.
156. Cruse: *Crisis, op. cit.,* p. 269 (italics in original).
157. DuBois: *Autobiography, op. cit.,* p. 291.

Chapter 2: Political and Social Segregation

1. Meier: *Negro Thought in America 1880–1915,* p. 4.
2. See Hirshson, *op. cit.,* pp. 48 and 178.
3. See Harlan, *op. cit.,* p. 6.

4.   See Furnas, *op. cit.*, p. 853.
5.   Jean H. Baker: *Affairs of Party*, p. 242.
6.   Drake and Cayton, *op. cit.*, vol. 1, p. 377.
7.   Hirshson, *op. cit.*, pp. 103, 168, 216.
8.   Harlan, *op. cit.*, pp. 14 and 25.
9.   *Ibid.*, pp. 165, 350.
10. *Ibid.*, p. 338.
11. Lewis M. Steel, quoted in Lockard, *op. cit.*, p. 219.
12. Gonzales, *op. cit.*, pp. 92 and 106
13. Penn Kimball: *The Disconnected*, p. 3.
14. See *ibid.*, pp. 11, 35, 88.
15. See Cruse: *Plural*, pp. 202–203.
16. See Clark, *op. cit.*, p. 158.
17. See Manning Marable: *Black American Politics*, pp. 180–185.
18. Kimball, *op. cit.*, p. 176.
19. William V. Shannon: "The Age of the Bosses," *American Vistas, op. cit.*, p. 62.
20. Kimball, *op. cit.*, p. 17.
21. *Ibid.*, p. 21.
22. Drake: "The Social and Economic Status of the Negro in the United States," *Anatomies, op. cit.*, p. 220; see Tom Hayden: *The Great Society Reader, op. cit.*, p. 491.
23. See Myrdal, *op. cit.*, p. 731.
24. Quoted in Rosengarten, *op. cit.*, p. 499.
25. See Robert S. Lynd and Helen Merrill Lynd: *Middletown in Transition*, p. 408.
26. See James West: *Plainville, U.S.A.*, p. 83.
27. Drake and Cayton, *op. cit.*, vol. 1, p. 113 (italics in original).
28. *Ibid.*, p. 175.
29. Herbert J. Gans: "The White Exodus to Suburbia," *Cities in Trouble*, p. 45.
30. Glazer: "Introduction," *ibid.*, p. 11.
31. Gans, *op. cit.*, *ibid.*, p. 45.
32. Martin Kilson: "Black Politics: A New Power," *The Seventies*, p. 303.
33. Cruse: *Plural, op. cit.* (italics in original).
34. *Ibid.*, p. 202.
35. Charles V. Hamilton: "On Parity and Political Empowerment," *The State of Black America*, p. 114.
36. Harrington: *The New American Poverty*, p. 135.
37. Clark, *op. cit.*, p. 156.
38. Gary Orfield: "Separate Societies: Have the Kerner Warnings Come True?," *Quiet Riots: Race and Poverty in the United States*, p. 105.
39. Marable, *op. cit.*, p. 244.
40. Clark, *op. cit.*, p. 156.
41. Woodward: "Capitulation to Racism," *Black History, op. cit.*, p. 335 (italics in original).
42. Hirshson, *op. cit.*, p. 101.

43. Harlan, *op. cit.*, p. 384.
44. DuBois: *The Souls of Black Folk*, p. 57.
45. Arna Bontemps and Jack Conroy: *They Seek a City*, p. 196.
46. Addison Gayle, Jr.: *The Way of the New World: The Black Novel in America*, p. 80.
47. Richard Bardolph: *The Negro Vanguard*, p. 190.
48. See Myrdal, *op. cit.*, p. 305.
49. Louis E. Lomax, *op. cit.*, pp. 19, 20, 54.
50. Frazier: *On Race Relations, op. cit.*, p. 216.
51. Harlan, *op. cit.*, p. 129.
52. DuBois, quoted in *ibid.*, p. 134.
53. Wright: *The Long Dream*, p. 71.
54. Frazier: *Negro Youth at the Crossways*, p. 65.
55. Drake and Cayton, *op. cit.*, vol. 2, p. 563 (italics in original).
56. Frazier: *On Race Relations, op. cit.*, p. 209.
57. Drake and Cayton, *op. cit.*, vol. 2, p. 724.
58. See *ibid.*, p. 728.
59. Rap Brown: *Die Nigger Die*, p. 7.
60. Cruse: "Revolutionary Nationalism and the Afro-American," *Black Fire, op. cit.*, p. 56.
61. Hughes: *The Langston Hughes Reader, op. cit.*, p. 342.
62. Wright: *The Long Dream, op. cit.*, p. 71.
63. Wright: *American Hunger, op. cit.*, p. 14.
64. Baraka: *Home*, pp. 114–115.
65. Wright: *American Hunger, op. cit.*, p. 5.
66. Drake: "The Social and Economic Status of the Negro," *op. cit., Anatomies*, p. 204.
67. Wright: *The Long Dream, op. cit.*, p. 158.
68. Gayle, *op. cit.*, p. 159.
69. Claude McKay: *Home to Harlem*, p. 274.
70. See DuBois: *The Souls of Black Folk, op. cit.*, p. 17.
71. Ellison: *Invisible Man, op. cit.*, pp. 190 and 382.
72. Lomax, *op. cit.*, p. 21.
73. Wright: *The Long Dream, op. cit.*, p. 35.
74. See Myrdal, *op. cit.*, p. 724.
75. See Sophonisba Breckinridge: "The Color Line in the Housing Problem," Lynch, *op. cit.*, p. 139.
76. See Wright: *Native Son*, p. 110.
77. Albert B. Cleage, Jr.: *The Black Messiah*, p. 182.
78. Kilson: "Blacks and Neo-ethnicity in American Political Life," *Ethnicity, op. cit.*, p. 240.
79. Wright: *White Man, Listen!*, p. 109.
80. Irving Kristol: "The Negro Today Is Like the Immigrant," *Cities in Trouble, op. cit.*, p. 152.
81. Handlin, *op. cit.*, p. 177.
82. See Lincoln: *Sounds of the Struggle, op. cit.*, p. 202.

83. Kilson: "Blacks and Neo-ethnicity," *Ethnicity, op. cit.,* p. 240.
84. Dollard, *op. cit.,* p. 175.
85. Bruno Bettelheim and Morris Janowitz: *Social Change and Prejudice,* pp. 267–268.
86. Quoted in Robert Dahl: *Who Governs?,* p. 234.
87. Hasia R. Diner, quoted in Cruse: *Plural, op. cit.,* note 114, p. 147.
88. William Kornblum: *Blue Collar Community,* p. 34.
89. *Ibid.,* p. 22.
90. *Ibid.,* p. 30.
91. Cruse: *Crisis, op. cit.,* p. 261.
92. Barbara Greenleaf: *American Fever,* p. 200 (italics in original).
93. James Boggs: "Black Power—A Scientific Concept Whose Time Has Come," *Black Fire, op. cit.,* p. 109. See Robert Conot: *American Odyssey,* p. 74.
94. Hughes: "Autobiography," *The Langston Hughes Reader, op. cit.,* p. 336.
95. Wright: *American Hunger, op. cit.,* p. 5.
96. Kornblum, *op. cit.,* p. 4.
97. See Moyers, pp. 70–71.
98. See Andrew Greeley: *The Most Distressed Nation,* p. 238.
99. See Kornblum, *op. cit.,* pp. 73, 202–203, 212.
100. See Novak, *op. cit.,* p. 74; Peter Binzen: "The White Schools or White Town," *ibid.,* p. 114.
101. Kilson: "Blacks and Neo-ethnicity," *Ethnicity, op. cit.,* pp. 259 and 257.
102. Novak, *op. cit.,* p. 61.
103. Ryan: *White Ethnics, op. cit.,* p. 94.
104. Quoted in Moyers, *op. cit.,* p. 71.
105. Greeley, *op. cit.,* pp. 226, 240, 245.
106. Thomas Sowell: *Ethnic America,* p. 39.
107. *Ibid.,* pp. 111 and 127.
108. Novak, *op. cit.,* p. 25.
109. *Ibid.,* p. 250.
110. *Ibid.,* p. 254.
111. *Ibid.,* p. 255.
112. *Ibid.,* p. 168.
113. See Albert Vorspan: "Blacks and Jews," *Black Anti-Semitism and Jewish Racism, op. cit.,* p. 205.
114. See Nathan Perlmutter and Ruth Ann Perlmutter: *The Real Anti-Semitism in America,* p. 182.
115. Quoted in Nat Hentoff: "Introduction," *Black Anti-Semitism and Jewish Racism, op. cit.,* p. xxi.
116. Rabbi Jay Kaufman: "Thou Shalt Surely Rebuke Thy Neighbor," *ibid.,* p. 66.
117. *Ibid.,* pp. 72–73.
118. Cruse: "My Jewish Problem and Theirs," *op. cit., ibid.,* p. 185.
119. Earl Raab: "The Black Revolution and the Jewish Question," *ibid.,* p. 31.

120. E. Digby Baltzell: *The Protestant Establishment*, p. 386.
121. Jacob Riis: *A Ten Years War*, p. 64.
122. Woodward: *The Burden of Southern History, op. cit.*, p. 113.
123. Wright: *American Hunger, op. cit.*, p. 40.
124. Bozell, Brent, quoted in George H. Nash: *The Conservative Movement*, p. 215.
125. Harrington: *The Other America, op. cit.*, p. 84.
126. See Dollard, *op. cit.*, p. 364.
127. Lloyd Warner: "A Methodological Note," Drake and Cayton, *op. cit.*, vol. 2, p. 781 (italics in original).
128. Allison Davis, Burleigh B. Gardner, Mary R. Gardner: *Deep South*, p. 338.
129. See Charles A. Reich: *The Greening of America*, pp. 122 and 124.
130. Carmichael, quoted in *Black Voices from Prison*, p. 9.
131. See Michael Wallace: "The Uses of Violence in American History," *Myth and the American Experience, op. cit.*, vol. 2, pp. 401 and 410.
132. *Ibid.*, p. 397.
133. *Ibid.* (italics in original).
134. *Ibid.*, p. 410.
135. *Ibid.*, pp. 408–409.
136. Rap Brown, *op. cit.*, p. 38.
137. Wright: "The Man Who Went to Chicago," *Eight Men*, p. 180.
138. Cruse: *Crisis, op. cit.*, p. 317.
139. DuBois: "Black America," *Negro: An Anthology*, p. 101.
140. Erskine Caldwell: *Deep South*, p. 137.
141. Ellison: *Shadow and Act, op. cit.*, p. 92.
142. Walter White: "A Man Called White," *Growing Up Black*, p. 18.
143. Myrdal, *op. cit.*, p. 561.
144. Michael Wallace: "The Uses of Violence," *op. cit.*, *Myth*, p. 402.
145. Paul Cheviny, quoted in Lockard, *op. cit.*, p. 169.
146. Raab: "Forward: Ending the Past: Equal Opportunity and Desegregation," *American Race Relations, op. cit.*, p. 25.
147. Raab and Lipset: "The Prejudiced Society," *op. cit., ibid.*, p. 34.
148. John Herbers: "The Kerner Report: A Journalist's View," *Quiet Riots, op. cit.*, pp. 17–18.

Chapter 3: Black Poverty: The Effect of Segregation

1. Raab: "Introduction," *op. cit., American Race Relations*, p. 18 (italics in original).
2. David Hamilton: "Poverty Is Still with Us—and Worse," *Quiet Riots, op. cit.*, p. 37.
3. Michael S. March: "Coverage, Gaps, and Future Directions of Public Programs," *Poverty in Affluence*, p. 173.
4. David Swinton: "The Economic Status of Black America," *The State of Black America, op. cit.*, p. 13.

5. Wilson, Aponte, Kirschenman, Wacquant: "The Ghetto Underclass and the Changing Structure of Urban Poverty," *Quiet Riots*, p. 131.

6. Gary Sandelur, *op. cit., ibid.*, p. 70.

7. See William McDougall: *The Group Mind*, passim.

8. Heinz: "The Problem of 'Pariahs,' " *op. cit., Max Weber and Sociology Today*, p. 248.

9. Nikki Giovanni: *Gemini*, p. 81.

10. Dwight L. Dumond: "The Controversy over Slavery," *Paths of American Thought*, p. 103.

11. Frederickson, *op. cit.*, p. 7.

12. See Gutman, *op. cit.*, p. 81.

13. Robert Williams: *Negroes with Guns*, p. 119.

14. Norman O. Brown: *Life Against Death*, p. 10.

15. *Ibid.*, p. 12.

16. Raab: "Introduction," *op. cit., American Race Relations*, p. 14.

17. *Ibid.*

18. Ellison: *Shadow and Act, op. cit.*, p. 298.

19. H. L. Mencken: *A Mencken Chrestomathy*, p. 192.

20. Drake and Cayton, *op. cit.*, vol. 1, pp. 18 and 29.

21. Meier and Rudwick: "Black Violence in the Twentieth Century: A Study in Rhetoric and Retaliation," *Along the Color Line, op. cit.*, p. 229.

22. Drake and Cayton, *op. cit.*, vol. 1, p. 175 (see also note 28, ch. 2).

23. Alain Locke: "The New Negro," *The New Negro: An Interpretation*, p. 11.

24. *Ibid., passim.*

25. See Gossett, *op. cit.*, p. 340.

26. Hughes: *The Big Sea*, p. 51.

27. Elizabeth Stevenson: *Babbitts and Bohemians*, p. 215.

28. See Cruse: *Crisis, op. cit.*, p. 38.

29. Hughes: *The Big Sea, op. cit.*, p. 228.

30. Jeanne Noble: *Beautiful, Also, Are the Souls of My Black Sisters*, p. 142.

31. Paula Giddings: *When and Where I Enter* (uncorrected galleys), p. 178.

32. DuBois, quoted in Arnold Rampersad: *The Art and Image of W.E.B. DuBois*, p. 199.

33. Frazier: "Some Effects of the Depression on the Negro in Northern Cities," *The Black Urban Condition, op. cit.*, p. 210.

34. Myrdal, *op. cit.*, p. 295.

35. R. and H. Lynd, *op. cit.*, p. 465.

36. Claude McKay: "Harlem Runs Wild," *The Black Urban Condition, op. cit.*, p. 249.

37. Myrdal: *Challenge to Affluence*, p. 44.

38. Quoted in Bennett, *op. cit.*, p. 299.

39. Clark and Kirwan, *op. cit.*, p. 231.

40. William L. Evans: "The Negro in Chicago Industries," *The Black Urban Condition, op. cit.*, p. 205.

41. Hughes: *The Big Sea, op. cit.*, p. 334.
42. Clark and Kirwan, *op. cit.*, pp. 365–366.
43. Drake and Cayton, *op. cit.*, vol. 2, p. 583.
44. Giddings, *op. cit.*, p. 345.
45. See William Kelly: "Where St. Louis' Negroes Work," *The Black Urban Condition, op. cit.*, p. 161.
46. Cruse: *Plural, op. cit.*, p. 177 (italics in original).
47. Drake and Cayton, *op. cit.*, vol. 2, p. 543.
48. Meier and Rudwich: *From Plantation to Ghetto, op. cit.*, p. 240.
49. William Leuchtenburg: "The Roosevelt Reconstruction: Retrospect," *America's Recent Past*, p. 237.
50. See Myrdal: *American Dilemma, op. cit.*, pp. 258, 264, 260, 343.
51. See Everett Carl Ladd, Jr., with Charles D. Hadley: *Transformations of the American Party System*, pp. 130 and 134.
52. See Clark and Kirwan, *op. cit.*, p. 296.
53. Quoted by Bardolph, *op. cit.*, p. 202.
54. Howard Florance: "What Really Happened," *America's Recent Past, op. cit.*, p. 206.
55. Bunche, quoted in Joseph P. Lash: *Eleanor: The Years Alone*, p. 130.
56. See Lash: *Eleanor and Franklin*, p. 869.
57. Thomas Gladwin: *Poverty U.S.A.*, p. 77.
58. Harris and Wilkins: "Introduction," *Quiet Riots, op. cit.*, p. xxii.
59. Moynihan: "The Moynihan Report," *The Moynihan Report and the Politics of Controversy*, p. 63.
60. Laura Carper: "The Negro Family and the Moynihan Report," *Poverty: Views from the Left*, p. 204.
61. See Oscar Lewis: "The Cult of Poverty," *Poverty in Affluence, op. cit.*
62. Charles Valentine: *Culture and Poverty*, p. 13.
63. Gladwin, *op. cit.*, p. 97.
64. Clark, *op. cit.*, p. xxii.
65. Wilson: *The Truly Disadvantaged, op. cit.*, p. 38.
66. Thernstrom: "Is There Really a New Poor?," *Poverty: Views from the Left, op. cit.*, p. 89.
67. See Thernstrom: "Poverty in Historical Perspective," *On Understanding Poverty*, p. 179.
68. See Zahova D. Blum and Peter H. Ross: "Social Class Research and Images of the Poor: A Bibliographic Review," Appendix, *ibid.*, p. 395.
69. See Gladwin, *op. cit.*, p. 41.
70. Wilson, *op. cit.*, p. 20.
71. Otis Dudley Duncan: "Inheritance of Poverty or Inheritance of Race," *On Understanding Poverty, op. cit.*, p. 87.
72. See Kerner Commission: "Riots: Causes and Future Choices," *Poverty in Affluence, op. cit.*, p. 191.
73. Gladwin, *op. cit.*, p. 78.
74. Bennett: "The White Problem in America," *Black on Black*, p. 106.
75. Moynihan: "The Moynihan Report," *op. cit.*, p. 160.

76. Moynihan, quoted in *ibid.*, p. 51.
77. Carper, *op. cit., Poverty: Views from the Left*, p. 197.
78. Elizabeth Herzog: "Is There a Breakdown of the Negro Family?," *The Moynihan Report, op. cit.*, p. 351.
79. James Farmer, *ibid.*, p. 411.
80. See Harrington: *The New American Poverty, op. cit.*, pp. 148, 174, 179.
81. Robert Lekachman: "Between Apostles and Technicians," *The Seventies, op. cit.*, p. 85.
82. Harrington: *The New American Poverty, op. cit.*, p. 204.
83. Valentine, *op. cit.*, pp. 142 and 82.
84. Herbert Aptheker: *Afro-American History: The Modern Era*, pp. 39 and 83.
85. *Ibid.*
86. *Ibid.*, p. 258.
87. Clark, *op. cit.*, pp. 15–16.
88. *Ibid.*, p. 128.
89. Herbers, *op. cit., Quiet Riots*, p. 21.
90. Clark, *op. cit.*, pp. 15–16.
91. Wade Nobles and Lawford Goddard: "Drugs in the Afro-American Community: A Clear and Present Danger," *The State of Black America, op. cit.*, p. 175.
92. Claude Brown, quoted in Silberman: *The Moynihan Report, op. cit.*, p. 441.
93. Rap Brown, *op. cit.*, p. 25.
94. John O. Calmore: "To Make Wrong Right: The Necessary and Proper Aspirations of Fair Housing," *The State of Black America, op. cit.*, p. 88.
95. Wilson, Aponte, Kirschenman, Wacquant, *op. cit., Quiet Riots*, p. 131.
96. See Lynn Curtis: "Thomas Jefferson, the Kerner Commission and the Retreat of Folly," *ibid.*, p. 179.
97. "Conclusion," *The State of Black America, op. cit.*, p. 186.
98. Wright: "Introduction," *Black Metropolis*, vol. 1., *op. cit.*, p. xxiii.
99. Gladwin, *op. cit.*, p. 19.
100. Moynihan: "The Professionals and the Pool," *On Understanding Poverty, op. cit.*, pp. 4 and 14.
101. Gettleman and Mermelstein: *The Great Society Reader, op. cit.*, pp. 49–50.
102. Elinor Graham, *ibid.*, p. 223 (italics in original).
103. Ronald Radosh, *ibid.*, p. 292.
104. Gettleman and Mermelstein, *ibid.*, p. 179.
105. Morris Janowitz: *The Last Half Century*, pp. 465 and 469.
106. Graham: *The Great Society Reader, op. cit.*, p. 225.
107. Graham, quoted in *ibid.*, p. 175.
108. Rap Brown, *op. cit.*, p. 75.
109. Harrington: *The New American Poverty, op. cit.*, p. 21.

110. *Ibid.*, p. 15.
111. *Ibid.*, p. 76.
112. Cruse: *Plural, op. cit.*, pp. 330–331.
113. Harrington: *The New American Poverty, op. cit.*, p. 30.
114. *Ibid.*, p. 27.
115. Orfield, *op. cit., Quiet Riots*, p. 105.
116. Harrington: *The New American Poverty, op. cit.*, p. 33.
117. John Jacob: "Black America, 1988: An Overview," *The State of Black America, op. cit.*, p. 2.
118. Janowitz, *op. cit.*, p. 162.
119. Bruno Stein: *On Relief*, p. 39.
120. Harrington: *The New American Poverty, op. cit.*, pp. 174 and 148.
121. Gore Vidal: "The Second American Revolution," *The Second American Revolution and Other Essays*, p. 270.
122. Swinton, *op. cit., The State of Black America*, p. 35.
123. *Ibid.*, pp. 35–36.
124. Jacob, *op. cit., ibid.*, p. 1.
125. Adams, Duncan, Rodgers: "The Persistence of Urban Poverty," *Quiet Riots, op. cit.*, p. 86.
126. Bart Landry: *The New Black Middle Class*, pp. 108 and 148.
127. Robert Hill, quoted in Alphonso Pinkney: *The Myth of Black Progress*, p. 100.
128. See Pinkney, *ibid.*, p. 102.
129. Landry, *op. cit.*, p. 70.
130. Pinkney, *op. cit.*, p. 102.
131. Wilson, *op. cit.*, p. 109.
132. Harrington: *The New American Poverty, op. cit.*, p. 123 (italics in original).
133. Wilson, *op. cit.*, p. 111.
134. Cruse: *Plural, op. cit.*, p. 369.
135. Lesuw, Schnare, Struyk: "Housing," *The Urban Predicament, op. cit.*, p. 160.
136. Calmore, *op. cit., The State of Black America*, p. 98.
137. Pinkney, *op. cit.*, p. 83.
138. Edward C. Banfield: *The Unheavenly City*, p. 76 (italics in original).
139. Wilson, *op. cit.*, p. 110.
140. Janowitz, *op. cit.*, p. 388.
141. Cruse: *Plural, op. cit.*, p. 389 (italics in original).
142. *Ibid* (italics in original).
143. Wilson, *op. cit.*, p. 138.
144. *Ibid.*, p. 56.
145. See Valentine, *op. cit.*, pp. 113 and 129.
146. Wilson, *op. cit.*, pp. 12 and 100–102.
147. *Ibid.*, pp. 46 and 103.
148. Lloyd Warner, Marchia Mesker, Kenneth Fells: *Social Class in America*, p. 25.

149.   Orfield, *op. cit., Quiet Riots*, p. 119.
150.   James B. Conant: "Schools and Northern Negro Slums," *American Race Relations, op. cit.*, p. 155.
151.   Glazer and Moynihan, *op. cit.*, p. 46.
152.   Wilson, *op. cit.*, p. 43.
153.   *Ibid.*, p. 100.
154.   *Ibid.*, p. 12.
155.   See Riis: *How the Other Half Lives*, p. 112.
156.   Stein, *op. cit.*, p. 37.
157.   *Ibid.*, p. 32.
158.   Quoted in Harrington: *The New American Poverty, op. cit.*, p. 68.
159.   Pinkney, *op. cit.*, p. 2.
160.   Kovel, *op. cit.*, pp. 212 and 217.
161.   Ellison: *Invisible Man, op. cit.*, p. 382.
162.   Joel Williamson: *New People*, p. 62.
163.   DuBois: "The Dusk of Dawn," *Black on Black, op. cit.*, p. 32.
164.   James Boggs: "The Revolutionary Struggle for Black Power," *The Black Seventies*, p. 42.
165.   George Jackson: "Letter to Fay Stender," June 12, 1970, *Soledad Brother*, p. 277.
166.   George Jackson: *Blood in My Eye*, p. 51.
167.   Sidney M. Wilhelm, Edwin Powell, quoted in Lincoln: *Sounds of the Struggle, op. cit.*, p. 186.
168.   Baldwin: *No Name in the Street*, p. 129.
169.   Nobles and Goddard, *op. cit., The State of Black America*, p. 179.
170.   George Cain: *Blueschild Baby*, pp. 116 and 138.
171.   *Ibid.*
172.   Price M. Cobbs: "Valuing Diversity: The Myth and the Challenge," *The State of Black America, op. cit.*, p. 155.

Chapter 4: Self-help and Community

1.   Meier: "Frederick Douglass's Vision for America: A Case History in Nineteenth-Century Negro Protest," Meier and Rudwick: *Along the Color Line, op. cit.*, p. 9.
2.   Benjamin Quarles: *Frederick Douglass*, p. 101.
3.   Brawley: *Negro Builders and Heroes*, p. 66.
4.   Quoted in Meier, *op. cit., Along the Color Line*, p. 22.
5.   *Syracuse Daily Standard*, quoted in Quarles, *op. cit.*, p. 102.
6.   Quarles, *ibid.*, p. viii.
7.   *Ibid.*, p. 272.
8.   Quoted in *ibid.*, p. 148.
9.   Quoted in *ibid.*, p. 221.
10.   Quoted in Brawley: *Negro Builders and Heroes, op. cit.*, p. 65.
11.   Quoted in *ibid.*, p. 91.

12. Booker T. Washington: *Up from Slavery*, p. 198 (italics in original).

13. DuBois, quoted in Bennett: *Before the Mayflower, op. cit.*, p. 279.

14. Washington, quoted in Brawley: *A Social History of the American Negro, op. cit.*, p. 304.

15. See Meier: "Booker T. Washington: An Interpretation," *Black History, op. cit.*, p. 343.

16. Harlan, *op. cit.*, p. 85.

17. Washington, *op. cit.*, p. 119.

18. Washington, quoted in Meier: *Negro Thought in America, op. cit.*, p. 83.

19. Washington: "Cast Down Your Bucket Where You Are," *Negro Protest Thought, op. cit.*, p. 15.

20. Harlan, *op. cit.*, p. 204.

21. Meier: *Negro Thought in America, op. cit.*, p. 93.

22. See Cruse: *Crisis, op. cit.*, p. 18.

23. Washington, quoted in Meier: *Negro Thought in America, op. cit.*, p. 106.

24. DuBois: *The Souls of Black Folk, op. cit.*, p. 43.

25. See Harlan, *op. cit.*, p. 22.

26. DuBois, quoted in "Preface," *ibid.*, p. x.

27. *New York Evening Post*, quoted in *ibid.*, p. 363.

28. Harlan: "Preface," *ibid.*, p. 244.

29. *Ibid.*, p. 244.

30. See *ibid.*, pp. 26, 49, 104, 95.

31. See Meier: "Booker T. Washington and the Negro Press"; "Booker T. Washington and the Rise of the NAACP," *Along the Color Line, op. cit.*, p. 61.

32. Meier: *Negro Thought in America, op. cit.*, p. 228.

33. Harlan, *op. cit.*, p. 33.

34. *Ibid.*, p. 50.

35. Washington, quoted in *ibid.*, p. 34.

36. Meier: *Negro Thought in America, op. cit.*, p. 257.

37. Washington: *Negro Protest Thought, op. cit.*, p. 5.

38. See Stokely Carmichael and Charles V. Hamilton: *Black Power*, p. 134.

39. Harlan, *op. cit.*, p. 26.

40. Monroe Trotter, *Boston Guardian*, Dec. 20, 1902, *Negro Protest Thought, op. cit.*, p. 27.

41. Harlan, *op. cit.*, p. 24.

42. Washington, quoted in Brawley: *Negro Builders and Heroes, op. cit.*, p. 151.

43. Washington: *Negro Protest Thought, op. cit.*, p. 14.

44. DuBois: *Against Racism, op. cit.*, p. 138.

45. See Harlam, *op. cit.*, p. 218.

46. Frazier: *On Race Relations, op. cit.*, p. 315.

47. Harlan, *op. cit.*, p. 226.

48. Dubois, quoted in Frazier: *The Negro in the United States, op. cit.,* p. 460.
49. Washington: *Up from Slavery, op. cit.,* p. 142.
50. Harlan, *op. cit.,* p. 205.
51. *Ibid.,* pp. 187f and 190.
52. *Ibid.,* pp. 321, 310, 384.
53. *Ibid.,* p. 248.
54. See DuBois, quoted in *ibid.,* p. x.
55. DuBois: *The Souls of Black Folk, op. cit.,* p. 150.
56. Dubois: *Against Racism, op. cit.,* p. 114.
57. See Frazier: *The Black Bourgeoisie,* p. 26 and *passim.*
58. Lomax, *op. cit.,* p. 54.
59. Frazier: *The Negro in the United States, op. cit.,* pp. 289 and 298.
60. See Cruse: "Revolutionary Nationalism and the Afro American," *op. cit., Black Fire,* p. 56.
61. Landry, *op. cit.,* pp. 25 (italics in original) and 30.
62. See Frazier: *The Black Bourgeoisie, op. cit.,* p. 69.
63. Frazier: *On Race Relations, op. cit.,* pp. 263 and 287.
64. Landry, *op. cit.,* p. 39.
65. Myrdal: *An American Dilemma, op. cit.,* p. 885.
66. See Rudwick and Meier: "Attorneys Black and White: A Case Study of Race Relations Within the NAACP," *Along the Color Line, op. cit.,* pp. 130, 134, 156.
67. Frazier: *The Black Bourgeoisie, op. cit.,* pp. 108–109.
68. DuBois: *Against Racism, op. cit.,* pp. 297, 139, 149.
69. See Jean Toomer: "Natalie Mann," *The Wayward and the Seeking,* pp. 255f.
70. Landry, *op. cit.,* pp. 64 and 59.
71. Ellison: "Introduction," *Shadow and Act, op. cit.,* p. xx.
72. DuBois: *The Gift of Black Folk,* pp. 327–328.
73. DuBois, quoted in Frazier, *The Negro in the United States, op. cit.,* p. 334.
74. Frazier, *ibid.,* p. 18.
75. Margaret Walker: *Jubilee,* p. 46.
76. DuBois: *Against Racism, op. cit.,* p. 153.
77. Meier: *Negro Thought in America, op. cit.,* p. 218.
78. Brawley: *A Social History of the American Negro, op. cit.,* p. 66.
79. Charles V. Hamilton: *The Black Preacher in America,* p. 21.
80. Drake and Cayton, *op. cit.,* vol. 2, p. 679.
81. Rudolph Fisher: "Vestige," *The New Negro, op. cit.,* and "Revival," *ibid.,* p. 90.
82. Maya Angelou: *Singin and Swingin and Gettin' Merry Like Christmas,* p. 33.
83. Cleage: *op. cit.,* p. 5.
84. Frazier, quoted in Hamilton, *op. cit.,* p. 116.
85. James A. Joseph: "Has Black Religion Lost Its Soul?," *The Black Seventies, op. cit.,* p. 73.

86. Cleage, *op. cit.*, pp. 85 and 113.
87. E. David Cronan: *Black Moses*, p. 179.
88. DuBois, quoted in Harlan, *op. cit.*, p. 300.
89. Daisy Bates: "The Long Shadow of Little Rock," *Growing Up Black, op. cit.*, p. 35.
90. Quoted in Giddings, *op. cit.*, p. 97.
91. Giddings: *In Search of Sisterhood*, p. 107.

Chapter 5: Agitation for Civic Equality

1. Larry Neal: "New Space: The Growth of Black Consciousness in the Sixties," *The Black Seventies, op. cit.*, p. 15.
2. Carmichael: "Toward Black Liberation," *op. cit., Black Fire*, p. 128.
3. Roland Barthes: *Writing Degree Zero*, p. 58.
4. Myrdal: "Preface," *An American Dilemma, op. cit.*, p. lxxvii (italics in original).
5. *Ibid.*, p. 928.
6. Ellison: *Shadow and Act, op. cit.*, p. 313 (italics in original).
7. Giddings: *When and Where I Enter, op. cit.*, p. 295.
8. Carmichael: "Toward Black Liberation," *op. cit., Black Fire*, p. 125.
9. Noble, *op. cit.*, p. 275.
10. Saul Bellow: *The Dean's December*, p. 207.
11. Malcolm X: *Autobiography of Malcolm X*, pp. 245–46.
12. Carmichael and Hamilton: "The Concept of Black Power," *The Social Rebel in American Literature*, p. 100 (italics in original).
13. Malcolm X: *The Speeches of Malcolm X*, p. 34.
14. Cruse: *Crisis, op. cit.*, p. 548.
15. Cruse: *Plural, op. cit., passim.*
16. DuBois, quoted in Marable, *op. cit.*, p. 160.
17. Washington: "The Future of the American Negro," *Negro Protest and Thought, op. cit.*, p. 15.
18. DuBois: "An Open Letter to the Southern People," *Against Racism, op. cit.*, p. 20.
19. DuBois: *Autobiography, op. cit.*, p. 264.
20. Washington: *Up from Slavery, op. cit.*, p. 25.
21. DuBois: *Autobiography, op. cit.*, p. 297.
22. DuBois: "Crisis, April, 1934," *Black Nationalism in America*, p. 291.
23. DuBois: *Autobiography, op. cit.*, p. 136.
24. DuBois, quoted in Rampersad, *op. cit.*, p. 62.
25. DuBois: *The Gift of Black Folk, op. cit.*, p. 339.
26. DuBois: *The Souls of Black Folk, op. cit.*, p. 22.
27. DuBois: *Autobiography, op. cit.*, p. 120.
28. Lincoln: "The Black Muslims in America," *op. cit., American Race Relations*, pp. 181–182.
29. M. G. Cooke: "Introduction," *Modern Black Novelists*, p. 9.

30. DuBois: *Autobiography, op. cit.*, p. 75.
31. *Ibid.*, p. 71.
32. *Ibid.*, pp. 75 and 79.
33. Rampersad, *op. cit.*, p. 1.
34. *Ibid.*, p. 67.
35. DuBois: *Autobiography, op. cit.*, p. 243.
36. DuBois: "My Evolving Program for Negro Freedom," *What the Negro Wants, op. cit.*, pp. 58–59.
37. DuBois: *Against Racism*, pp. 145–146.
38. *Ibid.*, p. 17.
39. DuBois: *Autobiography, op. cit.*, p. 411.
40. DuBois: "My Evolving Program for Negro Freedom," *op. cit., What the Negro Wants*, p. 36.
41. DuBois: *Autobiography, op. cit.*, p. 296.
42. DuBois: *The Souls of Black Folk, op. cit.*, p. 138.
43. DuBois: *Autobiography, op. cit.*, p. 63.
44. DuBois: "The Spirit of Modern Europe," *Against Racism, op. cit.*, p. 60.
45. *Ibid.*, pp. 67–68.
46. DuBois, quoted in Bontemps: *One Hundred Years of Negro Freedom*, p. 193.
47. DuBois: *Autobiography, op. cit.*, p. 335.
48. *Ibid.*, p. 393.

Chapter 6: Black Communality and Black Urban Militance

1. Glazer: "Introduction," *Cities in Trouble, op. cit.*, p. 9.
2. Quoted in Cruse: *Plural, op. cit.*, pp. 216–217.
3. DuBois: "Dusk of Dawn," *op. cit., Black on Black*, p. 32.
4. Baraka: *Home, op. cit.*, p. 114.
5. Baldwin: *Nobody Knows My Name*, p. 29.
6. Lomax, *op. cit.*, p. 64.
7. James Weldon Johnson: "The Book of Negro Poets," *Voices from the Harlem Renaissance*, p. 288.
8. Clark: "Introduction," *op. cit.*, p. xxiii (italics in original).
9. Glazer and Moynihan, *op. cit.*, p. 27.
10. Hughes: "Esthete in Harlem," *Voices from the Harlem Renaissance*, p. 98.
11. Drake and Cayton, *op. cit.*, vol. 2, p. 654.
12. Marable, *op. cit.*, p. 227.
13. Frazier: *Negro Youth at the Crossroads, op. cit.*, pp. 46, 78, 49.
14. See Silberman: *Crisis in Black and White, op. cit.*, p. 231.
15. Swinton: "The Economic Status of Black America," *op. cit., The State of Black America*, p. 37.
16. Thomas R. Brooks: *Walls Come Tumbling Down*, p. 277.
17. Hosea Williams, quoted in Marable, *op. cit.*, p. 209.

18. Maurice Charney: "James Baldwin's Quarrel with Richard Wright," *Five Black Writers*, p. 251.
19. Baldwin: "Many Thousands Gone: Richard Wright's 'Native Son,' " *Images of the Negro in American Literature*, pp. 241f.
20. Robert Bone: "The Novels of James Baldwin," *ibid.*, p. 280.
21. Lyndon Johnson: Howard University Address, June 4, 1965, *The Moynihan Report and the Politics of Controversy, op. cit.*, p. 130.
22. Gans: "The Negro Family: Reflections on the Moynihan Report," *ibid.*, p. 451.
23. Nobles and Goddard: "Drugs in the Afro-American Community," *op. cit., The State of Black America*, p. 179 (see also note 169, ch. 3).
24. Giovanni: *A Poetic Equation: Conversations Between Nikki Giovanni and Margaret Walker*, p. 105.
25. Ethel Waters: "His Eye Is on the Sparrow," *Growing Up Black, op. cit.*, p. 160.
26. Clark, *op. cit.*, p. 109.
27. Rainwater and Yancey: *The Moynihan Report and the Politics of Controversy, op. cit.*, p. 31.
28. Huey P. Newton: *Revolutionary Suicide*, p. 260.
29. Malcolm X: *Autobiography, op. cit.*, p. 169.
30. *Ibid.*, p. 183.
31. George Jackson: Letter, June 10, 1970, *Soledad Brother, op. cit.*, p. 27.
32. George Jackson: Letter to Fay Stender, April 1970, *ibid.*, p. 49.
33. Eldridge Cleaver: *Soul on Ice*, pp. 17 and 186.
34. Reich, *op. cit.*, p. 255 (italics in original).
35. George Jackson: Letter to His Mother, June 29, 1968, *Soledad Brother, op. cit.*, p. 168.
36. "Preface," *ibid.*, p. 8.
37. George Jackson: Letter, June 10, 1970, *ibid.*, p. 40.
38. Angela Davis: *An Autobiography*, pp. 253 and 305.
39. Knight: *Black Voices from Prison, op. cit.*, p. 15.
40. *Ibid.*, p. 23.
41. Saunders Redding: "The Alien Land of Richard Wright," *Five Black Writers, op. cit.*, p. 6.
42. Giovanni: *A Poetic Equation, op. cit.*, pp. 30 and 33 (italics in original).
43. Baldwin: "Many Thousands Gone," *Notes of a Native Son*, p. 42.
44. Chester Himes: "Dilemma of the Negro Novelist in the United States," *Beyond the Angry Black*, p. 56.
45. Redding: "No Day of Triumph," *Black Voices*, p. 301.
46. See Alice Walker: *The Color Purple*, p. 87.
47. Wright: *Black Boy*, p. 65.
48. Malcolm X: *Autobiography, op. cit.*, p. 251 (italics in original).
49. William Faulkner: *The Mansion*, p. 299.
50. Hughes: *The Big Sea, op. cit.*, p. 39.
51. Quoted in Giddings: *When and Where I Enter, op. cit.*, p. 102.
52. Zora Neale Hurston: *Mules and Men*, p. 85.

53. "Glossary," *ibid.*, pp. 254–255.
54. Malcolm X: *Autobiography, op. cit.*, p. 311.
55. See Baldwin: "In Search of a Majority," *Nobody Knows My Name, op. cit.*, p. 131.
56. Knight: *Black Voices from Prison, op. cit.*, p. 183.
57. Norman O. Brown: *Life Against Death, op. cit.*, pp. 302, 290, 235.
58. See Kardiner and Ovesey: "Psychodynamic Inventory," *Beyond the Angry Black, op. cit.*, p. 96.
59. Rudwick and Meier: "Black Violence in the Twentieth Century," *op. cit., Along the Color Line*, p. 229.
60. Quoted in Harlan, *op. cit.*, p. 34.
61. Locke: "The New Negro," *Voices from the Harlem Renaissance, op. cit.*, p. 52.
62. Locke: "The New Negro," *op. cit., The New Negro*, pp. 1, 10, 11.
63. *Ibid.*, p. 11 (see also notes 23 and 24, ch. 3).
64. Locke: "The Legacy of the Ancestral Arts," *ibid.*, pp. 254–255.
65. Locke: "Negro Youth Speaks," *ibid.*, p. 51.
66. See Frazier: "Durham: Capital of the Black Middle Class," *ibid.*, pp. 333f.
67. Frazier, quoted in Cruse, *Crisis, op. cit.*, p. 156.
68. Cruse, *ibid.*, pp. 84 and 52.
69. George Kent: "Patterns of the Harlem Renaissance," *The Harlem Renaissance Remembered*, p. 48.
70. Warrington Hudlin: "The Renaissance Re-examined," *ibid.*, p. 275.
71. Marcus Garvey: "Aims of the Universal Negro Improvement Association," *Negro Protest Thought, op. cit.*, p. 85.
72. *Ibid.*, p. 86.
73. *Ibid.*, p. 91.
74. Locke, quoted in Cronan, *op. cit.*, p. 186.
75. See Cronan, *Ibid.*, p. 212.
76. *Ibid.*, p. 107.
77. J. W. Johnson: "Marcus Garvey," *American Literature by Negro Authors*, p. 177.
78. McKay, quoted in Cruse, *Crisis, op. cit.*, p. 58.
79. DuBois: *Autobiography, op. cit.*, p. 273.
80. Malcolm X, quoted in Eugene Victor Wolfenstein: *The Victims of Democracy: Malcolm X and the Black Revolution*, p. 311.
81. Cronan: "Marcus Garvey: "One Aim! One God! One Destiny!," *Black History, op. cit.*, p. 404.
82. Cronan: *Black Moses, op. cit.*, p. 13.
83. *Ibid.*, p. 16.
84. Harlan, *op. cit.*, p. 281; Cronan: *Black Moses, op. cit.*, p. 70.
85. Cronan: *ibid.*, pp. 52, 61, 79.
86. Cruse: *Crisis, op. cit.*, p. 332.
87. Cronan: *Black Moses, op. cit.*, p. 121.
88. Garvey, quoted in Marable: *op. cit.*, p. 63.

89. Locke, quoted in Cronan: *Black Moses, op. cit.,* p. 186.

90. Arthur S. Link: *American Epoch,* p. 245.

91. Kelly Miller, quoted in Cronan: *Black Moses, op. cit.,* p. 143.

92. Quoted in *ibid.,* p. 143.

93. Cruse: *Crisis, op. cit.,* p. 294.

94. Locke: "The New Negro," *op. cit., Voices from the Harlem Renaissance,* p. 53.

95. Cronan: *Black Moses, op. cit.,* p. 203.

96. See Cruse: *Crisis, op. cit.,* pp. 40, 45, 172, 286.

97. A. Philip Randolph: "The Messenger, Dec. 1919," *Negro Protest Thought, op. cit.,* p. 79.

98. Randolph, quoted in Cruse: *Crisis, op. cit.,* p. 172.

99. Cruse, *ibid.,* p. 329.

100. Randolph: "Second National Negro Congress," *Negro Protest Thought,* p. 203.

101. Bontemps: *One Hundred Years of Negro Freedom, op. cit.,* p. 238.

102. Randolph, quoted in Marable: *op. cit.,* p. 83.

103. Marable, *ibid.,* p. 84.

104. Wolfenstein, *op. cit.,* p. 180.

105. Randolph: "National Negro Congress Leaflet, 1940," *Negro Protest Thought, op. cit.,* p. 198.

106. Randolph: "March on Washington Presents a Program for Negroes," *What the Negro Wants, op. cit.,* p. 135.

107. Randolph: "National Negro Congress Leaflet, 1940," *op. cit., Negro Protest Thought,* p. 198.

108. "March on Washington," *op. cit.,* p. 137.

109. See Drake and Cayton, *op. cit.,* vol. 2, pp. 745 and 754.

110. "NAACP Report 1919," *Negro Protest Thought, op. cit.,* p. 65 (italics in original).

111. DuBois: *Autobiography, op. cit.,* pp. 326 and 334.

112. Marable, *op. cit.,* p. 164.

113. E. U. Essien-Udom: *Black Nationalism,* p. 45.

114. Meier and Rudwick: "The Origins of Nonviolent Direct Acion in Afro-American Protest: A Note on Historical Discontinuities," *Along the Color Line, op. cit.,* p. 315.

115. *Ibid.,* p. 323.

116. Meier and Rudwick: "Integration vs. Segregation: The NAACP and CORE Face a Challenge from Within," *ibid.,* pp. 242 and 251.

117. See *Negro Protest Thought, op. cit.,* p. 212.

118. Baldwin, quoted in Richard Dalfiume: "The 'Forgotten Years' of the Negro Revolution," *America's Recent Past, op. cit.,* p. 309.

119. Andrew Hacker: *The End of the American Era,* p. 97.

120. Alfred Kazin: *A Walker in the City,* p. 141.

121. Drake and Cayton, *op. cit.,* vol. 2, p. 754.

122. *Ibid.,* vol. 1, p. 111.

123. *Ibid.,* vol. 2, p. 754.

124. Baldwin, quoted in Dalfiume, *op. cit., America's Recent Past,* p. 309.
125. John G. Killens: *And Then We Heard the Thunder,* p. 202.
126. Maxwell Geismar: "The Shifting Illusion," *American Dreams, American Nightmares,* p. 57.
127. Essien-Udom, *op. cit.,* p. 55.
128. *Ibid.,* p. 211.
129. Lincoln: *The Black Muslims,* p. 247.
130. See Essien-Udom, *op. cit.,* pp. 153 and 155.
131. *Ibid.,* p. 80.
132. *Ibid.,* p. 167.
133. *Ibid.,* p. 184.
134. Quoted in *ibid.,* p. 255.
135. Essien-Udom, *ibid.,* pp. 256 and 182.
136. *Ibid.,* p. 66.
137. Lincoln: *Signs of the Struggle, op. cit.,* pp. 57–58.
138. Bellow: *Herzog,* p. 67 (italics in original).
139. See Lincoln: *The Black Muslims, op. cit.,* p. 115.
140. *Ibid.,* p. 100.
141. William James: *Varieties of Religious Experience,* p. 186.
142. Essien-Udom, *op. cit.,* p. 185.
143. *Ibid.,* p. 71.
144. Cleage, *op. cit.,* p. 178 (see also notes 76 and 77, ch. 2).

Chapter 7: The Black Movement of the Sixties

1. Landry, *op. cit.,* p. 72.
2. Giddings: *When and Where I Enter, op. cit.,* pp. 270–271.
3. Ladd and Hadley: *Transformation of the American Party System, op. cit.,* p. 223.
4. Ellison: *Shadow and Act, op. cit.,* p. 297.
5. Marcuse: *La Fin de l'Utopie, op. cit.,* p. 112 (author's translation).
6. See Jesse Pitts: "The Counter-Culture," *The Seventies, op. cit.,* pp. 132–133.
7. *Ibid.*
8. Bobby Seale: *Seize the Time,* p. 365.
9. See James Forman: *The Making of Black Revolutionaries,* pp. 437 and 476.
10. Hosea Williams, quoted in David J. Garrow: *Bearing the Cross,* p. 548.
11. Marcuse: *L'Homme Unidimensionnel, op. cit.,* p. 241 (author's translation; italics in original).
12. *Ibid.,* p. 254 (author's translation).
13. Marcuse: *La Fin de l'Utopie, op. cit.,* p. 43.
14. See Jean-Michel Palmier: *Marcuse et la Nouvelle Gauche,* p. 467.
15. Anton C. Zijderveld: *The Abstract Society,* p. 132.
16. Joan Didion: *The White Album,* p. 39.
17. Martin Luther King, Jr.: "The Rising Tide of Racial Consciousness," *A*

Testament of Hope: The Essential Writings of Martin Luther King, Jr., p. 145.

18. Giddings: *When and Where I Enter, op. cit.*, pp. 271f.
19. Ellison: "Introduction," *Shadow and Act, op. cit.*, p. xv.
20. Charles U. Smith: "The Sit-ins and the New Negro Student," *American Race Relations Today*, p. 71.
21. Brooks, *op. cit.*, p. 282.
22. King: "Looking for New Industry," *A Testament of Hope, op. cit.*, p. 115.
23. *Brown v. Board of Education of Topeka*, 1954, quoted by Anthony Lewis in *The New York Times: Portrait of a Decade*, p. 24.
24. Chief Justice Earl Warren, quoted in *ibid.*, p. 29.
25. King, quoted by Garrow, *op. cit.*, p. 56.
26. King, quoted by Bennett: *What Manner of Man*, p. 60.
27. King: "The Strength to Live," *A Testament of Hope, op. cit.*, p. 508.
28. See Jerry Tallmer: "A Man with a Hard Head," *Martin Luther King, Jr.: A Profile*, p. 4.
29. Bennett: *What Manner of Man, op. cit.*, p. 61.
30. See Martin Luther King, Sr.: *An Autobiography*, p. 82.
31. Cruse: *Plural, op. cit.*, p. 224.
32. Bennett: *What Manner of Man, op. cit.*, p. 193.
33. William Robert Miller: "The Broadening Horizons: Montgomery, America, the World," *King: A Profile, op. cit.*, p. 65.
34. King: "Stride Toward Freedom," *A Testament of Hope, op. cit.*, p. 428.
35. Forman, *op. cit.*, p. 85.
36. See Garrow, *op. cit.*, p. 85.
37. King: "Love, Law, and Civil Disobedience," *A Testament of Hope, op. cit.*, p. 45.
38. James Washington: "Introduction," *ibid.*, p. xiv.
39. King: "The Power of Nonviolence," *ibid.*, p. 14.
40. King: "Love, Law, and Civil Disobedience," *ibid.*, p. 49.
41. Clark: "Interview," *ibid.*, p. 331.
42. King, *ibid.*, p. 334.
43. King: "Nonviolence: The Only Way to Freedom," *ibid.*, p. 58.
44. King: "The Burning Tide in the South," *ibid.*, p. 97.
45. King, quoted in Bennett: *What Manner of Man, op. cit.*, p. 65.
46. "Playboy Interview," *A Testament of Hope, op. cit.*, p. 365.
47. Meier: "Conservative Militant," *King: A Profile, op. cit.*, p. 146.
48. Vincent Harding: "The Crisis of Powerless Morality," *ibid.*, p. 184.
49. See Meier, *op. cit., ibid.*, p. 147.
50. Garrow, *op. cit.*, p. 276.
51. NAACP woman worker, quoted in Reese Cleghorn: "Crowned with Crisis," *King: A Profile, op. cit.*, p. 125.
52. King: "Equal Now: The President Has the Power," *A Testament of Hope, op. cit.*, p. 155.
53. Brooks, *op. cit.*, p. 169.

54. Garrow, *op. cit.,* p. 264.
55. King: "Where Do We Go from Here?," *A Testament of Hope, op. cit.,* p. 576.
56. Cruse: *Plural, op. cit.,* p. 242 (see also notes 72–85, ch. 4).
57. Lincoln: "Introduction," *King: A Profile, op. cit.,* p. xiii.
58. King: "Stride Toward Freedom," *Negro Protest Thought, op. cit.,* p. 265.
59. Bunche, quoted in Myrdal: *An American Dilemma, op. cit.,* p. 808.
60. King, quoted in Garrow, *op. cit.,* p. 47.
61. King, quoted in *ibid.,* p. 91.
62. King, quoted in *ibid.,* p. 273.
63. King, quoted in Lewis M. Killian: *The Impossible Revolution?,* p. 75.
64. King, quoted in Garrow, *op. cit.,* p. 540.
65. Malcolm X: *Autobiography, op. cit.,* p. 364.
66. King, quoted in Garrow, *op. cit.,* p. 563.
67. Quoted in *ibid.,* p. 572.
68. King, quoted in *ibid.,* p. 564.
69. King, quoted in David Halberstam: "When 'Civil Rights' and 'Peace' Join Forces," *King: A Profile, op. cit.,* p. 202.
70. King, quoted in *ibid.*
71. King, quoted in Garrow, *op. cit.,* p. 546.
72. King, quoted in *ibid.* p. 696.
73. King, quoted in *ibid.* p. 592.
74. Clark, *op. cit.,* p. 218.
75. Forman, *op. cit.,* p. 336.
76. Malcolm X, quoted in *ibid.,* p. 333.
77. Forman, *ibid.,* pp. 315 and 255.
78. Hosea Williams, quoted in Garrow, *op. cit.,* p. 547.
79. King: *A Testament of Hope, op. cit.,* p. 404.
80. See Garrow, *op. cit.,* p. 553.
81. Quoted in *ibid.,* p. 602.
82. Meier: "Conservative Militant," *op. cit., King: A Profile,* p. 155.
83. Julius Lester: *Search for the New Land,* p. 154.
84. Cruse: *Plural, op. cit.,* pp. 223–224.
85. Forman: *op. cit.,* p. 216.
86. *Ibid.,* p. 148.
87. *Ibid.,* p. 376.
88. *Ibid.,* p. 362.
89. *Ibid.,* p. 237.
90. Lewis, *op. cit.,* p. 130.
91. Rap Brown, *op. cit.,* p. 61.
92. Schlesinger, quoted in Forman, *op. cit.,* p. 382.
93. Forman, *ibid.,* pp. 460 and 470.
94. Rap Brown, *op. cit.,* pp. 53 and 63.
95. Forman, *op. cit.,* p. 381.
96. See Brooks, *op. cit.,* p. 259.
97. See Forman, *op. cit.,* p. 496.

98. Giovanni: *A Poetic Equation, op. cit.,* p. 120.
99. See Forman, *op. cit.,* p. 521.
100. *Ibid.,* p. 435.
101. Halberstam, quoted in Harry S. Ashmore: *Hearts and Minds,* p. 382.
102. Forman, *op. cit.,* pp. 376–377.
103. Carmichael and Hamilton, *op. cit.,* p. 38.
104. Rap Brown, *op. cit.,* p. 130.
105. See Forman, *op. cit.,* p. 451.
106. King: "Black Power Defined," *A Testament of Hope, op. cit.,* p. 307.
107. "The Trumpet of Conscience," *ibid.,* p. 651.
108. Kilson, *op. cit.,* p. 247.
109. Killian, *op. cit.,* p. 105.
110. Forman, *op. cit.,* pp. 456 and 446.
111. Angela Davis, *op. cit.,* p. 170.
112. Hosea Williams, quoted in Garrow, *op. cit.,* p. 547.
113. Gladwin, *op. cit.,* p. 35.
114. Brooks, *op. cit.,* p. 239.
115. Quoted in Palmier, *op. cit.,* p. 508 (author's translation).
116. Norman O. Brown, *op. cit.,* p. 292.
117. See Marcuse: *La Fin de l'Utopie, op. cit.,* p. 17 (see also notes 11–16, ch. 7).
118. George Jackson: *Blood in My Eye, op. cit.,* p. 44.
119. Cleage, *op. cit.,* p. 12.
120. *Ibid.,* p. 131 (see also notes 76 and 77, ch. 2; notes 83–86, ch. 4; notes 142–144, ch. 6).
121. *Ibid.,* pp. 35 and 28.
122. Baraka: "The Last Days of the American Empire," *Black Writers of America,* p. 754 (italics in original).
123. See *Black Nationalism in America, op. cit.,* p. 1.
124. Angela Davis, *op. cit.,* p. 374.
125. Giovanni: *Gemini, op. cit.,* p. 107.
126. Stephen Schneck: "LeRoi Jones, or Poetics and Policemen, or Trying Heart, Bleeding Heart," *Five Black Writers, op. cit.,* p. 194.
127. Cruse: *Crisis, op. cit.,* p. 466.
128. Baraka: *Daggers and Javelins,* p. 46.
129. *Ibid.,* p. 109.
130. *Ibid.,* p. 112.
131. Seale, *op. cit.,* p. 271.
132. *Ibid.,* p. 238.
133. Angela Davis, *op. cit.,* p. 150.
134. Thomas Landess and Richard Quinn: *Jesse Jackson and the Politics of Race,* p. 75.
135. Gwendolyn Brooks: *Report from Part 1,* p. 204.
136. *Ibid.,* p. 205.
137. Quoted in Landess and Quinn, *op. cit.,* p. 77.
138. Cleaver, quoted in Reginald Major: *A Panther Is a Black Cat,* p. 71.

139. See Seale, *op. cit.*, p. 4.
140. Newton, *op. cit.*, p. 53.
141. *Ibid.*, p. 66.
142. Newton: *In Search of Common Ground: Conversations with Erik H. Erikson and Huey P. Newton*, p. 87.
143. Quoted in Major, *op. cit.*, p. 60.
144. Seale, *op. cit.*, pp. 99 and 139.
145. See Major, *op. cit.*, pp. 12 and 24.
146. Seale, *op. cit.*, p. 72.
147. *Ibid.*, p. 63.
148. Newton: *Revolutionary Suicide, op. cit.*, p. 135.
149. Seale, *op. cit.*, p. 63.
150. *Ibid.*, p. 125.
151. Newton: *Revolutionary Suicide, op. cit.*, p. 122.
152. Newton: *In Search of Common Ground, op. cit.*, p. 23.
153. Jervis Andersen: "The Agonies of Black Militancy," *The Seventies, op. cit.*, p. 295.
154. Don A. Schanche: *The Panther Paradox*, p. 164.
155. "Foreword," *ibid.*, p. ix.
156. Thomas Brooks, *op. cit.*, p. 272.
157. Lester, *op. cit.*, p. 154.
158. Newton: *Revolutionary Suicide, op. cit.*, p. 106.
159. Newton, quoted in Seale, *op. cit.*, p. 117.
160. Seale's Random House editor, *ibid.*, p. 23 note.
161. Newton: *In Search of Common Ground, op. cit.*, p. 27 (italics in original).
162. *Ibid.*, p. 28.
163. George Jackson: *Blood in My Eye, op. cit.*, p. 11.
164. Newton: *Revolutionary Suicide, op. cit.*, p. 70.
165. Newton: *In Search of Common Ground, op. cit.*, p. 30.
166. See George Jackson: *Blood in My Eye, op. cit.*, p. 187.
167. Newton: *In Search of Common Ground, op. cit.*, p. 37.
168. *Ibid.*, p. 36.
169. *Ibid.*, p. 35.
170. Newton: *Revolutionary Suicide, op. cit.*, p. 113.
171. Seale, *op. cit.*, p. 4.
172. Cleaver, quoted in Schanche, *op. cit.*, p. 43.
173. Newton: *Revolutionary Suicide, op. cit.*, p. 76.
174. Tom Wolfe: "Radical Chic," *Radical Chic and Mau-Mauing the Flak Catchers*, p. 42.
175. Newton: *Revolutionary Suicide, op. cit.*, p. 4.
176. *Ibid.*, p. 5.
177. Forman, *op. cit.*, p. 538.
178. Major, *op. cit.*, p. 162.
179. *Ibid.*, p. 157.

180. Wolfenstein, *op. cit.*, p. 344.
181. Quoted in Major, *op. cit.*, p. 158.
182. Newton: *Revolutionary Suicide, op. cit.*, p. 120.
183. Major, *op. cit.*, pp. 57, 104, 109; see Schange, pp. 165 and 221.
184. Major, *op. cit.*, p. 178.
185. *Ibid.*, p. 33.
186. *Ibid.*, p. 32.
187. Cruse: *Plural, op. cit.*, pp. 222–223.
188. Max Stanford: "Revolutionary Action Movement Manifesto," *Black Nationalism in America, op. cit.*, p. 512.
189. Stanford: "Letter from Jail," 1968, *ibid.*, p. 515.
190. See *ibid.*, pp. 518–520.
191. *Ibid.*, pp. 551–553.
192. Wolfenstein, *op. cit.*, p. 367.
193. Harry B. Shaw: *Gwendolyn Brooks*, p. 76.
194. Seale, *op. cit.*, p. 4; see note 139, ch. 7.
195. Malcolm X: *Autobiography, op. cit.*, p. 153.
196. Archie Epps: "Introduction," *The Speeches of Malcolm X, op. cit.*, p. 58.
197. Malcolm X, quoted in "Epilogue," *Autobiography, op. cit.*, p. 391.
198. Malcolm X: *ibid.*, p. 125.
199. Malcolm X: speech at Harvard, March 24, 1961, *The Speeches of Malcolm X, op. cit.*, pp. 115–116.
200. *Ibid.*, p. 118.
201. Malcolm X: *Autobiography, op. cit.*, p. 269.
202. *Ibid.*, p. 12 (italics in original).
203. *Ibid.*, pp. 26–27 (italics in original)
204. *Ibid.*, p. 36.
205. *Ibid.*, p. 43.
206. *Ibid.*, p. 90.
207. *Ibid.*, p. 139.
208. *Ibid.*, p. 2.
209. *Ibid.*, p. 31.
210. Wolfenstein, *op. cit.*, p. 14.
211. Malcolm X: *Autobiography, op. cit.*, p. 15.
212. *Ibid.*, p. 187; see Wolfenstein, *op. cit.*, p. 204.
213. Malcolm X: *Autobiography, op. cit.*, pp. 75 and 287.
214. *Ibid.*, p. 163.
215. Malcolm X, quoted in Wolfenstein, *op. cit.*, p. 291.
216. Malcolm X: "The Ballot or the Bullet," speech in Cleveland, April 3, 1964, *Malcolm X Speaks*, p. 40.
217. Malcolm X: *Autobiography, op. cit.*, pp. 95 and 121.
218. *Ibid.*, p. 75.
219. *Ibid.*, p. 287 (italics in original).
220. Epps: "Introduction," *op. cit., The Speeches of Malcolm X*, p. 29; Haley: "Epilogue," *op. cit., Autobiography of Malcolm X, op. cit.*, p. 410.

221. Malcolm X, *ibid.*, p. 266 (italics in original).
222. Breitman: "A Declaration of Independence," *Malcolm X Speaks, op. cit.*, p. 19.
223. Malcolm X: "The Leverett House Forum," March 18, 1964, *The Speeches of Malcolm X, op. cit.*, p. 134.
224. Malcolm X: "The Ballot or the Bullet," *Malcolm X Speaks, op. cit.*, p. 26.
225. Malcolm X "The Harlem 'Hate-Gang' Scare," *ibid.*, pp. 68–69.
226. See Essien-Udom, *op. cit.*, p. 297.
227. Malcolm X: *Autobiography, op. cit.*, p. 289 (italics in original).
228. Essien-Udom, *op. cit.*, p. 306.
229. Malcolm X: speech at Harvard, March 24, 1961, *op. cit.*, *The Speeches of Malcolm X*, p. 125.
230. Malcolm X, quoted in "Introduction," *ibid.*, p. 81.
231. Carter G. Woodson: "The Association for the Study of Negro Life and History, 1947," *Black Nationalism in America, op. cit.*, p. 315.
232. See Malcolm X: "A Declaration of Independence," *op. cit.*, *Malcolm X Speaks*, p. 21.
233. Malcolm X: "The Ballot or the Bullet," *op. cit.*, *ibid.*, p. 304.
234. Wolfenstein, *op. cit.*, p. 304.
235. Malcolm X: "The Ballot or the Bullet," *op. cit.*, *Malcolm X Speaks*, pp. 38–39.
236. *Ibid.*, p. 41.
237. Malcolm X: "The Leverett House Forum," *op. cit.*, *The Speeches of Malcolm X*, p. 158.
238. Malcolm X: "Prospects for Freedom in 1965," *Malcolm X Speaks, op. cit.*, p. 150; Malcolm X: "The Ballot or the Bullet," *op. cit.*, *ibid.*, p. 40.
239. Breitman: "On Black Nationalism," *ibid.*, p. 213.
240. Malcolm X: "Segregation or Integration: A Debate," *Negro Protest Thought, op. cit.*, p. 363.
241. Malcolm X: "The Black Revolution and Its Effects upon the Negroes of the Western Hemisphere," *Malcolm X Speaks, op. cit.*, p. 217.
242. Malcolm X: "After the Bombing," p. 160.
243. Malcolm X: speech at Audubon, Dec. 20, 1964, *ibid.*, p. 121.
244. See Malcolm X: "Dollarism and Capitalism," *ibid.*, p. 199.
245. Malcolm X: "Interview with Milton Henry," *ibid.*, p. 83.
246. Malcolm X: "The Black Revolution," *ibid.*, p. 52.
247. Malcolm X: "The Leverett House Forum," *op. cit.*, *The Speeches of Malcolm X*, p. 135.
248. *Ibid.*, p. 136.
249. Malcolm X: "On Politics," *Malcolm X Speaks, op. cit.*, p. 203.
250. *Ibid.*
251. Malcolm X: "The Ballot or the Bullet," *op. cit.*, *ibid.*, p. 28.
252. Malcolm X, *ibid.*, p. 111.
253. Malcolm X: "Prospects for Freedom," *op. cit.*, *ibid.*, p. 150.
254. Malcolm X, *ibid.*, p. 111.

255. See Epps: "Introduction," *op. cit., The Speeches of Malcolm X*, p. 37.
256. Malcolm X: "Harvard Law School Forum," Dec. 16, 1964, *ibid.*, p. 171.
257. Malcolm X: "Message to the Grass Roots, 1963," *Malcolm X Speaks, op. cit.*, p. 8.
258. Wolfenstein, *op. cit.*, p. 324.
259. Malcolm X, *Malcolm X Speaks, op. cit.*, p. 106.
260. Malcolm X: "To Mississippi Youth," Dec. 31, 1964, *ibid.*, p. 146.
261. Malcolm X: "Speech at Audubon," *op. cit., ibid.*, p. 129.
262. Malcolm X: "The Ballot or the Bullet," *op. cit., ibid.*, p. 31.
263. Malcolm X: "Interview with Milton Henry," *op. cit., ibid.*, p. 81.
264. Malcolm X: "Harvard Law School Forum," *op. cit., The Speeches of Malcolm X*, p. 173.
265. Malcolm X: "Appeal to African Heads of State," *Malcolm X Speaks, op. cit.*, pp. 72–77.
266. Malcolm X: "Interview with Milton Henry," *op. cit., ibid.*, p. 79.
267. See *The New York Times*, August 13, 1964: "Dispatch by M. S. Handler," *ibid.*, pp. 85–87.
268. Wolfenstein, *op. cit.*, p. 331.
269. "After the Bombing," *Malcolm X Speaks, op. cit.*, p. 160.
270. Giddings: *When and Where I Enter, op. cit.*, p. 301.
271. Cruse: *Crisis, op. cit.*, p. 361.
272. Ashmore, *op. cit.*, p. 443.
273. Jordan, quoted in *ibid.*, p. 451.
274. Baraka: "Malcolm Remembered," *Selected Poetry*, p. 288.
275. Forman, *op. cit.*, pp. 389f.
276. Norman Mailer: *Cannibals and Christians*, p. 42.
277. Kilson: "Blacks and Neo-ethnicity in American Political Life," *op. cit., Ethnicity*, p. 259.
278. Killian, *op. cit.*, p. 132 (italics in original)
279. Rabbi Jay Kaufman: "Thou Shalt Surely Rebuke Thy Neighbor," *op. cit., Black Anti-Semitism and Jewish Racism*, p. 63.
280. Lester: "A Response," *ibid.*, p. 234.
281. Ashmore, *op. cit.*, p. 388.
282. See George Jackson: "To John Gerass," *Blood in My Eye, op. cit.*, p. 183.
283. Schanche, *op. cit.*, p. .208.
284. George Jackson: "Letter to a Comrade," March 28, 1971, *Blood in My Eye, op. cit.*, p. 4.
285. George Jackson: "To John Gerass," *op. cit., ibid.*, p. 187.
286. Newton: *In Search of Common Ground, op. cit.*, p. 35.
287. Forman, *op. cit.*, p. 59.
288. Newton: *Revolutionary Suicide, op. cit.*, pp. 48 and 5.
289. Bayard Rustin, quoted in Garrow, *op. cit.*, p. 602.
290. Malcolm X: *Autobiography, op. cit.*, p. 138.
291. *Ibid.*, p. 378.

292. Boggs: "The Revolutionary Struggle for Black Power," *op. cit., The Black Seventies*, p. 177.

293. Rap Brown, *op. cit.*, p. 131.

294. Ashmore, *op. cit.*, p. 455.

295. Henry Martin: "Letter from Abroad," Nov. 23, 1969, *The Black Seventies, op. cit.*, p. 177.

296. Cruse: *Crisis, op. cit.*, p. 362.

297. Charles Kadushin: *The American Intellectual Elite*, p. 244.

298. Allen Tate, quoted in Sterling Brown: "Count Us In," *What the Negro Wants, op. cit.*, p. 323.

299. Kadushin, *op. cit.*, p. 291.

300. Peter H. Rossi: "Researchers, Scholars and Policy Makers: The Politics of Large Scale Research," *The Contemporary University: U.S.A.*, p. 126.

301. Bellow: *Mr. Sammier's Planet*, p. 33.

302. Susan Sontag: "In 'Blues for Mr. Charlie,' " *Against Interpretation*, p. 152.

303. Mailer: "Of a Fire on the Moon," *The Long Patrol*, p. 705.

304. See W. J. Weatherby: *Squaring Off Mailer Against Baldwin*, p. 37.

305. Woodward: *The Burden of Southern History, op. cit.*, pp. 129–130.

306. See William Styron: "The Death-in-Life of Benjamin Reid," *This Quiet Dust*, p. 112.

307. See William Styron: "Conversations with Douglas Barzelay and Robert Sussman, 1968," *Conversations with William Styron*, p. 108.

308. Styron: "The Joint," *This Quiet Dust*, p. 144.

309. Daniel J. Boorstin: *The Decline of Radicalism*, pp. 121 and 125–133 (italics in original).

310. Anderson: "The Man Who Became a Woman," *op. cit., The Portable Anderson*, p. 492.

311. Kimball, *op. cit.*, p. 261.

312. Cruse: *Plural, op. cit.*, p. 354 (italics in original).

313. Clarence Lusane, quoted in Marable, *op. cit.*, p. 282.

314. See Joseph Kimes: "Changing Roles in the New South," *American Race Relations Today, op. cit.*, pp. 57f.

315. See David S. Broder: *The Party's Over*, pp. 207f.

316. Kimball, *op. cit.*, p. 249.

317. Andrew Hacker, *op. cit.*, p. 125.

318. Samuel Lubell: *The Future of American Politics*, p. 104.

319. Marable, *op. cit.*, p. 301.

320. Kimball, *op. cit.*, pp. 53 and 98.

321. Conan: "Schools and the Northern Slums," *op. cit., American Race Relations Today*, p. 153.

322. Killian, *op. cit.*, p. 140.

323. Marcuse: *L'Homme Unidimensionnel* p. 165.

324. Palmier, *op. cit.*, p. 467 (author's translation).

325. Quoted in Giddings: *When and Where I Enter, op. cit.*, p. 297.

326. Quoted in *Black Nationalism in America, op. cit.*, p. 198 (see also notes 11–16 and 115–118, ch. 7).

Chapter 8: White Monoculturism

1. Melville J. Herskovits: *The American Negro*, p. 82.
2. Langston Hughes: "Theme for English B," *The Langston Hughes Reader*, *op. cit.*, p. 109.
3. See Palmier, *op. cit.*, p. 342.
4. See Marcuse: *Eros et Civilisation*, pp. 36 and 100–102.
5. Norman O. Brown: *Life Against Death*, *op. cit.*, p. 292.
6. *Ibid.*, p. 281 (see also notes 115–118, ch. 7).
7. See Barthes: *Mythologies*, p. 141.
8. Norman O. Brown, *op. cit.*, p. 290.
9. See Ishmael Reed: "The Great Tenure Battle of 1977: Interview with Jan Ewing," *Shrovetide in Old New Orleans*, p. 227.
10. Janowitz, *op. cit.*, p. 309.
11. Glazer and Moynihan, *op. cit.*, p. 313.
12. Leslie A. Fiedler: *Waiting for the End*, p. 72.
13. Glazer and Moynihan, *op. cit.*, p. 309.
14. Vertamae Smart-Grosvenor: "Skillet Blond," Amiri Baraka and Amina Baraka: *Confirmation: An Anthology of Afro-American Women*, uncorrected galleys, p. 394.
15. Albert Einstein, Cecyle S. Neidle: *The New Americans*, p. 309.
16. Claude-Edmonde Magny: *The Age of the American Novel*, p. 228.
17. Vidal: *Two Sisters*, p. 92.
18. Magny, *op. cit.*, pp. 226–227.
19. Richard Chase: "The Classic Literature: Art and Idea," *Paths of American Thought*, *op. cit.*, pp. 62–63.
20. Barthes: "Martians," *The Eiffel Tower*, p. 29.
21. Vidal: *Two Sisters*, *op. cit.*, p. 92.

Chapter 9: The Stereotype of the Black Beast

1. Seymour Gross: "Introduction," *Images of the Negro in American Literature*, *op. cit.*, p. 2.
2. See Sterling Brown: "A Century of Negro Portraiture in American Literature," *Black Voices*, *op. cit.*
3. Sterling Brown: "Negro Characters as Seen by White Authors," *Dark Symphony*, p. 139.
4. Thomas Wolfe: *Look Homeward, Angel*, *op. cit.*, pp. 136 and 310.
5. Thomas Wolfe: *The Web and the Rock*, p. 156.
6. Fiedler: *Waiting for the End*, *op. cit.*, p. 125.
7. Atlanta *News*, Sept. 10, 1874, *Great Issues of American History*, *op. cit.*, pp. 43–44.
8. Baldwin: *Giovanni's Room*, p. 51.
9. Ellison: *Shadow and Act*, *op. cit.*, p. 41.

10. See Baldwin: *No Name in the Street, op. cit.,* p. 102.
11. Baldwin: "Many Thousand Gone," *op. cit., Partisan Review,* p. 107.
12. Ellison: *Invisible Man, op. cit.,* p. 16.
13. See Baldwin: "Introduction," *Nobody Knows My Name, op. cit.,* p. xiv.
14. Wright: *The Long Dream, op. cit.,* p. 78.
15. Quoted in Bennett: *Before the Mayflower, op. cit.,* pp. 242–243.
16. See I. A. Newby: *Jim Crow's Defense,* p. 37.
17. *Ibid.,* p. 92.
18. Faulkner: *Sartoris,* p. 279.
19. Quoted in Calvin C. Hernton: "Frontspiece," *Sex and Racism in America.*
20. G. Stanley Hall, quoted in Newby, *op. cit.,* p. 39.
21. John Howard Griffin: "Dark Journey," *Beyond the Angry Black, op. cit.,* p. 42.
22. Hernton, *op. cit.,* p. 4.
23. Reed: *Reckless Eyeballing,* p. 55.
24. Thomas Nelson Page, quoted in Sterling Brown: "Negro Characters," *op. cit., Dark Symphony,* p. 156.
25. Reed: *Reckless Eyeballing, op. cit.,* p. 8.
26. Hughes: "Shakespeare in Harlem," James A. Emanuel: *Langston Hughes,* p. 53.
27. Fiedler: "Negro and Jew: Encounter in America," *Breakthrough,* p. 343.
28. See Marcuse: *Eros et Civilisation, op. cit.,* p. 27.
29. Hernton: *op. cit.,* p. 176 (italics in original).
30. Fiedler: *Waiting for the End, op. cit.,* p. 115.
31. See Myrdal: *An American Dilemma, op. cit.,* p. 591.
32. See Dollard, *op. cit.,* p. 317.
33. See Griffin: "Dark Journey," *op. cit., Beyond the Angry Black,* p. 42.
34. Hernton, *op. cit.,* p. 112.
35. Nancy M. Tischler: *Black Masks,* p. 104.
36. Fiedler: "Negro and Jew," *op. cit., Breakthrough,* p. 342.
37. Myrdal: *An American Dilemma, op. cit.,* p. 591.
38. Fiedler: "Preface," *Love and Death in the American Novel,* p. xxi.
39. *Ibid.,* pp. 147–148.
40. Boorstin: *Genius of American Politics,* p. 173.
41. Melville, quoted in Sidney Kaplan: "Herman Melville and the American National Sin," *Images of the Negro, op. cit.,* p. 141.
42. Walt Whitman, quoted in *ibid.,* p. 162.
43. Wright: *The Outsider,* p. 159.
44. Ellen Glasgow: *Barren Ground,* p. 281.
45. See Glasgow: *In This Our Life,* p. 75.
46. Frederick P. W. McDowell: *Ellen Glasgow and the Ironic Art of Fiction,* p. 94.
47. Magny, *op. cit.,* p. 199.
48. Sartre, quoted in *ibid.,* note 22, p. 204.

49. Faulkner, quoted in "Introduction," *Black Voices, op. cit.,* p. 43.
50. Richard H. King: *A Southern Renaissance,* p. 34.
51. Howard Odum, quoted in *ibid.,* p. 41.
52. Allen Tate: "To the Lacedemonians," *Poems 1922–1947,* p. 18.
53. Sterling Brown, quoted in Tischler, *op. cit.,* p. 31.
54. John Crowe Ransom: "Reconstructed but Unregenerate," *I'll Take My Stand,* p. 14.
55. See Michael O'Brien: *The Idea of the American South,* pp. 205–207.
56. Richard King, *op. cit.,* p. 60.
57. See Stark Young: "Not in Memoriam, but in Defense," *I'll Take My Stand, op. cit.*
58. Frank Owsley: "The Irrepressible Conflict," *ibid.,* p. 77.
59. Owsley, *ibid.,* p. 77.
60. Robert Penn Warren: *Brother to Dragons,* p. 116.
61. *Ibid.,* p. 87.
62. Tate: "After Calhoun," *Poems 1922–1947, op. cit.,* pp. 86–87.
63. Tate: "The Swimmer," *Poems,* p. 179.
64. Tate: "Sonnets at Christmas," *Poems 1922–1947, op. cit.,* p. 51.
65. Tate: "Sonnets of the Blood, III," *ibid.,* p. 167.
66. Warren: *Meet Me in the Green Glen,* p. 370 (italics in original).
67. Davenport, *op. cit.,* p. 175.
68. See James Korges: *Erskine Caldwell,* p. 38.
69. John Eden Hardy: "Eudora Welty's Negroes," *Images of the Negro, op. cit.,* p. 225.
70. See Flannery O'Connor: "Everything That Rises Must Converge," *The Complete Stories, passim.*
71. Dorothy Walters: *Flannery O'Connor,* pp. 118 and 136.
72. Robert Coles: *Flannery O'Connor's South,* p. 37.
73. Styron: *This Quiet Dust, op. cit.,* p. 13 (italics in original).
74. Styron: *Lie Down in Darkness,* p. 69.
75. Styron: *The Confessions of Nat Turner,* p. 173.
76. *Ibid.,* p. 92.
77. *Ibid.,* p. 232.
78. *Ibid.,* p. 156.
79. *Ibid.,* p. 207.
80. *Ibid.,* p. 401 (italics in original).
81. *Ibid.,* p. 426.
82. Gayle: *The Way of the New World, op. cit.,* p. 285.
83. Bennett: "Nat's Last White Man," *William Styron's Nat Turner,* p. 10.
84. Davenport: "Preface," *op. cit.,* p. vii.
85. Dollard, *op. cit.,* pp. 372 and 375.
86. Hughes: "Simply Heavenly," *The Langston Hughes Reader, op. cit.,* pp. 272–273.
87. See Sinclair Lewis: *Kingsblood Royal, passim.*
88. Willa Cather: *Sapphira and the Slave Girl,* p. 290.
89. Carlos Baker: *Ernest Hemingway,* p. 274.

90.   Ernest Hemingway: *To Have and Have Not,* pp. 73 and 75.

91.   James R. Mellow: *Invented Lives,* pp. 420 and 438.

92.   Richard Lehan: "Focus on F. Scott Fitzgerald's *The Great Gatsby,*" *American Dreams, American Nightmares, op. cit.,* pp. 108 and 110.

93.   Robert Bone: "The Background of the Negro Renaissance," *Black History, op. cit.,* p. 416.

94.   Hughes: *The Big Sea, op. cit.,* p. 225.

95.   Vachel Lindsay: "The Congo," *Literature of the United States,* vol. 2, p. 947.

96.   See Gross: "Introduction," *op. cit., Images of the Negro,* p. 9.

97.   Ben Hecht: *A Thousand and One Afternoons in Chicago,* p. 226.

98.   See Elizabeth Ammons: *Conflicting Stories,* p. 103.

99.   Gertrude Stein, quoted in John Malcolm Brinnin: *The Third Rose,* p. 320.

100. Gertrude Stein: *Everybody's Autobiography,* p. 109.

101. Gertrude Stein: *The Autobiography of Alice B. Toklas,* p. 292.

102. See Reed: *Shrovetide, op. cit.,* note, p. 227.

103. Bruce Kellner: *Carl Van Vechten and the Irreverent Decades,* p. 209.

104. Countee Cullen: *One Way to Heaven,* p. 99.

105. See Reed: *Mumbo Jumbo, passim,* especially pp. 55f.

106. Hurston, quoted in David L. Lewis: *When Harlem Was in Vogue,* p. 98.

107. Kellner, *op. cit.,* p. 210.

108. Carl Van Vechten: *Nigger Heaven,* pp. 89–90 and 107.

109. Benjamin Brawley, quoted in Arna Bontemps: "Introduction," *The Harlem Renaissance Remembered, op. cit.,* p. 22.

110. Kellner, *op. cit.,* p. 209.

111. Van Vechten, quoted in David Lewis, *op. cit.,* p. 98.

112. Alice Dunbar-Nelson, quoted in Gloria T. Hull: *Color, Sex and Poetry,* p. 88.

113. Cruse: *Crisis, op. cit.,* p. 32.

114. Mabel Dodge, quoted in *ibid.*

115. Warren Hudlin: "The Renaissance Re-examined," *op. cit., The Harlem Renaissance Remembered,* p. 275.

116. Sterling Brown: "Negro Characters," *op. cit., Dark Symphony,* p. 164.

117. Gross: "Introduction," *op. cit., Images of the Negro,* p. 13.

118. Truman Capote: *Other Voices, Other Rooms,* p. 127.

119. Capote: *The Grass Harp,* p. 10.

120. John W. Aldridge: *After the Lost Generation,* p. 219.

121. Capote: *Answered Prayers,* pp. 33–34.

122. Norman Podhoretz, "My Negro Problem—and Ours," *The Commentary Reader,* p. 382.

123. See Jack Kerouac: *On the Road,* pp. 148–149.

124. Tom Wolfe: *Radical Chic, op. cit.,* p. 42.

125. Mailer: *The White Negro,* p. 4.

126. *Ibid.,* p. 8.

127. Baldwin: "The New Lost Generation," *The Price of the Ticket,* p. 308.

128. Mailer, quoted in Weatherby, *op. cit.,* p. 37.

129. Mailer: *Existential Errands*, p. 308.
130. Mailer: "Of a Fire on the Moon," *The Long Patrol*, p. 705.
131. Mailer: *Existential Errands, op. cit.*, p. 308.
132. Mailer: "Of a Fire on the Moon," *op. cit., The Long Patrol*, p. 705.
133. Mailer: *Existential Errands, op. cit.*, p. 309.
134. Mailer, quoted in Weatherby, *op. cit.*, p. 205.
135. See Mailer: *An American Dream*, p. 186.
136. Mailer: *Why Are We in Vietnam?*, pp. 161 and 26.
137. *Ibid.*, p. 208.
138. Jennifer Bailey: *Norman Mailer, Quick Change Artist*, p. 77.
139. Mailer: *Why Are We in Vietnam?, op. cit.*, p. 208.
140. Gayle: *The Way of the New World, op. cit.*, pp. 39 and 279.
141. Baldwin: *Nobody Knows My Name, op. cit.*, p. 228.
142. See Irving Malin: *Jews and Americans*, pp. 123 and 80; See Leslie Fiedler: "Negro and Jew: Encounter in America," *Breakthrough, op. cit.*, p. 342.
143. Nat Hentoff: "Introduction," *Black Anti-Semitism and Jewish Racism*, p. xi.
144. Baldwin: "Negroes Are Anti-Semitic Because They Are Anti-white," *The Price of the Ticket, op. cit.*, p. 430.
145. See Cruse: "My Jewish Problem and Theirs," *Black Anti-Semitism and Jewish Racism, op. cit., passim.*
146. Ellison: *Shadow and Act, op. cit.*, p. 130.
147. Seymour Krim: "Ask for a White Cadillac," *Beyond the Angry Black, op. cit.*, pp. 111f.
148. Philip Roth: *Reading Myself and Others*, p. 228.
149. Bellow: "Looking for Mr. Green," *Mosby's Memoirs and Other Stories*, p. 100.
150. Bellow: *Mr. Sammler's Planet, op. cit.*, pp. 49 and 210.
151. Martin Luther King, Jr.: "Letter from Birmingham Jail," April 16, 1963, *The Reform Spirit in America*, p. 366.
152. Bellow: *The Adventures of Augie March*, p. 378.
153. Roth: *Reading Myself and Others, op. cit.*, pp. 224, 231, 227.
154. Bernard Malamud: "Black Is My Favorite Color," *Idiots*, p. 18.
155. Sidney Richman: *Bernard Malamud*, p. 139.
156. Malamud: "Angel Levine," *The Magic Barrel*, p. 53.
157. Malamud: *The Tenants*, p. 54.
158. *Ibid.*, p. 146.
159. *Ibid.*, p. 61 (italics in original).
160. *Ibid.*, p. 54.
161. *Ibid.*, p. 165.
162. *Ibid.*, p. 169.
163. Ben Siegel: "Through a Glass Darkly: Bernard Malamud's Painful Views of the Self," *The Fiction of Bernard Malamud*, p. 139.
164. Malamud: *The Tenants, op. cit.*, p. 173.
165. Mark Schechner: "Jewish Writers," *The Harvard Guide to Contemporary Literature*, p. 205.

Chapter 10: The Stereotype of the Contented Slave

1. See Sterling Brown: "Negro Characters," *op. cit., Dark Symphony,* pp. 139f.
2. See Tischler, *op. cit.,* pp. 17 and 61.
3. Roanis Bradford, quoted in Sterling Brown: "Negro Characters," *op. cit., Dark Symphony,* p. 139.
4. Sterling Brown: *The Negro in American Fiction,* p. 50.
5. Booker T. Washington: *Up from Slavery, op. cit.,* p. 10.
6. Glasgow: *The Woman Within,* p. 52.
7. Bellow: *Herzog, op. cit.,* p. 81.
8. See John O. Killens: "The Confession of Willie Styron," *William Styron's Nat Turner, op. cit.,* p. 43.
9. Styron: "Interview with Michael West, 1977," *Conversations, op. cit.,* p. 228.
10. Newby, *op. cit.,* p. 104.
11. Mark Sullivan: *The Education of an American,* vol. 1, p. 119.
12. Newby, *op. cit.,* p. 178.
13. *Ibid.,* p. 70.
14. Henry Louis Gates, Jr.: *Figures in Black,* pp. 25 and 21.
15. Thomas Jefferson, quoted in *ibid.,* p. 5.
16. Jefferson, quoted in Houston A. Baker, Jr.: *The Journey Back,* p. 8.
17. Jefferson, quoted in H. L. Gates, *op. cit.,* p. 5.
18. McDowell, *op. cit.,* p. 63.
19. Glasgow: *In This Our Life, op. cit.,* p. 400.
20. Glasgow: *Barren Ground, op. cit.,* pp. 281–282.
21. Katherine Anne Porter: "The Old Order," *The Leaning Tower and Other Stories,* p. 35.
22. Porter, quoted in Joan Givner: *Katherine Anne Porter: A Life,* p. 452.
23. See Caldwell: *A Place Called Estherville, passim.*
24. Caldwell: *Georgia Boy,* p. 119.
25. Korges: *op. cit.,* p. 38.
26. Caldwell: *A Place Called Estherville, op. cit.,* p. 214.
27. See Korges, *op. cit.,* p. 20.
28. See Thomas Wolfe: *The Web and the Rock, op. cit.,* p. 18.
29. Thomas Wolfe: *Look Homeward, Angel, op. cit.,* pp. 524 and 96.
30. *Ibid.,* p. 408.
31. Wright: *The Long Dream, op. cit.,* p. 142.
32. See Robert Coughlan: *The Private World of William Faulkner,* p. 90.
33. Faulkner, quoted in David Minter: *William Faulkner: His Life and Work,* p. 212.
34. Malcolm Cowley: *The Faulkner-Cowley File,* p. 107.
35. Faulkner, quoted in *ibid,* p. 111.
36. See John Faulkner: *My Brother Bill,* p. 268.
37. See Faulkner: *The Mansion, op. cit.,* p. 34.
38. See Faulkner: "The Compsons," *The Portable Faulkner,* p. 756.

39. See Faulkner: *Sartoris, op. cit.,* p. 83.
40. Newby, *op. cit.,* p. 78.
41. Faulkner: *Requiem for a Nun,* p. 208 (see also note 49, ch. 9).
42. Baldwin: *No Name in the Street, op. cit.,* p. 45.
43. Magny, *op. cit.,* p. 230.
44. Faulkner: *Sartoris, op. cit.,* p. 83.
45. Faulkner: "Mountain Victory," *Collected Stories of William Faulkner,* p. 769.
46. Faulkner: *The Sound and the Fury,* pp. 106–107.
47. Styron: *Lie Down in Darkness, op. cit.,* p. 61.
48. Styron: *Sophie's Choice,* p. 513.
49. Arthur M. Schlesinger, Jr.: "The Causes of the Civil War: A Note on Historical Sentimentalism," *Black History, op. cit.,* p. 223.
50. Hamlin Garland: *A Daughter of the Middle Border,* p. 132.
51. William Dean Howells, quoted in H. L. Gates, *op. cit.,* p. 23.
52. Howells, quoted in H. Baker, *op. cit.,* p. 150.
53. See H. L. Gates, *op. cit.,* pp. 14 and 24.
54. Cather: *Sapphira and the Slave Girl, op. cit.,* p. 111.
55. Anderson: "Dark Laughter," *Dark Symphony, op. cit.,* p. 166.
56. Anderson, quoted in "Introduction," *Images of the Negro, op. cit.,* p. 7.
57. John Updike: *Buchanan Dying,* p. 25.
58. Updike: *Rabbit Redux,* p. 47.
59. *Ibid.,* p. 13.
60. *Ibid.,* p. 103.
61. Updike: *Self-consciousness,* p. 65.
62. Sterling Brown: *The Negro in American Fiction, op. cit.,* p. 88.
63. Alice Childress: "Trouble in Mind," *Black Theater,* p. 213.
64. James Farrell, quoted in Sterling Brown, *The Negro in American Fiction, op. cit.,* p. 176.
65. Eugene O'Neill: *All God's Chillun Got Wings,* p. 40.
66. *Ibid.,* p. 71.
67. O'Neill: *The Iceman Cometh,* p. 39.
68. Malamud: *Dubin's Lives,* p. 343.
69. Tischler, *op. cit.,* p. 13.
70. Barthes: *Roland Barthes,* p. 90 (italics in original).
71. Podhoretz, *op. cit., Commentary Reader,* p. 387.
72. See H. Baker: "Introduction," *op. cit.,* p. xiii.
73. H. L. Gates, *op. cit.,* p. 141.
74. Podhoretz, *op. cit., Commentary Reader,* p. 387.

Chapter 11: The Stereotype of the Mulatto

1. Sterling Brown: "Negro Character," *op. cit., Dark Symphony,* p. 139.
2. Tischler, *op. cit.,* p. 17.
3. *Ibid.,* p. 87.
4. Sterling Brown: "Negro Character," *op. cit., Dark Symphony,* p. 139.

5. Baldwin: *Blues for Mr. Charlie,* p. 49.

6. See Erlene Stetson: "Introduction," *Black Sister,* p. xx; see also Francoise Wonner: *Autobiographical Voices,* p. 6.

7. Wright: *The Long Dream, op. cit.,* pp. 64–65.

8. Joel Williamson: *New People,* p. 12.

9. Wright: *Lawd Today,* p. 134.

10. Bennett: *Before the Mayflower, op. cit.,* p. 265.

11. Hernton, *op. cit.,* p. 50 (italics in original).

12. *Ibid.,* pp. 21 and 42.

13. Chester Himes: *If He Hollers Let Him Go,* p. 126.

14. See Baraka: "Dutchman," scene 2, *Black Theater, op. cit.*

15. See James Weldon Johnson: "The White Witch," Jean Wagner: *Black Poets of the United States,* p. 371.

16. Ted R. Spivey: *Revival,* p. 21.

17. Fiedler: *The Return of the Vanishing American,* p. 178.

18. Toni Morrison: *Sula,* p. 113.

19. Pauline Hopkins, quoted in Jane Campbell: *Mythic Black Fiction,* p. 38.

20. Tischler, *op. cit.,* p. 65.

21. Himes: "A Nigger," *Black on Black,* p. 129.

22. Malcolm Cowley: *Exiles Return,* pp. 236–237.

23. Thomas Wolfe: *The Web and the Rock, op. cit.,* p. 140.

24. See Faulkner: "The Bear," *Portable Faulkner, op. cit.,* p. 312.

25. See Faulkner: "Wash," *ibid.,* p. 18.

26. Philip Blair Rice: "Faulkner's Crucifixion," *William Faulkner: Three Decades of Criticism,* p. 381.

27. Faulkner: *Absalom, Absalom!,* p. 207.

28. Faulkner: "The Old People," *Go Down, Moses,* p. 168.

29. Magny, *op. cit.,* p. 191.

30. Faulkner: *Absalom, Absalom!, op. cit.,* p. 198 (italics in original).

31. Magny, *op. cit.,* p. 220.

32. Faulkner, quoted in Edith Brown Douds: "Recollections of William Faulkner and the Bunch," *William Faulkner of Oxford,* p. 53.

33. Faulkner, quoted in Robert Coughlan, *op. cit.,* p. 140.

34. Minter, *op. cit.,* p. 250.

35. Faulkner, quoted in Cowley: *The Faulkner-Cowley File, op. cit.,* p. 155.

36. Faulkner: *Light in August,* p. 227.

37. John L. Langley, Jr.: "Joe Christmas: The Hero in the Modern World," *Three Decades of Criticism, op. cit.,* pp. 269 and 273.

38. See Kazin: "The Stillness of *Light in August,*" *ibid.,* p. 251.

39. See Richard P. Adams: "Focus on William Faulkner's 'The Beal,'" *American Dreams, American Nightmares, op. cit.,* pp. 128–134.

40. Magny, *op. cit.,* p. 223 (italics in original).

41. Faulkner: "Delta Autumn," *Go Down, Moses, op. cit.,* p. 363.

42. Faulkner: *Soldier's Pay,* p. 302.

43. See Faulkner: *The Mansion, op. cit.,* p. 309.

44. See Minton, *op. cit.,* p. 233.

45. See Stephen B. Oates: *William Faulkner, the Man and the Artist*, p. 306.
46. Faulkner, quoted in Ilse DuSoir Lind: "The Design and Meaning of *Absalom, Absalom!*," *Three Decades of Criticism, op. cit.*, p. 296.
47. Tate, quoted in Sterling Brown: "Negro Characters," *op. cit., Dark Symphony*, p. 150.
48. Tischler, *op. cit.*, p. 17.
49. Tate: "The Ancestors," *Poems 1922–1947, op. cit.*, p. 9.
50. Tate: "Sonnets of the Blood, VIII," *ibid.*, p. 171.
51. Tate: "Elegy," *ibid.*, p. 89.
52. Warren: *Band of Angels*, p. 209.
53. See Warren: *Wilderness*, p. 151.
54. W. J. Cash: *The Mind of the South*, p. 327.
55. Williamson, *op. cit.*, p. 63.
56. Cather: *Sapphira and the Slave Girl, op. cit.*, p. 290.
57. Ellison: *Invisible Man, op. cit.*, p. 121.
58. Stoddard, quoted in Newby, *op. cit.*, p. 135.
59. Stoddard, quoted in *ibid.*, p. 134.
60. Christopher Lasch: *The New Radicalism in America*, p. 65.
61. Reta Childe Dorr, quoted in *ibid.*, p. 52.
62. Noble, *op. cit.*, p. 299.
63. Giddings: "Preface," *When and Where I Enter, op. cit.*, p. 6.
64. Lasch, *op. cit.*, p. 66.
65. Giddings: *When and Where I Enter, op. cit.*, p. 340.
66. Lasch, *op. cit.*, p. 57 (italics in original).
67. Giddings: *When and Where I Enter, op. cit.*, p. 55.
68. *Ibid.*, p. 46.
69. Page Smith, *op. cit.*, p. 657.
70. See Giddings: *When and Where I Enter, op. cit.*, pp. 126–127.
71. See Noble, *op. cit.*, p. 297.
72. *Ibid.*, p. 299.
73. Didion, *op. cit.*, pp. 112, 113, 115.
74. Giddings: *When and Where I Enter, op. cit.*, pp. 303 and 308.
75. Noble, *op. cit.*, p. 300.
76. Giddings: *When and Where I Enter, op. cit.*, p. 297.
77. Noble, *op. cit.*, p. 300.
78. See David M. Gordon: " 'Rebellion' in Context: A Student's View of Students," *The Contemporary University U.S.A.*, p. 292.
79. See Baldwin: *No Name in the Street, op. cit.*, p. 128.
80. See Mailer: *Cannibals and Christians, op. cit.*, p. 28.
81. Baraka: *Home, op. cit.*, p. 136.
82. Baraka, quoted in Werner Sollors: *Amiri Baraka/LeRoi Jones: The Quest for a "Populist Modernism,"* p. 25.
83. Mailer: "The Sixth Presidential Paper—A Kennedy Miscellany," *The Presidential Papers*, p. 159.
84. *Ibid.*, p. 160.
85. Mailer: *Cannibals and Christians, op. cit.*, p. 114.

86. See Mailer: *Why Are We in Vietnam?, op. cit.,* p. 161.
87. *Ibid.,* p. 110.
88. See Weatherby, *op. cit.,* pp. 37 and 65.
89. Kazin: *Bright Book of Life,* p. 257.
90. Gayle: *The Way of the New World, op. cit.,* pp. 106–108.
91. Mailer: *An Americana Dream, op. cit.,* p. 125.
92. *Ibid.,* p. 186.
93. Mailer: "Of a Fire on the Moon," *op. cit., The Long Patrol;* p. 707.
94. Mailer: "Of a Fire on the Moon," *op. cit., ibid.,* p. 139.
95. Jennifer Bailey: *Norman Mailer, op. cit.,* p. 103.
96. Mailer: "Contribution to a *Partisan Review* Symposium," *Existential Errands, op. cit.,* p. 307.
97. Mailer: *Why Are We in Vietnam?, op. cit.,* p. 208.
98. Gayle: *The Way of the New World, op. cit.,* pp. 280 and 271.
99. See Mailer: *Genius and Lust,* pp. 185–189.
100. Norman O. Brown: *Life Against Death, op. cit.,* p. 44.
101. Irving Malin: *New American Gothic,* p. 129 (italics in original).
102. Roth: *Reading Myself and Others, op. cit.,* p. 135.
103. See Robert Lowell: "For the Union Dead," *Selected Poems,* p. 136.
104. Lowell: "Two Walls," *History,* p. 169.
105. J. M. Linebarger: *John Berryman,* p. 85.
106. *Ibid.,* p. 135.
107. Malamud: *The Tenants, op. cit.,* p. 93.
108. Fiedler: *Love and Death in the American Novel, op. cit.,* p. 366.
109. Barthes: *Roland Barthes, op. cit.,* p. 69 (italics in original).
110. Fiedler: *Love and Death in the American Novel, op. cit., passim.*
111. Fiedler: "The Jig Is Up," *Waiting for the End, op. cit.,* p. 130.
112. Fiedler: *The Second Stone,* especially p. 180.
113. Fiedler: "The Jig Is Up," *Waiting for the End, op. cit.,* p. 136.
114. Bellow: *Herzog, op. cit.,* p. 67 (italics in original; see also note 138, ch. 6).
115. Bellow: *Mr. Sammler's Planet, op. cit.,* p. 49 (see also note 150, ch. 9).
116. Robert Dutton: *Saul Bellow,* p. 160.
117. Bellow: *Mr. Sammler's Planet, op. cit.,* pp. 210, 162, 89, 145.
118. *Ibid.,* p. 66.
119. Bellow, quoted in Lionel Trilling: *Beyond Culture,* p. 230.
120. Bellow, quoted in Philip Rahv: "Saul Bellow's Progress," *Essays on Literature and Politics,* p. 65.
121. Updike: "Nakedness," *Too Far to Go,* p. 184.
122. Updike: *The Coup,* pp. 46, 135, 174.
123. Updike: "Marching Through Boston," *Too Far to Go, op. cit.,* p. 74.
124. Updike: *Rabbit Redux, op. cit.,* p. 114.
125. *Ibid.,* p. 311.
126. Updike: "Marching Through Boston," *Too Far to Go, op. cit.,* p. 88.
127. Updike: *Bech Is Back,* p. 192.

128. Updike: *The Coup, op. cit.,* p. 53.
129. Updike: *Bech Is Back, op. cit.,* p. 43.
130. Updike: "Re Rabbit Redux," *Hugging the Shore,* p. 859.
131. Updike: *Buchanan Dying, op. cit.*
132. Barthes: *Mythologies, op. cit.,* p. 43 (italics in original).
133. Sontag: *Against Interpretation, op. cit.,* p. 154.
134. *Ibid.,* p. 152.
135. Joyce Carol Oates: *Because It Is Bitter, and Because It Is My Heart,* p. 23.
136. *Ibid.,* p. 82.
137. Myrdal: *An American Dilemma, op. cit.,* p. 928 (italics in original).
138. Ellison: *Shadow and Act, op. cit.,* pp. 315–316.
139. Barthes: *Mythologies, op. cit.,* p. 141.
140. Himes: "Essays," *Black on Black, op. cit.,* p. 229.
141. Warren, quoted in Gross, "Introduction," *op. cit., Images of the Negro,* pp. 25–26.
142. Ashmore: "Where Have All the Liberals Gone?," *The Establishment and All That, op. cit.,* p. 65.
143. Schlesinger: "The Struggle for Freedom," *op. cit., Black History,* p. 31.

Chapter 12: The Black Dialectic with Respect to the Stereotype of the Black Beast

1. DuBois: *The Souls of Black Folk, op. cit.,* p. 17 (see also note 70, ch. 2).
2. Bernard W. Bell: *The Afro-American Novel and Its Tradition,* p. 79.
3. See Baldwin: *Nobody Knows My Name, op. cit.,* p. 29.
4. Baraka: *Daggers and Javelins, op. cit.,* p. 325.
5. Wright: *Black Boy, op. cit.,* p. 65.
6. See Reed: *Mumbo Jumbo, op. cit.*
7. Bell: "Introduction," *op. cit.,* p. xii.
8. See Wright: *American Hunger, op. cit.,* p. 45.
9. William Kelley, quoted in Michel Fabre: *La Rive Noire,* p. 281.
10. Lincoln: *Sounds of the Struggle, op. cit.,* p. 33.
11. Herskovits: *The American Negro, op. cit.,* p. 21.
12. H. Baker: *Singers of Daybreak,* p. 7 (italics in original).
13. Nella Larsen: *Passing,* p. 180.
14. See Gayle: *The Way of the New World, op. cit.,* p. 311.
15. Fiedler: "Negro and Jew: Encounter in America," *op. cit., Breakthrough,* p. 340.
16. Baldwin: *Giovanni's Room, op. cit.,* p. 129.
17. Vidal: *The Second American Revolution, op. cit.,* p. 152.
18. Hughes: *Not Without Laughter,* p. 45.
19. Reed: *Mumbo Jumbo, op. cit.,* p. 168.
20. Alice Walker: *The Color Purple, op. cit.,* p. 166.

21. Nathan A. Scott, Jr.: "The Dark and Haunted Tower of Richard Wright," *Five Black Writers, op. cit.,* p. 22.
22. Gayle: *The Way of the New World, op. cit.,* p. 179.
23. *Ibid.,* p. 179.
24. See Marcuse: *L'Homme Unidimensionnel, op. cit.,* p. 165 (author's translation).
25. George Moses Horton: "On Liberty and Slavery," *The Poetry of the Negro 1746–1970,* p. 11.
26. H. Baker: *The Journey Back, op. cit.,* p. 123.
27. See Baraka: "Introduction," *The Motion of History and Other Plays,* p. 16.
28. Saunders Redding: "To Make a Poet Black," *From the Dark Tower,* p. 159.
29. DuBois: *"The Crisis,* October, 1920," *Black Nationalism in America, op. cit.,* p. 286.
30. Frazier: *On Race Relations, op. cit.,* p. 103.
31. Craig H. Werner: "The Briar Patch as Modernist Myth: Morrison, Barthes and Tar-Baby As Is," *Critical Essays on Toni Morrison,* p. 151 (italics in original).
32. See Bell, *op. cit.,* p. 63.
33. See Hugh M. Gloster: "Sutton E. Griggs: Novelist of the New Negro," *The Black Novelist,* pp. 13–14.
34. See Bontemps: "Black Thunder," *From the Dark Tower, op. cit.,* p. 87.
35. Robert Hayden: "Middle Passage," "Ballad of Nat Turner," "John Brown," *Collected Poems.*
36. David Littlejohn: *Black on White,* p. 6.
37. *Ibid.,* p. 66 (italics in original).
38. *Ibid.,* p. 163 (italics in original).
39. Bell, *op. cit.,* p. 186.
40. Bernard Appel: "Personal Impressions," *Richard Wright: Impressions and Perspectives,* p. 76.
41. Bell, *op. cit.,* p. 160.
42. Wright: *White Man, Listen!, op. cit.,* p. 131.
43. Reed: *Shrovetide, op. cit.,* p. 44.
44. *Ibid.,* p. 46.
45. Wright: "The Man Who Lived Underground," *Afro-American Literature: An Introduction,* p. 31.
46. *Ibid.,* pp. 40 and 57.
47. Quoted in Russell Carl Brignano: *Richard Wright: An Introduction to the Man and His Works,* p. 158.
48. Kingsley Widmer: "The Existent Darkness: Richard Wright's *Outsider,*" *Five Black Writers, op. cit.,* pp. 53 and 56.
49. See Widmer: "Black Existentialism: Richard Wright," *Modern Black Novelists,* p. 83.
50. Margaret Walker: *Richard Wright: Daemonic Genius,* p. 35.
51. Wright, quoted in Brignano, *op. cit.,* p. 126.

52. Baldwin: "Everybody's Protest Novel," *Notes of a Native Son, op. cit.,* p. 19.
53. Himes: *My Life of Absurdity,* p. 8.
54. Wright: "Introduction," *White Man, Listen!, op. cit.,* p. 17.
55. Baldwin: "Everybody's Protest Novel," *op. cit., Notes of a Native Son,* p. 19.
56. Toomer: *Cane,* p. 218.
57. Wright, quoted in Margaret Walker: *Daemonic Genius, op. cit.,* p. 282.
58. Wright: *Black Boy, op. cit.,* p. 228.
59. Daniel Aaron: "Richard Wright and the Communist Party," *Wright: Impressions and Perspectives, op. cit.,* p. 46.
60. Wright: "Blueprint for Negro Writing," *Voices from the Harlem Renaissance, op. cit.,* p. 397.
61. Wright: "The American Problem," *Wright, Impressions, op. cit.,* p. 15.
62. Wright: *American Hunger, op. cit.,* p. 14.
63. Wright: *White Man, Listen!, op. cit.,* p. 130.
64. Edward A. Watson: *Wright: Impressions and Perspectives, op. cit.,* p. 168.
65. Stephen Soitos: "Black Orpheus Refused: A Study of Richard Wright's 'The Man Who Lived Underground,' " *Richard Wright: Myths and Realities,* p. 16.
66. Wright: "Blueprint for Negro Writing," *op. cit., Voices from the Harlem Renaissance,* p. 398.
67. Margaret Walker: *Daemonic Genius, op. cit.,* pp. 93 and 206.
68. Bell, *op. cit.,* p. 166.
69. Wright: *Pagan Spain,* p. 17.
70. Brignano, *op. cit.,* p. 32.
71. Margaret Walker: "Richard Wright," *Wright: Impressions and Perspectives, op. cit.,* p. 65.
72. Margaret Walker: *Daemonic Genius, op. cit.,* pp. 91 and 245.
73. Baldwin: "Alas, Poor Richard," *The Price of the Ticket, op. cit.,* p. 285.
74. Wright: *Black Boy, op. cit.,* p. 33.
75. Wright: *Pagan Spain, op. cit.,* p. 138 (italics in original).
76. Wright: *Black Power,* p. 254.
77. *Ibid.,* pp. 116–117.
78. Fabre: *La Rive Noire, op. cit.,* p. 191 (author's translation).
79. Wright: *Black Power, op. cit.,* p. 67.
80. Léopold Senghor, quoted in Fabre: *La Rive Noire, op. cit.,* p. 195 (author's translation).
81. See Wright: *White Man, Listen!, op. cit.,* pp. 82 and 99.
82. Wright: *American Hunger, op. cit.,* p. 44.
83. Margaret Walker: *Daemonic Genius, op. cit.,* p. 83.
84. Aaron: "Richard Wright and the Communist Party," *op. cit., Wright: Impressions and Perspectives,* p. 46.
85. *Ibid.,* p. 41.
86. Margaret Walker: *Daemonic Genius, op. cit.,* p. 57.
87. Wright: *American Hunger, op. cit.,* p. 123.

88. *Ibid.,* p. 40.
89. Wright: *Pagan Spain, op. cit.,* p. 1.
90. See Margaret Walker: *Daemonic Genius, op. cit.,* pp. 13 and 42.
91. Wright: *The Long Dream, op. cit.,* pp. 315 and 276.
92. Baldwin: "Alas, Poor Richard," *op. cit., Nobody Knows My Name,* p. 215.
93. Himes: *A Case of Rape,* p. 28.
94. Himes: *If He Hollers Let Him Go, op. cit.,* p. 187.
95. *Ibid.,* p. 153.
96. *Ibid.,* p. 156.
97. *Ibid.,* p. 187.
98. Himes: "Foreword," *op. cit., Black on Black,* pp. 7–8.
99. Himes: *My Life of Absurdity, op. cit.,* p. 27.
100. *Ibid.,* p. 13.
101. See Himes: "Now Is the Time! Here Is the Place," "Negro Martyrs Are Needed," *Black on Black, op. cit.,* pp. 213f and 232f.
102. Himes: "Prediction," *ibid.,* p. 286.
103. Himes: *The Quality of Hurt,* p. 59.
104. Himes: *My Life of Absurdity, op. cit.,* p. 144.
105. *Ibid.,* p. 155.
106. *Ibid.*
107. Bell, *op. cit.,* p. 186.
108. Reed: *Shrovetide, op. cit.,* p. 143.
109. *Ibid.,* p. 41.
110. H. Baker: *The Journey Back, op. cit.,* p. 126.
111. Baldwin: "Many Thousands Gone," *Images of the Negro, op. cit.,* p. 241.
112. Quincy Troupe: "Foreword," *James Baldwin: The Legacy,* p. 17.
113. Baldwin, quoted in Weatherby: *Artist on Fire,* p. 350.
114. Baldwin: *Tell Me How Long the Train's Been Gone,* pp. 444 and 71.
115. Baldwin, quoted in Weatherby: *Artist on Fire, op. cit.,* p. 283; see Cruse: *Crisis, op. cit.,* p. 489.
116. Baldwin: *Tell Me How Long the Train's Been Gone, op. cit.,* p. 330.
117. Baldwin: "Everybody's Protest Novel," *op. cit., The Price of the Ticket,* p. 33.
118. Baldwin: *James Baldwin, Nikki Giovanni: A Dialogue,* p. 23.
119. Fabre: *La Rive Noire, op. cit.,* p. 206 (author's translation).
120. Baldwin: *Baldwin, Giovanni, op. cit.,* p. 15.
121. Baldwin: *A Rap on Race,* p. 10.
122. See Bone: "The Novels of James Baldwin," *op. cit., Images of the Negro,* p. 272.
123. Gayle: *The Way of the New World, op. cit.,* p. 266.
124. Cruse: *Crisis, op. cit.,* p. 297.
125. Baldwin: *A Rap on Race, op. cit.,* pp. 41–42.
126. L. D. Aldridge, quoted by S. E. Anderson: "Revolutionary Black Nationalism and the Pan African Idea," *The Black Seventies, op. cit.,* p. 112.
127. Hoyt Fuller: "The New Black Literature," *The Black Aesthetic,* p. 365.

128. Don L. Lee: "Black Poetry of the '60s," *ibid.*, p. 239 (italics in original).

129. Larry Neal: "The Black Arts Movement," *ibid.*, p. 273.

130. Sollors, *op. cit.*, p. 193.

131. Giovanni: *Conversations, op. cit.*, pp. 35 and 33 (italics in original).

132. Giovanni: "The True Import of Present Dialogue, Black vs. Negro," *Black Feeling Black Talk Black Judgment*, p. 20.

133. Giovanni: "Records," *Ibid.*, p. 67.

134. Judy Simmons, Stephen Henderson: *Understanding the New Black Poetry*, p. 365.

135. Ebon: "The Prophet's Warning or Shoot to Kill," *ibid.*, p. 349.

136. Carolyn Rodgers: "U Name This One," *Black Sister, op. cit.*, p. 183.

137. Gwendolyn Brooks: *Report from Part One, op. cit.*, p. 84.

138. Gwendolyn Brooks: "To Prisoners," *To Disembark*, p. 45.

139. Brooks: "First Fight, Then Fiddle," quoted in Harry B. Shaw: *Gwendolyn Brooks, op. cit.*, p. 114.

140. Baraka: "Black Art," *Black Magic*, p. 116.

141. Baraka, quoted in Sollors, *op. cit.*, p. 186.

142. Baraka: *Dutchman, op. cit., Black Theater*, p. 515.

143. Baraka: *The Slave, Selected Plays and Prose of Amiri Baraka/LeRoi Jones*, p. 118.

144. Baraka: *A Black Mass, Four Black Revolutionary Plays*, p. 31.

145. See Sollors, *op. cit.*, p. 182.

146. Baraka: "The World Is My Poem," *Selected Poetry, op. cit.*, p. 177.

147. Baraka: "Reality Is Dealt With," *ibid.*, p. 157.

148. Baraka: "Leadbelly Gives an Autograph," *ibid., p.* 65.

149. Baraka: "Love Is the Presence of No Enemy," *ibid.*, p. 219.

150. Baraka: "Introduction," *Four Black Revolutionary Plays, op. cit.*, p. vii.

151. Baraka and Fundi: *In Our Territories*, p. 8.

152. Seale, *op. cit.*, p. 4 (see also note 139, ch. 7).

153. Baraka and Fundi, *op. cit.*, pp. 5 and 9.

154. Baraka: "Black Art," *op. cit., Black Magic*, p. 155.

155. Baraka, quoted in Sollors, *op. cit.*, p. 256 (italics in original).

156. Baraka: "New Sense," *Tales*, p. 96.

157. Don L. Lee: "The Wall," *Understanding New Black Poetry, op. cit.*, p. 335.

158. Don L. Lee: "Two Poems," *ibid.*, p. 332.

159. Cruse: *The Black Seventies, op. cit.*, p. 29.

160. Henderson: *Understanding the New Black Poetry, op. cit.*, p. 17.

161. H. Baker: "Introduction," *The Journey Back, op. cit.*, p. xi.

162. Baraka: "Introduction," *The Motion of History, op. cit.*, p. 16.

163. H. Baker: *The Journey Back, op. cit.*, p. 97.

Chapter 13: Black Attitudes Toward Integration

1. Gates, *op. cit.*, p. 21 (see also note 14, ch. 10).

2. *Ibid.*, p. 30.

3. Fabre: *La Rive Noire, op. cit.,* p. 23.
4. Gates, *op. cit.,* p. 93.
5. Wright: *Black Boy, op. cit.,* p. 222.
6. Baldwin: *A Rap on Race, op. cit.,* p. 39.
7. H. Baker: *The Journey Back, op. cit.,* p. 37.
8. See Barbara Christian: *Black Feminist Criticism,* p. 4.
9. Harriet E. Wilson: *Our Nig,* pp. 108 and 12.
10. H. Baker: *The Journey Back, op. cit.,* p. 47.
11. *Ibid.,* p. 58.
12. Baraka: *The Autobiography of LeRoi Jones,* p. 92 (italics in original).
13. DuBois: *Autobiography, op. cit.,* p. 169 (see also notes 65–73, ch. 2).
14. Peter Revell: *Paul Laurence Dunbar,* p. 17.
15. *Ibid.,* p. 20.
16. Charles Chesnutt: quoted in *ibid.,* p. 22.
17. See Russell Ames: "Social Realism in Charles W. Chesnutt," *The Black Novelist, op. cit.* (see also note 52, ch. 10).
18. Dunbar: "We Wear the Mask," *Complete Poems,* p. 71.
19. Dunbar, quoted in Revell, *op. cit.,* p. 163.
20. Dunbar, quoted in *ibid.,* p. 52.
21. Revell, *ibid.,* p. 162.
22. Wagner, *op. cit.,* p. 98.
23. Revell, *op. cit.,* p. 113.
24. Sterling Brown: *The Negro in American Fiction, op. cit.,* p. 84 (italics in original).
25. Dunbar: "Chrismus on the Plantation," *Complete Poems, op. cit.,* p. 138.
26. Revell, *op. cit.,* p. 165.
27. Dunbar, quoted in Redding: "American Negro Literature," *Afro-American Literature, op. cit.,* p. 273.
28. See Revell, *op. cit.,* p. 91.
29. Gates, *op. cit.,* p. 182.
30. J. N. Johnson, quoted in Henderson, *op. cit.,* p. 73.
31. Revell, *op. cit.,* p. 52.
32. Dunbar: "When Malindy Sings," *Complete Poems, op. cit.,* p. 82.
33. Dunbar, quoted in Revell, *op. cit.,* p. 49.
34. Dunbar: "When All Is Done," *Complete Poems, op. cit.,* p. 113.
35. Dunbar, quoted in Revell, *op. cit.,* p. 126 (italics in original).
36. Johnson, quoted in Bell, *op. cit.,* p. 87.
37. Johnson, quoted in Lewis, *op. cit.,* p. 146.
38. Angelina Grimké, quoted in Hull, *op. cit.,* p. 118.
39. See Christian, *op. cit.,* pp. 168f.
40. See Campbell, *op. cit.,* pp. 22–32.
41. Johnson: *The Autobiography of an Ex-Coloured Man,* p. 18.
42. *Ibid.,* p. 14.
43. *Ibid.,* p. 156.
44. *Ibid.,* p. 56.
45. *Ibid.,* p. 144.

46. *Ibid.*, p. 145.
47. D. Lewis, *op. cit.*, p. 115.
48. *Ibid.*, p. 117.
49. *Ibid.*, 120.
50. *Ibid.*, p. 95.
51. *Ibid.*, p. 227.
52. *Ibid.*, p. 174.
53. Toomer, quoted in Cynthia Kerman and Richard Eldridge: *The Lives of Jean Toomer*, p. 189.
54. Toomer: "Being American," *The Wayward and the Seeking*, *op. cit.*, p. 93.
55. Toomer: "Reflections of an Earth-Being," *ibid.*, p. 20.
56. Toomer, quoted in Kerman and Eldridge: *The Lives of Jean Toomer*, *op. cit.*, p. 84.
57. Toomer: "Fern," *Cane*, *op. cit.*, p. 26.
58. Toomer: "Withered Skin of Berries," *The Wayward and the Seeking*, *op. cit.*, pp. 139–140.
59. D. Lewis, *op. cit.*, p. 68.
60. Toomer: "Fern," *Cane*, *op. cit.*, p. 31.
61. Toomer: "Being American," *op. cit.*, *The Wayward and the Seeking*, p. 123.
62. See Wagner, *op. cit.*, p. 277.
63. Toomer: "Cane," *Understanding the New Black Poetry*, *op. cit.*, p. 118.
64. Gérard Cordesse: "The Two Models in Cane," *Regards sur la Littérature Noire Américaine*, p. 13.
65. Toomer: "Avey," *Cane*, *op. cit.*, p. 84.
66. *Ibid.*, p. 88.
67. Toomer: "Theater," *ibid.*, p. 99.
68. Toomer: "Bona and Paul," *ibid.*, p. 145.
69. Toomer, quoted in Kerman and Eldridge: *The Lives of Jean Toomer*, *op. cit.*, p. 98.
70. Toomer, quoted in D. Lewis, *op. cit.*, p. 69.
71. Toomer, quoted in Kerman and Eldridge: *The Lives of Jean Toomer*, *op. cit.*, pp. 96 and 174.
72. Toomer: "Kabnis," *Cane*, *op. cit.*, pp. 158 and 200.
73. *Ibid.*, p. 212.
74. *Ibid.*, p. 224.
75. *Ibid.*, p. 226.
76. Toomer, quoted in Kerman and Eldridge: *The Lives of Jean Toomer*, *op. cit.*, p. 81.
77. Toomer: "Blue Meridian," *The Wayward and the Seeking*, *op. cit.*, p. 225.
78. Kerman and Eldridge: *The Lives of Jean Toomer*, *op. cit.*, p. 330.
79. Toomer, quoted in *ibid.*, p. 299.
80. *Ibid.*, p. 300.
81. Toomer: "Natalie Mann," *op. cit.*, *The Wayward and the Seeking*, p. 255.

82. Toomer, quoted in Kerman and Eldridge: *The Lives of Jean Toomer*, *op. cit.*, p. 371.

83. Toomer: "Split Men," *The Wayward and the Seeking*, *op. cit.*, p. 423 (italics in original).

84. Toomer, quoted in Kerman and Eldridge: *The Lives of Jean Toomer*, *op. cit.*, p. 301.

85. Gates, *op. cit.*, p. 224.

86. Toomer: "Natalie Mann," *op. cit.*, *The Wayward and the Seeking*, p. 280.

87. Redding: "The Negro Writer and His Relation to His Roots," *Black Voices*, *op. cit.*, p. 617.

88. Emanuel and Gross: *Dark Symphony*, *op. cit.*, p. 67.

89. George Kent: "Patterns of the Harlem Renaissance," *op. cit.*, *The Harlem Renaissance Remembered*, p. 27.

90. Cruse: *Crisis*, *op. cit.*, pp. 38 and 230.

91. Wallace Thurman, quoted in "The Infants of the Spring," *The Negro in American Fiction*, *op. cit.*, p. 146.

92. See Hiroko Sato: "Under the Harlem Shadow: A Study of Jessie Fauset and Nella Larsen," *The Harlem Renaissance Remembered*, *op. cit.*, pp. 69–80.

93. C. Bell, *op. cit.*, pp. 106 and 112.

94. Fauset, quoted in Amritjit Singh: *The Novels of the Harlem Renaissance*, p. 41.

95. Gayle: *The Way of the New World*, *op. cit.*, p. 126.

96. George Schuyler: "The Negro-Art Hokum," *Voices from the Harlem Renaissance*, *op. cit.*, p. 311.

97. Schuyler: "Our Greatest Gift to America," *ibid.*, p. 365.

98. Marianne B. Russell: "The Evolution of Style in the Poetry of Melvin B. Tolson," *Black Poets Between Worlds*, p. 13.

99. Tolson: "Dark Symphony," *The Poetry of the Negro*, *op. cit.*, pp. 140 and 149.

100. Tolson: "Libretto for the Republic of Liberia," *Black Poets Between Worlds*, *op. cit.*, p. 10.

101. Tolson: "Harlem Gallery," Jon Woodson: "Melvin Tolson and the Art of Being Difficult," *ibid.*, p. 36.

102. See Woodson, *ibid.*, pp. 23 and 38.

103. Larsen, *op. cit.*, p. 97.

104. D. Lewis, *op. cit.*, p. 231.

105. Gerald Early: "Introduction," *My Soul's High Song: The Collected Writings of Countee Cullen*, p. 22.

106. Rampersad: *The Life of Langston Hughes*, vol. 1, p. 63.

107. Cullen, quoted in D. Lewis, *op. cit.*, p. 77.

108. Cullen: "The Shroud of Color," *Black Poets of the United States*, *op. cit.*, p. 299.

109. See Cullen: "The Black Christ," *ibid.*, p. 304.

110. Cullen: "Pagan Prayer," *My Soul's High Song*, *op. cit.*, p. 93.

111. Cullen, quoted in *From the Dark Tower*, p. 73.
112. Cullen: "Heritage," *My Soul's High Song, op. cit.,* p. 107.
113. Cullen, quoted in Nicholas Canaday: "Major Themes in the Poetry of Countee Cullen," *The Harlem Renaissance Remembered, op. cit.,* p. 115.
114. Cullen, quoted in *From the Dark Tower, op. cit.,* p. 77.
115. Cullen, quoted in *ibid.,* p. 74.
116. Cullen: "A Thorn Forever in the Breast," from "The Black Poetry," *op. cit., Black Poets of the United States,* p. 304.
117. See "The Black Christ," *My Soul's High Song, op. cit.,* pp. 194f.
118. Georgia Johnson, quoted in Hull, *op. cit.,* p. 179.
119. See Georgia Johnson: "A Sunday Morning in the South," "Blue Blood," "Blue-Eyed Baby," *Black Female Playwrights.*
120. Hull, *op. cit.,* p. 72.
121. D. Lewis, *op. cit.,* p. 193.
122. Rampersad: *Life of Langston Hughes, op. cit.,* p. 119.
123. Thurman and Zora Neale Hurston, quoted in D. Lewis, *op. cit.,* p. 193.
124. Mae Gwendolyn Henderson: "Portrait of Wallace Thurman," *The Harlem Renaissance Remembered, op. cit.,* p. 167.
125. *Ibid.,* p. 165.
126. Hurston, *op. cit.,* p. 3.
127. Hurston: *Dust Tracks on a Road,* p. 233 (italics in original).
128. *Ibid.*
129. *Ibid.,* p. 326.
130. *Ibid.,* p. 218.
131. *Ibid.,* p. 328.
132. Hurston, quoted in Hezli V. Carby: "The Politics of Fiction, Anthropology, and the Folk: Zora Neale Hurston," *New Essays on "Their Eyes Were Watching God,"* p. 79.
133. Hurston: *Dust Tracks on a Road,* p. 60.
134. *Ibid.,* p. 116.
135. Quoted in Hull, *op. cit.,* p. 112.
136. See Hull, *ibid.,* p. 129.
137. Fenton Johnson, quoted in *Black Writers of America, op. cit.,* p. 456.
138. Grimké: "Under the Days," quoted in Hull, *op. cit.,* p. 152.
139. C. McKay: "Mulatto," *Voices from the Harlem Renaissance, op. cit.,* p. 182.
140. C. McKay: *Home to Harlem, op. cit.,* p. 10.
141. James De Jongh: *Vicious Modernism,* pp. 82–210.
142. Locke: "Spiritual Truancy," *Voices from the Harlem Renaissance, op. cit.,* p. 406.
143. C. McKay: "Tiger," *Black Writers of America, op. cit.,* p. 494.
144. C. McKay: "Outcast," *Afro-American Literature, op. cit.,* p. 109.
145. C. McKay: *Home to Harlem, op. cit.,* p. 274.
146. *Ibid.,* p. 263.
147. See D. Lewis, *op. cit.,* pp. 54 and 57.

148. See Cruse: *Crisis, op. cit.*, pp. 51–53.
149. C. McKay: *Banana Bottom, op. cit.*, p. 121.
150. Michael Stoll: "Claude McKay and the Cult of Primitivism," *The Harlem Renaissance Remembered, op. cit.*, p. 139.
151. Himes, quoted in "Introduction," *Black Voices, op. cit.*, p. 33.
152. DuBois: "On Being Black," *op. cit., Voices from the Harlem Renaissance*, p. 211.
153. Early: "Introduction," *op. cit.*, p. 59.
154. Hughes, quoted in D. Lewis, *op. cit.*, p. 83.
155. Hughes: "Simply Heavenly," *Langston Hughes Reader, op. cit.*, p. 258.
156. Hughes: "Passing," *ibid.*, p. 116.
157. Hughes, quoted in D. Lewis, *op. cit.*, p. 84.
158. Hughes, quoted in Weatherby, *Artist on Fire, op. cit.*, p. 116.
159. Ellison: "Richard Wright's Blues," *Black Writers of America, op. cit.*, p. 692.
160. Hayden: "The Web," *Collected Poems, op. cit.*, p. 42.
161. Hayden, quoted in Fred Fetron: "Portraits and Personal Characterization in the Poetry of Robert Hayden," *Black Poets Between Worlds, op. cit.*, p. 53.
162. S. E. Hyman: "Ralph Ellison in Our Times," *Ralph Ellison: A Collection of Critical Essays*, p. 51.
163. See Arthur Davis, *From the Dark Tower, op. cit.*, p. 208.
164. See Baldwin, quoted in Morris Dickstein: "Wright, Baldwin, Cleaver," *Wright: Impressions and Perspectives, op. cit.*, p. 185.
165. James McPherson: "Indivisible Man," *Critical Essays, op. cit.*, p. 44.
166. Richard Kostelanetz, quoted in *ibid.*
167. Jonathan Baumbach: "Nightmare of a Native Son: *Invisible Man* by Ralph Ellison," *Modern Black Novelists, op. cit.*, p. 64.
168. Littlejohn, *op. cit.*, pp. 110 and 157.
169. Ellison, quoted in McPherson, *op. cit., Critical Essays*, p. 44.
170. See *ibid.*, p. 46.
171. Gayle: *The Way of the New World, op. cit.*, p. 257.
172. Ellison: *Invisible Man, op. cit.*, p. 381.
173. Marcus Klein: "Ralph Ellison's Invisible Man," *Five Black Writers, op. cit.*, p. 99.
174. Ellison: *Invisible Man, op. cit.*, pp. 382–383.
175. Ellison, quoted in C.W.E. Bigsby: "From Protest to Paradox: The Black Writer at MidCentury," *The Fifties*, p. 231.
176. Ellison: "King of the Bingo Game," *Dark Symphony, op. cit.*, p. 274.
177. Tony Tanner: *City of Words*, p. 53.
178. Bigsby, *op. cit., The Fifties*, p. 233.
179. Bone: "Ralph Ellison and the Uses of Imagination," *Modern Black Novelists, op. cit.*, p. 48.
180. Ellison, quoted in *ibid.*, p. 53.
181. Ellison, quoted in Hyman, *op. cit., Critical Essays*, p. 39.
182. Ellison, quoted in Warren: "The Unity of Experience," *ibid.*, p. 25.

183. Ellison, quoted in Neal: "Ellison's Zoot Suit," *Critical Essays, op. cit.,* p. 64.

184. Ellison: *Shadow and Act, op. cit.,* p. 255.

185. Reed: *Shrovetide, op. cit.,* p. 88.

186. Colin MacInnes: "Dark Angel: The Writings of James Baldwin," *Five Black Writers, op. cit.,* p. 120.

187. Reed: *Shrovetide, op. cit.,* p. 135.

188. Baldwin, quoted in *Artist on Fire, op. cit.,* p. 33.

189. Baldwin: "The Last Interview," *The Legacy, op. cit.,* p. 205.

190. Troupe: "Foreword," *ibid.,* p. 12.

191. Baldwin: *A Rap on Race, op. cit.,* p. 143.

192. Baldwin: *Dialogue with Giovanni, op. cit.,* p. 35.

193. Troupe: "Foreword," *op. cit., The Legacy,* p. 17.

194. Baldwin: "Dialogue in Black and White," *ibid.,* p. 148.

195. Baldwin, quoted in *Artist on Fire, op. cit.,* p. 350 (see also note 113, ch. 12).

196. Baldwin: "Dialogue in Black and White," *op. cit., The Legacy,* p. 158.

197. Baldwin, quoted in *Artist on Fire, op. cit.,* p. 2.

198. Baldwin, quoted in MacInnes, *op. cit., Five Black Writers,* p. 140.

199. Baldwin: "No Name in the Street," *The Price of the Ticket, op. cit.,* p. 474 (see also note 43, ch. 6).

200. Baldwin, quoted in *Artist on Fire, op. cit.,* p. 140.

201. Reed: *Shrovetide, op. cit.,* p. 135.

202. Baldwin: *Nobody Knows My Name, op. cit.,* p. 29 (see also note 5, ch. 6).

203. Margaret Mead: *A Rap on Race, op. cit.,* p. 239.

204. Baldwin: "The Last Interview," *op. cit., The Legacy,* pp. 191, 189, 190.

205. Robert Lanz, quoted in *Artist on Fire, op. cit.,* p. 276.

206. Weatherby, *ibid.,* p. 2.

207. Campbell, *op. cit.,* p. 108.

208. See Bone: *The Negro Novel in America,* pp. 226 and 234.

209. Bone: "The Novels of James Baldwin," *op. cit., Images of the Negro,* p. 285.

210. *Ibid.,* p. 287.

211. Baldwin: "The New Lost Generation," *The Price of the Ticket, op. cit.,* p. 308 (see note 127, ch. 9).

212. Toomer: "Natalie Mann," *The Wayward and the Seeking, op. cit.,* p. 262.

213. Sterling Brown: *The Negro in American Fiction, op. cit.,* p. 145.

214. Schuyler, quoted in Lewis, *op. cit.,* p. 92.

215. Fenton Johnson: *Black Writers in America, op. cit.,* p. 456.

216. Larsen, *op. cit.,* p. 129.

217. Rudolph Fisher, quoted in Emanuel and Gross: *Dark Symphony, op. cit.,* p. 111.

218. Cullen: *One Way to Heaven, op. cit.,* p. 187.

219. Cleaver, *op. cit.,* p. 178.

220. Baldwin: *Dialogue with Giovanni, op. cit.,* p. 40.

221. Hernton, *op. cit.*, p. 62 (italics in original).
222. *Ibid.*, p. 61.
223. *Ibid.*, p. 66.
224. Wright: *The Long Dream, op. cit.*, p. 363.
225. Fabre: *The Unfinished Quest of Richard Wright*, p. 48.
226. Margaret Walker: *Daemonic Genius, op. cit.*, pp. 163 and 310.
227. Wright: *American Hunger, op. cit.*, p. 12.
228. Quoted in Fabre: *Unfinished Quest, op. cit.*, p. 477 (italics in original).
229. Himes: *Lonely Crusade*, p. 69.
230. Himes: *The Primitive*, p. 21.
231. Himes: *A Case of Rape, op. cit.*, p. 84.
232. *Ibid*, p. 89.
233. Himes: *The Quality of Hurt, op. cit.*, p. 285.
234. Himes: *If He Hollers Let Him Go, op. cit.*, p. 123.
235. Himes: *The Quality of Hurt, op. cit.*, p. 137.
236. *Ibid.*, p. 4.
237. Himes: *My Life of Absurdity, op. cit.*, p. 155.
238. Vidal: *Myron*, p. 88 (italics in original).
239. Malcolm X: *Autobiography, op. cit.*, p. 67.
240. Baraka: *Autobiography, op. cit.*, p. 224.
241. *Ibid.*, p. 232.
242. Cleaver, *op. cit.*, p. 8.
243. *Ibid.*, pp. 14 and 17.
244. Malcolm X: *Autobiography, op. cit.*, p. 121.
245. Baraka: "Black Dada Nihilismus," *Selected Poetry, op. cit.*, p. 41.
246. Cain, *op. cit.*, p. 99.
247. Etheridge Knight: *Black Voices from Prison, op. cit.*, p. 19.
248. Malcolm X: *Autobiography, op. cit.*, p. 95.
249. Cain, *op. cit.*, pp. 92 and 93.
250. Himes: *Lonely Crusade, op. cit.*, p. 305.
251. *Ibid.*, p. 306.
252. Himes: *The Quality of Hurt, op. cit.*, p. 285.
253. Cecil Brown: *The Lives and Loves of Mr. Jiveass Nigger*, p. 154.
254. *Ibid.*, p. 8.
255. *Ibid.*, p. 7.
256. *Ibid.*, p. 110.
257. See Baldwin: *Dialogue with Giovanni, op. cit.*, pp. 49 and 55.
258. See Alice Walker: *The Third Life of Grange Copeland, passim.*
259. Giovanni: "Make Up," *Cotton Candy on a Rainy Day*, p. 80.
260. Mary Burgher: "Images of Self and Race in the Autobiographies of Black Women," *Sturdy Black Bridges*, p. 116.
261. Carole Gregory: "A Freedom Song for the Black Woman," *Black Sister, op. cit.*, p. 188.
262. Stetson: "Introduction," *Ibid.*, p. xvii.
263. Christian: "The Contrary Women of Alice Walker: A Study of Female Protagonists in *In Love and Trouble*," *Black Feminist Criticism, op. cit.*, pp. 44–45.

264. Hurston: *Their Eyes Were Watching God*, p. 29.
265. Gwendolyn Bennett: "Heritage," *Black Sister, op. cit.*, p. 77.
266. Christian: "Ritualistic Process and the Structure of Paule Marshall's *Praisesong for the Widow*," *Black Feminist Criticism, op. cit.*, p. 25.
267. Sojourner Truth: *Black Sister, op. cit.*, p. 25.
268. Hughes: "The Negro Mother," *Langston Hughes, op. cit.*, p. 119.
269. Gwendolyn Brooks: "The Last Quatrain of Emmett Till," *The Bean Eaters*, p. 26.
270. Baldwin: *A Rap on Race, op. cit.*, p. 48.
271. Hull: "Black Women Poets from Wheatley to Walker," *Sturdy Black Bridges, op. cit.*, p. 69.
272. William Gardner Smith: *Return to Black America*, p. 7.
273. Carolyn Rodgers: "It Is Deep," *Sturdy Black Bridges, op. cit.*, p. 378.
274. See Frazier: *The Black Bourgeoisie, passim*; Moynihan, Moynihan Report, *op. cit., passim*.
275. See Himes: *The Third Generation*.
276. Ntozake Shange: *Betsey Brown*, p. 206.
277. Jessie Fauset: "Touché," *Black Sister, op. cit.*, p. 63.
278. Hernton, *op. cit.*, pp. 123 and 61.
279. Alice Walker: *Meridian*, pp. 107 and 106.
280. Carole Gregory: "A Freedom Song," *Black Sister, op. cit.*, p. 189.
281. Toni Morrison, quoted in Giddings: *When and Where I Enter, op. cit.*, p. 307.
282. Hernton, *op. cit.*, p. 135.
283. Morrison: *The Bluest Eye*, p. 139.
284. Giovanni: *Dialogue with Baldwin, op. cit.*, pp. 49 and 58.
285. Alice Walker: *The Temple of My Familiar*, pp. 253 and 273.
286. Angelou: *Gather Together in My Name*, p. 141.
287. Giddings: *When and Where I Enter, op. cit.*, p. 328.
288. Reed: *Reckless Eyeballing, op. cit.*, p. 26.
289. *Ibid.*, p. 8 (see also note 25, ch. 9).
290. Christian: "Trajectories of Self-definition: Placing Contemporary Afro-American Fiction," *op. cit.*, p. 179.
291. Kardiner and Ovesey, *op. cit., Beyond the Angry Black*, p. 100.
292. Giovanni: "Being and Nothingness," "I Am," "Introspection," *Cotton Candy, op. cit.*, pp. 89, 233, 25.
293. Carolyn Rodgers: "Poem for Some Black Women," *Black Sister, op. cit.*, p. 177.
294. Noble, *op. cit.*, p. 192.

Chapter 14: Black Racial Memory

1. Sterling Brown: *The Negro in American Fiction, op. cit.*, p. 145.
2. Williamson, *op. cit.*, p. 63.
3. Baldwin: *A Rap on Race, op. cit.*, p. 124.
4. Toomer: "Blue Meridian," *op. cit., The Wayward and the Seeking*, p. 239 (italics in original).

5. *Ibid.,* p. 232.
6. Herskovits, *op. cit.,* p. 33.
7. *Ibid.,* p. 16.
8. Williamson: "Preface," *op. cit.,* p. xi.
9. Larsen, *op. cit.,* p. 36.
10. See Arthur Davis: "Trends in Negro American Literature," *Dark Symphony, op. cit.,* p. 523.
11. Comer, *op. cit.,* p. 191.
12. Alice Walker: *The Third Life of Grange Copeland, op. cit.,* p. 196.
13. Gates: "Introduction: On Bearing Witness," *Bearing Witness,* p. 5.
14. Comer, *op. cit.,* p. 191.
15. Julian Mayfield: "Into the Mainstream and Oblivion," *Dark Symphony, op. cit.,* p. 560.
16. Werner, *op. cit., Critical Essay on Toni Morrison,* p. 151.
17. Ellison, quoted in George Kent: "Ralph Ellison and Afro-American Folk and Cultural Tradition," *Critical Essays, op. cit.,* p. 162.
18. H. Baker: *The Journey Back, op. cit.,* p. 121.
19. See Michael G. Cooke: *Afro-American Literature in the Twentieth Century,* p. 5.
20. See Wright: *Black Power, op. cit.*
21. Baraka: *Autobiography, op. cit.,* pp. 310–311.
22. Himes: *Cotton Comes to Harlem, passim,* especially p. 36.
23. Alice Walker, quoted in Christian: "The Black Woman Artist as Wayward," *Alice Walker, op. cit.,* p. 49.
24. Alice Walker: *The Temple of My Familiar, op. cit.,* p. 147.
25. Quoted in Abiola Irele: "Negritude: Literature and Ideology," *Modern Black Novelists, op. cit.,* p. 19.
26. Locke: *From the Dark Tower, op. cit.,* pp. 56–57.
27. Lester, *op. cit.,* p. 57.
28. Gwendolyn Brooks: *Report from Part One, op. cit.,* p. 25.
29. Baraka and Fundi, *op. cit.,* p. 58.
30. Reed: *Mumbo Jumbo, op. cit.,* p. 5.
31. DuBois, quoted in Robert Stepto: *From Behind the Veil,* p. 54.
32. H. Baker: *The Journey Back, op. cit.,* pp. 133–134 (italics in original).
33. Gwendolyn Brooks: *Report from Part One, op. cit.,* p. 87 (italics in original).
34. *Ibid.,* p. 45.
35. Hurston: *Mules and Men, op. cit.,* p. 3 (see also note 126, ch. 13).
36. Sterling Brown: *The Negro in American Fiction, op. cit.,* p. 154.
37. Toomer: *Cane, op. cit.,* p. 31.
38. Campbell, *op. cit.,* pp. 152 and 151.
39. Bell, *op. cit.,* p. 36.
40. See Campbell, *op. cit.,* p. 7.
41. *Ibid.,* p. 99.
42. Henderson: *Understanding the New Black Poetry, op. cit.,* pp. 62 and 66.

43. Campbell: "Introduction," *op. cit.,* p. x.
44. See Alice Walker: *Living by the Word,* p. 36.
45. Frazier: *On Race Relations, op. cit.,* p. 103.
46. Toni Morrison, quoted in Bettye J. Parker: "Complexity: Toni Morrison's Women—An Interview Essay," *Sturdy Black Bridges, op. cit.,* p. 253.
47. Sunday O. Anozie: "Negritude, Structuralism, Deconstruction," *Black Literature and Literary Theory,* p. 107.
48. *Ibid.,* p. 117.
49. *Ibid.,* pp. 115–116.
50. Senghor, quoted in *ibid.,* p. 116.
51. Reed: *Shrovetide, op. cit.,* p. 10.
52. See Lafcadio Hearn: "Letters of Ozias Midwinter," *Letters from the Raven,* p. 168.
53. Bronners, *ibid.,* p. 167.
54. Reed: *Shrovetide, op. cit.,* p. 75.
55. Hurston: *Mules and Men, op. cit.,* p. 229.
56. Charles Chesnutt: *Conjure Tales, passim.*
57. Shange: *Sassafras, Cypress and Indigo,* p. 5.
58. H. Baker: *The Journey Back, op. cit.,* p. 12.
59. Jayne Cortez: "Orisha," *Black Sister, op. cit.,* p. 151.
60. H. Baker: *The Journey Back, op. cit.,* p. 19.
61. Gwendolyn Brooks: "Riders to the Blood-Red Wrath," *Selected Poems,* pp. 116–117.
62. Locke, quoted in *From the Dark Tower, op. cit.,* p. 59.
63. Cullen: "Brown Girl," *Black Poets of America, op. cit.,* p. 317.
64. Kattie M. Combo: "Black Sister," *Black Sister, op. cit.,* p. 135.
65. Baraka: "A Poem for Black Hearts," *Black Magic, op. cit.,* p. 112.
66. George Kent, quoted in H. Baker: *The Journey Back, op. cit.,* p. 1.
67. Gwendolyn Brooks: "Riders to the Blood-Red Wrath," *op. cit., Selected Poems,* p. 117.
68. Campbell: "Introduction," *op. cit.,* p. ix.
69. See Ellison: *Shadow and Act, op. cit.,* p. 249.
70. See Douglass, quoted in John F. Callahan: *In the Afro-American Grain,* p. 28.
71. See Baraka: *Black Music,* pp. 14, 16, and *passim.*
72. See Gates: *Figures in Black, op. cit.,* p. 36.
73. Bell, *op. cit.,* p. 36.
74. Wright: "The Man Who Went to Chicago," *Eight Men, op. cit.,* p. 168.
75. Baldwin: *No Name in the Street, op. cit.,* p. 189.
76. Cleaver: "The White Race and Its Heroes," *America and Its Discontents, op. cit.,* p. 263.
77. Gwendolyn Brooks: "Riders to the Blood-Red Wrath," *op. cit., Selected Poems,* p. 118 (see also notes 20–27, ch. 1).
78. See Marianne B. Russell: "Evolution of Style in the Poetry of Melvin B. Tolson," *op. cit., Black Poets Between Worlds,* p. 11.

79. Tolson: "Dark Symphony," *op. cit., Black Writers of America,* p. 671.
80. H. Baker: *The Journey Back, op. cit.,* p. 70.
81. Ellison, quoted in *ibid.,* p. 59.
82. Hayden: "American Journal," *Collected Poems, op. cit.,* p. 192.
83. *Ibid.,* p. 194.
84. Neal, quoted in *From the Dark Tower, op. cit.,* p. 227.
85. H. Baker: *The Journey Back, op. cit.,* p. 142.
86. H. Baker: *Singers of Daybreak, op. cit.,* p. 90.
87. DuBois, quoted in H. Baker: *The Journey Back, op. cit.,* p. 124.
88. Cooke: "Preface," *Afro-American Literature in the Twentieth Century, op. cit.,* p. x (italics in original).
89. Henderson: *Understanding the New Black Poetry, op. cit.,* p. 62.
90. H.L. Gates, Jr.: *Figures in Black, op. cit.,* p. 36.
91. See Hurston: *Mules and Men, op. cit.,* p. 85.
92. See Thadious M. Davis: "Walker's Celebration of Self in Southern Generations," *Alice Walker,* pp. 25f.
93. Alice Walker: "Interview," *Sturdy Black Bridges, op. cit.,* p. 136.
94. H. L. Gates, Jr.: "Introduction," *op. cit., Bearing Witness,* p. 5 (italics in original).
95. Reed: *Mumbo Jumbo, op. cit.,* pp. 204 and 6 (italics in original).
96. Anozie, *op. cit., Black Literature and Literary Theory,* p. 118 (italics in original).
97. See Bell: "Introduction," *op. cit.,* p. xiii.
98. F. O. Mathiessen, quoted in Bell, *ibid.,* p. 21.
99. See Michael Awkward: *Inspiring Influences,* p. 49.
100. Redding, quoted in *Afro-American Literature: An Introduction, op. cit.,* p. 1 (see also note 28, ch. 12).
101. H. L. Gates, Jr.: "The Master's Race: On Canon Formation and the Afro-American Tradition," *Loose Canons,* p. 33.
102. Henderson: *Understanding the New Black Poetry, op. cit.,* p. 17 (see also note 160, ch. 12).
103. Neal, quoted in *ibid.*
104. H. Baker: *Singers of Daybreak, op. cit.,* p. 5.
105. June Jordan: *Civil Wars,* p. 87.
106. H. L. Gates, Jr.: *Figures in Black, op. cit.,* p. 39.
107. *Ibid.,* p. 36.
108. Stepto: "Preface," *op. cit.,* p. ix.
109. Ellison: *Invisible Man, op. cit.,* p. 307.
110. H. L. Gates, Jr.: *Figures in Black, op. cit.,* p. 49.
111. See Michael McKean, quoted in "Introduction," *Intertextuality and Contemporary American Fiction,* p. xvi.
112. Reed: "I Am a Cowboy in the Boat of Ra," *Afro-American Literature: An Introduction, op. cit.,* p. 152.
113. Baldwin: "The Devil Finds Work," *The Price of the Ticket, op. cit.,* p. 631.
114. Lincoln: *The Avenue, Clayton City,* p. 30.

115. Rap Brown: "Rap's Poem," *Understanding the New Black Poetry, op. cit.*, p. 187.
116. Hughes: "Ask Your Mama; Twelve Moods for Jazz," quoted in Emanuel: *Langston Hughes, op. cit.*, p. 167.
117. Rampersad: *The Life of Langston Hughes*, vol. 2, *op. cit.*, p. 167.
118. See H. L. Gates, Jr.: *Figures in Black, op. cit.*, p. 51.
119. Reed: *Shrovetide, op. cit.*, pp. 259 and 271.
120. Paule Marshall: *Praisesong for the Widow*, p. 38.
121. H. Baker: *Singers of Daybreak, op. cit.*, p. 13.
122. H. Baker: *The Journey Back*, p. 31.
123. *Ibid.*, p. 135.
124. *Ibid.*, p. 39.
125. Toomer, quoted in H. L. Gates, Jr.: *Figures in Black, op. cit.*, p. 201.
126. Christian: "Creating a Universal Literature: Afro-American Women Writers," *op. cit.*, p. 161.
127. Toni Morrison: *Sula, op. cit.*, p. 118.
128. Campbell, *op. cit.*, p. 140.
129. Alice Walker: *Meridian, op. cit.*, p. 213.
130. Alice Walker: *The Color Purple, op. cit.*, p. 110.
131. H. L. Gates, Jr.: *Figures in Black, op. cit.*, p. 174.
132. Ferdinand de Saussure: *Course in General Linguistics*, p. 122 (italics in original).
133. Johnson: *The Autobiography of an Ex-Coloured Man, op. cit.*, p. 75 (italics in original).
134. H. L. Gates, Jr.: *Figures in Black, op. cit.*, p. 177.
135. H. Baker: *The Journey Back, op. cit.*, p. 20.
136. Hayden: "Names," *Collected Poems, op. cit.*, p. 171.
137. Hayden: "El-Haji Malik El-Shabazz," *ibid.*, pp. 88–89.
138. Kimberly Benston: "I Yam What I Am: The Topos of Un(naming) in Afro-American Literature," *Black Literature and Literary Theory, op. cit.*, p. 152.
139. Bell, *op. cit.*, p. 334.

Chapter 15: Black Cultural Commitment

1. Stepto: "Preface," *op. cit.*, p. ix.
2. Bell, *op. cit.*, p. 284.
3. *Ibid.*, p. 246.
4. H. L. Gates, Jr.: *Figures in Black*, pp. 274 and 276.
5. Gloria Naylor: *The Women of Brewster Place*, p. 86.
6. H. L. Gates, Jr.: *Figures in Black, op. cit.*, p. 275.
7. Alice Walker, quoted in Deborah McDonnell: "The Changing Game: Generations, Connections and Black Novelists," *Alice Walker, op. cit.*, p. 142.
8. Quoted in H. L. Gates, Jr.: "The Blackness of Blackness: A Critique of

the Sign and the Signifying Monkey," *Black Literature and Literary Theory, op. cit.,* p. 316.

9. *Ibid.,* p. 293.
10. Quoted in Reed: *Shrovetide, op. cit.,* p. 99.
11. Hurston: *Their Eyes Were Watching God, op. cit.,* p. 210.
12. Tolson: "Harlem Gallery," *op. cit., Black Poets Between Worlds,* p. 36.
13. Quoted in H. Baker: "To Move Without Moving: Creativity and Commerce in Ralph Ellison's Trueblood Episode," *Black Literature and Literary Theory, op. cit.,* p. 231.
14. Sterling Brown: *The Negro in American Fiction, op. cit.,* p. 144.
15. *Ibid.,* p. 75.
16. *Ibid.,* p. 98.
17. See Baldwin: *Blues for Mister Charlie, op. cit.,* p. 49 (see also note 5, ch. 11).
18. Johnson, *Autobiography of an Ex-Coloured Man, op. cit.,* p. 211.
19. Alice Walker: "The Thing Itself," *Horses Make a Landscape Look More Beautiful,* p. 62.
20. Chesnutt: "The Wife of His Youth," *Black Writers of America, op. cit.*
21. Hughes: "Mulatto," *Dark Symphony, op. cit.,* p. 206 (italics in original).
22. See Arthur Davis: "The Tragic Mulatto Theme in the Works of Langston Hughes," *Five Black Writers, op. cit.,* p. 171.
23. Wright: *American Hunger, op. cit.,* p. 13 (see also note 62, ch. 12).
24. See Ellison: *Shadow and Act, op. cit.,* p. 101.
25. Henry Miller: "Amanda," from "Big Sur," Mailer: *Genius and Lust, op. cit.,* p. 567.
26. Anozie, *Black Literature and Literary Theory, op. cit.,* p. 107 (see also note 47, ch. 14).
27. See H. L. Gates, Jr.: *Figures in Black, op. cit.,* p. 274; "What's in a Name?: Some Meanings of Blackness," *Loose Canons, op. cit.,* p. 138.
28. Gerard William Barrax: "Black Narcissus," *Afro-American Literature: An Introduction, op. cit.,* p. 146.
29. Elizabeth S. Foster: "Notes," Herman Melville: *The Confidence-Man: His Masquerade,* p. 296.
30. Norman O. Brown: *Hermes the Thief,* p. 18.
31. Stetson: "Introduction," *op. cit., Black Sister,* p. xviii.
32. Senghor, quoted in Anozie, *op. cit., Black Literature and Literary Theory,* p. 107 (italics in original).
33. See *ibid.,* p. 121.
34. Jay Edwards: "Structural Analysis of the Afro-American Trickster Tale," *ibid.,* p. 90.
35. Victor Turner, quoted in Stepto, *op. cit.,* p. 69.
36. Stepto, *ibid.,* p. 167.
37. H. L. Gates, Jr.: *Figures in Black, op. cit.,* p. 123.
38. *Ibid.,* p. 93.
39. Toomer: *Cane, op. cit.,* p. 236.
40. Kerman and Eldridge: *The Lives of Jean Toomer, op. cit.,* p. 342.
41. Toomer: *Cane, op. cit.,* p. 200.

42. Lindsay Barrett: "The Tide Inside, It Rages," *Black Fire, op. cit.,* p. 153.
43. Gayle: *The Way of the New World, op. cit.,* p. 168.
44. Redding: "The Negro Writer and His Relation to His Roots," *op. cit., Black Voices,* p. 617 (see also note 12, ch. 12).
45. See H. Baker: *The Journey Back,* p. 1.
46. George Kent, quoted in *ibid.*
47. Hughes: "The Negro Speaks of Rivers," *The Langston Hughes Reader, op. cit.,* p. 88.
48. Morrison: *Beloved,* pp. 166 and 36.
49. Baldwin: "This Morning, This Evening, So Soon," *The Best Short Stories by Negro Writers,* p. 215.
50. Toomer: *Cane, op. cit.,* p. 112.
51. Toomer, quoted in Cooke: *Afro-American Literature in the Twentieth Century, op. cit.,* p. 187.
52. Billie Holiday, quoted in Angelou: *The Heart of a Woman,* p. 9.
53. Stepto, *op. cit.,* p. 67.
54. See Ellison: "Flying Home," *Dark Symphony, op. cit.,* p. 270.
55. See Alice Walker: "One Child of One's Own," Marianne Hirsh: "Clytemnestra's Children: Writing (Out) the Mother's Anger," *Alice Walker, op. cit.,* p. 35.
56. Shange: *Betsey Brown, op. cit.,* p. 35.
57. Shange: *Sassafras, Cypress and Indigo, op. cit.,* p. 224.
58. See H. Baker: "To Move Without Moving," *op. cit., Black Literature and Literary Theory,* pp. 222f.
59. Himes: *A Case of Rape, op. cit.,* p. 14.
60. See Morrison: *The Bluest Eye, passim,* especially p. 189.
61. See Faulkner: *Absalom, Absalom!, op. cit.*
62. Irma McClaurin: "Chain," *Black Sister, op. cit.,* p. 199.
63. See H. Baker: "To Move Without Moving," *Black Literature and Literary Theory, op. cit.,* p. 235.
64. Morrison: *The Bluest Eye, op. cit.,* p. 189.
65. *Ibid.,* p. 188.
66. *Ibid.,* p. 9.
67. *Ibid.,* p. 90.
68. Margaret Walker: *For My People,* p. 13.
69. Cruse: *Crisis, op. cit.,* p. 202.
70. Johnson: *Autobiography of an Ex-Coloured Man, op. cit.,* pp. 76–77.
71. McKay: "Negro Dancers," *The New Negro, op. cit.,* p. 215.
72. Gwendolyn Brooks: "A Song in the Front Yard," *Selected Poems, op. cit.,* p. 6.
73. Gwendolyn Brooks: "I Love These Little Booths at Benvenuti's," *ibid.,* p. 59.
74. Jayne Cortez: "Under the Edge of February," *Black Sister, op. cit.,* p. 154.
75. Cain, *op. cit.,* p. 19.
76. *Ibid.,* p. 66.

77. Hughes, quoted in Rampersad: *The Life of Langston Hughes,* vol. 2, *op. cit.,* p. 312 (italics in original).

78. Ossie Davis: *Purlie Victorious, Black Theater, op. cit.,* p. 447.

79. Giovanni: "Nikki-Rosa," *Black Sister, op. cit.,* p. 234.

80. See Benston: "I Yam What I Am," *Black Literature and Literary Theory, op. cit.,* pp. 152f.

81. Naylor: *Linden Hills,* p. 254.

82. Gwendolyn Brooks: "The Life of Lincoln West," *To Disembark, op. cit.,* p. 29.

83. Gwendolyn Brooks: *Report from Part One, op. cit.,* p. 152.

84. Gwendolyn Brooks, quoted in R. B. Miller: " 'Define . . . the Whirlwind': Gwendolyn Brooks's Epic Signs for a Generation," *Black American Poets Between Worlds, op. cit.,* p. 172.

85. Alice Walker: *The Color Purple, op. cit.,* p. 176.

86. Hughes: "Here to Stay," Rampersad: *The Life of Langston Hughes,* vol. 2, *op. cit.,* p. 231 (italics in original).

87. Naylor: *Brewster Place, op. cit.,* pp. 62–63.

88. Margaret Walker, quoted in Richard Barksdale: "Margaret Walker: Folk Orature and Historical Prophecy," *Black American Poets Between Worlds, op. cit.,* p. 107.

89. Margaret Walker: *For My People, op. cit.,* p. 13.

90. V. F. Calverton: "The Growth of Negro Literature," *Negro Anthology, op. cit.,* p. 79.

91. Johnson: "The Book of American Negro Poetry," *Black Writers in America, op. cit.,* p. 483.

92. Cited in Al Frazier: "To Be or Not to Bop: A Biography of Dizzy Gillespie," Amiri Baraka and Amina Baraka: *The Music,* p. 231.

93. Lester, *op. cit.,* p. 57 (see also notes 27, ch. 14).

94. Cruse: *Crisis, op. cit.,* p. 189.

95. Baraka: *Black Music, op. cit.,* p. 16.

96. Baraka: "Rhythm and Blues and New Black Music," *The Black Aesthetic, op. cit.,* p. 118.

97. Baraka: *Black Music, op. cit.,* p. 13.

98. William C. Handy: *Father of the Blues,* p. 121.

99. *Ibid.,* p. 120.

100. Baraka: "Blues, Poetry, and the New Music," *The Music, op. cit.,* p. 262.

101. See Barbara Bowen: "Untroubled Voice: Call and Response in *Cane,*" *Black Literature and Literary Theory, op. cit.,* p. 189.

102. Handy, *op. cit.,* p. 74.

103. Peter Labrie: "The New Breed," *Black Fire, op. cit.,* p. 64.

104. Ellison, quoted in Bone: "Ralph Ellison and the Uses of the Imagination," *op. cit., Modern Black Novelists,* p. 47.

105. Baraka: *Black Music, op. cit.,* p. 176.

106. Cooke: *Afro-American Literature in the Twentieth Century, op. cit.,* p. 131.

107. Handy, *op. cit.*, p. 76.
108. Hughes, quoted in Rampersad: *The Life of Langston Hughes*, vol. 2, *op. cit.*, p. 145.
109. Handy, *op. cit.*, p. 157.
110. *Ibid.*, p. 82.
111. Baraka: "The Phenomenon of *Soul* in Afro-American Music," *The Music, op. cit.*, p. 275 (italics in original).
112. Ellison, quoted in Bone, *op. cit.*, *Modern Black Novelists*, p. 49.
113. Ellison: "Richard Wright's Blues," *op. cit.*, *Black Writers in America*, p. 693.
114. Baldwin: "Sonny's Blues," *ibid.*, p. 742.
115. William Melvin Kelley: "Cry for Me," *Dark Symphony, op. cit.*, p. 465.
116. *Ibid.*, p. 469.
117. Hurston: *Dust Tracks on a Road, op. cit.*, p. 52.
118. Ellison: "Introduction," *Shadow and Act, op. cit.*, p. xiv.
119. Baraka: "The Phenomenon of *Soul*," *op. cit.*, *The Music*, p. 270.
120. Cooke: *Afro-American Literature in the Twentieth Century, op. cit.*, p. 31.
121. Toni Morrison, quoted in "Introduction," *Critical Essays on Toni Morrison, op. cit.*
122. Angelou: *Singin and Swingin, op. cit.*, p. 33 (see also note 82, ch. 4).
123. See Marshall: *Praisesong for the Widow, op. cit.*, pp. 249–254.
124. Jacques Lacan: "The Insistence of the Letter in the Unconscious," *Structuralism*, p. 133.
125. Blyden Jackson: "The Negro's Image of the Universe as Reflected in His Fiction," *Black Voices, op. cit.*, p. 627.
126. Ellison: "Interview with Richard Stern," *ibid.*, p. 659.
127. Hughes: *Not Without Laughter, op. cit.*, p. 313.
128. *Ibid.*, p. 267.
129. Hughes, quoted in Emanuel: *Langston Hughes, op. cit.*, p. 137.
130. Himes: *If He Hollers Let Him Go, op. cit.*, pp. 5–6.
131. Shange: *Sassafras, Cypress and Indigo, op. cit.*, p. 27.
132. Arthur Davis: "Trends in Negro American Literature," *op. cit.*, *Dark Symphony*, p. 525.
133. Rudolph Fisher: "Common Meter," *Black Voices, op. cit.*, pp. 84–85.
134. Cruse: *Crisis, op. cit.*, p. 9 (italics in original).
135. Baraka: "Blues, Poetry and the New Music," *op. cit.*, *The Music*, p. 264.
136. *Ibid.*
137. Cruse: *Crisis, op. cit.*, pp. 65–66.
138. Hughes: *The Big Sea, op. cit.*, p. 209.
139. Hughes, quoted in Rampersad: *The Life of Langston Hughes*, vol. 2, *op. cit.*, p. 189.
140. Rampersad, *ibid.*, pp. 317–318.
141. Ihab Hassan: *Contemporary American Literature*, p. 133 (italics in original).

142. Rodgers: *The Black Aesthetic, op. cit.,* p. 214.
143. See Stetson: *Black Sister, op. cit.,* p. 52.
144. Emanuel: *Langston Hughes, op. cit.,* p. 146.

Chapter 16: Black Aesthetic Forms

1. H. L. Gates, Jr.: "The Blackness of Blackness," *op. cit., Black Literature and Literary Theory,* p. 297.
2. *Ibid.*
3. Stepto, *op. cit.,* p. 81.
4. DuBois, quoted in *ibid.,* p. 74.
5. DuBois, quoted in *The Music, op. cit.,* p. 270.
6. Stepto, *op. cit.,* p. 65.
7. See *ibid.,* p. 63.
8. DuBois: *The Souls of Black Folk, op. cit.,* p. 17.
9. *Ibid.,* p. 20.
10. DuBois: "Of the Coming of John," *ibid.,* pp. 166f.
11. DuBois: "Of the Meaning of Progress," *ibid.,* p. 64.
12. William J. Schafer: "Ralph Ellison and the Birth of the Anti-Hero," *Critical Essays, op. cit.,* p. 125.
13. Johnson: *The Autobiography of an Ex-Coloured Man, op. cit.,* p. 221 (italics in original).
14. *Ibid.,* p. 20.
15. *Ibid.,* p. 74.
16. *Ibid.,* p. 181.
17. *Ibid.,* p. 56 (see also note 44, ch. 13).
18. See *ibid.,* p. 120.
19. *Ibid.,* p. 7.
20. *Ibid.,* p. 194.
21. *Ibid.,* p. 210.
22. *Ibid.,* p. 211.
23. Rachel Blau Du Plessis: "Power, Judgment, and Narrative in a Work of Zora Neale Hurston: Feminist Culture Studies," *New Essays on "Their Eyes Were Watching God," op. cit.,* p. 118.
24. Hurston: *Dust Tracks on a Road, op. cit.,* pp. 331 and 115.
25. Hurston: *Their Eyes Were Watching God, op. cit.,* p. 9.
26. *Ibid.,* p. 112.
27. *Ibid.,* p. 156.
28. *Ibid.,* p. 218.
29. *Ibid.,* p. 161.
30. *Ibid.,* p. 169.
31. *Ibid.,* p. 206.
32. *Ibid.,* p. 20.
33. Nellie McKay: "Crayon Enlargements of Life: Zora Neale Hurston's *Their Eyes Were Watching God,*" *New Essays, op. cit.,* p. 54.
34. Hurston: *Moses, Man of the Mountain,* p. 54.

35. *Ibid.*, p. 82.
36. *Ibid.*, p. 104.
37. *Ibid.*, p. 184.
38. *Ibid.*, p. 174.
39. *Ibid.*, p. 151.
40. *Ibid.*, p. 253.
41. *Ibid.*, p. 281.
42. *Ibid.*, p. 351.
43. See Rampersad: *The Life of Langston Hughes*, vol. 1, *op. cit.*, p. 323.
44. Hughes, quoted in *ibid.*, vol. 2, p. 286 (italics in original).
45. Rampersad, *ibid.*, p. 133.
46. Hughes, quoted in *ibid.*, vol. 1, p. 184.
47. Hughes, quoted in Wright: *White Man, Listen!*, *op. cit.*, p. 142.
48. Hughes, quoted in Rampersad: *The Life of Langston Hughes*, vol. 2, *op. cit.*, p. 368.
49. Rampersad, *ibid.*, vol. 1, p. 375.
50. See Hughes: *I Wonder as I Wander*, p. 122.
51. See Rampersad: *The Life of Langston Hughes*, vol. 2,, *op. cit.*, p. 14.
52. *Ibid.*, p. 119.
53. Emanuel: *Langston Hughes*, *op. cit.*, p. 141.
54. Smith, quoted in Rampersad: *The Life of Langston Hughes*, vol. 2, *op. cit.*, p. 179.
55. Bontemps, quoted in *ibid.*, p. 113.
56. Hughes: "Motto," *ibid.*, p. 263.
57. George Kent: "Hughes and the Afro-American Folk and Cultural Tradition," *Langston Hughes*, *op. cit.*, pp. 17–18.
58. See Himes: "Foreword," *Black on Black*, *op. cit.*, p. 7.
59. Himes: *My Life of Absurdity*, *op. cit.*, p. 182.
60. Himes: "Baby Sister," *Black on Black*, *op. cit.*, p. 12.
61. A. Robert Lee: "Harlem on My Mind: Fictions of a Black Metropolis," *The American City: Literary and Cultural Perspectives*, p. 81.
62. Ellison, quoted in Hyman: "Ralph Ellison in Our Time," *op. cit.*, *Critical Essays*, p. 44.
63. Neal: "Ralph Ellison's Zoot Suit," *ibid.*, p. 76.
64. Earl Rovit: "Ralph Ellison and the American Comic Tradition," *ibid.*, p. 152.
65. Ellison, quoted in "Introduction," *ibid.*, p. 3.
66. Neal: "Ralph Ellison's Zoot Suit," *ibid.*, p. 71.
67. Ellison, quoted in Hyman: "Ralph Ellison in Our Time," *ibid.*, p. 54 (italics in original).
68. Ellison, quoted in Shafer: "Ralph Ellison and the Birth of the Anti-Hero," *ibid.*, p. 119.
69. Ellison: *Invisible Man*, *op. cit.*, p. 9.
70. Baker: *The Journey Back*, *op. cit.*, p. 161.
71. Ellison, quoted in Bone: "Ralph Ellison and the Uses of the Imagination," *Critical Essays*, *op. cit.*, pp. 105–106.

72. Susan L. Blake: "Old John in Harlem: The Urban Folktales of Langston Hughes," *Langston Hughes, op. cit.,* p. 128.
73. Benston: "I Yam What I Am," *op. cit., Black Literature and Literary Theory,* p. 161.
74. Ellison: *Invisible Man, op. cit.,* p. 383.
75. Benston: "I Yam What I Am," *op. cit., Black Literature and Literary Theory,* p. 161.
76. Ellison, quoted in Callahan, *op. cit.,* p. 184.
77. Marcus Klein: *After Alienation,* p. 91; see Ellison: *Shadow and Act, op. cit.,* ch. 3.
78. Cooke, *op. cit.,* pp. 25–26.
79. Morrison: *The Bluest Eye, op. cit.,* p. 9.
80. *Ibid.,* p. 81.
81. *Ibid.,* p. 189.
82. Christopher Norris: *Derrida,* p. 42.
83. Morrison: *The Bluest Eye, op. cit.,* p. 25.
84. *Ibid.,* p. 189.
85. See *ibid.,* p. 160.
86. *Ibid.,* p. 151.
87. *Ibid.,* p. 190.
88. Morrison, quoted in Christian: "Community and Nature: The Novels of Toni Morrison," *Black Feminist Criticism, op. cit.,* p. 54.
89. Morrison: *Sula, op. cit.,* p. 118 (see also note 127, ch. 14).
90. *Ibid.,* p. 112.
91. Deborah McDonell: " 'The Self and the Other': Reading Toni Morrison's *Sula* and the Black Female Text," *Critical Essays on Toni Morrison, op. cit.,* p. 80.
92. *Ibid.,* p. 22.
93. *Ibid.,* p. 119.
94. *Ibid.,* p. 147.
95. Redding: "The Negro Writer and His Relation to His Roots," *op. cit., Black Voices,* p. 617 (see also note 44, ch. 15).
96. Morrison: *Song of Solomon,* p. 336.
97. Morrison: *Tar Baby,* p. 210.
98. Eleanor W. Traylor: "The Fabulous World of Toni Morrison: *Tar Baby,*" *Confirmation, op. cit.,* p. 401.
99. Morrison: *Tar Baby, op. cit.,* p. 243.
100. *Ibid.,* p. 162.
101. *Ibid.,* p. 270.
102. Susan Willis: "Eruptions of Funk: Historicizing Toni Morrison," *Black Literature and Literary Theory, op. cit.,* p. 268.
103. Morrison: *Beloved, op. cit.,* p. 89.
104. *Ibid.,* p. 198.
105. Hull, *op. cit.,* p. 129.
106. Georgia Johnson, quoted in *ibid.,* p. 163.
107. Hayden: "Incense of the Luck Virgin," *Collected Poems, op. cit.,* p. 34.

108. Morrison: *Beloved, op. cit.,* p. 140.

109. *Ibid.,* p. 251.

110. *Ibid.,* p. 127.

111. Morrison: *Jazz,* p. 9.

112. *Ibid.,* p. 209.

113. See Campbell, *op. cit.,* p. 150.

114. See David Bradley: *The Chaneysville Incident,* p. 390.

115. *Ibid.,* p. 428.

116. *Ibid.,* p. 262.

117. Ernest Gaines: *A Gathering of Old Men,* p. 31.

118. *Ibid.,* p. 38.

119. *Ibid.,* p. 92.

120. Alice Walker: *The Third Life of Grange Copeland, op. cit.,* p. 207 (italics in original).

121. Alice Walker: "Each One, Pull One," *Horses Make a Landscape, op. cit.,* p. 51.

122. Alice Walker: "Talking to My Grandmother Who Died Poor," *Good Night Willie Lee, I'll See You in the Morning,* pp. 46–47.

123. Alice Walker: *In Search of Our Mothers' Gardens,* p. 250 (italics in original).

124. Alice Walker: "Each One, Pull One," *op. cit., Horses,* p. 53 (italics in original).

125. Alice Walker: *In Search of Our Mothers' Gardens, op. cit.,* p. 17 (italics in original).

126. *Ibid.,* p. 128.

127. *Ibid.,* p. 156.

128. Alice Walker, quoted in Thadious M. Davis: "Walker's Celebration of Self in Southern Generations," *Alice Walker, op. cit.,* p. 27 (italics in original).

129. Alice Walker: *In Search of Our Mothers' Gardens, op. cit.,* p. 226.

130. Alice Walker: *In Search of Our Mothers' Gardens, op. cit.,* p. 85 (italics in original).

131. *Ibid.,* p. 232.

132. Alice Walker, quoted in Mary Helen Washington: "An Essay on Alice Walker," *Sturdy Black Bridges, op. cit.,* p. 136.

133. Morrison: *Tar Baby, op. cit.,* p. 281.

134. Alice Walker: *Meridian, op. cit.,* pp. 96 and 89.

135. Alice Walker, quoted in John F. Callahan: "The Hoop of Language: Politics and the Restoration of Voice in *Meridian,*" *Alice Walker, op. cit.,* p. 83.

136. Alice Walker; *Meridian op. cit.,* p. 199.

137. *Ibid.,* p. 200 (italics in original).

138. H. L. Gates, Jr.: "Color Me Zora: Alice Walker's (Re)Writing of the Speakerly Text," *Intertextuality and Contemporary American Fiction, op. cit.,* p. 151.

139. Hurston, quoted in Awkward, *op. cit.,* p. 52.

140. Awkward, *ibid.*, p. 51.
141. Hurston, quoted in H. L. Gates, Jr.: "Color Me Zora," *op. cit.*, *Intertextuality and Contemporary American Fiction*, p. 149.
142. Hurston, quoted in Awkward, *op. cit.*, p. 113.
143. Hughes, quoted in H. L. Gates, Jr.: "Color Me Zora," *op. cit.*, *Intertextuality and Contemporary American Fiction*, p. 152.
144. Toomer: *Cane*, *op. cit.*, p. 236.
145. Alice Walker: *The Color Purple*, *op. cit.*, p. 167.
146. H. L. Gates, Jr.: "Criticism in the Jungle," *Black Literature and Literary Theory*, *op. cit.*, p. 5.
147. Soyinka: "The Critic and Society: Barthes, Leftocracy and Other Mythologies," *ibid.*, p. 50.
148. Ludwig Wittgenstein: *Tractatus Logico-Philosophicus*, Proposition 4.002, p. 37.
149. Alice Walker: *The Temple of My Familiar*, *op. cit.*, p. 301.
150. John Edgar Wideman: *The Lynchers*, p. 183.
151. Alice Walker: *In Search of Our Mothers' Gardens*, *op. cit.*, p. 5.
152. Alice Walker: *Living by the Word*, *op. cit.*, p. 82.
153. Alice Walker: *The Temple of My Familiar*, *op. cit.*, p. 300.
154. *Ibid.*, p. 125.
155. *Ibid.*, p. 169.
156. *Ibid.*, p. 28.
157. *Ibid.*, p. 83.
158. Hurston, quoted in Awkward, *op. cit.*, p. 20.
159. Wittgenstein: *Tractacus*, *op. cit.*, Proposition 4.003, p. 39.
160. Gaines: "Introduction," *The Autobiography of Miss Jane Pittman*, p. ix.
161. Alice Walker: *The Temple of My Familiar*, *op. cit.*, p. 170.
162. William Melvin Kelley: *A Different Drummer*, p. 120.
163. *Ibid.*, p. 123.
164. *Ibid.*, p. 167.
165. Awkward, *op. cit.*, p. 132.
166. Naylor: *The Women of Brewster Place*, *op. cit.*, p. 86 (see also note 5, ch. 15).
167. Awkward, *op. cit.*, p. 99 (italics in original); see also p. 105.
168. Naylor: *Linden Hills*, *op. cit.*, p. 9.
169. *Ibid.*, p. 17 (italics in original).
170. *Ibid.*, p. 57 (italics in original).
171. Naylor: *Mama Day*, p. 8.
172. *Ibid.*, p. 218.
173. *Ibid.*, p. 262.
174. *Ibid.*, p. 219.
175. *Ibid.*, p. 175.
176. *Ibid.*, p. 295.
177. *Ibid.*, p. 308.
178. See *ibid.*, p. 230.
179. Hurston, quoted in Awkward, *op. cit.*, p. 15.
180. *Bailey's Cafe*, p. 28.

181. Jamaica Kinkaid: *A Small Place*, p. 31.
182. Morrison: "Life in His Language," *The Legacy, op. cit.,* p. 76.
183. Shange: "No More Love Poems," *Black Sister, op. cit.,* p. 273.
184. Angelou: *Gather Together in My Name, op. cit.,* p. 78.
185. Angelou: *Singin and Swingin, op. cit.,* p. 28.
186. Angelou: *The Heart of a Woman, op. cit.,* p. 172.
187. See *ibid.,* p. 37.
188. See Angelou: *Gather Together in My Name, op. cit.,* p. 141 (see also note 286, ch. 13).

Chapter 17: Black Postmodern Forms

1. O'Donnell and Davis: "Introduction," *Intertextuality and Contemporary American Fiction, op. cit.,* p. xii.
2. Alan Singer: "The Ventriloquism of History," *ibid.,* p. 73.
3. *Ibid.,* p. 74.
4. See Heide Ziegler: "The Erotics of Contemporary Parody," *ibid.,* p. 60.
5. Barthes, quoted in Linda Hutcheon: "Historiographic Metafiction," *ibid.,* p. 8.
6. Hutcheon, *ibid.*
7. Ziegler: "The Erotics of Contemporary Parody," *op. cit., ibid.,* p. 59.
8. Clarence Major: *My Amputations*, p. 141.
9. John Matthews: "The Ideology of Parody in John Barth," *Intertextuality and Contemporary American Fiction*, p. 47.
10. Mead: *A Rap on Race, op. cit.,* p. 256.
11. Reed: *Flight to Canada*, p. 96.
12. Reed: *The Free-lance Pallbearers*, p. 2.
13. *Ibid.*
14. *Ibid.,* p. 127.
15. *Ibid.,* p. 97.
16. *Ibid.,* p. 103.
17. *Ibid.,* p. 132.
18. Reed: *Mumbo Jumbo, op. cit.,* p. 204.
19. Johnson, quoted in *ibid.,* p. 211.
20. Reed, *ibid.,* p. 80 (italics in original).
21. *Ibid.,* p. 212.
22. *Ibid.,* p. 39.
23. *Ibid.,* p. 203.
24. Derrida: "Edmond Jabes and the Question of the Book," *Writing and Difference*, p. 77.
25. Reed: *Mumbo Jumbo, op. cit.,* p. 130.
26. Derrida: "Edmond Jabes and the Question of the Book," *op. cit., Writing and Difference*, p. 77.
27. See Jean-Paul Sartre: *Nausea*, pp. 218f.
28. Reed: *Mumbo Jumbo, op. cit.,* p. 204.
29. Reed: *Yellow Back Radio Broke-Down*, p. 16.
30. Reed: *Shrovetide, op. cit.,* p. 261.

31. Reed: *Yellow Back, op. cit.,* p. 165.
32. *Ibid.,* p. 34.
33. *Ibid.,* p. 36.
34. *Ibid.,* p. 53.
35. *Ibid.,* p. 152.
36. Singer: "The Ventriloquism of History," *op. cit., Intertextuality and Contemporary American Fiction,* p. 75.
37. Reed: *The Terrible Twos,* p. 60.
38. Reed: *Flight to Canada, op. cit.,* p. 7.
39. *Ibid.,* p. 10.
40. *Ibid.,* p. 82.
41. Benston: "I Yam What I Am," *op. cit., Black Literature and Literary Theory,* p. 152.
42. Reed: *Flight to Canada, op. cit.,* p. 179.
43. Reed: *Shrovetide, op. cit.,* p. 2.
44. Reed: *Flight to Canada, op. cit.,* p. 89.
45. *Ibid.,* p. 88.
46. *Ibid.,* pp. 88–89.
47. *Ibid.,* p. 81.
48. Wittgenstein: *Tractatus, op. cit.,* Proposition 5.6, p. 155 (italics in original).
49. Reed: *Flight to Canada, op. cit.,* p. 36.
50. *Ibid.,* p. 144.
51. Reed: *The Last Days of Louisiana Red,* pp. 125 and 172.
52. Major, *op. cit.,* p. 205.
53. Reed: *Flight to Canada, op. cit.,* p. 149.
54. *Ibid.,* p. 82.
55. Edgar Allan Poe: "The Raven," *The Complete Tales and Poems of Edgar Allan Poe,* p. 944.
56. Reed: *Flight to Canada, op. cit.,* p. 178.
57. Wittgenstein: *Tractatus, op. cit.,* Proposition 5.64, p. 117.
58. *Ibid.,* Proposition 5.634.
59. Geneva Smitherton, quoted in Awkward, *op. cit.,* p. 10.
60. Cooke: *Afro-American Literature, op. cit.,* p. 7.
61. Reed, quoted in James A. Snead: "Repetition as a Figure of Black Culture," *Black Literature and Literary Theory, op. cit.,* p. 64.
62. Reed: *Reckless Eyeballing, op. cit.,* p. 54.
63. Reed: *The Last Days of Louisiana Red, op. cit.,* p. 336.
64. Baldwin: *Blues for Mr. Charlie, op. cit.,* p. 42.
65. Hutcheon: "Historiographic Metafiction," *op. cit., Intertextuality and Contemporary American Fiction,* p. 13.
66. Reed: *The Last Days of Louisiana Red, op. cit.,* p. 17 (see also notes 15–17, ch. 17).
67. Reed: *The Terrible Twos, op. cit.,* p. 133.
68. Hutcheon: "Historiographic Metafiction," *op. cit., Intertextuality and Contemporary American Fiction,* p. 13.

69. Reed: *The Terrible Twos, op. cit.*, p. 115.
70. *Ibid.*, p. 176.
71. See Reed: *The Terrible Threes*, p. 76.
72. *Ibid.*, p. 77.
73. Reed: *The Terrible Twos, op. cit.*, p. 121.
74. Reed: *The Terrible Threes, op. cit.*, p. 148.
75. *Ibid.* (italics in original).
76. Snead: "Repetition as a Figure of Black Culture," *op. cit., Black Literature and Literary Theory*, p. 71.
77. H. L. Gates, Jr.: "The Blackness of Blackness," *op. cit., ibid.*, p. 311.
78. *Ibid.*
79. Reed: *The Terrible Threes, op. cit.*, p. 165.

BIBLIOGRAPHY

Afro-American Literature: An Introduction, ed. by Robert Hayden, David J. Burroughs, and Frederick R. Lapides. New York: Harcourt Brace Jovanovich, 1971.

Aldridge, John. *After the Lost Generation.* New York: McGraw-Hill, 1951.

Alice Walker, ed. by Harold Bloom. New York: Chelsea House, 1989.

America and Its Discontents, ed. by Robie Macauley and Larzer Ziff. Waltham, Mass.: Xerox College, 1971.

The American City: Literary and Cultural Perspectives, ed. by Graham Clarke. London: Vision, 1988.

American Dreams, American Nightmares, ed. by David Madden. Carbondale, Ill.: Southern Illinois University Press, 1970.

American Race Relations Today, ed. by Earl Raab. New York: Anchor, 1962.

American Vistas, ed. by L. Dinnerstein and K. Jackson. New York: Oxford University Press, 1971.

America's Recent Past, ed. by F. D. Mitchell and R. O. Davis. New York: Wiley, 1969.

Ammons, Elizabeth. *Conflicting Stories.* New York: Oxford University Press, 1991.

Anatomies of America, ed. by Philip Ehrensatt and Amitai Etzioni. New York: Macmillan, 1969.

Anderson, Sherwood. *The Portable Sherwood Anderson.* New York: Viking, 1949.

Angelou, Maya. *Gather Together in My Name.* New York: Random House, 1974.

———. *The Heart of a Woman.* New York: Random House, 1981.

———. *I Know Why the Caged Bird Sings.* New York: Random House, 1969.

———. *Singin' and Swingin' and Gettin' Merry like Christmas.* New York: Random House, 1976.

Aptheker, Herbert. *Afro-American History: The Modern Era.* Secaucus, N.J.: Citadel, 1973.

Arendt, Hannah. *Crisis of the Republic.* New York: Harcourt Brace, 1969.

Ashmore, Harry. *Hearts and Minds.* New York: McGraw-Hill, 1987.

Awkward, Michael. *Inspiring Influences.* New York: Columbia University Press, 1988.

Bailey, Jennifer. *Norman Mailer: Quick Change Artist.* London: Barnes and Noble, 1979.

Baker, Carlos. *Ernest Hemingway.* New York: Scribner, 1969.

Baker, Houston. *The Journey Back.* Chicago: University of Chicago Press, 1980. *Signs of Daybreak.* Washington, D.C.: Howard University Press, 1974.

Baker, Jean H. *Affairs of Party.* Ithaca, N.Y.: Cornell University Press, 1983.

Baldwin, James. *The Amen Corner.* New York: Dial, 1968.

———. *Another Country.* New York: Dial, 1962.

———. *Blues for Mr. Charlie.* New York: Dial, 1964.

———. *Giovanni's Room.* New York: Dial, 1956.

———. *Go Tell It on the Mountain.* New York: Grosset & Dunlap, 1953.

———. *Just Above My Head.* New York: Dial, 1979.

———. *The Legacy,* ed. by Quincy Troupe. New York: Simon & Schuster, 1989.

———. *Nobody Knows My Name.* New York: Dial, 1961.

———. *No Name in the Street.* New York: Dial, 1972.

———. *Notes of a Native Son.* Boston: Beacon, 1957.

———. *The Price of the Ticket.* New York: St. Martin's, 1985.

———. *A Rap on Race.* New York: Lippincott, 1972.

———. *Tell Me How Long the Train's Been Gone.* New York: Dial, 1968.

Baldwin, James, and Nikki Giovanni. *A Dialogue.* Philadelphia: Lippincott, 1973.

Baltzell, E. Digby. *The Protestant Establishment.* New York: Random House, 1964.

Banfield, Edward C. *The Unheavenly City.* Boston: Little, Brown, 1968.

Baraka, Amiri. *The Autobiography of LeRoi Jones.* New York: Freundlich, 1984.

———. *Black Magic.* New York: Bobbs Merrill, 1969.

———. *Black Music.* New York: Morrow, 1967.

———. *Daggers and Javelins.* New York: Quill, 1984.

———. *Four Black Revolutionary Plays.* New York: Bobbs Merrill, 1969.

———. *Home.* New York: Morrow, 1960.

———. *The Motion of History and Other Plays.* New York: Morrow 1978.

———. *Selected Plays and Poetry of Amiri Baraka/LeRoi Jones.* New York: Morrow, 1979.

———. *Selected Poetry of Amiri Baraka/LeRoi Jones.* New York: Morrow, 1979.

———. *The System of Dante's Hell.* New York: Grove, 1963.

———. *Tales.* New York: Grove, 1967.

Baraka, Amiri, and Amina Baraka. *Confirmation: An Anthology of African American Women.* New York: Morrow, 1983 (uncorrected galleys).

———. *The Music.* New York: Morrow, 1987.

Baraka, Amiri, and Fundi. *In Our Terribleness.* New York: Bobbs Merrill, 1970.

Bardolph, Richard. *The Negro Vanguard.* New York: Holt, Rinehart & Winston: 1959.

Barthes, Roland. *The Eiffel Tower,* trans. by Richard Howard. New York: Hill & Wang, 1979.

———. *Mythologies,* trans. by Annette Lavers. New York: Hill & Wang, 1972.

———. *Roland Barthes,* trans. by Richard Miller. New York: Noonday, 1977.

———. *Writing Degree Zero,* trans. by Annette Lavers and Colin Smith. Boston: Beacon, 1970.

Basic Issues of American Democracy, ed. by H. M. Bishop and S. Hendel. New York: Appleton-Century-Crofts, 1970.

Bearing Witness, ed. by H. L. Gates, Jr. New York: Pantheon, 1991.

Bell, Bernard W. *The Afro-American Novel and Its Tradition.* Amherst, Mass.: University of Massachusetts Press, 1987.

Bellow, Saul. *The Adventures of Augie March.* New York: Viking, 1963.

———. *The Dean's December.* New York: Harper & Row, 1982.

———. *Mr. Sammler's Planet.* New York: Viking, 1970.

———. *Mosby's Memoirs and Other Stories.* New York: Viking, 1951.

Bennett, Lerone, Jr. *Before the Mayflower.* Chicago: Johnson, 1964.

———. *What Manner of Man.* Chicago: Johnson, 1964.

Bettelheim, Bruno, and Morris Janowitz. *Social Change and Prejudice.* New York: Free Press, 1975.

Beyond the Angry Black, ed. by John A. Williams. New York: Free Press, 1975.

The Black Aesthetic, ed. by Addison Gayle. New York: Doubleday, 1971.

Black Anti-Semitism and Jewish Racism, ed. by Richard Baron. New York: Arbor House, 1968.

Black Female Playwrights, ed. by Kathy A. Perkins. Bloomington, Ind.: Indiana University Press, 1990.

Black Fire, ed. by LeRoi Jones and Larry Neal. New York: Morrow, 1968.

Black History, ed. by Melvin Drummer. New York: Anchor, 1969.

Black Literature and Literary Theory, ed. by H. L. Gates, Jr. New York: Methuen, 1984.

Black Nationalism in America, ed. by John H. Bracey, August Meier, and Elliot Rudwick. Indianapolis: Bobbs Merrill, 1970.

The Black Novelist, ed. by Robert Hemenway. Columbus, Ohio: Merrell, 1970.

Black on Black, ed. by Arnold Adell. Toronto: Macmillan, 1968.

Black Poets Between Worlds, ed. by R. Baxter Miller. Knoxville, Tenn.: University of Tennessee Press, 1981.

The Black Seventies, ed. by Floyd B. Barbour. Boston: P. Sargent, 1970.

Black Theater, compiled by Lindsay Patterson. New York: New American Library, 1971.

Black Voices, ed. by Abraham Chapman. New York: New American Library, 1968.

Black Voices from Prison, ed. by Etheridge Knight. New York: Pathfinder, 1970.

Black Writers of America, ed. by R. Barksdale and K. Kinnamon. New York: Macmillan, 1972.

Blauer, Bob. *Black Loves, White Loves.* Berkeley, Calif.: University of California Press, 1989.

Bone, Robert. *The Negro Novel in America.* New Haven, Conn.: Yale University Press, 1969.

Bontemps, Arna. *One Hundred Years of Negro Freedom.* New York: Dodd Mead, 1961.

Bontemps, Arna, and Jack Conroy. *They Seek a City.* New York: Hill & Wang, 1945.

Boorstin, Daniel. *The Decline of Radicalism.* New York: Random House, 1969.

———. *Genius of American Politics.* Chicago: University of Chicago Press, 1953.

Bradley, David. *The Chaneysville Incident.* New York: Harper & Row, 1981.

Brawley, Benjamin. *Negro Builders and Heroes.* Chapel Hill, N.C.: University of North Carolina, 1937.

———. *A Social History of the American Negro.* New York: Macmillan, 1921.

Breakthrough, ed. by Irving Malin and Irwin Stark. New York: McGraw-Hill, 1964.

Brignano, Russell Carl. *Richard Wright: An Introduction to the Man and His Work.* Pittsburgh: University of Pittsburgh Press, 1970.

Brinnin, John Malcolm. *The Third Rose.* Boston: Little, Brown, 1959.

Broder, David. *The Party's Over.* New York: Harper & Row, 1972.

Brooks, Gwendolyn. *The Bear Eaters.* New York: Harper & Row, 1960.

———. *Report from Part I.* Detroit: Broadside, 1972.

———. *Selected Poems.* New York: Harper & Row, 1963.

———. *To Disembark.* Chicago: Third World, 1981.

Brooks, Thomas. *Walls Come Tumbling Down.* Englewood Cliffs, N.J.: Prentice Hall, 1970.

Brown, Cecil. *The Lives and Loves of Mr. Jiveass Nigger.* New York: Farrar, Straus & Giroux, 1969.

Brown, H. Rap. *Die Nigger Die!* New York: Dial, 1969.

Brown, Norman O. *Hermes the Thief.* New York: Vintage, 1969.

———. *Life and Death.* New York: Modern Paperback Library, 1959.

Brown, Sterling. *The Negro in American Fiction.* New York: Quadrangle, 1969.

Butler, Octavia. *Imago.* New York: Warner, 1989.

Cain, George. *Blueschild Baby.* New York: Dell, 1970.

Caldwell, Erskine. *Deep South.* New York: Signet, 1969.

———. *Georgia Boy.* New York: Duell Sloan & Pearce, 1943.

———. *A Place Called Estherville.* London: Falconor, 1950.

Callahan, John C. *In the Afro-American Grain.* Chicago: University of Illinois Press, 1988.

Campbell, Jane. *Mythic Black Fiction.* Knoxville, Tenn.: University of Tennessee Press, 1986.

Capote, Truman. *Answered Prayers.* New York: Random House, 1987.

———. *The Grass Harp.* New York: Random House, 1951.

———. *One Christmas.* New York: Random House, 1982.

———. *Other Voices, Other Rooms.* New York: Random House, 1948.

Carmichael, Stokely, and Charles Hamilton. *Black Power*. New York: Random House, 1967.

Cash, W. J. *The Mind of the South*. New York: Vintage, 1941.

Cather, Willa. *Sapphira and the Slave Girl*. New York: Knopf, 1963.

Chesnutt, Charles. *Conjure Tales*, retold by Ray Anthony Shepard. New York: Dutton, 1973.

Christian, Barbara. *Black Feminist Criticism*. New York: Pergamon, 1985.

Cities in Trouble, ed. by Nathan Glazer. Chicago: Quadrangle, 1970.

Clark, Kenneth. *Dark Ghetto*. New York: Harper & Row, 1965.

Clark, Thomas, and Albert Kirnan. *The South Since Appomattox*. New York: Oxford University Press, 1967.

Cleage, Albert B., Jr. *The Black Messiah*. New York: Sheed & Ward, 1969.

Cleaver, Eldridge. *Soul on Ice*. New York: Delta, 1969.

Coles, Robert. *Flannery O'Connor's South*. Baton Rouge, La.: Louisiana State University Press, 1980.

Comer, James. *Beyond Black and White*. New York: Quadrangle, 1972.

The Commentary Reader, ed. by Norman Podhoretz. New York: Atheneum, 1966.

Conot, Robert. *American Odyssey*. New York: Morrow, 1974.

Contemporary University: U.S.A., ed. by Robert S. Morison. Boston: Beacon, 1967.

Cooke, M. G. *Afro-American Literature in the Twentieth Century*. New Haven, Conn.: Yale University Press, 1984.

————. *Modern Black Novelists*. Englewood Cliffs, N.J.: Prentice Hall, 1971.

Coughlin, Robert. *The Private World of William Faulkner*. New York: Harper, 1953.

Cowley, Malcolm. *The Faulkner-Cowley File*. New York: Penguin, 1966.

————. *Exile's Return*. New York: Viking, 1951.

Critical Essays on Toni Morrison, ed. by Nellie Y. McKay. Boston: G. K. Hall, 1987.

Cronan, E. David. *Black Moses*. Madison, Wis.: University of Wisconsin Press, 1967.

Cruse, Harold. *The Crisis of the Negro Intellectual*. New York: Morrow, 1967.

————. *Plural but Equal*. New York: Morrow, 1987.

Cullen, Countee. *My Soul's High Song: The Collected Writings of Countee Cullen*, ed. by Gerald Early. New York: Doubleday, 1991.

————. *One Way to Heaven*. New York: Capes, 1932.

Curti, Merle. *The Growth of American Thought*. New York: Harper, 1953.

Dahl, Robert. *Who Governs?* New Haven, Conn.: Yale University Press, 1961.

Dark Symphony, ed. by James A. Emanuel and Theodore L. Gross. New York: Free Press, 1968.

Davenport, Garven. *The Myth of Southern History*. Nashville, Tenn.: Vanderbilt University Press, 1967.

Davis, Allison; Burleigh B. Gardner; and Mary R. Gardner. *Deep South*. Chicago: Phoenix, 1965.

Davis, Angela. *An Autobiography*. New York: Random House, 1974.

De Jongh, James. *Vicious Modernism.* New York: Cambridge University Press, 1990.

Derrida, Jacques. *Writing and Difference,* trans. by Alan Bass. Chicago: University of Chicago Press, 1978.

Didion, Joan. *The White Album.* New York: Simon & Schuster, 1979.

Dollard, John. *Caste and Class in a Southern Town.* New York: Harper, 1957.

Drake, St. Clair, and Horace R. Cayton. *Black Metropolis.* New York: Harper & Row, 1962.

DuBois, W.E.B. *Against Racism,* ed. by Herbert Aptheker. Amherst, Mass.: University of Massachusetts Press, 1985.

———. *The Autobiography of W.E.B. DuBois.* New York: International Publications, 1968.

———. *The Gift of Black Folk.* New York: Stratford Allen, 1924.

———. *The Souls of Black Folk.* New York: Crest, 1961.

Dunbar, Paul Laurence. *Complete Poems.* New York: Dodd Mead, 1913.

Dutton, Robert. *Saul Bellow.* New York: Twayne, 1971.

Ellison, Ralph. *Invisible Man.* New York: Random House, 1952.

———. *Shadow and Act.* New York: Random House, 1953.

Emanuel, James. *Langston Hughes.* New York: Twayne, 1967.

Essien-Udom, E. U. *Black Nationalism.* New York: Dell, 1962.

The Establishment and All That. Santa Barbara, Calif.: *Center Magazine*/Center for the Study of Democratic Institutions, 1970.

Ethnicity: Theory and Experience, ed. by Nathan Glazer and Daniel P. Moynihan. Cambridge, Mass.: Harvard University Press, 1975.

Evans, Richard. *Contested Terrain.* New York: Basic Books, 1979.

Fabre, Michel. *La Rive Noire.* Paris: Lieu Commun, 1986.

———. *The Unfinished Quest of Richard Wright,* trans. by Isabel Barzun. New York: Morrow, 1973.

Faulkner, John. *My Brother Bill.* New York: Trident, 1963.

Faulkner, William. *Absalom, Absalom!* New York: Modern Library, 1951.

———. *Collected Stories of William Faulkner.* New York: Random House, 1950.

———. *Go Down Moses.* New York: Random House, 1942.

———. *Light in August.* New York: Modern Library, 1950.

———. *The Mansion.* New York: Random House, 1955.

———. *The Portable Faulkner.* New York: Viking, 1946.

———. *Requiem for a Nun.* New York: Random House, 1951.

———. *Sartoris.* New York: Harcourt Brace, 1951.

———. *Soldier's Pay.* New York: Liveright, 1926.

———. *The Sound and the Fury.* New York: Modern Library, 1946.

Ferkiss, Victor. *Technological Man.* New York: New American Library, 1969.

The Fiction of Bernard Malamud, ed. by Richard Astro & Jackson Benson, Corvallis, Oreg.: Oregon State University Press, 1977.

Fiedler, Leslie A. *Love and Death in the American Novel.* New York: Criterion, 1960.

———. *The Return of the Vanishing American.* New York: Stein & Day, 1968.

──────. *The Second Stone.* New York: Stein & Day, 1963.

──────. *Waiting for the End.* New York: Stein & Day, 1964.

The Fifties, ed. by W. French. Deland, Fla.: Everett/Edwards, 1970.

Five Black Writers, ed. by Donald Gibson. New York: New York University Press, 1970.

Forman, James. *The Making of Black Revolutionaries.* New York: Macmillan, 1972.

Frazier, E. Franklin. *The Black Bourgeoisie.* New York: Collier, 1962.

──────. *The Negro in the United States.* New York: Macmillan, 1957.

──────. *Negro Youth at the Crossroads.* Washington, D.C.: Schocken, 1940.

Frederickson, George M. *White Supremacy.* New York: Oxford University Press, 1981.

From the Dark Tower, ed. by Arthur P. Davis. Washington, D.C.: Howard University Press, 1974.

Furnas, J. C. *The Americans,* vol. 2. New York: Capricorn, 1969.

Gaines, Ernest. *The Autobiography of Miss Jane Pittman.* New York: Dial, 1971.

──────. *A Gathering of Old Men.* New York: Dial, 1983.

Garlin, Hamlin. *A Daughter of the Middle Border.* Gloucester, Mass.: Sagamore, 1971.

Garrow, David J. *Bearing the Cross.* New York: Morrow, 1986.

Gates, Henry Louis, Jr. *Figures in Black.* New York: Oxford University Press, 1987.

──────. *Loose Canons.* New York: Oxford University Press, 1992.

Gates, John. *The Story of American Communism.* New York: Nelson, 1958.

Gayle, Addison. *The Way of the New World: The Black Novel in America.* New York: Doubleday, 1976.

Giddings, Paula. *In Search of Sisterhood.* New York: Morrow, 1988.

──────. *When and Where I Enter.* New York: Morrow, 1984.

Giovanni, Nikki. *Black Feeling, Black Talk/Black Judgement.* New York: Morrow, 1979.

──────. *Cotton Candy on a Rainy Day.* New York: Morrow, 1978.

──────. *Gemini.* Middlesex, U.K.: Penguin, 1976.

──────. *My House.* New York: Morrow, 1972.

──────. *Those Who Ride the Winds.* New York: Morrow, 1983.

Giovanni, Nikki, and Margaret Walker. *A Poetic Equation: Conversations Between Nikki Giovanni and Margaret Walker.* Washington, D.C.: Howard University Press, 1974.

Givner, Joan. *Katherine Anne Porter: A Life.* New York: Simon & Schuster, 1982.

Gladwin, Thomas. *Poverty U.S.A.* Boston: Little, Brown, 1967.

Glasgow, Ellen. *Barren Ground.* New York: Modern Library, 1933.

──────. *This Is Our Life.* New York: Grosset & Dunlap, 1941.

Glazer, Nathan, and Daniel P. Moynihan. *Beyond the Melting Pot.* Cambridge, Mass.: M.I.T. Press, 1970.

Goldman, Eric. *Rendezvous with Destiny.* New York: Vintage, 1955.

Gornick, Vivian. *The Romance of American Communism.* New York: Basic Books, 1977.

Gossett, Thomas F. *Race: The History of an Idea in America.* New York: Schocken, 1965.

Great Issues in American History, vol. 2, ed. by Richard Hofstadter. New York: Vintage, 1958.

The Great Society Reader, ed. by M. E. Gettleman and D. Mormelstein. New York: Random House, 1967.

Greeley, Andrew. *That Most Distressful Nation.* Chicago: Quadrangle, 1972.

Greenleaf, Barbara. *American Fever.* New York: Four Winds, 1970.

Gutman, Herbert G. *Work, Culture and Society in Industrial America.* New York: Knopf, 1976.

Hacker, Andrew. *The End of the American Era.* New York: Atheneum, 1977.

Hacker, Louis M. *The Triumph of American Capitalism.* Berkeley, Calif.: University of California Press, 1940.

Hamilton, Charles V. *The Black Preacher in America.* New York: Morrow, 1972.

Handlin, Oscar. *Race and Nationality in American Life.* New York: Anchor, 1957.

Handy, W. C. *Father of the Blues,* ed. by Arna Bontemps. New York: Macmillan, 1944.

Harlan, Louis R. *Booker T. Washington, the Wizard of Tuskegee.* New York: Oxford University Press, 1983.

The Harlem Renaissance Remembered, ed. by Arna Bontemps. New York: Dodd Mead, 1972.

Harrington, Michael. *The New American Poverty.* New York: Holt, Rinehart & Winston, 1984.

———. *The Other America.* New York: Macmillan, 1963.

The Harvard Guide to Contemporary Literature, ed. by Daniel Hoffman. Cambridge, Mass.: Harvard University Press, 1979.

Hassan, Ihab. *Contemporary American Literature.* New York: Ungar, 1973.

Hayden, Robert. *Collected Poems,* ed. by Frederick Glaysher. New York: Liveright, 1985.

Hearn, Lafcadio. *Letters from a Raven.* New York: Brentano, 1907.

Hecht, Ben. *A Thousand and One Afternoons in Chicago.* Chicago: Covici-McGee, 1921.

Hemingway, Ernest. *To Have and Have Not.* New York: Scribner, 1937.

Henderson, Stephen. *Understanding the New Black Poetry.* New York: Morrow, 1973.

Hernton, Calvin. *Sex and Racism in America.* New York: Grove, 1966.

Herskovits, Melville J. *The American Negro.* Bloomington, Ind.: Southern Illinois University Press, 1968.

Himes, Chester. *Black on Black.* London: Michael Joseph, 1975.

———. *A Case of Rape.* Washington, D.C.: Howard University Press, 1984.

———. *Cotton Comes to Harlem.* London: Panther, 1967.

———. *If He Hollers Let Him Go.* New York: Chatham, 1973.

————. *Lonely Crusade.* New York: Chapman, 1947.

————. *My Life of Absurdity.* New York: Doubleday, 1976.

————. *The Primitive.* New York: New American Library, 1955.

————. *The Quality of Hurt.* New York: Doubleday, 1972.

————. *The Third Generation.* New York: Chatham, 1954.

Hirshson, Stanley B. *Farewell to the Bloody Shirt.* Bloomington, Ind.: Indiana University Press, 1962.

Hughes, Langston. *The Big Sea.* New York: Hill & Wang, 1940.

————. *I Wonder as I Wander.* New York: Hill & Wang, 1956.

————. *The Langston Hughes Reader.* New York: Braziller, 1958.

————. *Not Without Laughter.* New York: Knopf, 1930.

Hull, Gloria T. *Color, Sex and Poetry.* Bloomington, Ind.: Indiana University Press, 1987.

Hurston, Zora Neale. *Dust Tracks on a Road.* Chicago: University of Illinois Press, 1982.

————. *Moses, Man of the Mountain.* Chicago: University of Illinois Press, 1984.

————. *Mules and Men.* Chicago: University of Illinois Press, 1978.

————. *Their Eyes Were Watching God.* Chicago: University of Illinois Press, 1978.

I'll Take My Stand, intro. by Louis R. Rubin, Jr. New York: Harper, 1962.

Images of the Negro in American Literature, ed. by Seymour L. Gross and John Edward Hardy. Chicago: University of Chicago Press, 1966.

Intertextuality and Contemporary American Fiction, ed. by Patrick O'Donnell and Robert Davis. Baltimore: Johns Hopkins University Press, 1989.

In Their Place, ed. by Lewis H. Carlson and George Colburn. New York: Wiley, 1972.

Jackson, George. *Blood in My Eye.* New York: Random House, 1972.

————. *Soledad Brother.* Middlesex, U.K.: Penguin, 1971.

Jacobs, Jane. *The Death and Life of Great American Cities.* New York: Vintage, 1961.

James, William. *Varieties of Religious Experience.* New York: Modern Library, 1978.

Janowitz, Morris. *The Last Half Century.* Chicago: University of Chicago Press, 1978.

Johnson, James Weldon. *The Autobiography of an Ex-Coloured Man.* New York: Arden, 1979.

Jones, Gayl. *Corregidora.* New York: Random House, 1975.

Jordan, June. *Civil Wars.* Boston: Beacon, 1961.

Kadushin, Charles. *The American Intellectual Elite.* Boston: Little, Brown, 1974.

Kazin, Alfred. *Bright Book of Life.* Boston: Little, Brown, 1971.

————. *A Walker in the City.* New York: Harcourt Brace, 1951.

Kelley, William Melvin. *A Different Drummer.* New York: Doubleday, 1962.

Kellner, Bruce. *Carl Van Vechten and the Irreverent Decades.* Norman, Okla.: University of Oklahoma Press, 1968.

Kerman, Cynthia, and Richard Eldridge. *The Lives of Jean Toomer.* Baton Rouge, La.: Louisians State University Press, 1987.

Kerouac, Jack. *On the Road.* New York: Signet, 1957.

Key, V. O., Jr. *Public Opinion and American Democracy.* New York: Knopf, 1967.

Killens, John G. *And Then We Heard the Thunder.* New York: Knopf, 1963.

Killian, Lewis M. *The Impossible Revolution?* New York: Random House, 1968.

Kimball, Penn. *The Disconnected.* New York: Columbia University Press, 1972.

Kincaid, Jamaica. *A Small Place.* New York: New American Library, 1988.

King, Martin Luther, Jr. *A Testament of Hope,* ed. by James M. Washington. New York: Harper & Row, 1986.

———. *Why We Can't Wait.* New York: Signet, 1964.

King, Martin Luther, Sr., with Clayton Riley. *Daddy King: An Autobiography.* New York: Morrow, 1980.

King, Richard. *A Southern Renaissance.* New York: Oxford University Press, 1980.

Klein, Marcus. *After Alienation.* New York: World, 1964.

Korges, James. *Erskine Caldwell.* Minneapolis: University of Minnesota Press, 1969.

Kornblum, William. *Blue Collar Community.* Chicago: University of Chicago Press, 1974.

Kosinski, Jerzy. *Pinball.* London: Arrow, 1983.

Kovel, Joel. *White Racism.* New York: Pantheon, 1970.

Ladd, Everett Carl, Jr., with Charles D. Hadley. *Transformations of the American Party System.* New York: Norton, 1975.

Landess, Thomas, and Richard Quinn. *Jesse Jackson and the Politics of Race.* Ottawa, Ill.: Jameson, 1985.

Landry, Bart. *The New Black Middle Class.* Berkeley, Calif.: University of California Press, 1987.

Langston Hughes, ed. by Harold Bloom. New York: Chelsea, 1989.

Nella Larsen. *Passing.* New York: Arno, 1969.

Lasch, Christopher. *The New Radicalism in America.* New York: Knopf, 1965.

Lash, Joseph. *Eleanor: The Years Alone.* New York: Norton, 1972.

———. *Eleanor and Franklin.* New York: Norton, 1971.

Lester, Julius. *Search for the New Land.* New York: Dial, 1969.

Lewis, Anthony, and *The New York Times. Portrait of a Decade.* New York: Random House, 1964.

Lewis, David L. *When Harlem Was in Vogue.* New York: Knopf, 1981.

Lewis, Sinclair. *Kingsblood Royal.* London: Cape, 1948.

Lincoln, C. Eric. *The Avenue, Clayton City.* New York: Morrow, 1988.

———. *The Black Muslims.* Boston: Beacon, 1961.

———. *Sounds of the Struggle.* New York: Morrow, 1969.

Linebarger, J. M. *John Berryman.* New York: Twayne, 1974.

Link, Arthur S. *American Epoch.* New York: Knopf, 1955.

Literature of the United States, vol. 2, ed. by Walter Blair, Theodore Hornberger, and Randall Stewart. Chicago: Scott, Foresman, 1947.

Lockard, Duane. *The Perverted Priorities of American Politics.* New York: Macmillan, 1971.

Locke, Alain. *The New Negro: An Interpretation.* New York: A. & C. Boni, 1925.

Lomax, Louis. *The Negro Revolt.* New York: Harper & Row, 1963.

Lowell, Robert. *History.* New York: Farrar, Straus & Giroux, 1973.

———. *Selected Poems.* New York: Farrar, Straus & Giroux, 1976.

Lubell, Samuel. *The Future of American Politics.* New York: Harper & Row, 1977.

Lynch, Hollis R. *The Black Urban Condition.* New York: Crowell, 1973.

Lynd, Robert and Helen Merrill. *Middletown in Transition.* New York: Harcourt Brace, 1937.

Magny, Claude-Edmonde. *The Age of the American Novel,* trans. by Eleanor Hochman. New York: Ungar, 1972.

Mailer, Norman. *The American Dream.* New York: Dial, 1965.

———. *The Armies of the Night.* New York: New American Library, 1968.

———. *Cannibals and Christians.* New York: Dial, 1966.

———. *Existential Friends.* Boston: Little, Brown, 1968.

———. *Genius and Lust.* New York: Grove, 1976.

———. *The Long Patrol,* ed. by Robert Lucid. New York: World, 1971.

———. *Of a Fire on the Moon.* Boston: Little, Brown, 1969.

———. *The Presidential Papers.* Frogmore, England: Panther, 1977.

———. *The White Negro.* San Francisco: City Lights, 1970.

———. *Why Are We in Vietnam.* New York: Putnam, 1967.

Major, Clarence. *My Amputations.* New York: Fiction Collective, 1986.

Major, Reginald. *A Panther Is a Black Cat.* New York: Morrow, 1971.

Malamud, Bernard. *Dubin's Lives.* New York: Farrar, Straus & Giroux, 1977.

———. *Idiots.* New York: Farrar, Straus & Giroux, 1950.

———. *The Magic Barrel.* New York: Farrar, Straus & Giroux, 1950.

———. *The Tenants.* Middlesex, U.K.: Penguin, 1972.

Malcolm X. *The Autobiography of Malcolm X,* written with the assistance of Alex Haley. New York: Grove, 1966.

———. *Malcolm X Speaks,* ed. by George Breitman. New York: Grove, 1966.

———. *The Speeches of Malcolm X,* ed. by Archie Epps. London: Paragon, 1968.

Malin, Irving. *Jews and Americans.* Carbondale, Ill.: Southern Illinois University Press, 1965.

———. *New American Gothic.* Carbondale, Ill.: Southern Illinois University Press, 1962.

Marable, Manning. *Black American Politics.* London: Verso, 1985.

Marcuse, Herbert. *Eros et Civilisation,* trans. by Jean Guy Neny and Boris Fraenkel. Paris: Les Editions de Minuit, 1963.

———. *Le Fin de l'Utopie,* trans. by Roskopf and Wiebel. Neufchâtel, France: Seuil, 1968.

———. *L'Homme Unidimensionnel,* trans. by Monique Wittig. Paris: Les Editions de Minuit, 1968.

Marshall, Paule. *The Chosen Place, The Timeless People.* New York: Vintage, 1968.

———. *Praisesong for the Widow.* New York: Dutton, 1984.

Martin Luther King, Jr.: A Profile, ed. by Eric Lincoln. New York: Hill & Wang, 1970.

McDougall, William. *The Group Mind.* New York: Arno, 1973.

McDowell, Frederick P. W. *Ellen Glasgow and the Ironic Art of Fiction.* Madison, Wis.: University of Wisconsin Press, 1963.

McKay, Claude. *Banana Bottom.* New York: Harcourt Brace Jovanovich, 1961.

———. *Home to Harlem.* Chatham, N.J.: Chatham Bookseller, 1973.

Meier, August. *Negro Thought in America 1880–1915.* Ann Arbor, Mich.: Bobbs Merrill, 1963.

Meier, August, and Elliott Rudwick. *Along the Color Line.* Chicago: University of Chicago Press, 1976.

———. *From Plantation to Ghetto.* New York: Hill & Wang, 1970.

Mellow, James R. *Invented Lives.* London: Souvenir, 1980.

Melville, Herman. *The Confidence Man: His Masquerade,* ed. by Elizabeth Foster. New York: Hendricks, 1954.

Mencken, H. L. *A Mencken Chrestomathy.* New York: Knopf, 1956.

Minter, David. *William Faulkner: His Life and Work.* Baltimore: Johns Hopkins University Press, 1980.

Morrison, Toni. *Beloved.* New York: Knopf, 1987.

———. *The Bluest Eye.* London: Granada, 1981.

———. *Song of Solomon.* New York: Knopf, 1977.

———. *Sula.* New York: New American Library, 1973.

———. *Tar Baby.* New York: Knopf, 1981.

———. *Jazz.* New York: Knopf, 1992.

The Moynihan Report and the Politics of Controversy, ed. by Lee Rainwater and William Yancey. Cambridge, Mass.: M.I.T. Press, 1967.

Myrdal, Gunnar. *An American Dilemma.* New York: Harper, 1962.

———. *Challenge to Affluence.* New York: Pantheon, 1963.

Myth and the American Experience, vol. 2, ed. by Nicholas Corde and Patrick Gerster. Beverly Hills, Calif.: Glencoe, 1973.

Nash, George H. *The Conservative Movement.* New York: Basic Books, 1976.

Naylor, Gloria. *Bailey's Cafe.* New York: Harcourt Brace Jovanovich, 1992.

———. *Linden Hills.* New York: Ticknor & Fields, 1985.

———. *Mama Day.* New York: Vintage, 1989.

———. *The Women of Brewster Place.* Middlesex, U.K.: Penguin, 1983.

Negro Anthology, collected and ed. by Nancy Cunard; ed. and abridged by Hugh Ford. New York: Ungar, 1970.

Negro Protest Thought in the Twentieth Century, ed. by F. Broderick and A. Meier. New York: Bobbs Merrill, 1965.

Neidle, Cecyle S. *The New Americans.* New York: Twayne, 1967.

Newby, I. A. *Jim Crow's Defense*. Baton Rouge, La.: Louisiana State University Press, 1965.

Newton, Huey P. *In Search of Common Ground: Conversations with Eric H. Erikson and Huey P. Newton*. New York: Norton, 1978.

———. *Revolutionary Suicide,* written with the assistance of J. Herbert Blake. New York: Harcourt Brace Jovanovich, 1973.

Niebuhr, Reinhold. *Leaves from the Notebook of a Tamed Cynic*. Cleveland: World, 1957.

Noble, Jeanne. *Beautiful, Also, Are the Souls of My Black Sisters*. Englewood Cliffs, N.J.: Prentice Hall, 1978.

Norris, Christopher. *Derrida*. Cambridge, Mass.: Harvard University Press, 1987.

Novak, Michael. *The Rise of the Unmeltable Ethnics*. New York: Macmillan, 1971.

Oates, Joyce Carol. *Because It Is Bitter, and Because It Is My Heart*. New York: Dutton, 1990.

Oates, Stephen B. *William Faulkner: The Man and the Artist*. New York: Harper & Row, 1987.

O'Brien, Michael. *The Idea of the American South*. Baltimore: Johns Hopkins University Press, 1979.

O'Connor, Flannery. *The Complete Stories*. New York: Farrar, Straus & Giroux, 1984.

O'Neill, Eugene. *All God's Chillun Got Wings*. New York: Random House, 1934.

———. *The Iceman Cometh*. New York: Random House, 1946.

Palmier, Jean-Michel. *Marcuse et la Nouvelle Gauche*. Paris: Belfond, 1973.

The Partisan Review Anthology, ed. by William Phillips and Philip Rahv. London: Macmillan, 1962.

Paths of American Thought, ed. by Arthur M. Schlesinger, Jr., and Morton White. Boston: Houghton Mifflin, 1963.

Perlmutter, Nathan, and Ruth Ann Perlmutter. *The Real Anti-Semitism in America*. New York: Arden, 1982.

Petry, Ann. *The Street*. New York: Pyramid, 1966.

Pinkney, Alphonso. *The Myth of Black Progress*. New York: Cambridge University Press, 1984.

Poe, Edgar Allan. *The Complete Tales and Poems of Edgar Allen Poe*. New York: Modern Library, 1938.

The Poetry of the Negro 1746–1970, ed. by Langston Hughes and Arna Bontemps. New York: Hill & Wang, 1970.

Porter, Katherine Anne. *The Leaning Tower and Other Stories*. New York: Delta, 1962.

Poverty: Views from the Left, ed. by Jeremy Larner and Irving Howe. New York: Morrow, 1968.

Poverty in Affluence, ed. by R. E. Will and H. G. Vatler. New York: Harcourt Brace Jovanovich, 1970.

Quarles, Benjamin. *Frederick Douglass*. Washington, D.C.: Associated Publications, 1948.

Quiet Riots: Race and Poverty in the United States, ed. by F. R. Harris and R. W. Wilkins. New York: Pantheon, 1988.

Rahv, Philip. *Essays on Literature and Progress.* Boston: Houghton Mifflin, 1978.

Ralph Ellison: A Collection of Critical Essays, ed. by John Hersey. Englewood Cliffs, N.J.: Prentice Hall, 1974.

Rampersad, Arnold. *The Art and Image of W.E.B. DuBois.* Cambridge, Mass.: Harvard University Press, 1976.

———. *The Life of Langston Hughes,* 2 vols. New York: Oxford University Press, 1986–1988

Reed, Ishmael. *Flight to Canada.* New York: Random House, 1976.

———. *The Free-Lance Pallbearers.* New York: Doubleday, 1967.

———. *The Last Days of Louisiana Red.* New York: Random House, 1974.

———. *Reckless Eyeballing.* New York: St. Martin's, 1986.

———. *Shrovetide in Old New Orleans.* New York: Doubleday, 1978.

———. *The Terrible Threes.* New York: Atheneum, 1989.

———. *The Terrible Twos.* New York: St. Martin's, 1982.

———. *Yellow Back Radio Broke-Down.* Chatham, N.J.: Chatham Bookseller, 1975.

The Reform Spirit in America, ed. by Robert M. Walker. New York: Putnam, 1967.

Regards sur la Littérature Noire Américaine, ed. by Michel Fabre. Paris: Publications du Conseil Scientifique de la Sorbonne, 1980.

Reich, Charles A. *The Greening of America.* New York: Random House, 1970.

Renshaw, Patrick. *The Wobblies.* London: Blackwell, Eyre & Spottiswoode, 1967.

Revell, Peter. *Paul Laurence Dunbar.* Boston: Twayne, 1979.

Richard Wright: Impressions and Perspectives, ed. by David Ray and Robert Farnsworth. Ann Arbor, Mich.: University of Michigan Press, 1973.

Richard Wright: Myths and Realities, ed. by James Trotman. New York: Garland, 1988.

Richman, Sidney. *Bernard Malamud.* New Haven, Conn.: College University Press, 1966.

Riesman, David. *Individualism Reconsidered.* New York: Anchor, 1955.

Riis, Jacob. *How the Other Half Lives.* New York: Hill & Wang, 1957.

———. *A Ten Years' War.* Boston: Houghton Mifflin, 1900.

Rosegarten, Theodore. *All God's Dangers: The Life of Nate Shaw.* New York: Vintage, 1984.

Roth, Philip. *The Great American Novel.* New York: Holt, Rinehart & Winston, 1973.

———. *Reading Myself and Others.* New York: Farrar, Straus & Giroux, 1975.

Sartre, Jean-Paul. *La Nausée.* Paris: Gallimard, 1938.

Saussure, Ferdinand de. *Course in General Linguistics,* ed. by Charles Bailey and Albert Sechehaye in collaboration with Albert Riedlinger; trans. by Wade Baskin. New York: McGraw-Hill, 1959.

Schanche, Don A. *The Panther Paradox*. New York: McKay, 1970.

The Seventies, ed. by Irving Howe and Michael Harrington. New York: Harper & Row, 1972.

Shange, Ntozake. *Betsey Brown*. London: St. Martin's, 1985.

———. *Sassafras, Cypress and Indigo*. London: St. Martin's, 1982.

Shaw, Harry B. *Gwendolyn Brooks*. Boston: Twayne, 1980.

Silberman, Charles. *Crisis in Black and White*. New York: Vintage, 1947.

Simkins, Francis O. *The South Old and New*. New York: Knopf, 1947.

Singh, Amritjit. *The Novels of the Harlem Renaissance*. Garland, Pa.: Pennsylvania State University Press, 1976.

Smith, Page. *The Rise of Industrial America,* vol. 6. New York: McGraw-Hill, 1984.

Smith, William Gardner. *Return to Black America*. Englewood Cliffs, N.J.: Prentice Hall, 1970.

The Social Rebel in American Literature, ed. by R. H. Woodward and J. J. Clark. New York: Odyssey, 1968.

Sollors, Werner. *Amiri Baraka/LeRoi Jones: The Quest for a Populist Modernism*. New York: Columbia University Press, 1978.

Sontag, Susan. *Against Interpretation*. New York: Farrar, Straus & Giroux, 1966.

Sowell, Thomas. *Ethnic America*. New York: Basic Books, 1981.

Spivey, Ted R. *Revival*. Gainesville, Fla.: University of Florida Press, 1986.

The State of Black America, ed. by Janet Dewart. New York: National Urban League, 1989.

Stein, Bruno. *On Relief*. New York: Basic Books, 1971.

Stein, Gertrude. *The Autobiography of Alice B. Toklas*. New York: Harcourt Brace, 1933.

———. *Everybody's Autobiography*. New York: Random House, 1971.

Stepto, Robert. *From Behind the Veil*. Chicago: University of Illinois Press, 1979.

Stevenson, Elizabeth. *Babbitts and Bohemians*. New York: Macmillan, 1967.

Structuralism, ed. by Jacques Ehrmann. New York: Anchor, 1970.

Sturdy Black Bridges: Visions of Black Women in Literature, ed. by Roseann Bell, Bettye Parker, and Beverly Guy Sheftall. New York: Anchor, 1979.

Styron, William. *The Confessions of Nat Turner*. New York: Random House, 1967.

———. *Conversations with William Styron,* ed. by James L. W. West III. Jackson, Miss.: University of Mississippi, 1985.

———. *In the Clap Shack*. New York: Random House, 1973.

———. *Lie Down in Darkness*. New York: Random House, 1979.

———. *The Long March*. New York: Random House, 1952.

———. *Sophie's Choice*. New York: Bantam, 1982.

———. *This Quiet Dust*. New York: Random House, 1982.

Sullivan, Mark. *The Education of an American,* vol. 1. New York: Doubleday, 1938.

Symes, Lillian, and Travers Clements. *Rebel America*. Boston: Beacon, 1972.

Tanner, Tony. *City of Words.* New York: Harper & Row, 1971.

Tate, Allen. *Poems.* New York: Scribner, 1960.

———. *Poems 1922–1947.* New York: Scribner, 1953.

Teaford, John C. *The Unheralded Triumph.* Baltimore: Johns Hopkins University Press, 1984.

Thernstrom, Stephen. *The Other Bostonians.* Cambridge, Mass.: Harvard University Press, 1972.

This America, ed. by John D. Kern and Irwin Griggs. New York: Macmillan, 1942.

Three Decades of Criticism, ed. by Frederick J. Hoffman and Olga W. Vickery. New York: Harcourt Brace, 1963.

Tischler, Nancy. *Black Masks.* London: University Park, 1969.

Toomer, Jean. *Cane.* New York: Harper & Row, 1969.

———. *The Wayward and the Seeking,* ed. by Darwin T. Turner. Washington, D.C.: Howard University Press, 1980.

The Transformation of American Society, ed. by John A. Garraty. Columbia, S.C.: University of South Carolina Press, 1968.

Trilling, Lionel. *Beyond Culture.* New York: Viking, 1965.

Two Blocks Away, ed. by Charlotte Mayerson. New York: Holt, Rinehart & Winston, 1965.

Updike, John. *Bech Is Back.* New York: Knopf, 1982.

———. *Buchanan Dying.* New York: Knopf, 1974.

———. *The Coup.* New York: Knopf, 1978.

———. *Hugging the Shore.* New York: Knopf, 1983.

———. *Museums and Women.* New York: Knopf, 1956.

———. *Rabbit Redux.* New York: Knopf, 1971.

———. *Self-consciousness.* New York: Knopf, 1989.

———. *Too Far to Go.* New York: Fawcett, 1956.

The Urban Predicament, ed. by William Gorham and Nathan Glazer Washington, D.C.: Urban Institute, 1976.

Valentine, Charles. *Culture and Poverty.* Chicago: University of Chicago Press, 1968.

Van Vechten, Carl. *Nigger Heaven.* London: Knopf, 1926.

Vidal, Gore. *Myron.* New York: Random House, 1964.

———. *The Second American Revolution and Other Essays.* New York: andom House, 1982.

———. *Two Sisters.* Boston: Little, Brown, 1970.

Voices from the Harlem Renaissance, ed. by Nathan Irwin Huggins. New York: Oxford University Press, 1976.

Wagner, Jean. *Black Poets of the United States,* trans. by Kenneth Douglas. Urbana, Ill.: University of Illinois Press, 1973.

Walker, Alice. *The Color Purple.* New York: Harcourt Brace Jovanovich, 1975.

———. *Good Night, Willie Lee, I'll See You in the Morning.* New York: Harcourt Brace Jovanovich, 1982.

———. *Horses Make a Landscape Look More Beautiful.* New York: Harcourt Brace Jovanovich, 1984.

————. *In Search of Our Mothers' Gardens*. New York: Harcourt Brace Jovanovich, 1983.

————. *Living by the Word*. New York: Harcourt Brace Jovanovich, 1988.

————. *Meridian*. New York: Pocket, 1977.

————. *The Temple of My Familiar*. New York: Harcourt Brace Jovanovich, 1989.

————. *The Third Life of Grange Copeland*. New York: Harvest/Harcourt Brace Jovanovich, 1977.

Walker, Margaret. *For My People*. New Haven, Conn.: Yale University Press, 1942.

————. *Jubilee*. Boston: Houghton Mifflin, 1966.

————. *Richard Wright: Daemonic Genius*. New York: Warner, 1983.

Walters, Dorothy. *Flannery O'Connor*. New York: Twayne, 1973.

Warner, Lloyd, Marchia Mesker; and Kenneth Falls. *Social Class in America*. Chicago: Science Research Associates, 1949.

Warren, Robert Penn. *Band of Angels*. New York: Random House, 1955.

————. *Brother to Dragons*. New York: Random House, 1953.

————. *Meet Me in the Green Glen*. New York: Random House, 1971.

Washington, Booker T. *Up from Slavery*. New York: Dodd Mead, 1965.

Weatherby, W. J. *Squaring Off Mailer Against Baldwin*. New York: Donald Fine, 1977.

Max Weber and Sociology Today, ed. by Otto Stommer; trans. by Kathleen Morris. Oxford, U.K.: Oxford University Press, 1971.

West, James. *Plainville, U.S.A.* New York: Columbia University Press, 1945.

What the Negro Wants, ed. by Raylord W. Logan. Chapel Hill, N.C.: University of North Carolina Press, 1944.

White Ethnics, ed. by Joseph P. Ryan. Englewood Cliffs, N.J.: Prentice Hall, 1973.

Wideman, John Edgan. *The Lynchers*. New York: Henry Holt, 1973.

Wiebe, Robert. *The Search for Order*. New York: Hill & Wang, 1967.

William Faulkner: Three Decades of Criticism, ed. by Fred J. Hoffman and Olga W. Vickery. New York: Harcourt Brace, 1963.

William Faulkner of Oxford, ed. by James Webb and A. Wigfall Green. Baton Rouge, La.: Louisiana State University Press, 1965.

Williams, Robert. *Negroes with Guns*. New York: Marzan & Munzell, 1962.

Williams, Robin, Jr. *American Society*. New York: Knopf, 1960.

Williamson, Joel. *New People*. New York: Free Press, 1980.

William Styron's Nat Turner, ed. by John Hendrick Clarke. Boston: Beacon, 1968.

Wilson, Harriet E. *Our Nig*, ed. by H. L. Gates, Jr. New York: Vintage, 1982.

Wilson, William Julius. *The Truly Disadvantaged*. Chicago: University of Chicago Press, 1987.

Wish, Harvey. *The American Historian*. New York: Oxford University Press, 1960.

Wittgenstein, Ludwig. *Tractatus Logico-Philosophicus*, trans. by D. F. Pears and B.F.M. Guiness. London: Routledge & Paul, 1961.

Wolfe, Thomas. *Look Homeward Angel*. New York: Modern Library, 1929.

———. *The Web and the Rock*. New York: Sun Dial, 1940.

Wolfe, Tom. *Radical Chic, Mau-Mauing the Flak Catchers*. New York: Farrar, Straus & Giroux, 1970.

Wolfenstein, Eugene Victor. *The Victims of Democracy: Malcolm X and the Black Revolution*, Berkeley, Calif.: University of California Press, 1981.

Woodward, C. Vann. *The Burden of Southern History*. New York: New American Library, 1968.

———. *Reunion and Reaction*. Boston: Little, Brown, 1966.

———. *The Strange Case of Jim Crow*. New York: Oxford University Press, 1974.

Wright, Charles. *Absolutely Nothing to Get Excited About*. New York: Farrar, Straus & Giroux, 1973.

Wright, Richard. *American Hunger*. New York: Harper & Row, 1977.

———. *Black Boy*. New York: Harper, 1937.

———. *Black Power*. New York: Harper, 1954.

———. *Eight Men*. New York: Avon, 1961.

———. *Lawd Today*. New York: Avon, 1963.

———. *The Long Dream*. New York: Doubleday, 1958.

———. *Native Son*. New York: Harper, 1940.

———. *The Outsider*. New York: Perennial, 1965.

———. *Pagan Spain*. New York: Harper, 1954.

———. *White Man, Listen!* New York: Doubleday, 1957.

Zijderveld, Anton C. *The Abstract Society*. New York: Doubleday, 1971.

Zinn, Howard. *The Twentieth Century: A People's History*. New York: Harper & Row, 1980.

INDEX